THE CHALLENGE
TO POWER

THE CHALLENGE TO POWER

Money, Investing, and Democracy

JOHN C. HARRINGTON

CHELSEA GREEN PUBLISHING COMPANY
WHITE RIVER JUNCTION, VERMONT

Editor: Safir Ahmed
Managing Editor: Marcy Brant
Copy Editor: Collette Leonard
Designer: Peter Holm, Sterling Hill Productions
Design Assistant: Daria Hoak, Sterling Hill Productions

Recycled Paper

Chelsea Green sees publishing as a tool for cultural change and ecological stewardship. We strive
to align our book manufacturing practices with our editorial mission, and to reduce the impact
of our business enterprise on the environment. We print our books and catalogs on chlorine-free
recycled paper, using soy-based inks, whenever possible. Chelsea Green is a member of the Green
Press Initiative (www.greenpressinitiative.org), a nonprofit coalition of publishers, manufacturers,
and authors working to protect the world's endangered forests and conserve natural resources.
The Challenge to Power was printed on Perfection Antique Recycled, an 80 percent recycled paper
supplied by Maple-Vail.

Printed in the United States
First printing, September 2005
10 9 8 7 6 5 4 3 2 1

Library of Congress Cataloging-in-Publication Data
Harrington, John C., 1945-
  The challenge to power : money, investing, and democracy / John C.
Harrington.
     p. cm.
  Includes bibliographical references and indexes.
  ISBN 1-931498-96-2 (hardcover) — ISBN 1-931498-97-0 (pbk.)
  1. Investments—Moral and ethical aspects. 2. Social responsibility of
business. 3. Corporations—Political activity. 4. Stockholders' voting.
I. Title.
  HG4515.13.H38 2005
  332.63'2—dc22
                          2005022384

Chelsea Green Publishing Company
Post Office Box 428
White River Junction, VT 05001
(800) 639-4099

www.chelseagreen.com

CONTENTS

We Are Running Out of Time

We need to take back control of our money, our investments, our retirement funds, our jobs, our economic system, our lives, and our democracy. The global economy and world affairs are dominated by corporate oligopolies and a small group of corporate elites that are controlling our destiny with *our own* dollars.

The primary focus of this book is on money and socially responsible investing (SRI), and SRI's ability to create a dynamic, new, decentralized, noncorporate democratic economy which will not only maximize individual portfolio financial return and community wealth, but will also create a renewed social and environmental vision of the future. SRI is also necessary to save our democracy. We must act now. We can demand a better world. But we are running out of time.

The struggle for the control of our own capital is no longer an esoteric academic exercise. It is a necessity. The survival of our planet may depend upon it. Giant corporations, and increasingly a small number of them, from Wal-Mart to Microsoft, are defining the world we live in. Soon, our only economic choices will be whether to buy Pepsi or Coke, shop at Wal-Mart or Home Depot, bank at Citigroup or Bank of America, and see a movie on TV presented by Disney or General Electric.

Individual financial decisions will be just as limited. Do we invest in a scandal-ridden mutual fund, or through a brokerage firm providing insider stock deals to corporate management in exchange for large underwriting business? Better yet, do we turn over our tax preparation to a CPA firm that "cooks the books" for corporate clients, while it electronically transfers our personal financial information to its information technology (IT) subsidiary in India?

The excesses of corporate management's greed in the 1980s gave way to even more outrageous excesses in the 1990s. The music played, stock values increased, and no one believed that the party would ever end.

Of course, there was never any celebration for half of the world's population—the 2.8 billion people who live on less than the equivalent of two dollars per day, the more than one billion people who do not have access to safe water, the 840 million people who go hungry, or the one-third of all children under the age of five who suffer from malnutrition.[1]

The economic disparities are glaring and getting worse each year. The richest fifth of the world's population has access to 86 percent of the world's gross domestic product (GDP), while the poorest fifth has access to 1 percent. The assets of the world's three richest men, currently Bill Gates, Warren Buffet and Karl Albrecht, exceed the combined GDP of the world's forty-eight poorest countries.[2]

Meanwhile, millions of Americans are unemployed and if they find a job, it is at companies like Wal-Mart that pay barely above minimum wage, with little or no health benefits, which means taxpayers subsidize them. Many people are working more than one job just to support their families, and the underemployed, like those whose unemployment compensation has run out, are not even counted in the unemployment numbers. The savings rate has dived to 0.2 percent of disposable income[3] and by March 2005 consumer debt stood at over $2.12 trillion.[4] That's about $6,000 for every man, woman and child in the United States.

To understand whether our country, economy, and investors are being served by the present system, we first need to explore how and why Americans seem to be disengaged with the political process. Although voter turnout improved in the 2004 Presidential Election, it still represented less than 60 percent of the registered voters, and only about 17 percent of the youth vote. We will begin this book by exploring electoral politics and government institutions and whether they are responding to our democratic need for change and truly representing our interests as shareholders, taxpayers, voters, and citizens. And we'll review political and economic issues that must be addressed by responsible investors in this new millennium.

We need to ask the following questions: Are politicians and government bureaucrats being bought off to support the "corporatization" of our global economy? Is the privatization of the public sector healthy for democracy and competitive capitalism? Is there a viable countervailing power to corporate dominance of our air, water, and food, much less the U.S. political and economic system? Are our elected officials—local, state, and national—representing their taxpaying constituents or their corporate donors? Has corporate management become so powerful and democracy so weak that corporate democracy, intelligent consumerism, and SRI are the only remaining leverages available to the public to affect positive social, environmental, and political change? In this context, corporate democracy means one dollar, one vote, where shareholders' voting power equates to dollars invested; political decisions are made by the ability to control capital and leverage dollars and have nothing to do with participatory democracy or one person, one vote, as we know it. Have politicians, government, and democracy become irrelevant?

President George W. Bush was re-elected in 2004, this time by a majority of both the popular vote and the electoral vote; the same election delivered increased Republican majorities in both the Senate and House of Representatives. Was this a victory for democracy or a victory for corporate management which invested heavily in Republican candidates? As the *Wall Street Journal* reported on Nov. 4, 2004:

> In the next four years, drug makers, health-care companies, and financial-service concerns expect to benefit from Bush efforts to rein in legal costs and extend dividend and capital-gains tax cuts. Wall Street companies are looking for a flood of new investment if Mr. Bush succeeds in opening the Social Security system to privately-owned accounts. Fast-food chains are less worried about a higher minimum wage and auto makers about tighter fuel economy standards—both areas where a Kerry administration planned to make changes.

For the last four years, Americans have witnessed corrupt corporate management, with greedy Chief Executive Officers (CEOs) and Chief Financial Officers (CFOs), and record personal and corporate bankruptcies. From 1988 to 2000, the ratio of non-financial debt (consumer credit card) to the GDP held steady at about 1.8 to 1; now it is more than 2.0 to 1. From 2001 to the end of 2003, the economy added $1.3 trillion in gross domestic product and $4.2 trillion in debt, which means that for every new dollar of economic output, we've added $3.19 in new debt. In the first quarter of 2004, debt rose at an annual rate of 8.6 percent, more than double the growth of the economy. By December 31, 2004, our national debt stood at $7.6 trillion.

The number of new personal bankruptcies nationwide rose 7.8 percent to 1,625,813 from 1,508,578 for the year ending September 30, 2003, according to the Administrative Office of the U.S. Courts; personal and corporate filings doubled since 1994.[5] Thanks to corporate management's greed, fraud, incompetence, and a bad economy and market, more than sixty thousand companies sought bankruptcy protection in 2001. The ten largest companies filing for bankruptcy in 2001 reported employing about 140,500 while by September 30, 2002, the top ten bankrupt companies reported employing 444,600.[6] Of the twenty-four largest bankruptcies since 1980, twelve, or half, occurred in 2001 and 2002.[7] Welcome to the new millennium!

Meanwhile, excessive management compensation, lucrative severance plans, and outlandish corporate parties thrown at shareholders' expense are skyrocketing. This might lead one to believe that shareholders, the legal owners of corporations, receive the most benefit. Actually the majority of financial benefits accrue to an extremely small group of people worldwide—corporate officers, including CEOs and CFOs, as well as corporate board members. These are the elite of the elite, individuals who have managed to be at the right place at the right time. They have been educated at the right schools, have the right friends, and have had the political skills— or sheer luck—to have successfully obtained or retained positions within corporations to gain access to incredible wealth and power, for which the rest of the world's citizens suffer immensely. Not only does the majority of the world's population suffer economically due to this distorted global economic malice, but our environment, food and water supply, and in fact, most of the day-to-day, life-and-death decisions are in the hands of these non-elected, non-caring corporate elite.

The situation has been made worse because economic entities, called corporations, are legally treated as human beings and given the same civil liberties and rights as us mortals. The individuals running them are protected by a battery of attorneys, have limited legal and financial exposure, and heavily influence, if not totally control, the politicians and government bureaucrats that protect their corporate seal and "life" of state incorporation. What's wrong with this picture?

Capitalism in the traditional sense no longer exists, if it ever did, except for the small business merchants and those in many service sectors of the economy who actually compete in a relatively free marketplace, but are ultimately manipulated by large corporations that dominate their trade associations, i.e. Chambers of Commerce. These same giants of American enterprise control supply as well as demand (through manipulative use of the major media outlets and mass advertising). There are probably only about two hundred thousand people across the globe that control our natural resources, wealth, and truly act as self-appointed kings (or Niccolo Machiavelli's "princes"), preaching free enterprise while exercising authoritarian capitalism, feeding at the public trough, and privatizing everything that moves.

So how is the SRI community responding to this dismal state of affairs? We will review its struggle for vision, and an evaluation of some of the movement's founders' conflicts, successes, and failures. This review will identify SRI professional and trade organizations that have advanced the movement and illuminated early struggles within some of the first SRI firms, including Working Assets and Progressive Asset Management, as well as the problems encountered when socially committed firms such as Ben and Jerry's "go public."

For more than three decades now, I have been involved in the SRI movement. I began my SRI career in 1972 when, as an analyst for the California Legislative Assembly Office of Research, I wrote a report entitled *The State of California and Southern African Racism: California's Economic Involvement with Firms Operating in Southern Africa*. Suffice it to say the report was controversial, as was the divestment legislation I wrote for the Black Caucus in 1973. I wrote several additional reports and legislation advocating socially responsible investing. I served on a Sacramento city investment board and was a consultant for the California Legislature's Select Committee on Investment Priorities and Objectives. In 1980, Governor Jerry Brown created the Governor's Public Investment Task Force which I chaired. The task force issued a set of recommendations leading the way for both the California Public Employee Retirement System (CALPERS) and the California State Teachers Retirement System (CALSTRS) to adopt strong proxy voting and shareholder advocacy policies that continue to this day.

In 1983 several colleagues and I opened Working Assets Money Market Fund, a socially responsible mutual fund, and a year earlier, I had started my own investment advisory firm, Harrington Investments, Inc. (HII), which currently manages about $170 million in individual and institutional socially screened assets. Later, in 1987, I co-founded the Oakland, California-based Progressive Asset Management (PAM), a brokerage firm specializing in SRI and in 1996 I formed Global Partners, LLC, a high social impact venture fund primarily investing in small businesses specializing in organic and natural products as well as alternative energy systems. As such, I have been an "insider" in the SRI community and a witness to all its growing pains, struggles, and successes.

And so, in reviewing the SRI community's history, I will outline a few major debacles and policy and management errors, as well as success stories that have helped us advance SRI. There are also numerous enthusiastic, knowledgeable, and experienced folks who are currently exploring new directions and structures that address problems of legacy (when founders of SRI businesses move on or retire and need to insure that their social and environmental mission is adopted by a new group of owners). This is also the task of another group of SRI leaders which is creating an innovative business structure called Upstream 21. We'll see how this fits into other goals of SRI, especially as it relates to expanding democratic ownership to stakeholders and funding new, innovative green technology and other socially responsible private business opportunities.

We'll review and evaluate socially screened mutual funds—with a track record of at least ten years—to determine how well they have performed financially against each other and against standard indexes. Just as important, we'll look at the social criteria of each fund, evaluate how well the fund meets its social goals, and review its shareholder advocacy history—if it has one. We'll discover whether or not a mutual fund is innovative in taking a further step by investing a portion of its assets in Community Development Financial Institutions (CDFIs) such as community banks and credit unions, loan funds, microcredit enterprises, social venture funds or private placements, all of which may have a much more significant economic impact on local communities than passively screening stock portfolios.

We as shareholders are the owners, but the ownership responsibility is so distorted through multiple layers of administration and bureaucracy that most of us know little or nothing about our companies, much less have the ability to exert control. A mutual fund shareholder may invest in an index fund, sector fund or an aggressive growth equity fund, and have little knowledge of the companies that comprise the portfolio, much less be aware of the mutual fund adviser's ability to vote the fund's stock on behalf of the investor at literally dozens of annual shareholders meetings. "Don't ask, don't tell" takes on a whole new meaning.

Readers may be shocked to also learn that the charitable contributions made to environmental or social change organizations are at times turned into investments in companies that are causing the often irreversible environmental or social injury that such nonprofit organizations were created to repair or prevent in the first place. It is even difficult for donors to get many nonprofits to disclose this information. Never mind a donor's inability to find out how the organization voted its stock (perhaps that you donated) on a shareholder resolution that your church or pension fund may have introduced to address a particularly egregious corporate action or policy.

If SRI investors fund community-based organizations, we need to evaluate these financial intermediaries, discuss organizations that support charitable giving and philanthropic goals, and review their investment philosophy. Institutional investors—large philanthropic foundations, family trusts, and environmental and social justice organizations—invest their operational funds, endowments and reserves, in liquid securities, such as stocks, bonds, and mutual funds, as well as in non-liquid investment instruments. Some that invest in traditional stocks and bonds are often screened by portfolio managers, utilizing social and environmental criteria. However, many, if not most, of these institutions do not socially screen, and many have not even considered mission-based investing. Why not? Why the resistance?

On the other hand, as some nonprofit foundations and public interest organizations become more active at the shareholder level by voting stock, dialoguing with corporate management, joining shareholder coalitions, and endorsing environmental and human rights codes of conduct, will such actions encourage their larger cousins to adopt social investment policies consistent with social or environmental program objectives? Will some organizations follow the Sierra Club's lead and create mutual funds *reinforcing* the organization's primary mission—such as protecting the environment by investing in environmental businesses and screening polluters? Are we on the verge of a major shift where foundations become more of an activist with their ownership of capital? Will they join an increasing number of public pension funds, social justice foundations, colleges and endowments, family trusts, and private investors in challenging corporate management?

We will also look at a recent phenomena, within the last ten years, where a lot of social venture funds and associations—such as the Social Venture Network (SVN), Investors Circle, the Environmental Capital Network (ECN), and the Community Development Venture Capital Alliance (CDVCA), as well as an array of "angel" investors—have complemented and supplemented their investments with SRI private equity financing. Many of these organizations have joined growing community-based efforts to decentralize investment and consumer decision-making to democratize control of regional and local economies.

Any discussion of SRI also requires a review of retirement plans and the role of pension fund capital. Most employees of private pension plans, while they receive quarterly reports from their plan administrators or their employers who may control their individual 401(k) retirement plan, don't even know what companies make up their investment portfolio, and are totally unaware of how their employer votes their stock "exclusively for their benefit" as required by the Employee Retirement Income Security Act of 1974 (ERISA). Some plans, such as was the case with Enron, may be almost entirely invested in their own company's stock. If the company goes down, so do the retirees' future benefits.

A public employee may also be in the dark on such matters unless he or she is lucky enough to be in a large state or city plan like the California Public Employee Retirement System (CALPERS) or the New York City Employees Retirement System where attention has been focused in recent years on shareholder proxy voting, corporate governance, and issues of shareholder transparency. The overwhelming majority of public employees of most state and local government plans across the country are ignorant of their beneficial ownership and shareholder voting rights. Much of the voting of stock proxies is administered by government bureaucrats, and votes are cast overwhelmingly to favor corporate management's position. Not only do public employees have their stock voted against their own economic interests, some pension plans are investing in companies that are actually taking their jobs by privatizing the public sector. How about that—you own the company that eliminates your job!

We'll also focus our attention on the difference between investing in liquid, socially screened securities and indexes, and putting money to work directly in a community investment vehicle—both at home and abroad—as well as micro-enterprise lending.

And, if we are interested in influencing corporate behavior, we must take a hard look at the current rage—corporate codes of conduct. What are these codes and what are sustainability and corporate social responsibility (CSR)? Is CSR an oxymoron? And, if we accept corporate voluntary codes, are they just public relations devices, or are companies actually changing their conduct for the good of global society? How do concerned investors monitor these voluntary codes to ensure that corporate management will respect and implement them? Will there be an enforcement mechanism to ensure compliance, and will sanctions be imposed against bad actors?

We'll take a meaningful look at shareholder advocacy, including the efficacy of engaging in dialogue with management, filing and co-filing shareholder resolutions, and determining the results if a majority of shareholders adopt a resolution opposed by corporate management. Based upon the recent deluge of corporate fraud, accounting irregularities, and CEO excesses, will Wall Street reform? Have we witnessed a shareholder revolution that will lead to a new form of responsible capitalism, creating the basis of enlightened corporate leadership reminiscent of Plato's philosopher kings?

We in the SRI community need to look beyond our marketing and advertising to face the question head on: Is SRI really a force for progressive change? In an honest and open fashion, we need to appraise how successful we can be with passive social screening and shareholder advocacy. What are the pitfalls of relying only on social screening? Is there a difference between the social criteria and the actual implementation of a social investment strategy? Are we simply institutionalizing limited corporate democracy? Does corporate governance reform simply legitimize the undemocratic corporate structure and management control? If a company's management is treating its domestic employees well, should SRI turn a blind eye to its human rights violations in China? Should we invest in a company that advances the employment and compensation of women and minorities while killing its customers with lung cancer? When SRI mutual funds invest in "best of class" oil or chemical companies, does this add credibility to our profession or homogenize it into oblivion?

In the final chapter, I will review stakeholder and shareholder strategies and specific tactics that are being coordinated within the SRI community to gain leverage in the corporate boardroom. We will review the goals of SRI investors, as well as pension funds, mutual funds, labor unions, and other institutional investors, and evaluate NGO's and community investment strategies for democratizing the economy.

Economic control, leverage, or influence comes not from the barrel of a gun, but from the slide of a credit card, the press of computer keys (to make an Internet purchase, donate to a charity, or trade a stock), and the signing of a proxy to vote your shares. This book will primarily focus on investing, and what has been defined in the late twentieth and early twenty-first centuries as socially responsible investing.

The final chapter will also explore environmental fiduciary responsibility and review several projects underway aimed at dramatically increasing public disclosure of corporate financial risks associated with corporate activities, presently undisclosed, that may significantly increase costs to shareholders in the future.

Socially responsible investors need new strategies to challenge corporate power, including revisiting the corporate campaign originally designed and successfully implemented in the 1980s by Ray Rogers and others against the former textile giant, J. P. Stevens. It is important, in this regard, to follow the money and ask the following questions: Will the investment banks and brokerage firms on Wall Street introduce shareholder resolutions, and vote against the management of corporations in which they underwrite and make a market for their stock? How long will a Merrill Lynch or a Paine Webber have such a corporate client's business if they vote against corporate management? Will SRI practitioners, making money off Wall Street investment products, challenge the invisible hand that feeds them? Will mutual funds vote against corporate management while soliciting it for 401(k) and 403(b) business? Follow the money. It is one thing to screen a company from investment because it doesn't meet social or environmental criteria; it is another to work actively with other stakeholders to challenge corporate management's power, as well as Wall Street's largest financial services powerhouses.

How widely are corporations sharing our personal, financial, and medical information? Is technology being utilized by governments to spy on its citizens? Will this rush by corporations, especially technology and financial services businesses, to outsource U.S. jobs and confidential personal financial data overseas lead to greater productivity and savings for shareholders, or simply increase U.S. unemployment and Americans' identify theft?

Various shareholder strategies will be discussed, reviewed, and evaluated. Do corporate governance shareholder strategies by pension funds and other institutional investors advance progressive goals or simply distract investors from the real issue of corporate control over our economy and political system? Is corporate management really influenced at all by responsible shareholders' actions? Does more responsive and transparent corporate management lead to a more socially responsible company? Is a major structural overhaul of "capitalism" overdue? Will 2005 become George Orwell's *1984*? Should corporate management be seen as treasonous and unpatriotic for avoiding U.S. taxes, shipping jobs overseas, and doing business with our country's enemies?

Finally, this book will discuss a strategy that will build a long-term coalition of organizations and individuals, including shareholders, to provide a truly countervailing power against corporate management. From such a broad coalition of stakeholders comes a longer-term solution for developing more sustainable financial growth and security for investors, and more decentralized and democratic local, national, and global economic decision-making, inevitably more responsive to people than to short-term corporate profits. For socially responsible investing and democracy, it is time for a new beginning. We can truly change the world—but we're running out of time.

1

Are Politicians and Government Relevant?

mericans are free to decline to participate in the electoral process. This free choice has been exercised. Our nation's citizens are
refusing to participate in record numbers. The percentage of the voting-
age population who registered to vote in the 2000 election was at an all-
time low of 64 percent,[1] and only 55 percent reported actually voting
in the 2000 presidential election.[2] With all the publicity and fanfare of
the 2004 election, only 59.1 percent of registered voters exercised their
franchise. In the sixteen states that held primary elections in the spring
of 2002, on average only 16.2 percent of eligible voters went to the polls
to vote.[3] Democratic California Governor Gray Davis, who was recalled
on October 7, 2003, had been reelected to serve a second term less than
a year earlier by 14.63 percent of eligible voters and 20.53 percent of the
registered voters in California.[4]

It's not just who *isn't* voting, but who *is* voting that is also revealing. Much
of our country's growth is due to immigration (20 percent of California's
and 13 percent of Florida and New York's voting-age population are not citizens). Not only are immigrants not participating in our great democratic
tradition, but non-white people, young people, the working poor, renters,
and the less educated are voting in fewer numbers, and are clearly not represented in the halls of Congress or in our state legislatures. According to
recent census data, long-time homeowners, whites with higher income and
education, older married people, and women are all more likely to vote,
even if in declining percentages.[5]

According to a study, jointly conducted by the *Washington Post*, the Henry J.
Kaiser Family Foundation, and Harvard University, if current trends continue,

people sixty-five and older who vote in mid-term elections are likely to exceed young adults by a four to one ratio by 2022.[6]

The San Francisco-based Public Policy Institute of California surveyed more than five thousand Californians in 2004 on participation in civic activities and found that non-Hispanic whites, comprising 46.7 percent of the state's population, are twice as likely as Latinos, Blacks, and Asians to sign petitions, write elected officials, contribute money to candidates and issues, attend rallies, or volunteer for a political party.[7]

According to "The Vanishing Voter" national survey, among respondents thirty-four years of age and younger, those who agreed that "most politicians are liars or crooks" were 17 percent less likely to vote in 2000 than those who disagreed.[8] "Disgusted with politics" also came out at the top of the list of the reasons why non-registrants were not planning on registering to vote and second on the list of those that were registered to vote, but chose not to vote.[9]

Not only are young people not voting, but according to a Lake, Snell, Perry & Associates' survey from May 2002, which included eight focus groups at three sites in California, voters of all backgrounds believe the American political system is driven by money, particularly large contributions from wealthy special interests, and that elected officials are more responsive to big money than to people. African-Americans and Latinos particularly believed that they were shut out of politics and victimized by the decisions being made.[10]

Not surprisingly, according to investigative reporter Gregory Palast, as many as ninety-one thousand people, over half of them African-American, were not able to vote in the November 5, 2002 election in Florida. Not only were they blocked from voting in the 2000 election, they were not restored to the voter rolls until January 2003.[11]

About 20 percent of the registered non-voters in 2000 did not vote because they were not interested, felt their vote would not make a difference, or didn't like the candidates or campaign issues.[12] In California, voters in the November 2002 elections were so disgusted with the two major party candidates for Governor that the turnout was 30.92 percent of eligible voters and 43.37 percent of registered voters. Major party gubernatorial candidates in California spent well over $100 million on the election, saying absolutely nothing of importance or much relevance to voters. Little was said about the impending budget crisis in California until after the election, when Governor Davis announced an unbelievable $38 billion state budget deficit.

So while fewer Americans are participating in elections, the amount of money being spent on elections is skyrocketing. Meanwhile, the winner-takes-all elections and the two-party system are creating a racial divide in the country by pitting urban blacks and Latinos against rural and suburban whites. The same duopoly has frozen out third parties, and there is absolutely nothing to excite young voters, especially those seeking new ideas. Both Republicans and Democrats have gerrymandered districts using sophisticated computer programs, in an effort to perpetuate their own political careers. As a result, in the 2002 congressional elections, only four challengers beat House incumbents, the lowest number in American history.[13] Two years later, only seven incumbents in the House were defeated and four of them were in Texas, where the Republican-controlled legislature gerrymandered Democrats out of their seats.[14]

It is not much different in most state legislatures, where no changes occur in legislative districts unless the states have term limits. In many states, politicians have gerrymandered districts to protect themselves so effectively that no one even bothers to run against them. According to a *New York Times* op-ed: "In Arkansas, 75 percent of state legislative races this year were uncontested by either the Republicans or by the Democrats. The same was true of 73 percent of the seats in Florida, 70 percent in South Carolina, 62 percent in New Mexico."[15]

In presidential election years, many voters are also turned off by long and boring campaigns. According to Thomas E. Patterson, who oversaw "The Vanishing Voter" survey, campaigns are not delightfully long, they are numbingly long, and the front-loading of presidential primary elections—holding them earlier in the year—is why the overall turnout rate in primaries has fallen from nearly 30 percent to 17 percent since the 1970s.[16] The 2004 Democratic and Republican Party conventions in Boston and New York, respectively, were the largest political non-events of the campaign.

Overall voter turnout in the 2004 presidential election was improved by massive voter registration efforts and Get-Out-The-Vote (GOTV) drives by both major parties, as well as by such activist groups as MoveOn.org and Americans Coming Together. It remains to be seen, however, if this turnout level can be sustained and improved. Based upon historical data, I believe that the 2004 election was simply an exception to the trend of declining citizen and voter participation in the democratic process. Perhaps it is time for mandatory voting on the weekends with same day registration.

MONEY IN POLITICS

Besides long and boring campaigns, the influence of money also keeps people away from the polls. The facts speak for themselves: In 2000, Americans experienced the first ever presidential campaign over $100 million; since 1984 the presidential candidate who has raised the most money in advance of his party's primary elections has won every nomination; and no challenger to an incumbent politician spending under $900,000 won a seat in the House of Representatives in 2000.[17]

Fundraising records were set in 2004: John Kerry raised $249 million while George W. Bush raised $273 million. "The field of presidential candidates raised about $851 million (including public finance), a 70 percent increase over 2000," reported *The New York Times* on November 8, 2004. "National political parties raised more than $1 billion . . . this year's races for Congress and the White House are estimated to have cost roughly $3.9 billion, about a third more than they did four years ago, according to the Center for Responsive Politics, which tracks campaign spending."

Over the last decade, says the group Democracy 21, corporations gave $636 million to Republicans and $449 million to Democrats. These corporate gifts only point out that corporate management expected a slightly larger return on its investment from Republicans than from Democrats in the 2000 presidential election cycle. In 2004, corporate Political Action Committees (PACs) favored Republican congressional candidates ten to one.[18] The overwhelming investments in Republicans paid off since they expanded their majorities in both the House and Senate.

It is not really considered news anymore that corporations spend lots of money in national and state elections to get their way. As *In These Times* reported in 2002, Enron gave $2 million in the 2000 presidential campaign, tilting heavily towards Bush, and since 1989, has evenly divided $4 million to Democrats and Republicans running for federal office, while Arthur Anderson, Enron's accounting firm, lavished money on more than half the members of the House of Representatives and ninety-four of one hundred U.S. Senators in the past decade.

These corporate contributions were not unlike other corporate PAC (political action committee) and soft money contributions from WorldCom, Global Crossing, and numerous other corporate "good citizens," which split their money almost evenly between Democrats and Republicans. At long last, technology companies, including California's finest from Silicon Valley, stepped up to the plate to buy politicians in the 2002 election cycle. The *San Francisco Business Times* reported in 2002 that most Bay Area companies, such as Oracle ($268,734), Cisco ($182,038), and Siebel ($215,000) split their soft money between the two major parties, while Charles Schwab ($200,000), Safeway ($141,030), and Sequoia Capital ($195,271) gave all of their money to the Republican Party. The newspaper also reported that about three hundred companies that formed TechNet gave approximately $6 million to Bush and about $5 million to Al Gore during the 2000 general election, but until recently have been focusing on raising corporate PAC money from senior executives and top management to buy political influence following the passage of the Bipartisan Campaign Reform Act of 2002 (BCRA). Of the total $1.1 billion in soft money donations, large corporations doled out 87 percent.

On May 2, 2003, thanks to Senator Mitch McConnell (R-KY), who filed a suit to challenge the constitutionality of the campaign finance law, the BCRA was overturned in a 1,638-page decision handed down by a three-person federal district court. The ruling was immediately appealed by congressional supporters and the U.S. Supreme Court, by a one-vote majority, upheld BCRA, especially the two most important provisions: one banning unlim-

Top 10 Corporate Contributors *Total of Individual, Soft Money, and Political Action Committee Contributions*	
Company	**Total Contributions** **2000-2002 Election Cycles**
AT&T	$ 7,230,476
Microsoft	$ 6,000,383
Philip Morris	$ 5,418,898
SBC Communications	$ 5,096,486
Citigroup	$ 4,973,325
Goldman Sachs	$ 4,849,874
AOL Time Warner*	$ 4,607,253
Verizon Communications	$ 4,443,619
MBNA Corp	$ 4,292,877
United Parcel Service	$ 3,921,076

*Includes 2000 contributions form both America Online and Time Warner.
Source: Center for Responsive Politics

ited donations to political parties (soft money), and another barring outside groups from using donations from corporations to finance "hit" media ads right before election day. By December of 2003, the *Wall Street Journal* was reporting that dozens of special interest organizations had stepped in to accept wealthier donor money to avoid violating the ruling. Such groups include Americans for a Better Country, Americans for Job Security, Americans Coming Together, and The Partnership for America's Families. I feel more patriotic just reading the names of these organizations.

In his book, *Selling Out*, Mark Green, a Democratic candidate for mayor of New York City in 2002, encapsulates the corruption of the power of money on the democratic process: The 0.1 percent of Americans who contribute $1,000 or more to political candidates have far more influence than the other 99.9 percent; senators from the ten largest states must raise an average of over $34,000 a week, every week, for six years to stay in office; the cost of winning a congressional seat has risen ten-fold in twenty-four years; it is far easier for a working-class person to win a seat in the Russian Congress than in the American one; PAC money goes seven to one for incumbents over challengers (and 98 percent of House incumbents win); most other democracies get a 70 to 80 percent turnout of eligible voters, while in the United States it is half in presidential elections, one third in congressional elections, and often only one fifth in primaries.

Corporate contributions are only part of the story. In the halls of Capitol Hill and the state capitols, corporate lobbyists rule the day. At the national level, corporations have been able to use a loophole in the lobbying law to conceal their identities by forming over 135 lobbying coalitions. The Center for Responsible Politics, a nonpartisan group that analyzes campaign and spending by lobbyists, reported that on business tax issues alone, twenty-eight coalitions paid $5.4 million in 2000, but revealed little to nothing about their members. Most of these groups used the Big Five accounting firms as their lobbyists, including Arthur Anderson, which was found guilty of obstruction of justice for impeding the investigation into the Enron scandal.

Accounting firms' PACs have been busy soliciting money from their employees for years. In the 2000 election cycle, the American Institute of Certified Public Accounting (AICPAC) collected almost $1.4 million to influence politicians and almost evenly split $85 million in contributions to Democrats and Republicans between 1989 and 2001.[19] Not only does AICPAC spend lots of money on political activities, its individual members belly up to the bar as well. KPMG's PAC brought in more than $1.5 million from its employees in the 2002 election cycle, while Arthur Anderson's PAC collected $708,573, even though it's now out of business.[20]

Remember that AICPAC's former lawyer and lobbyist was Harvey Pitt, who later became Chairman of the Securities and Exchange Commission (SEC). Soon, Pitt brought in William Webster, the former head of the FBI and CIA, to head the newly created accounting oversight board to attempt to take the heat off accounting firms after the Enron, WorldCom, and Global Crossing scandals. Pitt, unfortunately, neglected to tell his fellow commissioners about Webster's role as head of the board of directors' auditing committee at U.S. Technologies, a company facing investor lawsuits alleging fraud. The resulting media exposure led Webster to withdraw his name and Pitt to resign from the SEC.

With Pitt and Webster gone, nothing really changed. It is an incestuous, insider world within the Beltway. Pitt was replaced by William Donaldson and Webster was replaced by William McDonough. Donaldson was co-founder of the investment banking and brokerage firm of Donaldson, Lufkin and Jenrette, and was Undersecretary of State for Henry Kissinger as well as serving in the Ford administration. McDonough spent twenty-two years at First Chicago Corporation and was then appointed president of the New York Federal Reserve. When he was head of the Federal Reserve, not surprisingly, he fiercely—and successfully—fought unionization of low paid security guards. McDonough was also an advisor to the World Bank and the bank's International Finance Corporation (IFC).

Corporations so dominate the political landscape that one drug company, Schering-Plough, was able to have an "unknown" senator quietly slip a provision in a military construction appropriations bill to extend the company's monopoly patent on the anti-allergy drug Claritin, which was due to expire at the end of 2002. Sales of Claritin hit $2.7 billion in 1999. It was not revenue the company wanted to lose.

According to a 2002 report from Public Citizen's Congress Watch, titled "The Other Drug War II," drug companies employ 623 lobbyists in Washington, DC. Overall, drug companies spent $78.1 million on lobbying in 2001, bringing the total lobbying bill for 1997–2001 to over $403 million. According to the book, *The People's Business*, there are more than one hundred thousand lawyers and lobbyists working in Washington, DC that so dominate the regulatory system that they often supply the language for proposed regulations themselves. It's a city constantly under siege by special interests. American citizens are so removed from the bubble within the beltway that we have no real representation.

To understand the extent to which corporate money influences government, we need only look at the power of the pharmaceutical industry, or "Big Pharma" as it is known. While hundreds of drug lobbyists are former congressional staff, twenty-three are former members of Congress. It is somewhat ironic for me to note that former Congressman Vic Fazio, a lobbyist at Clark & Weinstock who represents Eli Lilly & Co., the Pharmaceutical Research and Manufacturers of America (PhRMA) and Schering-Plough, was my staff colleague in the California State Legislature. Fazio ran the Assembly Democratic Consultants (the political arm of the lower house

Democrats in the California legislature) in the 1970s before he was elected to a state assembly seat, and was later elected to Congress. Unfortunately for Schering-Plough, the Claritin provision died, as did the company's stock price. According to Congress Watch, the drug's extension would have cost consumers an additional $7.3 billion. That would have been a handsome return on the $19.9 million Schering-Plough invested in lobbying and campaign contributions since the start of the 1996 election cycle.

Another congressional convert to the drug industry in 2004 was Representative James Greenwood (R-PA), the former chair of the Oversight and Investigations Subcommittee of the House Energy and Commerce Committee. Greenwood abruptly cancelled hearings into whether pharmaceutical companies had concealed evidence that antidepressant drugs may have induced suicide among children and adolescents, when the Biotechnology Industry Organization offered to appoint him president of the organization, "... for a fourfold salary increase to $650,000."[21]

The *Wall Street Journal* reported on November 4, 2004 that health care and drug companies contributed $26 million to Bush and the Republican Party because they believed that Democratic candidate John Kerry, unlike Bush, would allow Medicare to negotiate drug prices with the pharmaceutical companies and allow drug imports from Canada.

And since 9/11, drug companies have become quite patriotic. Eli Lilly & Co., for instance, had a special provision of its own slipped in at the eleventh hour into the 475-page Homeland Security bill in 2002, which protected Eli Lilly from being sued by the parents of autistic children who believe their child's condition was linked to Thimerosal, a mercury-based preservative made by the company that is used as a common ingredient in childhood vaccines. No one claimed authorship of the amendment—not the Lilly lobbyist, not the White House, not the Department of Health and Human Services, and not our new Senate Majority Leader Bill Frist of Tennessee, who had originally added the Lilly amendment to a different bill. Could this amazing and mysterious provision, which no one would claim, be connected to Lilly's $1.6 million campaign contribution to congressional politicians, of which 79 percent went to Republicans?

Frist lent pharmaceutical companies a hand again when he and more than two dozen Republican lawmakers wrote and called U.S. Trade Representative Robert Zoellick in an effort to protect lucrative drug patents. Thanks to pharmaceutical companies shelling out more than $50 million to help Republicans win control of Congress in November 2002, the industry celebrated a great victory when the United States, alone among the 144-member World Trade Organization (WTO), blocked a proposal for distributing patented medicines to less developed countries.[22]

Drug companies are ubiquitous in politics, and communicate their message throughout American society. Dozens of celebrities, including Lauren Bacall, Kathleen Turner, Rob Lowe, Larry King, and Montel Williams are paid large fees by companies such as Swiss drug maker Novartis AG to appear on television talk shows and morning news programs to discuss personal stories about ailments that afflict them or people near them. Often, they mention brand-name drugs without disclosing their financial ties to the drug manufacturers.[23]

Drug companies spend millions of dollars wining and dining doctors across the country, from emergency room physicians to general practitioners and dentists. It's not uncommon to find a "drug dealer" sitting in their outer offices, waiting to strike. My dentist refuses to see them, while my cousin, an emergency room physician in Austin, Texas, as well as my general practitioner in Napa, California, admit they enjoy a good dinner and wine occasionally with a drug maker's representative. I'm told that often there are more drug representatives waiting to see doctors than there are patients.

The influence of drug money reaches beyond our elected officials to our regulatory agencies. The FDA has been a little lax in monitoring the safety of drugs after it has approved them for sale. In the December 2004 issue of the *Journal of the American Medical Association*, its editorial board joined lawmakers and consumer advocates in calling for an independent agency to monitor the safety of drugs after it was discovered that Bayer knew for months after it released cholesterol-lowering drug Baycol in February 1998 that it might cause a rare and sometimes fatal muscular disorder.[24] This came after another drug company, Merck, withdrew its popular painkiller Vioxx after finding that people taking it were twice as likely to have heart attacks, strokes, and deaths compared with comparable medications. FDA drug-safety expert Dr. David Graham presented testimony before a U.S. Senate Committee in November 2004, saying that his supervisors tried to suppress his efforts to report the Vioxx problems. Recent clinical trials have found similar risks with Bextra and Celebrex.

Perhaps the problem lies in the FDA's advisory panels. Ten of the thirty-two FDA advisers who endorsed the continued marketing of painkillers were paid consultants for the companies providing those drugs.[25]

In October 2004, Democrats and Republicans in Congress adopted, and Bush signed into law, a $137 billion pre-election corporate tax give-away, including a $10 billion buyout for tobacco farmers, of which about 40 percent will go to non-farming quota holders, including millionaires, country clubs, and city dwellers. Supported by a coalition of multinational corporations, it finances shopping malls, supports ship builders such as defense contractor Northrop Grumman, aircraft leasing companies, the distilled spirits, wine and beer industries, producers of small jets, and the Alaska natural gas pipeline. Senator John McCain called the measure the "worst example of the influence of special interests I have even seen."

Ex-politicians so love Washington, DC that they never leave, even after they have served their terms of office. About 40 percent of members of Congress defeated in the 1992 elections went to work as lobbyists, and between 1988 and 1993 42 percent of all permanent Senate Committee staff directors became lobbyists, as did 34 percent of House chief staffers.[26] Not to be outdone by mere staff, departing Republican House member Billy Tauzin became the president and chief executive of PhRMA, the main drug lobbying group in Washington, DC. Tauzin was obviously rewarded for his work on the industry's behalf when he was chair of the House Energy and Commerce Committee, which had jurisdiction over drug industry issues, and directly involved in drafting a major prescription drug bill.

Tauzin's case speaks to a larger problem in Washington—the revolving door phenomena whereby corporate executives and government officials go back and forth between the public and private sector. For instance, at least five top deputies to former Homeland Security Secretary Tom Ridge are now security industry lobbyists, including Tim Hutchinson, now a lobbyist for ThermoElectron and CompuDyne, hustling his brother Asa

risk of breast and colon cancer. The European Commission banned the use of rBGH.

The FDA is so in love with Monsanto, that, according to *The Ecologist*, the agency's approval of rBGH was not just the handiwork of Michael Taylor, but of Margaret Miller, Deputy Director of the Office of New Animal Drugs, and Suzanne Sechen, lead reviewer of scientific data on rBGH for the FDA, who all have Monsanto ties.[30] If that isn't enough, John Gibbon, former Chair of the Congressional Office of Technology Assessment, was a ten-year Monsanto consultant; Marcia Hale, formerly an assistant to President Clinton, coordinates public affairs and corporate strategy for Monsanto in Britain; and Mickey Kantor, a longtime California Democratic party political hack and former U.S. trade representative and U.S. secretary of commerce, is on the Monsanto board of directors.[31] As former Texas Agricultural Commissioner Jim Hightower said, "They've eliminated the middleman. The corporations don't have to lobby anymore. They are the government." Hightower used to complain about Monsanto's lobbying the secretary of agriculture. That was before former Monsanto executive Ann Venamin *became* the secretary of agriculture.

The connection between Monsanto and government continues a long corporate tradition. Linda Fisher, the assistant administrator for EPA's Office of Pollution Prevention, Pesticides, and Toxic Substances in President Ronald Reagan's second administration, developed EPA's pesticide policy before joining Monsanto in 1995 as a lobbyist. Now she's back at EPA as deputy director.[32]

Corporate management of American's leading brokerage firms also makes sure our elected leaders gain preferential access to lucrative stock initial public offerings (IPOs). Former New York Senator Al D'Amato, Senator Judd Creg, Senator Jeff Bingaman, and others, Democrats and Republicans alike including congressional representatives' wives, have all cashed in on favored IPO stock allocations. While he ran Halliburton Corporation, Vice President Dick Cheney flipped some of the most sought-after IPO's, producing $45,000 in profits. During the 2000 presidential campaign, when questioned about IPO access, his spokeswoman said his broker gave him "no special consideration whatsoever." Terry McAuliffe, the former chair and fundraiser of the Democratic National Committee, was able to buy pre-IPO shares of Global Crossing for $100,000, which he later sold for an $18 million profit before the company collapsed.[33] I'm sure he also received no special consideration.

Corporate lobbyists also rule in numerous state legislatures, especially in key states such as California, New York, New Jersey, Texas, and Florida. Thanks in large part to term limits, most legislators serve so few years that they are entirely funded by the Third House (of lobbyists). This corporate control over the system is further reinforced by the fact that in forty-one of fifty states, legislators work part time and in thirty-three states, they have no legislative staff, whatsoever.[34] Guess who shows these part-time legislators, with little or no staff, the ropes? Guess who writes their legislation? Guess who hosts lunches, receptions, educational seminars, and special outings in exotic places? ALEC, that's who.

ALEC stands for American Legislative Exchange Council, and is controlled by corporations. ALEC sponsors ongoing state legislation to weaken environmental laws, build privatized prisons, deregulate energy (especially nuclear power), limit gun control, and support the tobacco industry.[35] Members include the NRA, Chevron, Arthur Anderson, Archer Daniels Midland, R. J. Reynolds Tobacco, Exxon, DuPont, Philip Morris, GTE, and on and on. You get the picture.

Special interests so rule the state legislative process that politicians often run campaigns on a platform of cleaning house, declaring that if they're elected they will change things, not be bought by corporate money, and no longer collect money from lobbyists. This was the campaign pledge by Republican gubernatorial candidate Arnold Schwarzenegger in 2003, when he ran in a special recall election in California against Democratic Governor Gray Davis. In his first year in office, Davis had accepted over $13 million in special interest funds. But as the *San Francisco Chronicle* reported on November 17, 2004, one year after taking office on a "reform" campaign, Schwarzenegger had accepted over $26 million from special corporate and other interests, ". . . deeply vested in the outcome of legislation and regulatory decisions in Sacramento, including financial companies, auto dealers, and manufacturers and health care concerns."

PROTECTING OUR PRIVACY

Privacy has always been a concern for U.S. citizens, but it has been the number one priority for U.S. Senator Phil Gramm, who successfully sponsored the Gramm-Leach-Bliley Act of 1999, when he was chairman of the Senate Banking Committee. That law allows financial institutions—banks, credit card companies, insurance firms, and brokerage houses—to take personal financial information on you, their customers, and sell it to other corporations under joint marketing agreements. Upon his retirement, Senator Gramm was rewarded by being hired by Swiss-based UBS Warburg (which owns Paine Webber). In January 2002 UBS Warburg acquired Enron Corporation's disgraced energy trading company. As a Senator, Gramm was the second-largest recipient of campaign money from Enron, taking $101,350 since 1989. His wife, Wendy, served on Enron's board of directors from 1993 to mid-2002, receiving between $915,000 and $1.8 million in salary, director fees, and Enron stock.

It certainly warms my heart to know that Phil and Wendy, who worked so hard for Enron, will now be able to share their financial expertise with UBS Warburg.

For four years running, California State Senator Jackie Speier attempted to pass legislation to prohibit banks, insurance companies, brokerage firms, and other financial service companies from selling personal data—names, addresses, bank balances, spending habits, and credit scores—to third parties without customer permission. Democrats and Republicans defeated the bill in the State Assembly in 2000, after corporations spent nearly $20 million in lobbying and campaign donations. In 2003, Speier re-introduced the bill, supported by Senate President Pro-Tem John Burton, and was adopted by the Senate but was killed again in an assembly committee.[36] The measure was opposed, among others, by Wells Fargo, Proividian Financial, Bank of America, Citigroup, Capital One, Fidelity Investments, Household International, JP Morgan Chase, and the California Chamber of Commerce. Speier said the trading and sale of personal financial information is a $900 million per year industry in California alone, with $500 million in profits. At the same time, a ballot initiative circulated by consumer groups called for banning financial institutions from sharing *any* information on customers, even among affiliates, without customers opting in.[37] Frightened legislators and a governor threatened with recall enacted it into law when they realized the consumer groups had collected over six hundred thousand signatures for the initiative to be placed on the 2004 ballot.

Those pesky local governments, especially in California, have also tried to protect consumers by approving ordinances to block banks from sharing information without getting prior customer approval. Bank of America and Wells Fargo attorneys teamed up to argue in U.S. District Court that federal law—which requires customers to opt *out*, instead of opting *in*, placing the burden on them to maintain their own privacy—supercedes state law. (Earlier in May, 2003, the U.S. Supreme Court rebuffed San Francisco and Santa Monica in their attempt to ban surcharges on ATMs and in a separate case, a federal judge ruled that federal law regulating the finance charges on bank mortgages superceded state law.)

Meanwhile, the financial institution lobby was hard at work trying to do an end run around Speier's law—it was busy working with the Republican-dominated Congress and the Bush administration and successfully re-authorized the federal Fair Credit Reporting Act in December 2003. Fortunately, a federal judge ruled in 2004 that the Fair Credit law could not pre-empt the Speier law, and only covered the sharing of information for credit reports, not financial privacy. The ruling against the American Bankers Association, the Consumer Bankers Association, and the Financial Services Roundtable, requires banks to give consumers the opportunity to opt out and prohibits the sale of information to a bank affiliate that isn't in the same line of business.[38]

Consumer privacy received a blow with the adoption of the Patriot Act after 9/11, which reduced civil liberties and allowed the breach of privacy. We live in a world of databases that collect information about us, including our medical history, education, religious affiliation, financial data, postal delivery, smoking habits, charitable donations, political ideology, ethnicity, and pet ownership, not to mention voting habits, gun registration, hunting and fishing licenses, and magazine subscriptions, all of which are offered for sale. One consumer profiling service, ChoicePoint, sells access to its public records databases to the IRS, FBI, and other federal agencies.[39] In February 2005, ChoicePoint publicly revealed that criminals may have gained access to confidential information on about one hundred forty thousand consumers, leading to possible identity theft. Bank of America and Time Warner, among others, have also "lost" computer tapes of customers, possibly revealing confidential information to identity thieves.

In December 2004, Bush signed into law the U.S. Intelligence Reform and Terrorism Prevention Act, which, among other things, requires the Department of Homeland Security to issue federal regulations mandating Social Security identification on birth certificates, along with DNA biometric markers. Eventually, all drivers' licenses will contain biometric markers that will be centralized in the department's database and linked to bank and credit card information. The national ID has arrived through the backdoor, with little debate or analysis.

The federal government is pushing technology, including hardware and software, to "modernize" the health care system by allowing data to be shared among institutions and government agencies. Plans call for creating a Health Information Technology Leadership Panel of industry executives and health care experts to advise the government on the costs and benefits of the technology. It is important that medical personnel have access to our medical records, prescription drugs taken, and recent immunizations, so they can provide us with proper medical care. But should pharmaceutical companies be able to buy this information? This may end up being another taxpayer subsidy to the technology companies as payback for their campaign contributions to the Bush administration. There is no limit to the role of government in subsidizing corporations, and as former Secretary of Health and Human Services Tommy Thompson said, "There is an absolute important role for government."

Corporations in the near future will be able to track American consumption patterns by radio frequency identification tags that will replace bar codes on products, so that computers can track every individual's purchase, and in some cases take pictures of consumers buying products. Gillette, Wal-Mart, and Proctor & Gamble may tie tracking devices on products to a consumer's credit card, so that not only will companies have a photo of a consumer, but be able to attach spending patterns to credit and debit card use.

Meanwhile, the Government Printing Office awarded four companies $378,000 in contracts to design new U.S. passports that will contain embedded chips storing personal data, including digitized data on a traveler's face, which can be accessed by electronic skimming devices.[40] The ACLU and twelve other organizations from North America, Europe, and Asia sent a letter to the International Civil Aviation Organization saying they were ". . . increasingly concerned that the biometric travel document initiative is part and parcel of a larger surveillance infrastructure monitoring movement of individuals globally."

Should we, however, congratulate our government regulators for securing peace and tranquility at the dinner table? So intense was public pressure on the Federal Trade Commission (FTC) and the Federal Communications Commission (FCC) that these agencies created the National Do Not Call Registry to thwart the evil empire of telemarketers. The irony is that AT&T, the company selected by the FTC to administer the program, has attracted the most telemarketing complaints in recent years. I'm happy to know that these complaints didn't affect the FTC's decision-making process, and that AT&T received $3.5 million in 2003 to manage the list because the company represented "the best value."[41]

There was not a dry eye in the house when we heard that the National Do Not Call Registry was going to cost telemarketing firms two million jobs. First, we wondered if these were jobs in the United States, or in India or Jamaica, or wherever, since our corporate friends have been going overseas for everything from tech support calls to phone sex. Now, we find out that most of these jobs might be spared because of the loopholes in the telemarketing regulations. Exemptions exclude long-distance phone companies, airlines, banks and credit unions, insurance companies, charities, telephone surveyors, and political organizations (ergo, *politicians*). Another sweet—and sweeping—exemption in the National Do Not Call Registry is for any company that already has a business relationship with you.

Commercial telemarketers went all the way to the U.S. Supreme Court to save those outsourced jobs, but the court ruled against them, saying the government could enact the registry to protect individual privacy. As of June, 2004, about 62 million phone numbers have been entered on the list.

Outsourcing has been prevalent in the health care industry, where medical transcription business is done in Asia to cut costs. X-rays and MRI scans are also transferred electronically to India for analysis. The American College of Radiology has already set up a task force to review the offshore transfer of radiology services. One radiologist told *The New York Times* in November 2003: "This teleradiology thing is another nail in the coffin of the job market. Who needs to pay us $350,000 a year if they can get a cheap Indian radiologist for $25,000 a year?"

David Lazarus, a columnist at the *San Francisco Chronicle*, has almost weekly revealed details of corporate outsourcing of private information on U.S. citizens. He has not only uncovered medical information that has been outsourced to Asia, but the transfer of customers' and clients' confidential financial data and tax information from financial and large accounting firms, including Charles Schwab and Bank of America, to Indian information technology companies. India does not have laws to protect U.S. citizens' privacy. This opens the door for massive identify theft, bribery, and extortion—all in the name of cutting corporate costs. According to Lazarus, few countries have laws to protect the security of confidential personal information, including medical records, credit histories, tax documents, bank, brokerage and insurance records, debt reports, and Social Security and credit card numbers.[42] Some or all of this information presently ends up in ten countries, including India, the Philippines, Ireland, Israel, Pakistan, Jamaica, Ghana, Mexico, Guatemala, and China.

For several years, computer firms such as Gateway have outsourced call centers to Southeast Asia, where customers seeking technical assistance and advice sometimes can't understand the staff to whom English is a second language. Lazarus discovered that many companies in India, for example, subcontract with catalog retailers like Lillian Vernon, to provide call center services, but they do not disclose to customers that workers in India may be listening in on calls in which credit card numbers and other personal information could be given out.[43]

At least with outsourced confidential financial data, there is only the risk of having your identification stolen. Major airlines outsource air-craft maintenance, and there is very little oversight to protect the flying public. In March 2004 the Wall Street Journal reported that the National Transportation Safety Board cited bad maintenance and lax federal over-sight as contributing to the 2003 crash of a U.S. Airways commuter flight. Already, Southwest Airlines and FedEx have outsourced most of their main-tenance, and Jet Blue sends its planes to El Salvador. For overseas mainte-nance only supervisors need to be licensed by the FAA, not each mechanic, as the airlines continue to furlough experienced mechanics. According to the *Journal*, the world-wide aircraft maintenance market is worth about $37 billion annually.

The $16 billion debt collection industry is now outsourcing to India, Mexico, and the Philippines, and may actually violate the federal Fair Credit Reporting Act by disclosing personal financial information. According to a December 6, 2004 report in the *Wall Street Journal*, companies such as General Electric, Citigroup, HSBC Holding PLC, and American Express are using their India-based staff to collect money from delinquent debtors.

In the Philippines, long-time U.S. military bases in Olongapo and Subic have been converted into business parks full of multinational corporations, as a burgeoning industry of staffing agencies for call centers has grown ram-pant with full-fledged "accent erasing" employee programs. These agencies try to transform Filipinos' native accents into Texan drawls for U.S.-based clients. Those who answer calls from customers in the United Kingdom are made to acquire British accents. Hollywood prevails in the Philippines!

The irony of outsourcing, especially computer and business processing, is that American firms are losing business to European companies. U.S.-based outsourcing firms won just a 44 percent share of commercial deals, down from 71 percent a year ago.[44]

In an October 21, 2003 article, *The Guardian* of England reported that a large number of U.K. businesses—including HSBC Bank, BT, British Airways, Prudential, Standard Chartered, Norwich Union, Bupa, Reuters, Abbey National, and Powergen—are moving their call centers to India, causing job loss among middle class IT jobs in the United Kingdom and the United States. The paper also said that according to a leaked consultancy report thirty thousand executive positions in the United Kingdom will go to India in the next five years, and an American firm, Forrester Research, predicted that the United States will lose 3.3 million white-collar jobs between now and 2015, mostly to India.

Summing up its depressing story, *The Guardian* waxed philosophical:

> This is the reality of the world order Britain established and which is sustained by the heirs of the East India Company, the multinational corporation. The corporations operate only in their own interests. Sometimes these interests will coincide with those of a disadvantaged group, but only by disadvantaging another.
>
> For centuries, we have permitted ourselves to ignore the extent to which our welfare is dependent on the denial of other peoples'. We begin to understand the implications of the system we have created only when it turns against ourselves.

If you've lost your job and you have to move, Applied Digital Solutions (ADS) can implant you with a microchip (VeriChip) and monitor you anywhere in the world, thanks to the Global Positioning Satellite (GPS) system. The VeriChip is a syringe-injectable radio-frequency device the size of the tip of a grain of rice which carries a unique ID number and other personal data that can be activated by an external scanner (remember the 2004 movie *The Manchurian Candidate*?) and transmitted to law enforcement agencies, medical monitors, or whomever. The ADS chief scientist involved in testing the device in Manhattan, Dr. Peter Zhou, was quoted as saying: "We will be a hybrid of electronic intelligence and our own souls."[45] In October 2004, the FDA approved the use of subdermal microchips for medical purposes.

The cry for national and personal security and the fear of terrorism in all forms have improved earnings forecasts for many corporations, especially technology companies. Fear has already become very profitable for many businesses feeding at the public trough. Biometric devices, including electronic monitors and surveillance camera technology, that record facial bone structures, iris scans, voices, and other physical attributes, are becoming more popular with federal security agencies. The Pentagon was temporarily barred by Congress from developing the Total Information Awareness (TIA) system to be used on U.S. citizens, but the Center for Democracy and Technology, a group that advocates online privacy, believes there are currently few constraints on government access to commercial databases legal under the Privacy Act and the U.S. Constitution. TIA would use software to search databases of passport applications, work permits, visas, driver's licenses, car rentals, airline ticket purchases, and arrests, as well as other financial, medical, or housing records, to nab suspected terrorists. After Congress demanded more details, TIA changed its name to Terrorism Information Awareness, changed its Web site, removed documents describing the project and its funding and is no longer granting interviews on the program.[46]

Lest we forget, John M. Poindexter, the former Reagan national security advisor, was a top official of the Pentagon's Defense Advanced Research Agency (DARPA), a $5 billion-a-year organization that is in charge of TIA. Poindexter was convicted of lying to Congress during the Iran-Contra affair of the 1980s, a conviction which was later reversed on the grounds that he had been given immunity for the testimony in which he lied.[47] Poindexter had the brilliant idea, which would have been funded by $8 million (they already spent only $600,000), to create a futures market for speculators to bet, and potentially profit, on terrorist events, such as using biological agents against Israel and the United States, as well as carrying out assassinations. The agency was going to start registering as many as one thousand traders.[48] Unfortunately, the Bush administration lost Poindexter when he resigned from DARPA. The *Wall Street Journal* explained that investors already speculate in a legitimate futures market based on death and destruction, and terror futures are not really anything new.

This concept originated in a report by Credit Suisse Group's Credit Suisse First Boston which said that decision markets had been proven to be uncannily accurate in predicting everything from Hollywood blockbusters to elections.[49] Supposedly this would be a way to create an alternative means of anticipating events by monitoring trading activity to gain insights on the likelihood of certain events. I'm sure they never thought that this would also be a way for wealthy traders including terrorists, to manipulate the futures markets to make money.

Larry Ellison, founder and CEO of Oracle Corporation, a software database company, has been adamant in his patriotic fervor in supporting a national ID card. Suffice it to say, that Larry's company would gladly donate the necessary software for such a system to the U.S. government; but would charge for maintenance and future software upgrades. This national ID system seems to be an updated version of the Pass system in the former apartheid white-minority-ruled South Africa. Shareholders of Oracle Corporation, Harrington Investments, Inc., and Walden Asset Management wrote a letter to Larry in January 2002, expressing our fear that such a national ID would limit civil liberties and personal freedom. As fiduciaries, we also asked a series of questions: Has our company considered the harm to its reputation from its involvement in a program that many see as severely eroding civil liberties? Has our company's general counsel determined the extent of legal liability and financial exposure? Has our company tested such software with existing customers to prove reliability, compatibility, and protection from being pirated? Has our company successfully supplied other municipal, state or foreign governments the same or similar software? Has our company provided software to, and is such data now being maintained by, a foreign government, police, and military for ID and surveillance purposes?

At the time of publication of this book, we had received no response from Larry, or Oracle Corporation.

THE CORPORATE RETURN ON INVESTMENT

What have the corporations received for exercising their God-given civic duty of feeding politicians' hunger for money? Here's one answer: In 1950, corporate taxes provided 26.5 percent of total federal revenue; by 2000, that had declined to 10 percent. In 1957, corporations supplied 45 percent of local property tax revenue to the states; by 1987, that was down to about 16 percent.[50]

According to a study done by the California Budget Project, corporate tax receipts were expected to provide 9.2 percent of the general fund revenues in 2003–2004, down from 14.4 percent in 1980–1981. New, increased and expanded corporate tax breaks are responsible for reducing state revenue by $4.6 billion in 2002–2003.

Tax avoidance is a great corporate game, as large, multinational, impersonal economic giants nimbly move from one tax haven to another, sometimes paying zero taxes in the United States. In 1999 Microsoft reported $12.3 billion in profits and paid no taxes. Enron paid no taxes in four of the last five years, while reporting $1.8 billion in profits. Even IBM—the favorite of the Nazis for providing the information technology to the Third Reich to move Jews to the death camps and ovens during World War II[51] and friends in technology of the South African apartheid system—received a U.S. tax rebate in 1997 while earning a paltry profit of $3.1 billion. All in all, the top corporations that paid zero taxes from 1996 to 1998—including AT&T, Bristol-Myers Squibb, Chase Manhattan, Enron, ExxonMobil, General Electric, Microsoft, Pfizer, and Philip Morris—gave $150.1 million to political campaigns from 1991 to 2001. Public Campaign, a group working for public financing of political campaigns, reports these corporations received $55 billion in tax breaks from 1996 to 1998 alone, and benefited from legislation that gutted the alternative minimum tax, allowing billions in rebates to select corporations.[52] That's not a bad return on their political investment. Of course, we, the American taxpayers, get shafted.

According to the General Accounting Office, more than 60 percent of U.S. corporations didn't pay any federal taxes for 1996 through 2000, five years "... when the economy boomed and corporate profits soared," reported the *Wall Street Journal* on April 6, 2004.

In generous states like California, taxpayers also get robbed by corporate giveaways. On December 15, 2004, the state's Franchise Tax Board gave $5 million in tax refunds to three companies that paid no state business income taxes in 2003. Another twenty-two "poor" companies were requesting $77 million in refunds.[53]

The most enterprising—and profitable—tax game of all is moving corporate assets overseas to avoid U.S. taxes. According to the Commerce Department, from 1983 to 1999, the value of American corporate assets in Bermuda, the Cayman Islands, and eleven other tax havens grew 44 percent more than their assets in Germany, England, and other countries with tax rates similar to the United States. One third of Enron's 2,832 subsidiaries are located in tax havens like the Cayman Islands.[54] This shift of assets—such as drug patents and ownership of corporate logos—makes their domestic operation appear less profitable and therefore less taxable. As the corporate tax base erodes, the burden shifts to individuals.

Columnist Arianna Huffington summarized the other benefits to corporations, besides tax breaks, in her book *Pigs At The Trough*: "The benefits of this offshore shell game extend well beyond a corporation's bottom line. Formerly red, white, and blue companies now sporting a Bermuda tan are also suddenly and conveniently immune to judgments against them in the U.S. courts, less accountable to their shareholders who are unable to file class action suits, and freed from a whole host of annoying government regulations."

Stuffy old accountants also promote leasing tax shelters for their corporate clients that cost the U.S. taxpayer billions a year in corporate tax deductions. A U.S. corporation will rent a foreign facility and then lease it back to a foreign public authority that owns and operates it. The company then claims depreciation over the life of the lease, no payments are made, and the foreign public authority never loses control of its assets. The corporation gets a tax break, lawyers and accountants earn large commissions and fees, and taxpayers lose. Following a congressional hearing on such practices, politicians appeared outraged, one of them saying, "Yet not one piece of tax legislation to curb tax shelter abuses has been enacted."[55] The result of this is that corporate income taxes represent only 9.4 percent of all federal tax receipts.[56]

As corporations paid fewer taxes, wealthy individuals were also rewarded by the Bush administration's tax cuts, enacted by Congress in 2003. This $350 billion (less than half sought by the White House) tax cut saves the average middle-class household about $217 a year, but will save $93,500 for those earning $1 million annually. About two-thirds of the tax break will go to 10 percent of Americans, while the bill will push the federal budget deficit to over $400 billion (total federal debt is about $7.6 trillion).[57] The working poor and middle class taxpayers are increasingly carrying the tax load while the wealthy and their corporations are subsidized. Of the $2 trillion in federal tax revenues collected each year, about one-half is generated by personal income tax and employer withholding. Another $500 billion is withheld from employees' paychecks for old age, disability, and unemployment insurance.[58]

That the rich are getting richer is more than a truism in America. The top four hundred individuals earned almost $70 billion in 2000, or about 1.09 percent of the total adjusted gross income.[59] This was more than twice the top four hundred's share for 1992. The average income for those four hundred was $174 million in 2000, nearly quadruple the $46.8 million average in 1992.[60]

The Rich Got Richer

Here are how much the top four hundred individual income-tax returns reported as adjusted gross income, their share of the nation's total, and the amount of annual income needed to qualify for this exclusive group.

Tax Year	Total Income for Top400 Returns	Reported Income of the Top 400 Returns as a Percent of Total Reported Individual Income	Cut Off to Make Top 400
2000	$69.57 billion	1.09%	$86.8 million
1999	$53.54 billion	0.91%	$67.4 million
1998	$44.20 billion	0.82%	$57.4 million
1992	$18.72 billion	0.52%	$24.4 million

SOURCE: INTERNAL REVENUE SERVICE STATISTICS OF INCOME DIVISION

According to the Institute for Policy Studies, the top two hundred corporations have combined sales greater than the sum total of the economies of 182 of the 191 countries in the world. These same two hundred companies have almost twice the economic clout in terms of annual income, as the poorest four-fifths of humanity. Of the largest one hundred economies in the world, fifty-three are corporations. And they have the same rights

President George W. Bush with Thailand Prime Minister Thaksin Shinawatra, whose family business received $160 million in loan guarantees from the U.S. Export-Import Bank to buy a satellite from an American firm, Loral Space and Communications, whose CEO Bernard Schwartz makes large contributions to U.S. politicians. *Source: Getty Images.*

under U.S. law as living, breathing citizens of the United States. (More on this wonderful legal irony and the genesis of most of our problems with corporations later in the chapter.)

Of course, our corporate friends also receive lucrative tax breaks, loopholes, or what is described in the California state budget as tax expenditures. A study by Jose Oyola, an assistant director at the General Accounting Office and an adjunct instructor at the University of Virginia, found that Cisco, Applied Materials, Inc., and Oracle receive millions of dollars in corporate tax breaks based on foreign sales intended to "help American exporters compete."[61] The study also reported that between 1991 and 2000, destitute companies such as Boeing and General Electric received $1.21 billion and $1.15 billion, respectively, in foreign sales tax breaks.

The federal government especially wanted to help Enron make a buck. This is the same Enron, whose eleven thousand employees lost $1.3 billion in retirement benefits because they didn't have a choice other than putting it all in Enron stock, and the same Enron that used about $7 billion in public funds to finance thirty-eight projects in twenty-nine countries.[62] In 1995, Ken Lay, the CEO of Enron told Congress: "Public finance agencies are the only reliable source of the financing that is essential for private infrastructure projects in developing countries."[63]

It's not just the struggling U.S. companies that the American taxpayer is subsidizing, but some downtrodden foreign companies as well. For instance, there's Thailand Prime Minister Thaksin Shinawatra, a billionaire whose family business, Asian telecommunications giant Shin Corporation, received a $160 million loan guarantee from the U.S. Export-Import Bank.[64] This loan guarantee was to help a Shin subsidiary, Shin Satellite, buy a new telecommunications satellite because Loral Space and Communications is the American supplier, and without the guarantee, Loral wouldn't finance the deal. Loral had Bernard Schwartz as chairman and CEO, a long-time Democratic Party donor who bankrupted GlobalStar after his company provided military technology to the Chinese government, but who still gives lots of money to politicians.

The U.S. Export-Import Bank is another taxpayer funded organization which uses loan guarantees to subsidize U.S. and foreign corporations which have lots of trouble getting funding on their own—companies like Boeing, Halliburton, General Electric, Northrop Grumman, Bechtel, Petroleos de Venezuela, Siemens, Chevron Texaco, and many, many others.[65]

It would be difficult to come up with a better case study of a corporation feeding at the public trough—despite a checkered past—than Halliburton. As America's number one oil services company, the nation's fifth-largest military contractor, and one of the biggest nonunion employers in the United States, Halliburton has benefited greatly from having friends in high places, like Vice President Dick Cheney, who ran the company from 1995–2000. Much of Halliburton's revenue is generated by U.S. and foreign government contracts, including the contract to add prison cells for alleged terrorists being held at Guantanamo, Cuba. The $9.7 million contract could grow to $300 million over the next four years.[66] In December 2001 the company was awarded a ten-year open-ended contract with the United States to provide military troops everything from mess halls and dorms to laundry services. According to a U.S. Army spokesman: "The overall anticipated cost of task orders awarded since contract award in December 2001 is approximately $830 million."[67] The company was also awarded a $17 million government contract in Iraq to put out oil well fires,[68] and a $1.2 billion contract to rebuild Iraq's oil industry in the southern part of the country.[69]

Halliburton's two subsidiaries, Dresser-Rand and Ingersoll-Dresser, helped rebuild Saddam Hussein's war-damaged oil fields in Iraq for $23.8 million. In 1991 Cheney told a group of oil company executives he was against getting rid of Hussein.[70] Back then he needed the dictator's money, and the elder Bush needed his oil. From 1997 to 2000 when Cheney was running Halliburton, two of its subsidiaries sold Hussein's government a total of $73 million in oil field supplies. It didn't violate U.S. sanctions at that time because Dresser-Rand and Ingersoll Dresser Pump Company, both of Halliburton's subsidiaries, were foreign.[71] Halliburton, like many patriotic companies mentioned earlier, uses off-shore subsidiaries to avoid U.S. taxes and other inconveniences—like being identified by the U.S. State Department as supporting suspected terrorist states.

One of the embarrassments that Halliburton hoped to avoid was government attention regarding its use of a Cayman Island subsidiary to operate in Iran. Halliburton has received a grand jury subpoena for documents, since U.S. law restricts American companies from doing business in countries (such as Iran) designated by the State Department as sponsors of terrorism, unless exempted by the Office of Foreign Assets Control (OFAC). It seems that OFAC recently referred its investigation of Halliburton to the U.S. Department of Justice.[72]

Halliburton is such an outstanding defense contractor that on December 13, 2002, the *Wall Street Journal* reported that the SEC had initiated a formal investigation into Halliburton's accounting practices, with regard to cost overruns on construction projects. In early August 2004, Halliburton agreed to pay $7.5 million to the SEC for failing to disclose how the company accounted for certain cost overruns which resulted in the company issuing misleading profit figures in 1998 and 1999. When Cheney was CEO, Halliburton paid the U.S. government $2 million in fines for consistently over-billing the Pentagon. In one case it charged the government $750,000 for work that actually cost only $125,000.[73] Christmas 2002 must have also been hard for Halliburton's corporate officers, since they agreed to pay $4 billion to settle more than three hundred thousand asbestos-related claims.[74]

Cheney was a true American patriot even while running Dallas-based Halliburton, building and maintaining energy facilities for $2.3 billion in government contracts and $1.5 billion in government financing and loan guarantees. While he was CEO, there was a dramatic increase in the number of Halliburton subsidiaries registered in tax havens—from nine in 1995 to forty-four in 2000. Halliburton's foreign customers were also able to have about $1.5 billion in loans guaranteed by the Export-Import Bank during

Cheney's term as company CEO. The company's taxes dropped from $302 million in 1998 to an $85 million *rebate* in 1999.[75]

Halliburton disclosed in 2002 that one of its units made "improper" payments of $2.4 million for favorable tax treatment to a Nigerian tax consultant who turned out to be an employee of a local tax authority.[76] Gosh, Halliburton reported making a bribe! It's unclear if Halliburton received a tax deduction for this.

Halliburton's troubles are never over, it seems. In late 2003 the Pentagon launched an investigation into whether Halliburton overcharged in $1.2 billion in fuel sales in Iraq.[77] It's ironic that $1.2 billion is also the amount of money Halliburton received from the U.S. Corps of Engineers to rebuild Iraq's oil industry. On August 12, 2004 *The New York Times* reported that a Pentagon audit found that Halliburton failed to adequately account for about $4.2 billion the company was paid for providing logistical support to troops in Iraq and Kuwait. Halliburton employees were reported to have accepted $6 million in illegal kickbacks. The FBI is investigating the company.

Besides being accused of overcharging on contracts in Afghanistan as well as Iraq, Halliburton was hit with a shareholder suit accusing the company of serial accounting fraud. Officials of Halliburton's partially-owned multibillion dollar TSKJ Bonny Island liquefied natural gas plant project in Nigeria are also being questioned about a $140 million slush fund used to funnel money through a British lawyer to gain the original plant contract by bribing Nigeria officials.[78] Halliburton, in a quarterly filing with the SEC, admitted ". . . that payments may have been made to Nigerian officials."[79]

Gerald W. McEntee, chair of the AFSCME Employee Pension Fund, who introduced shareholder resolutions in 2005 in an effort to force incumbent directors off the board, said: "The current situation at Halliburton represents the worst of corporate America: Cooking the books, doing business with terrorist states and cutting deals of questionable legality with oppressive regimes around the world. The Halliburton board has failed to properly monitor the company, leading to a drop in overall value of the company of more than $3 billion over five years."

McEntee added that shareholders will be hurt if Halliburton is convicted under the Foreign Corrupt Practices Act, since U.S. government contractors make up a large portion of Halliburton's revenues, and a conviction would ban the company from bidding on federal contracts. McEntee shouldn't worry, because Halliburton has done such a great job in Iraq and Afghanistan—at a cost of $10.5 billion—that the U.S. Army approved $9.4 million in bonus payments to the company's Kellogg Brown & Root subsidiary.[80]

Halliburton's troop-support project in Iraq was budgeted by the Army for $9.8 billion, and its subsidiary, KBR, has provided estimated costs of $16 billion—somewhat of a cost overrun. Halliburton operates more than 80 sites in Iraq at a cost of about $18 million a day, while the company estimated that by May 2005 it would need $28 million a day.[81] Once a military contractor has the government by the throat, taxpayers get squeezed.

In short, Halliburton gets to feed at the U.S. taxpayer trough and gets a tax rebate for moving more operations overseas—even after it is found to be over-billing the government. One relevant fact is that Cheney is still on Halliburton's payroll for approximately $180,000 a year in deferred compensation.

Halliburton's cozy relationship with the government is a continuation of a long American tradition. Another recent example is the Bechtel Corporation. George Shultz, a former secretary of the U.S. Treasury under President Richard Nixon and a former secretary of state under Reagan and now an advisor to Governor Schwarzenegger, was on the board of the privately-held Bechtel Corporation, serving as senior counsel. Shultz has served on Bush and Rumsfeld's Defense Policy Board, and is chairman of the advisory board of the Committee for the Liberation of Iraq. Bechtel CEO Riley Bechtel is on the President's Export Council; Bechtel senior vice president, Jack Sheehan, is on the influential Defense Policy Board; Bechtel senior vice president, Daniel Chao, serves on the U.S. Export-Import Bank advisory board; and twenty-one-year Bechtel veteran Ross Connelly is the executive vice president and chief operating officer for the U.S. Overseas Private Investment Corporation. From 1999 through 2002, Bechtel donated $1.3 million to political candidates.[82] In 2003, Bechtel received a $680 million contract to rebuild Iraq's infrastructure, including water, sewage, and power generation systems. There was no open and transparent bidding process.[83]

Corporate access to the Iraqi reconstruction should not come as a surprise to anyone who has monitored Pentagon business and defense contractors over the last fifty years. While Bechtel and Halliburton first come to mind, it is only because of their political visibility and connection to political starlets like George Schultz and Dick Cheney.

THE PRIVATIZATION TSUNAMI

Thirty to thirty-five companies, mostly run by retired military officers, dominate the Pentagon's list of contractors who provide a host of services—battlefield training, logistics, and military advice, operating weapons systems, gathering intelligence at home and abroad. During the Persian Gulf War in 1991, one of every fifty people on the battlefield was an American civilian under contract. By 1996, in Bosnia, the figure was one in ten, according to a report in the October 13, 2002 edition of *The New York Times*. The same newspaper story reported on other private military contractors, saying:

> In Bosnia, employees of DynCorp were found to be operating a sex-slave ring of young women who were held for prostitution after their passports were confiscated. In Croatia, local forces, trained by MPRI Corporation, used what they learned to conduct one of the worst episodes of 'ethnic cleansing,' an event that left more than 100,000 homeless and hundreds dead and resulted in war-crimes indictments. No employee of either firm has ever been charged in these incidents.

When Sean Penn spent time in Iraq, he was greeted and searched by a private militia armed with Kalasknikov rifles, questioned by a South African and a Texan, all paid for by DynCorp, a private military company (PMC). As Penn describes DynCorp:

PMCs, and there are many of them, tend to be staffed and directed by retired generals, CIA officers, counter terrorism professionals, retired Special Air Service men, Special Forces guys, and so on. DynCorp is a subsidiary of the benignly named Computer Services Corp. DynCorp forces are mercenaries. Their contracts have included covert actions for the CIA in Colombia, Peru, Kosovo, Albania, and Afghanistan.[84]

These private contractors feeding at the public trough are the new mercenaries. DynCorp is not alone. MPRI, formerly know as Military Professionals Resources, Inc., employs more than ten thousand former military personnel, including elite Special Forces. The company was sold to a publicly traded military contractor, L-3 Communications, for $40 million. The company's revenue exceeds $100 million a year. Call them what you will, but these are hired guns, owing allegiance only to a legal contract, wearing no uniform, but at the beck and call of faceless bureaucrats. What a way for a government agency to cover its tracks with non-uniformed mercenaries carrying out foreign policy by contract.

When MPRI went to human rights–deprived Equatorial Guinea, it was to train the Coast Guard to protect exploration by ExxonMobil off the African coast. When DynCorp goes to Colombia, it is involved in "aerial anti-narcotics" and all is paid for by U.S. taxpayers. But who controls these mercenary forces? In the battlefield a commander can't give orders to a contractor, and a contractor is not subject to the Uniform Code of Military Justice.

The London-based Hart Group, which has a large contract through the Army Corps of Engineers to guard energy facilities in Iraq, hires South African mercenaries, including assassins for the former apartheid government. In the early 1980s these hit men traveled to Zimbabwe, Botswana, and Zambia to murder opponents of white-minority rule. Other "freedom fighters" in Iraq, fighting for cash, include human rights violators from Augusto Pinochet's regime in Chile and Slobodan Milosevic's in Yugoslavia.[85]

Peter Singer, an analyst at the Brookings Institute in Washington and the author of *Corporate Warriors: The Rise of the Privatized Military Industry,* said: "While most people have not heard of this industry, it is a $100 billion-per-year business whose largest client is the U.S. government. But it has virtually no laws, oversight or any public understanding of how to deal with it."[86]

Representative Janice Schakowsky (D-IL) has been asking lots of questions about DynCorp's involvement in Colombia, but more importantly, questioning the privatization of global military operations, including Iraq. She was quoted in the June 22, 2003 *The New York Times Magazine* saying: "Is the U.S. military privatizing its missions to avoid public controversy or embarrassment—to hide body bags from the media and shield the military from public opinion? We talk a lot in Congress about how many U.S. troops are there and for how long, but not at all about the contractors. They don't have to follow the same chain of command, the military code of conduct may or may not apply, the accountability is absent and the transparency is absent—but the money keeps flowing."

According to a December 22, 2003 report in the *North Bay Progressive*, "The private sector is so firmly embedded in combat, occupation, and peacekeeping duties that the phenomenon may have reached the point of no return: the U.S. military would struggle to wage war without it."

In Iraq there are an estimated seventy-five thousand civilian employees of private contractors, of which about twenty thousand may be performing roles that probably would have been assigned to the U.S. military.[87] And ten companies in Iraq with billions of dollars in Defense Department contracts have paid more than $300 million in fines and penalties since 2000 ". . . to resolve allegations of bid rigging, fraud, delivery of faulty military parts and environmental damage."[88]

As Crenson and Ginsberg pointed out in *Downsizing Democracy*, an "essential requisite for the modern state is the ability to defend itself militarily. Here too the role of the ordinary citizens, once critical to national survival, is now much diminished." The authors note that constitutional protections limit the actions of the government, but not those of private firms. Public access under the Freedom of Information Act has also been held by the courts not to apply to private firms operating under government contracts. Crenson and Ginsberg write: "Whereas the federal government directly employs fewer than 2 million civilian workers, one recent study estimates that more than 12 million Americans are employed by a 'shadow government' of private corporations, universities, research laboratories, foundations, and state and municipal governments that hold government contracts, receive federal grants, or are required to carry out federal mandates."

The problems inherent in the military-industrial complex can be vividly seen in the dealings of Boeing with the Pentagon. Boeing, a publicly traded private defense contractor, needed to keep alive its Boeing 767 aircraft production line. The answer was an Air Force-sponsored one hundred aircraft lease program worth $20 billion to Boeing. Congressional representatives whoring themselves to Boeing for fat political donations and pork in their districts pushed ahead with the plan, even though the Federal Office of Management and Budget, General Accounting Office, and Congressional Budget Office reports all concluded that the deal would be more costly than if the Air Force simply bought the airplanes.[89] In July 2003 the General Accounting Office estimated that each 767 aircraft would cost $173 million, not $138 million as put forth by the Air Force and Boeing. The Air Force later released data bringing the final cost to $29.8 billion.[90]

Senator John McCain (R-AZ), a former presidential candidate, told *The New York Times*: "This is a great deal for Boeing Company and I'm sure is the envy of corporate lobbyists from one end of K Street to the other. But it is a lousy deal for the Air Force and the American taxpayer." The reason it was a great deal for Boeing is that if the Air Force were to buy the aircraft, Boeing would have to borrow to finance the production, thereby weakening its balance sheet. McCain released documents and emails showing how Boeing lobbyists and Air Force staff worked together to convince Congress to approve the deal. Specifically, documents indicated that one top Air Force official gave the company important financial data about a competing bid from Airbus.[91] She has since landed a new job—with Boeing. This Air Force official sold her house to a Boeing attorney working on the tanker-lease deal, while her daughter and son-in-law also worked for Boeing.[92] Boeing dismissed the two employees involved, and the Pentagon is investigating. McCain was quoted as saying "I've been concerned about the increasingly incestuous relationship between the Pentagon and the major defense corporations."[93] It echoes President Eisenhower's warning from more than fifty years ago about the military-industrial complex.

Boeing, which receives about one-half of its $49 billion in annual revenue from defense and space contracts, is also working with the Pentagon to get more financial assistance to support the company's Delta IV Rocket program as well as stretching the appropriations out over a longer period of time. A June 20, 2003 *Wall Street Journal* article said:

> By stressing the losses it faces down the road, Boeing also may be positioning itself to convince the Pentagon and U.S. Air Force officials to avoid punishing the company for allegedly improperly acquiring thousands of pages of internal documents dealing with rival Lockheed Martin's rocket program. The Justice Department and Air Force are conducting separate investigations of Boeing's actions. Boeing says it is cooperating with the probes.

The Air Force, as punishment to Boeing, transferred the purchase of $1 billion of rocket launchers to Lockheed, and will reimburse Lockheed for a $200 million investment to upgrade the company's Southern California facility so it can launch government spy, communications, and other satellites. Meanwhile both companies say they are losing money on most launches and argue that our government should be paying them more.[94] Lockheed and Boeing are now working together to lobby the Pentagon.

Defense contractor Lockheed, comprised of Lockheed, Martin Marietta, Loral, General Dynamics, and Titan Corp (recently purchased for $1.8 billion), agreed in August 2003 to pay $37.9 million to the government to settle charges that it inflated costs on several Air Force contracts. On the same day the company announced that it had received a $140 million contract from the FBI to develop a security system to protect the agency's computer network from hackers.[95]

Lockheed Martin exemplifies the relationship connecting corporations, foreign policy, and politicians. Claiming that Lockheed sells weapons banned by international law (anti-personnel mines and depleted-uranium weapons) and that the $27 billion company supports war and violates disarmament agreements, protestors have long attempted to shut down the Sunnyvale, California campus. According to the Center for Responsive Politics, Lockheed is the defense industry's top political donor, providing $2.2 million in 2002 to candidates and political parties. This is a small investment to make for billions in payback contracts. The Air Force continues to order new cargo planes after giving $2.6 billion to Lockheed Martin to buy fifty planes that still don't meet the military's requirements and can't even be flown in combat zones.[96]

It doesn't matter that planes can't fly in combat zones as long as Lockheed can be the "Number One" recipient of Pentagon primary contracts. In fiscal year 2003, the company took in $21.9 billion (80 percent of Lockheed's revenue comes from the U.S. government), Boeing had $17.3 billion, Northrop Grumman had $11.1 billion, and General Dynamics had $8.2 billion. In addition to funding key congressional supporters with campaign contributions, Lockheed's former executives have held government posts of secretary of the Navy, secretary of transportation, director of the national nuclear weapons complex, and director of the national spy satellite agency. Former executives have also served on the government's Defense Policy Board, the Defense Science Board, and the Homeland Security Advisory Council, which helps set military policy and select weapons systems. Danielle Brian of the Project on Government Oversight, a nonprofit organization that monitors government contracts, told The New York Times in November, 2004, that, "The fox isn't guarding the henhouse. He lives there."

Thanks to Edward Aldridge, a member of Lockheed Martin's board of directors, the company continues to have influence in Congress, with the Bush administration and with the Pentagon. Aldridge has been secretary of the Air Force, president of McDonnell Douglas Corporation, and more recently, under-secretary of defense. Before he left the Pentagon, he approved a $3 billion contract to build twenty Lockheed F/A 22 aircraft, after having long criticized the program as overpriced.[97] He has also been named as head of Bush's commission on space exploration, and wants to privatize the National Aeronautics and Space Administration (NASA).

It just so happens that Lockheed's United States Space Alliance operates "the space shuttle and does more business with NASA than any other contractor."[98] Privatizing NASA means more corporate opportunities to suck up taxpayer money. According to Alan Ross, a Washington lobbyist who advises companies seeking federal contracts: "The NASA budget is bigger than the gross domestic product of many South American countries. So the opportunities are there for great rewards."[99]

To make matters worse, many of the taxpayer-funded, multibillion dollar, lobbyist-inspired weapons systems we don't need, also don't work. Take, for example, the long-awaited anti-ballistic missile defense system. The December 2004 test firing of a missile to intercept an incoming mock warhead failed to get off the launch pad. So far, this useful weapon has cost the American taxpayers $130 billion and is expected to cost another $50 billion over the next five years.[100]

The most extreme case of the private sector's entrenched access to taxpayer money is the prison system, where two giants—Corrections Corporation of America (CCA) and Wackenhut Corporation—spend substantial sums of money to lobby state and local politicians and the Federal Bureau of Prisons to produce billions in corporate revenue. Investment banking and underwriters also fare very well when state bonds need to be sold to build more prisons. Mistreated prisoners have no right to bring suit in federal court over mistreatment in private prisons.

In California, prison guards are a potent lobby in the legislature, give generously to political campaigns, and perhaps as a result, were the least affected recently by severe budget cuts. Criminal justice is considered part of "Major State Infrastructure" in California and Department of Corrections (DOC)—with a $5.3 billion annual budget—oversees thirty-three prisons, thirty-eight correctional conservation camps, eleven youthful offender institutions, and twelve crime labs. When a group of German criminal justice experts were given an overview of California's system, they learned that the DOC employs nearly as many people as Germany imprisons. Germany, with a population of 82 million people has 56,000 inmates. California, with 34 million people, has 159,390.

As building and running prisons has become big business the private sector has expanded into law enforcement. The security business has been growing more than 7 percent a year, outpacing the growth of police by more than three times, and nationwide is a $33 billion industry. In 2002, California licensed 15,450 new security officers, for a total of 185,000. Of that number, an estimated 14,000 are licensed to carry guns.[101]

In many states there is no regulation or oversight at all regarding private security guards. In California, the most stringent, it took a three-hour class and an FBI criminal background check to become a security guard. In 2004 class requirements were raised to forty hours and minimal qualification in the use of firearms, batons, and pepper spray. The most comprehensive course is a twelve-week "Penal Code 832" class through California Community Colleges. According to Leo Hertoghe, professor emeritus and former chair of the department of criminal justice at California State University, Sacramento: "A ten-year-old could get an A-plus in that 832 class."[102]

Without civilian oversight and government control of armed security forces, anything can happen and usually does. An old friend of mine, Jerry Meszaros—a wonderful union organizer, the founding director of the St. Mark's "Bridges of Hope" Worker Center in Kansas City, and a founding board member of the Chicago-based National Interfaith Committee for Worker Justice—was shot and killed on August 13, 2003 by an off-duty, armed security guard who had been on the job only a few months. This killer was turned down initially when he attempted to first get a "license to carry," but persisted until he was successful. He had prior arrests for carrying a concealed weapon, aggravated assault, and obstructing an officer. He was stopping Jerry and his sister from going down a short one-way street to their home.

Is the tail wagging the dog? Do mercenaries, prison guards, private security firms, and defense contractors now control our government?

THE CORPORATION AS A PERSON

Besides controlling government through funneling money into politics, corporations received a great boost when the courts said they have the same rights as human beings. Some still believe that the now infamous *Santa Clara County v. Southern Pacific Railroad Company* decision of 1886 was really a "ruling" that breathed life into the corporate structure. Congress made no laws that corporations, which are chartered under state law, should be treated the same as living, breathing human beings. There was no state or federal court ruling, and no U.S. Supreme Court ever ruled on *Santa Clara*, or any other case, regarding the issue of corporate personhood. As Thom Hartmann explained in *Unequal Protection: The Rise of Corporate Dominance and the Theft of Human Rights:*

> In fact, to this day there has been no Supreme Court ruling that could explain why a corporation—with its ability to continue operating forever, a legal agreement that can't be put in jail and doesn't need fresh water to drink or clean air to breathe—should be granted the same constitutional rights our Founders explicitly fought for, died for, and granted to the very mortal human beings who are citizens of the United States to protect them against the perils of imprisonment and suppression they had experienced under a despot King.

In fact, Hartmann says that in the written record of the case, a court recorder noted and reported a simple statement of *opinion* by Chief Justice Waite. Before hearing arguments in the case, says Hartmann, Chief Justice Waite said: "The court did not wish to hear argument on the question whether the provision in the 14th Amendment to the Constitution, which forbids a State to deny to any person within its jurisdiction the equal protection of the laws, applies to these corporations. *We are all of the opinion that it does.*" This was followed by the actual decision delivered by Justice Harlan who explicitly said that the California Supreme Court was *not* ruling on the constitutional question of corporate personhood under the Fourteenth Amendment or any other amendment. So for over one hundred years, courts, lawyers and corporations have all been basing their arguments supporting corporate personhood on a falsehood.

To add further insult to legal injury, Hartmann notes that the court recorder, J. C. Bancroft Davis, a Harvard educated attorney and former assistant secretary of state to two presidents, was connected to the rail-roads, having served as president of the Newburgh and New York Railroad Company. This is the court recorder who wrote headnotes (a comment with no legal status) giving corporations the same rights as human beings.

No state or federal legislature passed a law or even discussed it; no amend-ment to the Constitution was deemed necessary. The citizens were simply informed that they had a mistaken view about corporations, if they were informed at all. Subsequent Supreme Courts never really considered the question, preferring instead to build on it. Neither the history nor the lan-guage of the Fourteenth Amendment justifies the belief that corporations are included within its protection. The language of the amendment itself does not support the theory that it applies to corporations. The first clause of Section One reads: "All persons born or naturalized in the United States, and subject to the jurisdiction thereof, are citizens of the United States and of the State wherein they reside." Certainly a corporation cannot be natu-ralized, and "persons" here is not broad enough to include corporations.

The first clause of the second sentence reads: "No State shall make or enforce any law which shall abridge the privileges or immunities of citi-zens of the United States." Efforts to persuade courts to allow corpora-tions to claim the protection of this clause have not been successful. The next clause reads: "Nor shall any State deprive any person of life, liberty, or property, without due process of law." It has not been decided that this clause prohibits a state from depriving a corporation of "life." The Court expressly held that the liberty guaranteed by the Fourteenth Amendment against deprivation without due process of law is the liberty of natural, not artificial persons. Thus, the words "life" and "liberty" do not apply to cor-porations, and of course they could not have been so intended to apply. No word in all this amendment gave any hint that its adoption would deprive the states of their long-recognized power to regulate corporations.

Corporations are artificial legal entities owned by stockholders, who may be humans or other corporations, pension funds, mutual funds, or the beneficial owners holding stock in street name. They are required by law to have officers and a board of directors (in small corporations these may all be the same people). In effect, the corporation is a collective of individuals with a special legal status and privileges not given to ordinary unincorporated businesses or groups of individuals or even to individuals themselves. Corporations are created by the state's granting of a charter.

America was founded upon democratic principles that distributed power among the legislative, judicial, and executive branches, so no one person or entity had the power inherent in a monarchy and that the *people* would participate in an electoral democracy. That concept worked fairly well for a long time. Over the last twenty years, however, there has been an immense shift in the balance of power towards multinational corporations and global trade organizations controlled by corporations.

The rise in corporate power began in 1886 with the U.S. Supreme Court and *Santa Clara County v. Southern Pacific Railroad*. At the time, railroads were the most powerful corporations in the country. Most of the nation's farmers were dependent on them to haul their crops and produce; even the manufacturing corporations were at their mercy when they needed coal, iron ore, finished steel, or any other materials transported. Lawyers for the railway corporations planned a national campaign to make corporations full, unqualified legal "persons"—demonstrated by the Supreme Court making several decisions in which this was an issue in 1877. In four cases that reached the Supreme Court, the railroads argued that they were protected by the Fourteenth Amendment from states regulating the maximum rates they could charge. In each case the Court did *not* render an opinion as to whether corporations were persons covered by the Fourteenth Amendment.

The perception that corporations have constitutional rights effectively inverts the relationship between these entities and the government. Recognized as persons, corporations lose much of their status as subjects of the government. Although artificial creations of their owners and the government, as legal persons they have a degree of immunity to government supervision. Endowed with the court-recognized right to influence both elections and the law-making process, corporations now dominate not just the U.S. and global economy, but also governments.

By the 1930s, corporations employed more than 80 percent of all workers and produced most of America's wealth. Many of the original ideas of the American Revolution were forgotten or watered down, and America increasingly became a corporate state, governed by a coalition of government and business interests. In the post-World War II years, corporations merged, consolidated, restructured, and metamorphosed into ever larger and more complex units of resource extraction, production, distribution, and marketing. By the 1990s, corporations put aside their traditional competitive feelings toward each other and forged tens of thousands of co-branding deals, marketing alliances, co-manufactured projects, and research and development agreements, and created a global network of common interests.

By 1997, fifty-three of the world's largest economies were not countries but corporations. Today, the top one hundred global companies control 33 percent of the world's assets, but employ only 1 percent of the world's workforce. General Motors is larger than Denmark; Wal-Mart bigger than South Africa. The mega-corporations roam freely around the globe, lobbying legislators, bankrolling elections, and playing governments off against each other to get the best deals. Their private hands control the bulk of the world's news and information flow.

Because of corporate personhood and a corporation's legal rights, the individual person has become a second-class citizen in the eyes of the law. A person who works for wages at a corporation loses his constitutional rights (such as free speech) when he steps onto corporate property. In any dispute with a corporate "person," an individual must pay for lawyers and courts; for a corporation, it is a tax-deductible expense. For a multinational corporation, a million dollars in legal costs hardly affects the bottom line. For a real person, a thousand dollars in legal costs may mean missing a month's rent or a mortgage payment. When ordinary people work together in a labor union, they are not afforded the same privileges as a corporate person.

Consider corporate contributions to politicians and their overall ability to influence political thought through the corporate media. Without ever giving a penny to a politician's campaign, the corporate media have an enormous amount of control over the political process through their ability to filter news and opinions. Dependent on other corporations for their own advertising income, they have no incentive to report the news impartially. The large media giants don't want to antagonize their advertisers by challenging the corporatization of truth. A perfect example is when CBS (owed by Viacom) refused to run a $2 million ad on Super Bowl Sunday for People for the Ethical Treatment of Animals, which asserted that restaurants which sell fried chicken, pork sausage, and fast-food burgers are responsible for ". . . making Americans fat, sick, and boring in bed."

The *Santa Clara v. Southern Pacific* fiasco was the beginning of the end of charter control, and today corporate charters are obtained in a few minutes by completing a form and paying a small fee to the secretary of state or some other state agency. State legislatures have mostly delegated the power to oversee the administration of corporate charters to state bureaucrats, but they still retain the power to revoke corporate charters and set the ground rules of corporate conduct. Only recently have citizens begun to question rubberstamp corporate charter approval and to raise issues about overall corporate conduct in a state.

THE CASE AGAINST UNOCAL

Besides securing "personhood" under the law, corporations have been getting away with activities overseas that would not be allowed under U.S. law. The case of Unocal Corporation is illustrative. On September 10, 1998, twenty-seven petitioners (individuals and organizations) filed a 129-page complaint with the California state attorney general requesting that he initiate judicial proceedings to revoke the corporate charter of giant petroleum conglomerate Unocal Corporation, under California Code of Civil Procedure Section 803 and California Corporations Code Section 1801. The complaint listed a host of charges against the company, including genocide and environmental destruction, unfair and unethical treatment of workers, and a list of "crimes against humanity": aiding the oppression of women, aiding the oppression of homosexuals, enslavement and forced labor, forced relocation of Burmese villages and villagers, killings, torture, and rape. Other charges accused the company of "complicity in gradual cultural genocide of tribal and indigenous people, usurpation of political power, and deception of the courts, shareholders and the public."[103]

The attorney general of California at that time, Dan Lungren, rejected the petition five days after it was filed. Current California attorney general, Bill Lockyer, has also said he has no intention of revoking Unocal's charter.

State attorney generals have acted in the past to revoke a corporation's charter whenever a private party gives them reason to believe that a company is breaking the law, or the governor of a state directs them to do so. According to the National Lawyer's Guild International Law Project for Human, Economic and Environmental Defense (HEED), the New York attorney general asked a court to revoke the charters of two tobacco industry "research" corporations, and a judge in Alabama, as a private citizen, asked a court to revoke the charters of the tobacco companies themselves. Even the former California attorney general, Evelle Younger, asked a court to revoke the charter of a private water company that was allegedly supplying impure water to its customers.[104]

Several of the counts against Unocal related to the company's operations in Burma (Myanmar), which has been ruled by the military since 1961 and is currently ruled by the State Law and Order Committee (SLORC), a group of military officers. SLORC allowed elections to take place in 1990, and the National League for Democracy (NLD), led by Aung San Suu Kyi, won with 81 percent of the vote. SLORC refused to abide by the election results, and Aung San Suu Kyi has been under house arrest ever since, with only a few free periods. Massive human rights abuses followed, and in 1997, the United States announced an embargo against the country, which included a ban on new investments by U.S. companies (the ban did not apply to companies already in Burma, such as Unocal.) The United States banned all imports from Burma in June 2003 after another military crackdown on the NLD. These sanctions block aid to the country from international lenders, freeze existing Burmese government assets in the United States and widen the ban on visas for the SLORC leadership. In 2004 the U.S. House and Senate overwhelmingly voted to renew economic sanctions and, President Bush signed a new import ban in July 2004.

Activists, human rights organizations, students, and the SRI community all joined forces in the mid-1990s to apply pressure on corporations operating in Burma—urging them to disengage and withdraw from supporting the Burmese economy, which mostly benefited the wealthy elite of the country and SLORC's generals. Aung San Suu Kyi supported the call for corporate disengagement and economic sanctions until the country returned to democratic rule.

Companies which had rushed into hot Asian markets and economies in the 1990s were asked to head for the door. Many companies did, including Levi Strauss, Hewlett-Packard, Heineken, Apple Computer, Motorola, Disney, and Kodak. Petroleum and natural gas companies had natural resource reasons to stay and resisted shareholders and activists.

Numerous government agencies, including the state of Massachusetts, began to adopt selective purchasing laws which had been used successfully in the anti-apartheid campaign in South Africa to put economic pressure on companies profiting from Burmese slavery and exploitation. These ordinances and statutory changes prohibited public contracts to buy products or services from companies found to be violating human and labor rights. Massachusetts enacted its law in 1996, three months before Congress authorized economic sanctions. Other state legislatures, including Maryland, also considered selective purchasing laws that targeted Nigeria, then ruled by a military junta, supported by oil and drug money, which was engaged in a brutal campaign to eliminate political opposition.

Under the threat of several states, including Maryland, enacting selective purchasing legislation, corporations represented by USA Engage, including Unocal, Chevron, ExxonMobil and Monsanto, "launched a furious campaign to defeat the selective purchasing proposal, arguing that sanctions are ineffective, unfairly disadvantage U.S. companies and undermine federal authority to make foreign policy," wrote Russell Mokhiber and Robert Weissman in the Multinational Monitor. "At the last minute, the Clinton administration intervened, saying Maryland's proposed law would violate U.S. trade treaty obligations. This tipped the balance against the bill. Big Business's lobbyists were smiling when they left Maryland."

The real selective purchasing battleground, however, was in the Massachusetts courts—not in the legislature, because the corporate lobbyists had already lost there. The National Fair Trade Council, another giant coalition of about six hundred U.S. manufacturing companies, filed suit in federal court in Boston in April 1998. The European Economic Union and Japan also filed a complaint against Massachusetts' law under the Government Procurement Agreement of the World Trade Organization (WTO), which forbids nation-states from using non-economic criteria in deciding contract bids. In late 1998, the court ruled against Massachusetts, saying that selective purchasing encroaches upon the federal government's ability to conduct foreign affairs. The case was appealed to the U.S. Supreme Court, but the corporate attorneys prevailed again in June 2000. In a flash, citizens—and local and state communities—lost the power to collectively decide which companies to do business with, based on their own values of democracy and human rights.

On the other hand, there was a silver lining to that cloud: the Supreme Court decision was narrowly worded and did not repeal those selective purchasing laws targeted at countries other than Burma, and did not say that other similar laws were unconstitutional. The Court did say that state and local governments could not pass laws that conflict with the federal government's right to conduct foreign policy enacted into federal law.

Unocal can't seem to get off the hook in Burma supporting the repressive military government with its oil revenue. Allegedly, Unocal hired and assisted the Burmese military to provide security for the company's construction of the Yadana Gas Pipeline in which villagers were forced into labor, their property seized, and many were beaten, raped and murdered. Roger Beach, chairman and CEO of Unocal, denied the allegations against the company and said that he was "proud of what we've accomplished there."[105] Unocal had bought into the Yadana pipeline in November 1992 with Total Fina Elf, a French oil company and operator of the $1.2 billion project. Total has a 31.2 percent stake while Unocal has 28.3 percent, Thailand 25.5 percent and Myanmar 15 percent.[106]

In 1996, fourteen Burmese villagers, represented by the International Labor Rights Fund, filed suit under the 1789 Alien Tort Claims Act (ATCA), which gives U.S. courts jurisdiction over human rights abuses overseas. In March 2000, Federal District Court Judge Ronald Lew ruled that the Burmese villagers' case should be heard in a California state court and found that "the evidence does suggest that Unocal knew that forced labor was being utilized and that the Joint Venturers benefited from the practice."[107] He also wrote that there was evidence that "the military forced plaintiffs and others, under threat of violence, to work on [Unocal's pipeline infrastructure] projects and to serve as porters for the military for days at a time."[108]

Despite stating that Unocal knew and benefited from "forced labor," Judge Lew remanded the case to state court on the grounds that the company didn't control the Burmese military and thus wasn't liable for its conduct under U.S. law. In June 2002, Los Angeles Superior Court Justice Victoria Chaney ruled that Unocal may be held liable for the conduct of the Burmese military government under the doctrine known as "vicarious liability," which holds that joint venture partners bear responsibility for each others' actions involving their common business.

In mid-December 2004, both the plaintiffs and Unocal announced that a settlement had been reached (the terms were still being negotiated), and would include an unspecified amount of money to pay villagers and to fund programs to improve living conditions for people in the region of the $1.2 billion pipeline. Heidi Quante, a spokesperson for the Burma Project in San Francisco, told the *Los Angeles Times* at the time that the fact that Unocal settled the case "speaks louder than any words they've spoken before. You would not settle if you did not think you were guilty." The fourteen villagers who filed suit are still in hiding today.

The ATCA of 1792 was originally enacted to prevent the United States from becoming a safe haven for seafaring pirates, permitting foreigners to sue one another in U.S. courts. It was expanded in a successful 1979 Brooklyn, New York case (*Filartiga v. Pena-Irala*), in which the family of a seventeen-year-old boy who had been tortured and murdered in Paraguay sued the policeman who had perpetrated the acts. *Filartiga* was upheld in a 1980 federal appeals court ruling. Since then, human rights lawyers have filed about two dozen suits against U.S. corporations. For example, one suit against Coca-Cola alleges that the company hired paramilitary units who murdered union organizers. Another suit pending in federal court in San Francisco would hold Chevron Texaco responsible for the shootings of Nigerian protestors by soldiers and police at oil company facilities. One more example is the filing of a suit in federal court in Washington in 2001 on behalf of eleven villagers in Aceh Province, Indonesia, alleging that they were victims of murder, torture, kidnapping, and rape by the military unit guarding ExxonMobil's gas field. At the request of ExxonMobil, in July 2002, the U.S. State Department wrote a letter to the judge in the case seeking to influence the court by saying that if the lawsuit is successful, it could undermine the Bush administration's war on terrorism and harm foreign investments in the country. The Bush administration has also asked an eleven-judge panel of the U.S. Court of Appeals to dismiss the Unocal suit.

To make matters even worse for insecure global enterprises, on November 11, 2002 a lawsuit was filed in federal court in the Eastern District of New York against twenty-two U.S. and European companies on behalf of the victims of apartheid in South Africa (*Khulsimani et al. v. Barclays et al.*). Defendant companies include Chevron Texaco, Citigroup, ExxonMobil, Fluor, Ford, General Motors, IBM, and J. P. Morgan Chase. Harrington Investments, Inc. added its name to an *amicus* (friend of the court) brief supporting the plaintiffs. The ATCA claim mentioned above was filed against a private firm, Drummond Company, operating in Colombia, for supporting paramilitary death squads allegedly murdering union members.[109]

The National Foreign Trade Council (NFTC), business organizations and the Bush administration urged the U.S. Supreme Court to invalidate the ATCA, in part arguing that courts enforcing the act would place U.S. corporations at a competitive disadvantage by only making U.S. companies, not foreign-based businesses, subject to litigation for human rights violations. To say the least, this argument was disingenuous, since these same corporations comprising the NFTC have adopted voluntary corporate codes of conduct. Harrington Investments joined the International Labor Rights Fund and other SRI firms and NGOs in support of the ATCA in an *amici* arguing that there was no legal basis for businesses to assert that their desire for further profit overrides the ATCA, which exists to prevent slavery, torture, extrajudicial killing, genocide, war crimes, crimes against humanity, and arbitrary detention. Public interest lawyers also argued that virtually all of the firms represented by the opponents of the ATCA participate in some form of corporate social responsibility (CSR) initiative and pledge to comply with social standards that far exceed the minimum standards of fundamental human rights under the ATCA. We said that unless these companies are misrepresenting their compliance with CSR, an argument that the ATCA was a hindrance to their economic competitiveness was ". . . simply incredible."

On June 28, 2004 the Supreme Court ruled against the Bush administration, business groups, and the Trade Council, maintaining the rights of foreign litigants to bring claims in U.S. federal court for human rights violations.

Terry Collingsworth, general council of the International Labor Rights Fund said that the "decision erases any doubt as to the validity of the ATCA for addressing egregious human rights cases, and sends a clear message to multinationals, who seek to profit from forced labor and torture of workers and other human rights victims."[110] Certainly the Supreme Court ruling against corporate interests also led to the decision by Unocal to settle the Burma case.

One more case worth looking at involves Nike and efforts to restrain the corporation's behavior abroad. Nike has had trouble with the issue of sweatshop labor at its factories for a long time. From Indonesia to Vietnam, Phil Knight, former CEO of the company and its largest shareholder, has defended the company, and was quoted in a January 10, 2003 story in the *Wall Street Journal*, saying Nike paid "on average, double the minimum wage as defined in countries where its products are produced" and that its workers "are protected from physical and sexual abuse." Mark Kasky, a Nike customer, sued in San Francisco Superior Court, claiming such statements amounted to false advertising.

Initially, the California court agreed with Nike that such statements, even if they were false, were protected by the First Amendment right to free speech, and an appellate court upheld the ruling. But in May 2002, the California Supreme Court ruled that Nike's propaganda was commercial speech and the company would be subject to the "truthfulness test" when it made statements about its products or operations. In its ruling, the Supreme Court cited a letter to the athletic directors at the University of

North Carolina (UNC) at Chapel Hill as evidence that the company had an "intended commercial audience." In 1997 Nike had signed an $11.6 million deal with UNC's athletic department to generate $6 to $8 million in annual revenue for Nike. The company, which was being bombarded by student protests over its sweatshops in foreign lands, ran full-page ads in the school newspaper, and unleashed a Nike representative, former UNC basketball coach Dean Smith, to protect Nike's lucrative contract.

Nike appealed the decision to the U.S. Supreme Court, which rejected the company's arguments by a 6 to 3 vote. The case then went to trial, which meant that if Nike was found guilty of lying relative to its commercial speech, the penalty could have been the disgorgement of all its profits in California.[111]

Nike was supported in court by the Bush administration, which had already warned that a ruling against Nike would give activists too many rights to sue companies. Nike was also supported by a barrage of *amici* briefs from ExxonMobil, Bank of America, Microsoft, Monsanto, Pfizer, and the ACLU. Supporters of Kasky filing an *amicus* brief included Domini Social Investments and Harrington Investments, Inc.

The case for Kasky was made by Adam M. Kanzer, general counsel and director of shareholder advocacy for Domini Social Investments, and Cynthia A. Williams, associate professor of law at the University Of Illinois College Of Law and the principal author of the *amicus* brief.

After five years and lots of lawyering, both sides agreed on an out-of-court settlement, providing $1.5 million over three years to the industry-supported Fair Labor Association (FLA). FLA is a nonprofit that promotes adherence to international labor standards and improved working conditions. Nike also agreed to continue its $500,000 minimum funding for after-hours worker education programs for two years, and to support small loan programs for workers at overseas facilities.

Most of the Kasky/SRI supporters don't think the settlement will have much impact on corporate reporting, transparency, or corporate accountability. Adam Kanzer of Domini wasn't happy about the money going to FLA: "I have concerns about the money going to FLA, as Nike is a founding member, and my understanding is that they have a significant influence over the FLA's agenda."[112] Clearly this was a victory for Nike, since the amount of cash involved was insignificant compared to what the company spends on its annual advertising budget and for sports stars' endorsements of Nike products (about $1.4 billion a year). But the pressure on Kasky and his lawyers to settle was likely significant. Nike has deep pockets and could have kept its attorneys going for years, whereas Kasky would have been required to endure a lengthy court appeals process, come up with more money, or require his attorneys to extend more pro bono time than they originally allocated. It proves another old adage: Those that have the gold, rule.

Everything a company says is commercial speech, and must be accurate. If Nike had succeeded in enlarging corporate political speech, it could have permanently undermined the most effective tool we have for holding corporations accountable—timely, accurate information. This would have been a huge step backwards at a time when investors need greater corporate transparency.

Nike is not the only company in trouble regarding commercial speech. People for Ethical Treatment of Animals (PETA) filed suit in the California Superior Court in Los Angeles against Kentucky Fried Chicken (KFC) and its parent company, Yum Brands, seeking an injunction to stop deceptive advertising. PETA contends that the chickens KFC buys from suppliers are abused through drugging, feeding, and slaughter practices, while the company on its Web site ("commercial speech") falsely claims that its chickens are handled humanely and do not suffer pain. PETA recently released a video that seems to graphically prove its claim.

There has been a *coup d'etat* against our democratic institutions and the administrative, legislative, and judicial branches of our government. The coup has been driven by money, wealth, and privilege. Corporate power reigns supreme in our land and most of our cherished traditions and institutions have been sacrificed to the god of money. Even the most sacred of our beliefs, free enterprise, has been corrupted. Corporations have turned competition into oligopoly. National, state, and local governments—including their regulatory agencies—have become partners of corporations, assisting them as they pillage the public treasuries.

The SRI community has attempted to develop alternatives to corporate power by creating businesses that represent a return to competition and the democratic control of capital. The first stage in this process is to build an underlying financial base of socially responsible capital, as well as investors dedicated to changing the traditional global corporate infrastructure. The ultimate purpose of this is to democratize capital allocation, focusing on community-based businesses and financial organizations, as opposed to the present centralized, global domination of our economic and political system by fewer and fewer large corporate entities which are controlled by a small group of wealthy individuals.

In thirty years, the SRI movement has accomplished its goal of creating a capital pool representing hundreds of thousands of individuals as well as institutional investors—public and private pension funds, retirement programs, family and charitable trusts, mission-based foundations, college and university endowments, social and environmental organizations, other NGOs, and socially screened funds. An underlying multi-layered, decentralized alternative economic community has evolved simultaneously, comprised of SRI mutual funds, community banks and credit unions, domestic and foreign loan funds, social venture funds, alternative trade organizations, microfinance entities, publicly and privately traded businesses, and nonprofit enterprises.

We now have the means to challenge corporate management and its captive regulators, politicians, and government bureaucrats by redirecting the flow of capital to community businesses and competitive enterprises. Changing the historical advance of wealth, power, and privilege will not be an easy task. Corporations have evolved into frightening instruments of economic and political power. Corporate management, however, has become so arrogant that it thought that the bull market would hide all of its unethical and criminal acts. Along with a three-year bear market, however, came public recognition that all was not perfect with oligopolistic capitalism. Not only did all boats not lift with the bull market, but the bear exposed an underbelly of corporate deceit and corruption.

2

Have Corporations Run Amok?

The financial services and investment banking industry has been plagued by scandals in recent years and each week seems to bring a fresh crime to the forefront. By now, everyone in America should know how much money stock analysts have earned pushing stocks of companies underwritten by their employers. One of many is Jack Grubman from Citigroup's Salomon Smith Barney, who earned about $20 million a year as a cheerleader for telecom stocks and walked away from Salomon with $32 million in cash and stock. He recommended WorldCom in the fall of 2000, when the price of the stock was $25, saying it would go to $87. Following WorldCom's bankruptcy, the company was renamed MCI, Inc. The stock currently trades around $20. Grubman, however, remained on the payroll of Salomon, earning $50,000 every three months helping the firm defend itself from legal claims.[1]

In that light, consider the fate of Kenneth A. Boss, a junior analyst at Salomon, who said he was fired from Salomon when he refused to revise his report which was critical of three office furniture companies, two of which had issued debt securities underwritten by Salomon. This was after the company announced reforms to end the entrenched practice of linking "research" to investment banking transactions.[2]

Over at WorldCom, CEO Bernard Ebbers, who has been charged with fraud and conspiracy, is asking the WorldCom bankruptcy court for $2 million for reimbursement of his legal bills.[3] WorldCom's messy $104 billion Chapter 11 filing in July 2002 set a record. This followed Enron's measly $67 billion filing in December 2001, after the energy company "restated" $586 million in profits. These little bankruptcies cost Americans about thirty-five thousand jobs and more than $1 billion in employee pensions.

At Enron, shareholders and former workers lost $29 billion. According to Bloomberg News, Enron's Chapter 11 recovery plan will pay creditors less than one-fifth of the estimated $67 billion they are owed.

WorldCom, the mother of all bankruptcies, was fined $500 million by the SEC for defrauding investors. Despite this, the company was awarded a $45 million contract to build a wireless phone network in Iraq. The contract was later voided. Two years later, under its new incarnation as MCI, the company was ranked eighth among all federal technology contractors, with a total of $772 million in government primary contracts. When informed of the $500 million SEC fine, Tom Schatz, president of Citizens Against Government Waste, told the Associated Press: "The $500 million is in a sense laundered by the taxpayers."

New York Attorney General Eliot Spitzer got Merrill Lynch to pay $100 million to settle a case he had filed alleging that Merrill analysts' recommendations were aimed at gaining additional investment banking business at the expense of investors who lost money by following bullish stock picks which the analysts disparaged in private.

Picking up on the Spitzer action, Massachusetts officials found that analysts for Credit Suisse First Boston (CSFB) were pressured to avoid writing negative stock evaluations on current or prospective investment banking clients of the firm. CSFB had opposed the securities industry's voluntary guidelines, which specifically prohibited analysts' pay from being linked to deals, and the Massachusetts secretary of state adopted the stronger recommendations made by Spitzer. It was all moot anyway, when the SEC rules took effect in July 2002 barring bankers from linking analysts' pay to deals. Of course, others got picked up as well, including Morgan Stanley and Goldman Sachs. These firms, including Citigroup and CSFB, agreed to pay the SEC $1.4 billion to end its investigation. It gives a whole new meaning to the cost of doing business.

In January 2002, CSFB paid the SEC $100 million to settle an investigation into a different issue—allegations that the firm was demanding kickbacks from customers who were awarded hot Initial Public Offering (IPO) allocations. IPOs are almost always underpriced, often by as much as 30 percent according to an analysis by Sanford C. Bernstein & Company.

From January 1999 to January 2001, telecom stocks alone had almost $10 billion in first day gains according to Thompson Financial. Ebbers, former CEO of WorldCom, received 869,000 shares in hot stocks from 1996 to 2000. Other WorldCom executives received thousands of shares as well.[4]

The SEC has now adopted rules requiring brokerage firms to break out company research ratings on stocks in terms of buy, hold, and sell. The rule made sense. As a September 13, 2002 article in the *Wall Street Journal* stated: "Just one in twenty-five of the companies that Merrill Lynch & Co. rates a sell are its own clients—meaning the vast majority of its sell ratings are on rival banks' clients—while Merrill has a banking relationship with six out of ten of the companies it rates a buy."

As the *Journal* also reported on July 27, 2004, ten of the largest brokerage firms began providing independent research as required by the 2003 SEC $1.4 billion settlement mentioned above. This was in response to allegations that there was no separation between a firm's investment banking, and its analysts providing glowing comments on the same firm-underwritten stocks. The companies included CSFB, Morgan Stanley, and Citigroup's Smith Barney; each is required to spend from $7.5 million to $75 million on independent research during the next five years.

Investment banking firms have also paid other firms to publish positive research reports on their underwriting customers. Bank of America (BA) paid U.S. Bancorp Piper Jaffray $400,000 for a report hyping Just for Feet's stock after BA sold $200 million of high-yield, high-risk ("junk") bonds for Just for Feet.[5] Piper Jaffray wound up paying a $32.5 million penalty—part of the same SEC $1.4 billion settlement. From 1999 to 2001, according to the NASD, the firm received more than $1.8 million from rivals in exchange for issuing reports and other services. Piper paid $430,000 to other firms to provide "research" for its own clients.[6] Is there anybody's research you would trust after this?

An issue that is finally getting some attention from both state and federal regulators is the sales practices of investment banking firms which sell their own mutual fund shares to bank clients. New York and Massachusetts allege that Morgan Stanley created improper financial incentives for its brokers to sell mutual funds that may not be in clients' best interests. More than 50 percent of the mutual funds sold by Morgan are proprietary, and as a company spokeswoman told *The New York Times* in July, 2003, "Morgan Stanley pays its brokers more for the sale of its proprietary funds and for fourteen other non-proprietary fund partners, than it does for selling nonproprietary funds."

In August 2004 the SEC voted unanimously to prohibit mutual fund management companies from directing trade to brokers as compensation for putting clients in their mutual funds.

The latest financial industry scandals, uncovered by state and federal regulators in September 2003, involved what are called late trading and improper market timing of mutual fund shares. Simply put, this means that some mutual fund managers and "preferred clients" were allowed to trade after the market closed to take advantage of lagging price movements as the net asset value (NAV) of mutual funds shares was computed. Companies caught up in this latest impropriety scandal include Putnam Investments and Morgan Stanley. Schwab has also admitted problems with some of its mutual funds, as have Alliance Capital, John Hancock, Janus, and many others.

Questioning the lack of oversight of the mutual fund industry, Arthur Levitt, former chair of the SEC, said: "I believe this is the worst scandal we've seen in fifty years, and I can't say I saw it coming."[7] The mutual fund scandal hasn't stopped the Investment Company Institute (ICI), which represents the mutual fund industry, from continuing to raise money for key congressional supporters. ICI raised $90,000 in the "Good Government 2004" campaign for four key Republicans on the House Financial Services Subcommittee, denying the donations had anything to do with the law-makers' support for its positions.[8] Its lobbyists included a former Newt Gingrich aide, a former SEC commissioner, and Steve Clark, a former Ameritech Corp. lobbyist and a close friend of Republican Michael Oxley, chair of the House Financial Services Committee.[9]

EXECUTIVE PRIVILEGES

Corporate scandals rarely affect executives' own pocketbooks. CEO pay went up in 2002 to an average of $7.4 million while stock prices plummeted, unemployment increased, revenue for the Fortune 500 companies fell 6 percent, profits were down 66 percent, and personal bankruptcy filings also set a new record high. A tax justice organization, United for a Fair Economy (UFE) in Boston, and the Institute for Policy Studies (IPS), a think tank in Washington, DC, linked executive compensation to employee layoffs, under-funded pension plans, and offshore tax havens. In a report released August 26, 2003, entitled: "Executive Excess 2003: CEOs Win, Workers and Taxpayers Lose," UFE and IPS found that:

- In 2001, the fifty largest companies that laid off the highest number of workers raised executive pay by an average of 40 percent.
- The thirty companies with the greatest unfunded pension liability paid their CEOs an average of 59 percent over the national median.
- At the twenty-four companies with the most offshore tax havens, CEOs earned 87 percent more than the median.

In 2002, IPS and UFE released a study, titled "Cooked Books Earned CEOs Big Dough," contending that "CEO's of companies under investigation for accounting irregularities earned 70 percent more from 1999 to 2001 than the average CEO at large companies." The study found that the top executives of twenty-three firms under investigation by the U.S. Department of Justice (DOJ) and the SEC earned an average of $62 million from 1999 to 2001, compared to an average of $36 million for CEO's listed in the annual *Business Week* executive pay survey. While the CEO's were collectively pocketing $1.4 billion during the study period, "the value of those firms plunged by $530 billion, about 73 percent of their total value." A total of 162,000 workers were laid off at these twenty-three corporations during this period.

The study also noted that Hewlett-Packard's former CEO, Carly Fiorina, got a 231 percent pay raise in 2002, as HP laid off a record 26,000 people, and the company's stock declined 15 percent. In 2005, Fiorina was fired by the HP board and received a $21 million severance package. AOL Time Warner CEO Gerald Levin received the biggest pay increase (1,612 percent), but only laid off 4,380 people in 2001.

In 1980 CEO's in the United States made forty-five times the pay of average workers. By 2002, they brought home 241 times as much. Now they make about three hundred times as much. By way of contrast, British CEO's made twenty-five times as much as workers, Canadian twenty-three times, and Germans thirteen times as much as workers. Since 1980 CEO pay in the United States has gone up 442 percent, adjusted for inflation, while average worker pay has risen a measly 1.6 percent.[10]

The same study showed that giving shareholders the least for their investment dollars in 2000–2002 was Larry Ellison at Oracle, who pulled in $781.4 million: shareholder return –61 percent. Next was Cendant's Henry Silverman, receiving $184.5 million: shareholder return, also –61 percent. He was followed by Cisco System's John Chambers with $157.6 million: shareholder return –76 percent. Last, but certainly not least, was Sun Microsystem's CEO Scott McNealy, with a measly $53.1 million: shareholders return –92 percent.

Despite all the noise over executive compensation, shareholder dismay, and a flurry of new shareholder resolutions addressing this issue, corporate management doesn't seem to have changed. In 2003 Steve Jobs of Apple pulled in almost $75 million, and John Chambers of Cisco drew almost $48 million.[11] Shareholders also got screwed by "retiring" sixty-two-year-old Bank of America Chairman Chad Gifford, who received a severance of $16.4 million, plus a lucrative consulting contract, corporate jet, company car, and another wad of dough in "incentives."[12]

Often, well-paid CEOs rise to the top, even if their companies don't. Secretary of the Treasury John Snow was paid more than $50 million for his twelve years as chairman of CSX as the company's profits fell and its stock lagged the market. The former chairman of Business Roundtable, an influential group of 157 CEO's from the largest corporations, Snow reportedly convinced SEC Chairman William Donaldson to support a weakened proxy access rule. Business Roundtable and the Chamber of Commerce have raised lots of money for George W. Bush's presidential campaign and the Republican National Committee and spent $12.8 million lobbying the federal government, including the White House, in 2003 and the first half of 2004.[13]

In September 2004 IPS and UFE released another report, concluding that CEOs who outsourced the greatest number of jobs overseas reaped larger pay and benefit increases in 2003. The study's authors mentioned George A. David, the chief of United Technologies, who received $70 million in 2003, and speculated that shareholder value could be increased by outsourcing David's job to India, where the highest paid CEO, Vivek Paul of Wipro— a major beneficiary of outsourcing—made a paltry $1 million.[14] One of Wipro's five largest customers is Microsoft, employing more than five thousand Wipro employees, from call centers to software development.

In 2003 Charles Schwab and Company—after it had eliminated over six thousand jobs and closed twenty branches—revealed in the company's proxy material that corporate directors were getting pay increases: about a 29 percent increase for board annual retainers ($45,000), a 40 percent increase for each board meeting ($2,800), and a 100 percent increase in compensation for each committee meeting ($2,000). As the August 20, 2003 *San Francisco Chronicle* reported, committee chairmen made about $157,000 while other directors made only about $147,000. It pays to play. A Schwab spokesperson told the *Chronicle*: "It's never an easy thing to lay off employees. But the additional expense for the compensation of board members, we think is a very good investment." In March 2004 Schwab CEO David Pottruck had his pay tripled to $3.6 million. In July 2004 Pottruck was terminated—with a parting gift from Schwab: a $6.2 million lump-sum payment plus a $1.63 million annually salary until January 2007, or until he gets a new job.[15]

Despite all the scandalous news in recent years about CEO excesses, not much has changed. William J. Shea, the third CEO in four years at Conseco, Inc., left in 2004 with a severance package of $13.5 million, following the company's $7.84 billion bankruptcy in 2002.[16] When he signed with Conseco, Shea received $45 million in cash and a $1.5 million pension every year for the rest of his life.[17] Shea's severance package was approved by the bankruptcy court.

Then there is the incredible tale of Richard Grasso, the former chairman of the New York Stock Exchange (NYSE), who received $140 million in deferred savings and retirement benefits as well as a meager $20 million

NYSE pay package in 2001.[18] The NYSE is supposed to provide oversight for the self-regulation of member firms. Grasso provided his brand of leadership by saying before he resigned that he would not accept another $48 million he was entitled to receive. Now the NYSE is suing to recover more of what it paid Grasso. He has counter-sued.

All of this begs the question: Don't corporate boards have unbiased compensation committees, who represent shareholders' interests, and can set executive compensation so that it is fair and impartial?

Until recently, the NYSE has been run by a twenty-seven-member board of directors which was fraught with conflicts; it had directors from companies the NYSE is supposed to regulate, including representatives of Bear Stearns, CSFB, Merrill Lynch, and Morgan Stanley. These industry insiders are joined by "public" outsiders, who included Carol Bartz from Autodesk, William Harrison, Jr. from J.P. Morgan Chase & Co., Andrea Jung from Avon Products, Mel Karmazin from Viacom, H. Carl McCall from HealthPoint, Juergen Schrempp from Daimler-Chrysler AG, and other "retirees" representing corporate interests.[19] I'm just relieved that the public is so well represented by these non-biased and non-interested "public" board members. John Reed, former Citicorp CEO, who replaced Grasso, has announced a slimmed-down board, but one still represented by retired corporate insiders like our good friend, Robert Shapiro, formerly of Monsanto.

In the fall of 2003, the NYSE strengthened its requirements for listing publicly traded companies on the exchange by requiring that company boards of directors must have a majority of independent directors, and that audit committees must be composed entirely of independent directors. The NYSE is now backtracking by weakening the definition of "independent" directors, and reducing the limitations on conflicts of interests. Some things never change.

In a December 2002 study, *The New York Times* found that of almost two thousand of the largest U.S. corporations, 420—or 20 percent—had compensation committees in 2001 with members who had business ties or other relationships with the CEO or the company. At more than seventy companies, the chairman of the compensation committee had such ties, and in nine cases the chairman was actually an executive of the company. These are only the connections that were disclosed; many others are not. This was the case with Frank Walsh, Jr., a former director and member of the compensation committee at Tyco, who pleaded guilty to charges of failing to report that Tyco had paid him $20 million for his role in a company deal. Interlocking directorates, or corporate officers serving on each others' boards of directors, has been the rule for many years, as well as directors who have open business ties with the company on whose board they serve. A perfect example, cited in the same *Times* article, is Clear Channel Communications, where only one of the five people on the compensation committee is free of potential conflicts. Both Vernon Jordan, Jr. and Alan Feld, who serve on the committee, work at Aken, Gump, Strauss, Hauer & Feld, the law firm working for Clear Channel.

Lavish compensation deals for corporate officers and board members have been a topic at the SEC, but also one on Capitol Hill. For example, the Senate Commerce Committee and Chairman John McCain must have been disappointed when eight CEOs ignored a committee request to testify on executive pay packages. They included Larry Ellison (Oracle), Michael Eisner (Disney), Leo Mullin (Delta Air Lines), and former CEO Jack Welch (General Electric).

These are the folks who own Congress: why should they have to appear and testify like ordinary people?

There are some moves afoot outside of the SEC or Capitol Hill to address the issue of executive compensation. Pension funds in California and around the world have formed the International Corporate Governance Network, which drafted a voluntary ten-point code of conduct calling for financial transparency and shareholder accountability. The code includes a prohibition of company loans and incentive schemes for executives, independent compensation committees, and a clear link between pay and performance.

In June 2003, the California Public Employee Retirement System (CALPERS) established its own executive pay standards tying compensation to performance and said it would vote its shares against compensation plans that award more than 5 percent of total equity compensation to the top five officers in any company. According to the Investor Responsibility

Research Center (IRRC), about 345 companies sought shareholder approval for stock-based compensation plans in 2001. In 73 percent of those cases, the plans involved dilution of the ownership of existing shareholders by between 3 percent and 10 percent. But in one-tenth of the companies, the dilution resulting from the executive compensations plans was more than 10 percent.[20]

Compensation is even better for corporate officers when a CEO can engineer a merger. With Harrah's taking over Caesar's for $5.2 billion, Caesar's CEO Wallace Barr takes in $120 million under a "change-of-control" provision in his contract. SouthTrust Corporation CEO Wallace Malone, Jr. will receive $59 million in "termination awards" over five years if he leaves SouthTrust when Wachovia takes over.[21] A merger between Anthem and WellPoint Health Networks netted WellPoint's CEO Leonard Schaeffer $47 million in benefits.[22] CALPERS voted against the deal, but it was overwhelmingly approved by shareholders. Better still, Gillette CEO James Kilts, who ran around to put a deal together with Proctor and Gamble, may receive up to $185 million in cash and stock under a complicated compensation package.[23]

A CEO's compensation package doesn't necessarily depend upon the profitability of the company or its stock price. Just ask John Antioco, the chief executive of Blockbuster, who has socked in $19 million in salary, bonuses, and stock options, while the company has lost $3 billion on almost $30 billion in revenue since the company went public in 1999, as the stock has steadily declined.[24]

Some would say that executive compensation packages negotiated by corporate management are excessive. But the *Wall Street Journal* reported on an amazing individual named Joseph Bachelder in June of 2003. Bachelder—a corporate attorney who negotiates compensation and severance packages for folks such as Jack Grubman of Salomon Smith Barney (Citigroup) who received $32 million in severance pay, and Dennis Kozlowski of Tyco International who is accused of robbing his company of $150 million in payments—believes, and wants you to believe, that he is "fighting for the underdog" and feels "like David going up against Goliath."

His tactics to gain lucrative severance packages—at the expense of shareholders—reminds me of extortion and bribery. "In severance negotiations, Mr. Bachelder plays a different set of cards," the *Journal* wrote. "He may appeal to directors' latent guilt, in cases when it is possible to argue that a fired executive is being made a scapegoat for problems that blindsided everyone. Other times, he reminds companies that terminated executives can be important witnesses in continuing litigation. When the sides come to terms, the client usually gets substantial severance pay, and the company gets assurances the ousted executive will respect confidential information and won't disparage the former employer."

Bachelder helped out Richard McGinn, a dismissed Lucent CEO. In 2003, Lucent settled shareholder suits alleging financial irregularities and overly aggressive sales practices by paying shareholders $568 million. As the *Journal* story reported, McGinn's severance package from Lucent was $5.5 million, "plus some help from Lucent in sorting out $4.3 million of personal bank loans he had taken out in boom times. In return, Mr. McGinn agreed to help Lucent for two years in connection with any lawsuits or regulatory requests."

Some company directors, including those at Disney, are starting to worry about personal liability regarding sweetheart compensation deals of the past. A Delaware Chancery Court ruled that a five-year-old shareholder suit against Disney and its directors could proceed to trial. The case contends Disney directors had almost no say in CEO Michael Eisner's hiring, or the departure, fourteen months later, of Michael Ovitz, a former Disney president who walked away with a package of over $100 million.[25] The suit contends that the compensation committee—which included Irwin Russell, Ovitz' personal attorney—spent less time considering the hiring of Ovitz than it did discussing Russell's $250,000 fee for negotiating Ovitz' contract.[26]

The Delaware Chancery Court may be on its way to spoiling the state's reputation as the country's leading corporate whore by ruling that an Oracle special litigation committee must look into stock sales made by its chairman and CEO, Larry Ellison, and other board members, which were rife with conflicts of interest. Oracle's special committee members did not disclose all the relationships that they had with Oracle through their employer, Stanford University, the $100 million house Ellison gave Stanford or the $170 million he donated for a scholarship program.[27]

Corporatization of Food

Do you wake up at night dreaming of Big Gulp, Big Mac or Supersize Fries? Have you ever wondered why your restaurant portions are so enormous? Or why you're given a gigantic drink container when you order a "medium" size, or why the large popcorn can be refilled for free (with lots of butter), and only costs twenty-five cents more than the medium one? Have you ever looked around America to see how large *we've* all become? Have you ever noticed how clothes sizes are changing—how you are getting bigger, but your clothes size is not? It is called clothing recalibration. My daughter Brenna moved down to a size zero from a size four almost overnight.

An article from the September 14, 2003 *New York Times* "Fashion Week/ Review" put it this way: "The clothes do convey a sort of reverse snobbishness in sizing, however. Those who are cable-thin and devoted to pretty things will have a hard time finding anything that fits. A size four is more or less equal to a size eight, and a particular red corduroy shirtdress in a size ten looked as if it could have accommodated all three sisters from 'Petticoat Junction.'"

The U.S. population is growing slower than the food supply, and corporations need us to eat more, more often and in larger portions. Agribusiness produces about 3,800 calories a day for every American—500 calories more than it produced thirty years ago and at least 1,000 more than most people need. There are now 227,208 fast food outlets in the United States, one for every one thousand people in this country.[28] In 2000, food companies generated nearly $900 billion in sales.

Of course, a lot of this corporate-pushed food is also genetically modified, and causes obesity as well. The U.S. surgeon general says three hundred thousand premature deaths per year are associated with obesity. That fact, however, doesn't stop the Bush administration from opposing the World Health Organization's (WHO) anti-obesity plan, which singles out specific types of foods, such as those with high fat and sugar content. And this is probably just a coincidental fact: the food industry gave $512,000 to the president's campaign.[29]

About 61 percent of Americans are considered overweight. According to the California Center for Public Health Advocacy (CCPHA), more than 25 percent of California's public school children are overweight and nearly 40 percent are considered unfit. The number of overweight teenagers has tripled in the past decade. According to the Centers for Disease Control and Prevention, 15 percent of children between the ages of twelve and nineteen are now overweight. Children have joined the ranks of Americans having gastric bypass surgery (stomach stapling), which have jumped overall from sixteen thousand in 1993 to over one hundred thousand in 2003.[30]

In 2003 CCPHA successfully pushed legislation to phase out California school districts' financial dependence on soft drink contracts and the bill, which became law on July 1, 2004, limits elementary schools to serving milk, water, and juice drinks, while middle schools can still offer sports drinks during school hours. Students can still bring sodas to school, and vending machines can still be used before and after school for fundraising events. High schools are not affected by the legislation. The bill had the support of a long list of health, medical, consumer, and educational groups, but the California Chamber of Commerce and the Grocery Manufacturers of America opposed it.

CCPHA reports that soda consumption has almost doubled in the last twenty years. According to the American Beverage Institute, the average American drinks 848 eight-ounce servings of soda each year, 630 in Mexico, 341 in Germany, 25 in China, and 10 in India.[31] That means Americans, on average, are drinking more than two servings of worthless sugar water per day and over sixteen per week, fattening themselves—and the beverage companies' coffers—in the process.

A study conducted by the Harvard School of Public Health in August 2004 concluded that sugar-sweetened beverages were linked to weight gain and Type 2 diabetes. One can of Coke or Pepsi contains 140–150 calories, or the equivalent of about ten teaspoons of sugar. Americans consume 52.3 gallons of soda a year, compared to 20.3 gallons of milk and 16.6 gallons of bottled water.[32]

Meanwhile, the sugar industry pumps money into our political system and reaps major subsidies in return. The federal government guarantees sugar producers inflated prices by restricting supply. As a *New York Times* editorial on November 29, 2003 noted: "Only about 15 percent of American sugar is imported under the quota rules, and while the world price is about seven cents a pound, American businesses that need sugar to make their products may pay close to twenty-one cents." As the *Times* reported, this nice little spread nets Florida's Fanjul "sugar kings" tens of millions annually, and costs Americans about $2 billion a year. The Fanjul family spent about $1 million in soft-money donations during the 2000 election cycle. Alfonso Fanjul, the chief executive of the family-controlled Flo-Sun company, served as Bill Clinton's Florida co-chairman in 1992.

According to the June 2004 issue of the *Journal of Food Chemistry and Analysis*, nearly one-third of the average American's calories come from junk food, beer, and sugary drinks, while only 10 percent comes from fruits and vegetables. According to the Centers for Disease Control (CDC), 98 percent of high schools have vending machines and snack bars, as do 74 percent of middle schools, and 43 percent of elementary schools. Moreover, about 20 percent of the nation's school districts offer brand name fast food and may serve fast foods on special days, such as McDonald's Wednesdays and KFC Fridays. Yum Brands, which owns KFC, has struggled with its ads to sell fried dead birds. Michael Markowitz, a branding consultant said: "The fundamental product offering—fried chicken—has been countertrend for years. Fried chicken is not a first tier choice for people any longer."[33]

Coke, which has for years cut deals with school districts for exclusive access, has one-upped its competitors. Coca-Cola Enterprises, Coke's largest bottler, became an official sponsor of the National PTA, which gave the company's senior vice president for public affairs and chief lobbyist a seat on the PTA board. The executive director of an advocacy group in Portland, Oregon, said: "It's a massive conflict of interest. The National PTA has a wonderful history in protecting and advocating for the health of children, and now it is part of the Coke marketing machine, because Coke literally helps to run it."[34]

Marketing to younger children is big business, and many cash-strapped school districts need any help they can get. According to James McNeal, a professor of marketing at Texas A&M and an authority on marketing to children: "Kids 4-to-12 spend on their own wants and needs about $30 billion a year. But their influence on what their parents spend is $600 billion. That's blue sky."[35] In July 2003, Coca-Cola pledged to stop marketing soda to children under the age of twelve, but found an alternative: market a twelve-ounce can of Swerve, made from skim milk and vitamins, with the same content as a twelve-ounce can of Coke and double the sodium. So first, the districts must wean the kids off Coke and onto Swerve—sort of like going from heroin to methadone. Besides that, this new sugary drink is perfect for Coke; since the government made deep cuts in the dairy farm program, milk is nearly as cheap a raw material as water.[36]

Even the $50 billion subsidized milk industry received a major boost when the Dietary Guidelines Advisory Committee, a thirteen-member panel which reports to the U.S. Department of Health and Human Services and Agriculture, recommended a 50 percent boost in milk consumption. This recommendation will be plugged into the food pyramid dietary guidelines for 2005. It will mean big profits for the dairy industry, including companies like Kraft Foods (owned by Philip Morris Tobacco), as federal nutrition programs, such as school lunch menus, are adjusted to conform to the federal guidelines.

Paul Hawken, one of the authors of *Natural Capitalism,* writing for *Utne* (May-June 2003), said: "McDonald's opens up 2,800 restaurants a year, and even the U.S. government has said that the doubling of childhood obesity and alarming growth in diabetes in the past twenty years is due to fast food. Right now, one out of every five meals in the United States is fast food, and they want that to be the case everywhere in the world. Coke says that it has achieved 10 percent of the total liquid intake of the world, and its goal is to go to 20 percent. Or is it 30 percent? These are absurd and devastating goals for corporations."

Hawken has been questioning the SRI community's investment in companies with allegedly sustainable business practices but whose own business models are not sustainable, including publicly traded food companies such as Wild Oats, Whole Foods Market, and Horizon Organic.

Food companies are facing increasing scrutiny by investors who believe in factoring in the risk of litigation and regulation regarding valuations. Many companies that mainly sell foods or drinks high in fat, sugar, or salt may lose market share to other healthier food companies according to a report by J.P. Morgan.[37] Says Jason Streets, an analyst at UBS Warburg: "The food and soft-drink industry will, in our opinion, have to change the products they sell, the way they label them and the way they market them. None of this is good for sales or profits and represents an absolute risk not factored into share prices currently."[38]

Labeling and transparency may provide some additional cover for corporate food processors and their distributors. The U.S. Food and Drug Administration (FDA) will require—beginning January 1, 2006—that food manufacturers list the product's trans fat content on the Nutrition Facts panel of the packaging, and predicts that such labeling could prevent up to 17,100 cases of coronary heart disease and up to 5,600 deaths a year. It will also save between $900 million and $1.8 billon a year in medical costs, lost productivity, and pain and suffering.[39] On the other hand, the FDA has made it easier for giant food companies to make health and nutrition claims while the European Union has proposed regulations which would ban marketing food as having a health benefit if it is also high in salt, sugar, or fat, even if it contains fortified vitamins and minerals.[40]

You may want to cheer the FDA for its trans fat labeling requirement, but past experience shows us that protecting consumers isn't very simple. In 1977, when a Canadian study linked saccharin to bladder cancer, the FDA proposed a ban on saccharin, but Congress instead put a label on Sweet 'n Low saying, "Use of this product may be hazardous to your health. This product contains saccharin, which has been determined to cause cancer in laboratory animals." In 2000, the FDA dropped this warning label because it was *convinced* (by whom, you might ask) that saccharin was no longer a health problem.

Naturally, the FDA never seriously considered a warning label on another artificial sweetener, aspartame, manufactured by the FDA's good friends at Monsanto under the brand name NutraSweet. There was some concern about connecting aspartame to brain cancer, but according to an August

12, 2003 *Wall Street Journal* article, ". . . most experts dismiss such claims as invalid." The artificial sweetener Splenda, or sucralose, is recommended in pregnancy books and by the American Diabetic Association, and is supposed to be safer than NutraSweet. But the *Napa Valley Register* reporter Kristin Ranuio wrote in an August 18, 2003 story that: "It turns out that there have been few studies on humans as to the safety of sucralose, but there have been tests done on animals. The poor little rats, mice and bunnies experienced problems such as shrunken thymus glands, enlarged liver and kidneys, reduced growth rates, decreased blood cell counts, diarrhea, extended pregnancies and even aborted pregnancies."

Investors as well as consumers have been warned repeatedly about the dangers of brand names such as McDonald's, Coca-Cola, and Kellogg. Based upon a weak global economic climate, most analysts feel brand name company stocks are overpriced. According to Jason James at HBC in London, consumers ". . . just don't want to go to McDonald's and eat the same thing; they are asserting their individuality. This may be anti-globalization backlash, or it may not be as overarching. Consumers may just want variety in their lives."[41]

Food companies, especially fast food establishments, are only going to change when consumers start demanding healthy, nutritional food. One leading children's marketing consultant says that companies listen when profits are at stake. "If it's going to hit the bottom line, they'll listen," he says. "You'd like them to have a conscience, but conscience and bottom line are not in the same paradigm in the corporate world."[42]

McDonald's—which operates 13,602 restaurants, spends about $1.5 billion a year on advertising, and is the target of many lawsuits linking its meals to obesity in children—has announced new initiatives to promote healthy lifestyles. Kraft Foods—part of tobacco giant Altria Group, Inc., and the biggest maker of processed genetically modified foods—said it planned to reformulate some of its products to improve nutritional content.

Every year food companies, nutritionists, and food and commodity groups representing the meat, dairy, and sugar industries battle it out to revise U.S. dietary guidelines. Federal school lunch programs, and billions of dollars, are at stake when the U.S. Department of Agriculture (USDA) publishes its eighty-page report every year. The food industry is particularly concerned that its ox will be gored due to rising obesity rates. This is especially true for the sugar and processed foods industries. According to the *Wall Street Journal*, during a 2000 revision, the Sugar Association successfully lobbied the U.S. Health and Human Services Department to change the wording of a recommendation that consumers should "limit" intake of sugar to "moderate" intake of sugar.[43] The Soft Drink Association was pleased with its lobbying success, saying: "We plan to work with the panel again to counter allegations from the activist community and public misconceptions that there is evidence to link sugar and obesity."[44]

Another major issue facing responsible investors is that of factory farms. These farms produce huge concentrations of manure that are stored in open lagoons and may become toxic. Spills and groundwater contamination are also a danger, as is airborne contamination of water from ammonia, which rises from lagoons and falls into low-lying rivers and estuaries. This was the subject of a Sierra Club report entitled, "The Rapsheet on Animal Factories," which identified the largest agricultural companies, including ConAgra, Tyson Foods, Cargill, and Smithfield farms.

Ultimately, the SRI community cannot avoid responding to health-related issues, such as genetic engineering and product labeling. SRI screened mutual funds are grappling with the problem of large food companies and their practices. Adam Kanzer, director of shareholder advocacy for Domini Social Investments, said: "It's definitely a problematic industry and it's something we have been looking at pretty closely over the last few months and trying to see if there is a different way to approach it."[45] The Domini Social Equity Fund currently invests in McDonald's, Wendy's International, Coca-Cola, and PepsiCo Inc. Calvert Group, the largest SRI-screened fund manager, is exploring nutrition issues but does not let it influence whether or not a company is included or excluded from a Calvert screened mutual fund portfolio.[46]

In the past, the United States has used foreign aid to pressure other nations to support U.N. initiatives or other American-sponsored action. Drugs are now becoming the latest weapon to force developing countries to accept bio-engineered food. Monsanto's profits need a boost, as do farmers who have bought GMO technology and lost European and third world markets. Greenpeace filed an ethics complaint with the American Medical Association against Senate Majority Leader Bill Frist (R-TN), who is an MD, for inserting language into an AIDS funding bill that tied AIDS dollars in Africa to accepting U.S.-supplied GMO food, saying Frist violated his professional and ethical responsibilities as a physician and engaged in medical blackmail.

HEALTH CARE AND TOBACCO

There is no longer any debate on whether the use of tobacco leads to increased health risks to the user and those exposed to second hand smoke.

In my 1992 book *Investing With Your Conscience*, I discussed "The Four Sins" exorcised from portfolios by early socially responsible investors: tobacco, alcohol, gambling, and weapons. Of the four, only tobacco companies have suffered financially from decreased demand in the United States due to increased public scrutiny and criticism, as well as investor rejection. The University of California, Stanford University, the University of Southern California, and the two largest California retirement systems (CALPERS and CALSTRS) still had over $700 million in tobacco stocks. When my book was published many public universities, churches, foundations, health centers, and hospitals had divested or would soon divest tobacco stocks.

In the Spring of 1997, CALPERS officials—representing 1.2 million members—met with the CEO of Philip Morris to assure him that they were not considering selling the company's stock, even though CALPERS' official position was that smoking was bad for the health of its beneficiaries, and even though it had been running aggressive antismoking campaigns.[47] The president of CALPERS, William Christ, said that Phillip Morris stock was a good investment and they did not intend to "respond to public pressure."[48] In 1998, CALPERS had over $1 billion invested in U.S. and international tobacco companies.[49]

Two years later, CALPERS divested $525 million in tobacco stocks and quoted Christ in its press release, saying: "The unprecedented amount of legal, regulatory and legislative action in the industry could substantially reduce our shareholder value in tobacco. Our decision means that we will have tobacco-free indices and benchmarks for all of our passively managed investments. This action was taken to protect our members' assets in the long-term."

No one knows just how many CALPERS beneficiaries died or became ill between 1997 and 2000 from smoking tobacco, and what that cost in lost productivity. Clearly, in 1997, Christ didn't see it as his fiduciary duty to protect either beneficiaries' health or their assets.

In early June 2000, the California State Teachers' Retirement System (CALSTRS) board of directors, which is responsible for the $114 billion California teachers' retirement system with over 630,000 beneficiaries, voted to strip its index funds of $238 million of tobacco stocks. Both CALPERS and CALSTRS have faced the same struggle: advocating a public policy of good health, providing health care for their members, and teaching school children the evils of smoking, while investing in companies that were killing and injuring their beneficiaries, increasing health care costs, and reducing productivity of their workers. In California, at the same time the city and the county of Los Angeles were participants in the national lawsuit against the tobacco industry, the L.A. City Employees' Retirement System held about $31.5 million in tobacco stocks and bonds, and L.A. County Employees' Retirement Association held $83.4 million in tobacco investments.[50]

The California divestment of tobacco stocks was influenced by the national lawsuit and the fear of a total collapse of the tobacco industry. In 1998, the tobacco companies agreed to pay more than $230 billion to various states over twenty-five years. Everyone claimed victory, but Crenson and Ginsberg have a different take on it in *Downsizing Democracy*: "The tobacco manufacturers agreed to the settlement for two reasons. First, they regarded the states as their most dangerous adversaries and feared numerous multibillion-dollar judgments that would have to be paid not from future earnings, but immediately, thus bankrupting most of the companies. In fact, the settlement actually gave the industry's most dreaded foes a stake—a $240 billion stake—in the tobacco manufacturers' survival and profitability. The industry calculated that the state governments, trial lawyers, and others receiving money under the tobacco settlement would now feel compelled to oppose any step that would prevent smokers from buying more cigarettes."

Also, as Crenson and Ginsberg point out, most of the settlement costs would be borne by smokers, most of whom are lower middle class workers.

It is unfortunate that CALPERS and CALSTRS board members didn't get a copy of the study Philip Morris commissioned a few years ago from Arthur D. Little, suggesting that the Czech government might benefit from smokers' premature deaths; with fewer years to live, smokers would require smaller pension benefits.[51] Arthur D. Little was also the consulting firm that worked with American companies and Leon Sullivan to justify continued U.S. investment in apartheid South Africa.

California pensions may divest, but the state still sides with tobacco, and without tobacco, the state budget deficit would be larger. Former Governor Gray Davis signed a bill guaranteeing state support of up to $2.3 billion in tobacco bonds sold to investors. This provided a small quick fix to the California budget, but means that the state has an incentive to keep people smoking so that the bonds will be repaid. California tobacco bonds were issued in anticipation of receiving funds that are part of a 1998 lawsuit settlement between companies and forty-five other states. If, at the end of the day, not enough people continue to smoke and keep the tobacco companies afloat, California taxpayers will be faced with additional debt to repay.

Fuzzy Math and Voodoo Economics

We should have known that this was a trend. In June 2001 the SEC fined Arthur Andersen, LLP $7 million for allowing Waste Management, Inc., to continue a series of "improper accounting practices" for several years, which inflated the company's earnings. In May of the same year Arthur Andersen had agreed to pay $110 million to settle a Sunbeam accounting fraud lawsuit. In 1998 Waste Management took a $3.5 billion charge based on accounting "irregularities," and Arthur Andersen agreed to pay $220 million to settle shareholder litigation.

Question: As auditors of Tyco since 1994, did PricewaterhouseCoopers (annual revenue: $8.1 billion) know about secret bonuses paid to Tyco executives and other irregularities? As the corporate scandals continued to hit, PricewaterhouseCoopers stayed in the headlines and paid $1 million to the SEC to settle a probe into alleged improper conduct related to its audits of SmarTalk Teleservices, a now bankrupt provider of prepaid telephone cards and wireless services.[52] The same PricewaterhouseCoopers agreed to pay $50 million to settle a shareholder class action lawsuit that charged the company with signing off on allegedly misleading financial statements by defense contractor Raytheon.[53] Raytheon's top executives had earlier agreed to pay $410 million to settle similar claims. It is just the cost of doing business for both defense contractors and our cherished auditors.

While it seems that the SEC is going to bar a PricewaterhouseCoopers partner from auditing in the future, the Manhattan district attorney's office announced that it will not bring criminal charges against Pricewater-houseCoopers for helping Tyco alter its books.[54] PricewaterhouseCoopers defended its audits of Tyco, advising it not to restate its financial results back to 1998, which was overruled by the SEC.[55] This all happened about the same time that the SEC chairman, William H. Donaldson, announced that thirty-six year insider and PricewaterhouseCoopers partner Donald Nicolaisen was being named chief accountant at the SEC.[56] He will work closely with the agency's Public Company Accounting Oversight Board to police the accounting industry. Apparently the SEC doesn't consider this a conflict, since about one-half of the SEC's chief accountants come from big accounting firms.

According to the *Wall Street Journal*, four large accounting firms dominate the landscape, creating their own oligopolistic empire. Besides PricewaterhouseCoopers, the other three (and their annual revenues) are: Deloitte & Touche ($5.9 billion), Ernst & Young ($4.5 billion) and KPMG ($3.2 billion).[57] The Big Four audit 99 percent of public company annual sales, even though 86 percent of the Fortune 1000 companies prefer to have more audit firms available.[58]

After the Big Five accounting firms became the Big Four with the implosion of Arthur Andersen, the SEC appointed a new Public Company Accounting Oversight Board to guard against conflicts and other auditing problems. The SEC chairman forgot to tell other commissioners that his appointee as oversight board Chair, William Webster, ran the audit committee for a publicly traded company whose executive was possibly involved in irregularities. Following Webster's resignation, the new board located its Washington, DC office in the same offices vacated by Arthur Andersen, and promptly voted themselves yearly salaries of $452,000 apiece ($560,000 for the new chair). Kayla Gillan—a member of the new board and formerly general counsel to CALPERS (where she was only paid $148,000)—said the high salaries (the president of the United States makes $400,000, and the chief justice of the Supreme Court receives $198,000) were justified because the board was not a federal agency but supported by fees from public companies and accounting firms.[59] She added further that personally, the move to DC was a trauma to her family and that at forty-four years old, her career was at risk.[60]

Gillan and her colleagues may well earn those big bucks, as members of the Big Four continue to stumble along with conflicts that are endemic to large oligopolistic enterprises. For example, KPMG LLP paid referral fees to its auditing customer, First Union Corp. (now Wachovia Corp.) for sending customers its way who needed tax shelters. KPMG, in some cases, made $400,000 or more per transaction.[61] How's that for a cozy symbiotic relationship? No problem with auditor independence here.

KPMG has refused to turn over tax documents to the Justice Department for its investigation of allegations that the firm pedaled abusive tax shelters—unlike PricewaterhouseCoopers and Ernst & Young, which paid off the government in fines.

The Enron, Tyco, WorldCom, Arthur Andersen, Global Crossings, and KPMG scandals are one more reason CALPERS and CALSTRS have pledged to vote against renewing the services of any auditor that has served a company for more than five years, or any auditor also performing consulting services for a company.

The SEC has issued guidelines that now require corporate audit committees to review and approve each and every time an auditing firm performs tax or consulting work, to limit conflicts of interest.

3

Growing Pains: The SRI Experience

In studying, living, and participating in history as global citizens, we hope to learn from our successes as well as our mistakes. That was what our country's citizens hoped for after Korea, Vietnam, and the Gulf War of 1991. But, alas, in 2003, the U.S. military invaded Iraq. This circumvented the United Nations Charter and violated international law and national sovereignty. The invasion has resulted in the deaths of thousands of American and Iraqi citizens. It has not only created a civil war but increased the threat of terrorism across the globe. Our government now has its eye on North Korea, Colombia, Syria, and Iran.

According to a now seemingly-visionary 2002 UBS Paine Webber report entitled "The American Empire? After Iraq," the geopolitical vulnerability of the United States lies with its enormous power, expanding imperial commitments, and the burdens of being an empire. The United States risks becoming increasingly isolated and disliked, and will be required to contend with a passive anti-American coalition consisting of Europe, Middle Eastern nations, and many developing countries. This hurts U.S. investors by (1) reducing the global popularity of major U.S. brands; (2) contributing to a weaker U.S. dollar; and (3) damaging U.S. exporters and multinational firms that need international cooperation on such matters as lowering trade barriers, protecting intellectual property, and managing international financial crises.

It doesn't seem like the Bush administration has learned much from the history of the Hapsburg Empire in the 1540s, or Britain in the 1820s. As of this writing, the United States has committed ground troops in Afghanistan, Iraq, Colombia, and Liberia, which has cost thousands of young Americans their limbs and lives; has alienated most of the world with its invasion and occupation of Iraq; increased defense and homeland security spending, increasingly infringing on individual American privacy rights; and is amassing a huge and growing budget and trade deficit for future generations of Americans.

Our country's thirst for international capital remains unabated, and the government's new doctrine of pre-emptive military strikes threatens not only our political relations with other countries, but also our ability to access foreign capital markets. David P. Bowers, chief global investment strategist for Merrill Lynch puts it this way: "America is more dependent on the rest of the world for capital than at any time in the past fifty years."[1] The American empire is already in peril.

GRASSROOTS OR ASTROTURF?

The socially responsible investment (SRI) community has a contemporary history that spans a little more than thirty years, but we need to ensure that, unlike our government and politicians, we learn and benefit from our mistakes. We need critical self-analysis and honest introspection. Self-examination is even more important as we begin to understand the complex and difficult job of blending social responsibility with traditional business practices, both in the profit and nonprofit sectors. This also holds true for business and professional associations and organizations that have been created as a result of the successful SRI movement. We need continually to question the quality of our growth as well as its quantity or size.

For example, have some social business trade groups already been "co-opted?" Businesses for Social Responsibility (BSR) was founded in 1992 by a group of small business leaders who were concerned about the lack of social and environmental consciousness among traditional business trade groups and wanted to serve as a progressive advocate for the small business community. Instead, BSR has been turned into a Who's Who of the corporate evil empire. Its members include British Petroleum (BP), ExxonMobil, Freeport-McMoRan Cooper & Gold, International Paper, Nike, Oracle,

Shell, Chevron Texaco, and Wal-Mart. BSR member companies have nearly $2 trillion in combined annual revenues. BSR has adopted SRI buzz words such as "sustainability" and "corporate social responsibility" (CSR). At its November 2004 conference, representatives of CSR came from exemplary companies such as AstraZeneca, The Gap, and Rio Tinto Limited. So much for a small business nonprofit professional group organized to express a progressive voice for free enterprise.

Taking over or totally funding—and controlling—small business organizations and professional associations has been a consistent strategy of corporate management. The Chamber of Commerce, originally founded and managed by small businesses, is increasingly financed and controlled by large companies.

On many political and economic issues, large corporations finance small business advocacy organizations to carry their water. On the November 2004 ballot in California, small business associations opposed Proposition 72, which would have required mid-sized and large companies to provide limited health care coverage to their employees. These associations, financed almost exclusively by big business (Wal-Mart alone donated $600,000 against Proposition 72), provided a perfect front group—waving the small business flag against Proposition 72—even though small businesses were not affected.

Not only do small business associations carry the water for large corporate overlords, but the Small Business Administration (SBA) recently reported that $2 billion in federal contracting money earmarked for small businesses primarily went to thirty-nine large corporations, including Titan, Raytheon, General Dynamics, and Hewlett-Packard.[2]

While large corporate financial services companies have slipped their representatives into some socially responsible business and investment trade and professional associations, progressive business folks and the SRI community have successfully created groups whose vision of the world is quite different than that of the American Petroleum Institute, the American Manufacturers Association, and the U.S. Chamber of Commerce.

Created in 1987, the Social Venture Network is comprised of more than four hundred progressive business people, investors, investment profes-

sionals, and founders and directors of nonprofit philanthropic foundations. In an earlier version of SVN's website which included a membership
directory, the description of members' vision read: "Our members believe
that today's dominant and economic paradigm promotes ever expanding
economic disparity and ever increasing resource extraction and consumption at the expense of the earth and future generations."

Progressive businesses and nonprofit organizations formed a national
coalition called the Business Alliance for Local Living Economies (BALLE),
which focuses on strengthening local independent businesses, keeping
money in the local community, reducing demand on environmental
resources, and preserving community character. Unlike the Chamber of
Commerce, it is not dominated by large corporations.

In 1992, a national nonprofit network of angel and institutional investors called Investors Circle (IC) was launched. IC brings together social
investors and entrepreneurs to do deals. Since its founding, IC has facili-
tated the investment of over $95 million in 150 socially responsible private
businesses and small social venture funds. The organization has about 110
members in twenty-four states and five countries. Some of the companies
financed through IC include Evergreen Solar—a solar power manufacturer
that went public in 2000, and Energia Global—a renewable energy company that was acquired by Italian electric utility Enel.

Another investment-related professional trade association is the
Community Development Venture Capital Alliance (CDVCA) (www.cdvca.
org), formed in 1993 and incorporated as a nonprofit in 1995. CDVCA
has more than one hundred members, including community development
venture capital funds, nonprofit community organizations, local banks
and credit unions, loan funds, foundations, and individuals. CDVCA holds
training sessions for its members and has a $6 million Central Fund (Fund
of Funds) to invest in venture capital funds which create jobs, encourage
minority and women ownership, support environmentally sustainable
business practices, and promote and create socially responsible business
enterprises.

Trade and professional associations tailored to the needs of the SRI community include the Social Investment Forum (SIF) (www.socialinvest.org),

and a more activist affiliate, the Shareholder Action Network (SAN) (www.shareholderaction.org). SIF's five hundred or so financial, professional, and institutional members use it for networking, education, research, conferencing, and advocacy. SAN serves as a clearinghouse for information, coordination, and analysis for shareholder action. Members participate in numerous conference calls regarding resolution advocacy and dialogue with corporate representatives. Membership is primarily comprised of social investment managers, brokers, planners, and other financial professionals.

SIF has evolved from a more participatory format—holding regular board meetings and conferences—to an organization focused on SRI research; the publication of a newsletter; and investment reports and studies relating to mutual fund and SRI manager performance, community investing, and industry trends. The president of the forum is Tim Smith, the former executive director of Interfaith Center on Corporate Responsibility (ICCR), now with Walden Asset Management.

Annual SRI conferences originally held by SIF have been replaced by the annual "SRI in the Rockies" Conference. In 2003 the fourteenth annual conference was held in Lake Tahoe, California, marking the eighth year that the conference was organized as a joint effort between SIF and First Affirmative Financial Network (FAF) (www.firstaffirmative.com). It was also co-hosted by Co-Op America (www.coopamerica.org), a national membership, nonprofit organization that supports SRI, "green," and responsible consumer behavior. FAF is a network of about 120 financial professionals who manage SRI assets for individual and institutional investors. Over four hundred socially responsible investment advocates attended the Lake Tahoe conference. The 2004 conference drew the largest attendance ever with over five hundred energetic participants.

BSR, SVN, IC, and other related business and venture capital groups, as well as SRI nonprofit organizations, such as SIF and "SRI in the Rockies," find their mission constantly challenged and confront criticism that SRI professionals and SRI businesses have become too "soft, fat, and successful." Questions have also been raised about whether the focus is on making money and changing the world (doing well while doing good), or simply appealing to liberal guilt while making money off a disillusioned investing public. Within such organizations, questions are constantly being asked if liberal small business people are more interested in participating in a new age social club, rather than politically and economically challenging corporations that care little for free enterprise or competition, but continue to widen the gap between the haves and the have-nots?

Is responsible investing, as it is currently practiced, a countervailing power to corporate management? Is socially screening or excluding companies from a portfolio enough? Have we become too fat and satisfied with the growing wealth that has been created by and for SRI professionals? Have we bought in to a corporate dialogue process that doesn't challenge corporate power but legitimizes and gives it a nice, perfumed scent? Do corporate governance shareholder resolutions simply fiddle while Rome burns with corporate management's greed? These questions need to be asked again and again.

Many believe that SRI professional organizations have been infiltrated with conservative investment and commercial bankers, corporate CEO's, new age venture capitalists, and small business folks preaching love and corporate reform—all believing that if only corporations add more visionary management and more minority and women board members, corporate capitalism will become more democratic, progressive, and enlightened. Robert Shapiro, former CEO of Monsanto, was given a forum at BSR to make a presentation on genetic engineering, while Monsanto spent millions in commercial propaganda to whitewash the possible health and environmental damages of genetic engineering.

The World Bank, in search of friends and money from SRI investors, sent Peter Woicke—head of the bank's International Finance Corporation (IFC)—to the 2004 "SRI in the Rockies" conference to promote privatization and other bank-funded projects in developing countries—and perhaps to counter the boycott campaign of World Bank bonds which are used to finance environmentally damaging extractive oil and gas projects. The World Bank recently rejected the most important recommendations of its own Civil Society study of its lending policies on oil, gas and mining, especially a recommendation calling for full prior informed consent of communities affected by large infrastructure projects.

There is a danger that "SRI in the Rockies" will become what BSR has become: a convenient forum for corporate propaganda and a way to gain credibility with social investors.

In the last twenty years, most of the writing devoted to SRI has been based on the premise that traditional investing is exclusively for financial gain, while SRI comprises a "triple bottom line" for investors, creating positive social and environmental benefits (or at the very least, avoiding harmful activities) while maximizing financial return. This premise has lulled a lot of SRI professionals and their clients into thinking that simply screening stocks traded in a secondary market will somehow rid them of guilt and responsibility, while gaining fabulous wealth. In fact, there are currently numerous so-called responsible mutual funds, financial planners, brokers, and investment advisory firms that passively screen but never write a letter to, or dialogue with, corporate management—and rarely vote in favor of a shareholder resolution, much less file one of their own. This passive screening has no impact on corporate management and may be used by Wall Street firms to gain access to an unsuspecting public's pocketbooks— hoodwinking folks into believing they are having a positive impact on the world through the use of their capital. The reality is that Wall Street is eager to commandeer the *language* of social responsibility, and promotes glitzy ads to create demand for SRI products and services in an effort to gain access to a growing and important politically progressive source of wealth, or as they say in the business, a "market niche."

There is no doubt that there is much more than a "triple bottom line" providing social, environmental, and financial return when investment decision making also considers such factors as a company's charitable donations policy, whether the company meets or excels at protecting its workers and the environment, or whether the company provides superior benefits for all of its employees—including domestic partners. Henry Ford believed he should pay his employees well enough so they could afford to buy automobiles. Companies that truly take care of business have been found to perform as well and often better than companies that ignore the reality of a changing workplace and changing worker needs and conditions. By the same token, a company that pollutes the environment, employs workers under sweatshop conditions, and fails to meet minimum environmental, OSHA, and equal employment standards, pays the price for defense attorneys, civil and criminal litigation, and local, state, and federal regulatory action. This is in addition to bad publicity, which destroys market share and creates what is now called "reputational risk." Shareholders pay the price for bad corporate citizenship.

For socially responsible business people, especially for those of us working in the financial services industry, SRI practices relate to both our clients' investment needs as well as our own internal business practices. The difficulty for all of us in the SRI business—profit as well as nonprofit—is not only succeeding financially, but also making sure we personally survive the journey. Socially responsible investing is an evolving art that constantly reflects changes in society, culture, technology, human relationships, ethics, and business practices. It is not static. Social and environmental screens change and evolve with society and the natural environment. SRI businesses that grew up in this milieu of social and political change and advocated like-minded and comprehensive social investment criteria created stresses and strains unique in the development of business enterprises.

Growth should not be the only measure of success. Often, growth in and of itself is not necessarily good. We must ask ourselves: Is the SRI movement having a positive impact upon global society and the environment? How can we continually update our strategy, tactics, goals and objectives to maintain not only SRI's effectiveness but also the passion? How can we bring in the younger generation while strengthening our social commitment?

It is important to expand our influence within the traditional financial and investment community, but not to the detriment of our ideals and long-term goals. We can't concentrate too much on being too pure, but, on the other hand, we can't be all things to all people. To some degree, we have already witnessed the homogenization of the SRI community.

A strong desire to advance responsible investing initially led me to colleagues in the same field; in 1983 it was Working Assets Management Company and Working Assets Money Fund, originally with seven relatively equal partners; in 1987, it was Progressive Asset Management (PAM), primarily with Peter Camejo; and, in 1996, WaterHealth International, Inc.

(WHI) with four other individuals, but primarily with Elwyn Ewald. My experiences convinced me that having complete control over my own business was the only way to achieve my personal and financial goals. This is the course I've set for Harrington Investments, Inc. (HII), and Global Partners, LLP. Jerry Dodson learned a lot sooner than I did, when he left as the first president of Working Assets in 1984 to start the Parnassus Fund. I guess some of us are slow learners.

While all three companies I was involved in founding are still alive today in one form or another (WHI emerged from Chapter 11 bankruptcy in late 2002), only one, Working Assets, actually met its financial and social goals and has excelled in both, under separate management teams and leadership. While PAM now has about 130 investors, the largest individual shareholder is still Peter Camejo (with 17 percent of the stock). PAM's president and CEO, Eric Leenson, has been able to keep the business marginally profitable with the help of Paradox Holdings Inc.'s Financial West Group which bought 40 percent of the business under an agreement approved by PAM shareholders in March 1999. PAM coordinates about fifty independent registered representatives throughout the United States. PAM now calls itself Progressive Asset Management Network. Financial West Group's ownership effectively represents control. PAM shares "trade" around seventeen cents, and there is almost no liquidity for the securities. All three businesses remain privately owned and managed, avoiding the disaster of going public and being gobbled up as part of the ongoing global corporate consolidation of business, i.e. Ben & Jerry's.

Starting a business in which there are several owners is like a complex marriage arrangement; no amount of planning, prenuptial agreements, background checks, psychological testing or encounter and focus groups can predict the future. Partners may think they are all on the same page, but this is seldom the case. As will be discussed, however, there are agreements that can protect the shareholders, investors, the integrity of the business, credibility of the partners, and insure a continuity of management's social goals and mission.

WORKING ASSETS

Working Assets (originally named Working Capital) is an amazing success story despite conflict among the partners from almost the first day of business. Its ultimate success had more to do with the strength and depth of board members' individual creativity rather than their collective wisdom. On the other hand, all of the partners brought together a rare combination of talent, ambition, knowledge and philosophical commitment. There was no lack of skills, education or drive. The main problem the group encountered was getting along personally—at least long enough for the business to survive and succeed.

Jerry Dodson, formerly of Continental Savings and Loan, clearly had the business credentials to serve as the president/CEO of Working Assets Management Company and the first president of Working Assets Money Fund. After departing from Continental, he had the time to coordinate the writing of our business plan and the expertise to get us through state and federal regulatory hurdles. He had help from Bob Wadsworth, a consultant who later made a career opening and registering mutual funds, eventually retiring and selling the business to UBS Warburg.

All seven of us—Brian Hatch, Peter Barnes, Julia Parzen, David Kim, Drummond Pike, Michael Kieschnick, and I—helped Dodson write the business plan. Portions of the plan were assigned to different partners based upon our respective professional strengths. Because of my twelve-year background in the California legislature and the socially responsible investment community, as well as my labor, political, and public sector connections, the institutional marketing plan was assigned to me.

Professionally, my career had taken several turns. I left my position as legislative advocate and later statewide political coordinator for the California State Council of Service Employees, SEIU, AFL-CIO, to open my consulting business, as well as to join Drexel Burnham Lambert in Los Angeles to study for the Series 7, NASD securities license exam. At Drexel, I joined with others to open an external investment advisory firm that would manage union assets, and specialize in targeting investments to create union employment while avoiding "union busters" and anti-union companies. Unfortunately, our plans were derailed when our principle investor lost most of his assets after his three small business investments failed.

My work at Drexel was the direct result of chairing the California Governor's Public Investment Task Force in 1980–1981, while employed by SEIU. When Dodson called me in 1981 to explore the creation of a socially responsible financial institution, we had already had some experience working together on the task force (he had chaired the Small Business Committee). Our initial discussions revolved around the creation of a bank, credit union, or savings and loan. We eventually hit upon the money market idea because we wanted a financial institution that would: be national in scope; appeal to a wide variety of investors; allow investors to easily access their money through check writing; permit investments to be socially screened; allow the partners to innovatively advertise; not be prohibitively expensive to manage and operate; and be structured to reduce the partners' need to come up with a great deal of their own money for initial capitalization. None of us had much in the way of savings or income, so the capital structure we finally agreed upon was a limited partnership (LP).

In the early 1980s, the LP was a perfect fit for us and for our investors. As the General Partners, we put up 5 percent of the initial capital and the LPs supplied the other 95 percent. The LPs had no liability, received 95 percent of the losses in the early years (until the 1986 Tax Act), and as the fund's assets and the management company's fee revenue grew, the LPs participated in 95 percent of the profits. The business plan and offering memorandum provided for a buyout of LPs based upon a formula of asset growth and management company success. This structure turned out to be both a blessing and a curse.

It is important to remember that we created Working Assets Management Company to be an investment advisor—as well as a mutual fund—owned by investors in the fund. The only real asset of an investment advisor is its investment contract—in this case our management company's contract with Working Assets Money Fund. The contract had to be renewed annually by the fund's outside members of the board of directors. Working

Assets Management Company created Working Assets Money Fund, the initial cost being amortized and paid back to the management company over several years. The management fee was also reduced to fund shareholders or subsidized by the management company in the early years, so the fund could compete on a yield basis with other larger and more traditional money market funds. Fund shareholders paid a management fee, including other costs related to fund expenses such as legal and accounting charges. The fee paid Working Assets Management Company, allowing the management company or adviser to market the fund.

Not unlike other small businesses' experiences in raising capital, it took much longer than we anticipated, and funds were raised primarily from family, friends, and colleagues. As was the case in drafting the business plan, each of the partners had different skills and contacts for fundraising. For example, Drummond Pike of Tides Foundation was well connected to the foundation world, Dodson was better connected to financial institutions and wealthy individuals in the Bay Area, and Brian Hatch of the California Professional Firefighters had connections with labor unions. Because of my connections to the SRI community, I put an advisory committee together of all of the well-known experts in the field to monitor and update our social criteria, while Michael Kieschnick almost single-handedly selected our first board of trustees. In 1984 we brought together the advisory board, the shareholders and staff of the Management Company, and the entire board of trustees at Asilomar Conference Center in Monterey, California, to review the social criteria and other aspects of Working Assets' operations. It was a great experience for all of us to connect and flesh out controversial social screening issues, from defining "repressive regimes" to identifying "capital flight."

The LP capital structure worked well for investors in the early years, but as the fund grew and the partners wanted to build a family of funds, the management company was limited by capital and legal restrictions. In other words, money generated from earnings could not be used to create new mutual funds—it had to be used for the original purpose, that is, to expand our efforts in marketing Working Assets Money Fund to benefit management company investors.

Dodson served as our first president and chairman of the board of the fund, but he was constantly being undermined and challenged by a couple of board members. The board was becoming fractionalized and, after less than a year, Dodson resigned as president to start his own company— Parnassus Asset Management—which in turn formed the Parnassus Fund, later adding other mutual funds. I reluctantly took over as president of Working Assets Management Company and lasted about a year, moving over to my own investment advisory business full-time as the feuding between factions on the board continued unabated.

In 1984, thanks primarily to Peter Barnes, Working Assets created a subsidiary to handle an affinity credit card service (Working Assets Funding Service), which provided Working Assets customers with a credit card. Every transaction provided a nickel to a fund created to finance progressive nonprofit, social justice, and environmental organizations. To this day that program and others have been of great service to the progressive community. Since 1985 Working Assets has donated over $46 million to nonprofit organizations all over the world.

The development of the affinity card was controversial. There was quite a debate at the board level as the credit card was seen by some as encouraging our investors to become spenders as well as savers. This was not unlike the storm that erupted between board members over whether or not the company should sell its customer lists to other firms for solicitation. Initially, I was successful in holding a majority of board members to a "no" vote, but later lost the vote when money became tight.

Another innovative idea that came from Peter Barnes was aggressive, hard hitting, and issue oriented advertising. Refer to Appendix A for an ad that was developed by Barnes that "pushed the envelope" for progressive, social, and environmental advertising. I believe that SRI mutual funds, investment advisors, and others in our field should go back to a more proactive and aggressive format, reminiscent of corporate campaigns, to raise social, environmental and political consciousness among investors.

Following Dodson's and my departure as corporate officers, Working Assets went through a crisis of leadership. After the board had settled upon a new president—through a rigorous and time consuming selection process—at the last minute it considered a new and untested candidate, who was hired on a split vote. The new president lasted less than a year, unsuccessfully attempting to merge his employee-owned buyout firm with Working Assets.

The personality rift on the board was finally resolved by the creation of two distinct and separate companies: Working Assets Management Company and Working Assets Funding Service. About half of the board members stayed with the money fund, while the remaining board members went with the credit card business. But, as in many human relationships, new conflicts arose on the successor Management Company board. The eventual solution was to oust the president and replace him with a lame duck president. Later the company was sold to private investors. These events followed my unsuccessful attempt to merge Working Assets with Progressive Asset Management when I failed to convince Dodson to sell his stock to me.

Working Assets, despite all of its problems, was ultimately successful. A great deal of the credit goes to Peter Barnes for his terrific ads, a successful South African divestment and disengagement national campaign, extensive marketing, and an SRI movement that became respectable and credible. The company began with a mission to create an enterprise that promoted socially responsible investing, and grew from a few dollars to over $250 million in assets when it was sold in 1992. All of the investors, including the founders, made money and advanced the national SRI movement.

The original Working Assets Money Fund was merged with Citizens Index, which is one fund in a large $660 million family of diversified socially screened mutual funds under the leadership of Sophia Collier. Now called Citizens Trust, the family includes Citizens Core Growth, Emerging Growth, Small Cap Core Growth, Global Equity, International Growth, Income, Value, and Citizens 300 Index Fund. Collier has proven to be a terrific businesswoman and a strong social and environmental advocate.

PROGRESSIVE ASSET MANAGEMENT

While I was serving as President of Working Assets, one of my clients introduced me to Peter Camejo—then an options trader and stockbroker at Prudential Bache—formerly with Merrill Lynch. I later learned that Camejo had an extensive political background, once running for president of the United States as a candidate for the Socialist Workers Party. He's now run for California Governor twice as a Green Party candidate, and was Ralph Nader's vice-presidential candidate in 2004.

When I met Camejo he was a very likeable guy, bright and energetic, who wanted to leave Prudential and planned to set up a brokerage firm "specializing in socially responsible investing." His idea was to recruit brokers and financial planners from Wall Street firms in the San Francisco Bay Area, raise capital primarily from family and friends, and launch the firm in San Francisco in late 1987. At that point in the evolution of SRI, I believed that it was extremely important for the community to have access to competitive brokerage services. The SRI movement had been successful in developing mutual funds and community investments, but still needed independent broker dealers to create a secondary market for high social impact investments. I agreed to serve as board chairman of the new company.

The first business plan was drafted in June 1987. The initial name of the firm was Progressive Investors, later changed to Progressive Asset Management (PAM). The creation of PAM (www.progressive-asset.com) was a joint effort by several activist stockbrokers and financial planners who wanted a financial services firm that reflected their political, environmental, and social values. All of the founders were from the San Francisco Bay Area, representing an eclectic diversity of ethnic, gender, sexual orientation, and social profiles highly representative of Bay Area talent.

One of the first decisions was where to open the PAM office. Camejo wanted it in the financial district of San Francisco. He wanted a big media splash and felt we would receive more credibility in the city—and we got both when we opened an office on Bush Street. We later moved to Oakland to save costs. The strong suit for PAM was its social and environmental roots and commitment. The weak part seemed to be limited financial services experience, management depth and talent, and the lack of numerous brokers with significant assets under management.

Start up capital was provided exclusively by selling preferred stock in the firm to socially responsible investors. A majority of the shares were purchased by Peter Camejo and his family. At Camejo's insistence stock was also issued to newly recruited brokers, a move which eventually led to excessive stock dilution. There was an early debate among founding brokers and planners as to the wisdom of issuing options as opposed to outright stock since PAM was not a cooperative or a collective. But Camejo believed that the stock was initially worthless anyway, so it was best to use as an incentive for brokers to join PAM.

Camejo also made a decision, against collective better judgment, to place brokers on the board of directors, including one who demanded a board seat when seeking employment with PAM, even though he had little brokerage experience and little knowledge of—and less experience with—SRI. Camejo's practice of adding brokers to the board and giving away shares to employees who took little financial risk led to repeated internal board confrontations. As one can imagine, having brokers on the board meant endless discussions over compensation and who gets the larger office.

Camejo also decided to open a branch office in Palo Alto, California, and hired a man who had no SRI experience but had a "story" of his track record as a producing broker and the number of producing brokers he promised to bring along with him. Not only did the new office manager not live up to his past production claims, but in a media interview which announced the opening of PAM's satellite office in Palo Alto, he disclosed that he was a member of the National Rifle Association (NRA). The broker's NRA connection was an embarrassment for PAM, as well as the Bay Area's socially responsible investment community. I was blindsided by Camejo's hiring decision, but fortunately the Palo Alto PAM office operation was short-lived.

Camejo had a habit of hiring brokers with no social conscience, including commodity traders with forecasts of great wealth and fortune. We learned the hard way that it was far better to train political progressives to be brokers than to expect conservatives to change stripes and be SRI advocates.

But Pam *did* have successes, a lot of which were based on providing many of the company's customers, individual and institutional, with special social products, including a series of low-income housing tax credit programs. Several were developed and sold to clients, including Sojourner Truth Garden Apartments in Davis, California; Visalia Garden Villas in Visalia, California; and Sunflower Norton Apartments in Los Angeles. Other programs, such as those in Harper Community in West Hollywood and Peter Claver Community in San Francisco provided low-income housing exclusively to those suffering with HIV and AIDS. Most of those sold were public programs, providing investors with federal tax credits, but no capital appreciation. These investments were popular since they returned credits for ten years. These and other low-income housing tax credit programs ultimately turned things over to nonprofit housing authorities so that, unlike private programs, the housing remained in low-income in perpetuity. Many of the programs were developed and marketed by Duncan Meany, a broker at PAM who specialized in affordable housing.

Camejo was also successful in launching the "IRA That Cares" program, where PAM would donate funds to the San Francisco AIDS foundation for every new account opened or transferred to PAM.

Another success for PAM was a model social screening program developed for institutional investors. It was designed as an introductory SRI product for pension funds, foundations, trusts, and other institutional and individual investors. A portfolio would receive a social and environmental evaluation, and then agree to screen for a variety of factors and compensate PAM by trading commissions (soft dollars). The program was run by Tom Van Dyck, an aggressive salesperson, broker, and spokesperson for PAM.

Unfortunately, Camejo and Van Dyck fought constantly. The final straw came when Camejo put the entire social screening team on the time clock— literally. Eventually, Van Dyck took his entire team to UBS Warburg Piper Jaffray in San Francisco to form a socially responsible investment division, which has been very successful.

WaterHealth International, Inc.

Think about this: Some 1.2 billion people in the world lack access to water. More than twice that number have no sanitation and in thirty years, most of the world will not have enough clean water to drink. About 70 percent of all fresh water goes to grow food and in many parts of the world, including the United States, North Africa and Asia, farmers can take up to 95 percent.[3]

According to Maude Barlow and Tony Clarke, authors of *Blue Gold*: "The hard news is this: humanity is depleting, diverting, and polluting the planet's fresh water resources so quickly and relentlessly that every species on earth—including our own—is in mortal danger."

In 1995, Ashok Gadgil, a staff scientist at the Lawrence Berkeley National Laboratory at the University of California in Berkeley, invented a water disinfection device called UV Waterworks. The device, about the size of a small suitcase, was able to disinfect about four gallons of water per minute by utilizing a 50-watt non-submerged UV bulb. UV Waterworks was able to deactivate the DNA of certain waterborne pathogens such as bacteria, viruses, and molds. The unit weighed only about fifteen pounds, had no moving parts, and required minimal maintenance. The major drawback was that, unlike the major competitor, chlorination, if the disinfected clean water was reinfected, it had to be disinfected again. Unlike chlorination, however, there was no change in the disinfected water's taste or smell. In many developing countries, people are unlikely to drink water that has been chlorinated because it affects smell and taste.

Gadgil had invented the device primarily to serve rural areas in third world countries, where waterborne diseases such as cholera, typhoid fever, gastroenteritis, dysentery, and infectious hepatitis annually kill more than 3.8 million children and impair the normal growth of 60 million additional children. Home-delivered, chlorinated tap water is uncommon in most parts of the world and two-thirds of the world population must fetch water from outside the home, much of which is contaminated by pathogens if it is not treated by boiling or other means.

While understanding that commercializing an invention for third world rural water disinfection was risky at best, I believed it was certainly needed. I had confidence that it would meet the strong social criteria for investing required by my clients and colleagues. At the same time, I knew it would be a risky start-up research and development business and therefore limited to only those investors that could bear the risk.

I had met three other people who were also interested in Gadgil's device— Elwyn Ewald, Doug Brunson, and Chris Grumm. As the chairman of the Northern California Support Association of the Ecumenical Development Cooperative Society (EDCS), now called Oikocredit (www.oikocredit.org), I had met Ewald in the early 1990's when he was working for the General Manager. EDCS, a global economic development organization that was created in 1975 by the World Council of Churches, had hired Ewald to represent it in the United States—primarily to raise capital for its Third World Cooperative lending organization. As chairman of the PAM Board from 1987 to 1992, I had worked with Ewald when I supervised and managed an offering of subordinated notes to fund EDCS. These notes were purchased by individual and institutional SRI investors, including the Ford Foundation's Program Related Investment (PRI). Ewald, having been asked to resign from EDCS by a new Dutch general manager in Amersfoort, the Netherlands, had extracted a sizable severance package which he wanted to invest in a start-up business. His former boss, Doug Brunson—an American who was retiring as the general manager of EDCS—also expressed an interest in participating. Prior to EDCS, Brunson, was an employee of IBM and ExxonMobil. Before working for EDCS, Ewald had been a lobbyist in Washington, DC for the Lutheran Church.

After initially capitalizing the business with our personal funds, in June 1996, the three of us and a friend of Ewald's, Chris Grumm, formed WaterHealth International (WHI) and signed a License Agreement with Lawrence Berkeley Lab for exclusive global royalty rights (except for India) to the UV Waterworks patent. In 1996 and in 1997, we raised two rounds of preferred stock investment capital for WHI to commercialize and market UV Waterworks, most of it from my clients, friends, and colleagues. Later in 1997, the company raised another round of capital, this time exclusively from the venture capital arm of Johnson & Johnson Company (JNJ).

WHI was plagued with all the classic problems of running a start-up business, including bad advice from big time legal and accounting firms. But the proverbial straw that broke the camel's back was when Ewald attempted to sell the company to the Darth Vader of corporations: Monsanto.

Ewald was wined, dined, and swept off his feet by Monsanto's Roundup-tongued devil Robert Shapiro, who entertained him in St. Louis. Shapiro expressed his vision of saving the rural poor with clean water (along with genetically modified seeds and lots of chemicals), while flaunting Monsanto's wealth—big budgets, staff for Ewald, and a partnership with the company that brought the world chemical defoliants in Vietnam, PCBs, and cancer-causing saccharin.

In conjunction with a threatened shareholder lawsuit against WHI and Monsanto, as well as a blown merger with American Home Products, Shapiro pulled the plug on WHI's deal. It was too late for Ewald to repair the damage. He, his wife, and friends on the board—which had ousted me as an officer of the company after I opposed the Monsanto deal—ended up alienating just about everyone who had invested in WHI. The company quickly ran out of funds, after spending over $6 million of investors' money.

In a desperate attempt to save the company, Ewald brought in Dr. Tralance Addy, owner of Plebys, a small health services company, and an employee of JNJ. Addy couldn't raise any more money, and eventually the company filed for bankruptcy under Chapter 11. Addy even tried to convince SRI investors to dilute themselves almost out of existence and give up their original redemption rights which allowed them to sell their shares back to the company. This request came after Ewald and his friends on the board had already stripped them of their shareholder rights and placed all power in his board of directors.

Addy did succeed in emerging from the bankruptcy in late 2002, an act which included ridding the company of yours truly and all of WHI's other socially responsible investors, with a promise to a Southern California bankruptcy judge that he would increase sales over 950 percent and raise another $10 million in a couple of years. (In the seven years of life, WHI had sold a grand total of about two hundred units.) He gave Ewald a job, and shared some WHI stock with Monsanto and JNJ. Thanks to bank-ruptcy laws written by and for corporate management, Addy ended up with almost 80 percent of WHI's stock.

As of February 2004, WaterHealth was majority-owned by Plebys International LLC (78.46 percent), with Ewald owning 7.31 percent, JNJ owning 5.18 percent, Monsanto at 3.23 percent, Eric Lemelson 2.84 percent, Richard Cortese 1.4 percent[4] and several other small investors, including the inventor of Waterworks, Ashok Gadgil. To talk his way into and out of Chapter 11, Addy promised to sell thousands of additional units and raise $10 million. Addy put in $2 million of his own money, and by late November 2004 announced that—thanks mostly to the World Bank's International Finance Corporation—he had raised another $1.8 million, far short of the amount he promised the federal bankruptcy court. This is another example of the apparent need for bankruptcy courts: to give cor-porate management the opportunity to eliminate shareholders and con-tinue to milk a corporation into perpetuity.

On April 28, 2004, Addy's law firm was successful in receiving a final decree and the Chapter 11 case was dismissed. If management has enough money, anything is possible.

The Dangers of Going Public

The Body Shop International, founded by Anita Roddick in 1976 to sup-port her two children, has grown into a publicly traded U.K. company operating in fifty countries, with over 1,900 outlets. It is considered a pre-mier socially responsible global company, with natural products, fair trade, and progressive environmental, social, and political views. The company also supports anti-corporate globalization work.

In early June 2001, the Guadalajara, Mexico-based Grupo Omnilife—Latin America's largest direct-to-consumer seller of nutritional supple-ments founded by Jorge Vergara Madrigal—reached a preliminary agree-ment to acquire the Body Shop for about $500 million.[5] Omnilife is, "outpacing Amway Corp's nutrition unit and Herbalife International, Inc., both of which entered the regional market earlier," and had 720,000 distributors in 1999.[6]

It is no wonder that Omnilife was not a good fit with Body Shop, and talks ended between the two in late June 2001. According to a June 27 report in the *Wall Street Journal Europe*, the deal was contingent on Omnilife's ability to borrow $250 million. Omnilife claimed that it had obtained loans from one Mexican and one foreign bank, but called the deal off because after doing its due diligence the company realized that the merger itself didn't make strategic sense.

In September 2001, the Body Shop issued a press release announcing that it had received "a number of unsolicited expressions of interest from third parties who were exploring the possibility of acquiring the company." None of the discussions would result in an offer that reflected the true value of the company, the release said, and reported a number of changes in management, including Anita and Gordon Roddick stepping down as co-chairs of the company but staying on as board members.

In an interview with Idealswork.com in 2002, Anita Roddick said: "Looking back, perhaps the biggest mistake we ever made was going on the stock market. Because it didn't allow you the freedom to have fun. It allows you lots of things, but not to have fun. I'm ambivalent about this, because I always used to think going into the stock market gave us enormous freedom in terms of the money that came through to build an organization that was so progressive and so altruistic and so out of the mold."

Jerry Greenfield and Ben Cohen who opened Ben & Jerry's Homemade in 1978, must feel the same way. When they were both twenty-eight years old they opened an ice cream parlor in an abandoned gas station, vowing to stay in business one year. Their successful socially responsible business welcomed the new money raised from the market when they went public, but they didn't duck the bullet by avoiding acquisition like the Body Shop. Ben & Jerry's is a South Burlington, Vermont-based company that since 1985 donated almost 8 percent of its pre-tax profits to charity, and purchased locally produced bovine growth hormone-free (Monsanto-free) milk for its ice cream. Ben & Jerry's developed a great brand name for its ice cream and was able to support a progressive political agenda.

On April 12, 2000, Ben & Jerry's Homemade, Inc. agreed to be acquired by the Anglo-Dutch consumer giant, Unilever. Initially, a competitive bid was made for the company, by Meadowbrook Lane Capital, an investment bank specializing in socially responsible projects. Meadowbrook included Ben Cohen and, ironically, Anita Roddick. If they had been successful in competing against Unilever to buy Ben & Jerry's, they would probably have delisted the stock and taken the company private again. Several groups were organized and rallies were held across the country to oppose the sale to Unilever.

According to Terry Mollner, a principle in Meadowbrook Lane Capital and a co-founder and board member of the Calvert Social Investment Fund, nothing could have stopped Unilever's buyout, because Ben & Jerry's attorneys ". . . had not baked into the legal documents the legal options that could prevent it. This means that board members would be sued if they did not accept the highest bid."[7] Welcome to the world of publicly traded companies.

Unilever successfully swallowed up Ben & Jerry's, initially allowing Cohen and Greenfield to stay involved with the company, keep a separate board, stay in Vermont, and pay Vermont dairy farmers a premium for their growth hormone-free milk. There was also a verbal agreement to allow Cohen to have veto power over a new CEO. Unilever contributed $5 million to the Ben & Jerry's Foundation, $5 million for minority-owned business start-ups, and $5 million to employees.[8]

The $5 million for start-ups went to a new Social Venture Fund run by Ben Cohen, and the $5 million to the Ben & Jerry's Foundation was in addition to an annual contribution of $1.1 million committed from Unilever to be maintained for ten years.[9]

Ben Cohen has not lost any of his radicalism or his ability to use the foundation to support progressive social and environmental change. He and co-founder Jerry Greenfield had hoped that their company would be able to have some social impact inside giant Unilever. Supposedly, Cohen was convinced to do the "deal" with Unilever when a company executive looked him in the eye during negotiations and said: "Ben, do you realize the opportunity you have here to help [Unilever] grow in its social commitment?"[10] Vermont Congressional

Representative Bernie Sanders also held out optimism: "My hope is that . . . Unilever will change its positions on agricultural issues and advocate for policies in Washington and elsewhere that preserve family farming in Vermont, instead of policies that drive family farmers off the land."[11]

Ben & Jerry's supporters asked: Will a socially committed, publicly-traded company like Ben & Jerry's, that is bought by Unilever, still carry out its original social mission? After Cohen, Greenfield, and other social investors were unable to take the company private and defeat Unilever's bid, they were able to extract a generous compromise from Unilever. They retained some independence, while gaining funds to continue their progressive work. Unfortunately, Unilever owns Ben & Jerry's, and can pull the plug at any time—excepting contractual obligations pursuant to their merger agreement. The tail of Ben & Jerry's does not wag big dog Unilever. It is owned and controlled by Unilever, even if the leash is long.

Mollner believed Unilever was sincere in its support of Ben & Jerry's social agenda. He wrote that Cohen and Greenfield "succeeded in having their social mission invited into the multinational corporation that purchased them with the possibility that it could spread throughout the company . . . and among other multinationals."[12]

When I was contemplating Mollner's words, Marjorie Kelly, publisher of *Business Ethics* magazine, reminded me of Jack Quarter's book *Beyond the Bottom Line: Socially Innovative Business Owners,* which studied eleven socially innovative firms in six countries that were merged or acquired by non-social firms. In every case, he found that these companies eventually reverted to traditional management practices. Social innovation was squeezed out every single time. When founders leave, a company goes public, or the firm is sold, chances are very good that the firm will begin the slide down the slope toward losing its mission.

Unilever has laid off one in five Ben & Jerry's employees, hired a CEO who was not approved by Ben Cohen, and has stopped donating 8 percent of pre-tax profits to the Ben & Jerry's Foundation—the company does donate $1 million annually, which was its original commitment. It is unclear if Unilever continues to honor its pledge to buy bovine growth hormone-free dairy products from Vermont farmers.[13]

Social investors also questioned Mollner's optimism about Ben & Jerry's ability to influence Unilever. Unlike Ben & Jerry's, Unilever is an ardent supporter of genetic engineering announcing proudly on its web site that: "Unilever supports the responsible use of modern biotechnology within the framework of effective regulatory control and provision of information about its use. The use of this technology to improve food crops can bring important benefits to mankind and individual applications should be judged on their merits."

As early as March 1998, Unilever was attacked by Friends of the Earth, Greenpeace, and the Genetic Engineering Network, for adding genetically engineered soya to Batchelor's Beanfeast—the first of the company's products to be labeled in Europe as containing genetically modified ingredients.[14]

Once a private company goes public, the entire game changes. Anita Roddick said it was no longer any fun, which is the identical statement I've heard from others that enjoy running a private company, especially a private family business. If you ask the same question of the current owners of Google, the Robert Mondavi Corporation, Ben & Jerry's (now Unilever), Greg Steltenpohl of Odwalla (now Coke), Will Rosenzweig of Republic of Tea (now part of New Age Beverages), or Kenny Ausebel of Seeds of Change (now part of Mars), what will be their answer? Was the mission lost for Ben & Jerry's, Odwalla, Republic of Tea, Seeds of Change, and the Robert Mondavi Corporation? The Mondavi family was in the process of taking parts of the company private again, as well as laying off over 360 people in the Napa Valley, when Constellation Brands Inc. launched an unsolicited $1.3 billion bid to take over the company. Shareholders sued Mondavi for not immediately considering the offer. Inevitably, Constellation bought Mondavi. Will the values of the Robert Mondavi family and their vision for the Napa Valley Community remain the same under Constellation Brands? Will the mission remain true for the new publicly traded Google? I have serious doubts.

Mike Gilliland, founder of Wild Oats Markets in 1984, took the company public in 1997 after he had built the firm into an organic grocery powerhouse with $1 billion in revenue. Four years later, after being pressured by the board of directors, he quit. Asked about going public, he told *Forbes*

Magazine: "I wish it didn't happen that way, but when you become a public company it's really not your baby anymore—the company takes on a life of its own. So I don't have any emotional trauma over it. A lot of the original people had left, or have since left."

Often, the precursor of an IPO is when the small business owner(s) take venture capital money. This invariably leads to the venture capitalists requiring the firm to commit to a future IPO as an "exit strategy" so they can receive a handsome return on their investment. As Gilliland explained to Forbes: "Going public with Wild Oats was inevitable. We took our first outside funding in 1991; after that we were down a different path—at some point you have to get your VC investors out. My advice is to hold out as long as you can before you take venture money."

Non-social venture capitalists care little about a company's social mission. Social venture capitalists, however, share or require a social or an environmental mission, and may not demand an IPO. Instead, they will require some kind of a "buy-back" of the social venture capital's investment over a specific period of time. This provides an incentive for the owner(s) to build the business and eventually buy out the social venture capitalists, to re-emerge again as the majority equity owners of the business.

The owners of private SRI businesses need to think long and hard before going public. Once a company does an IPO, the good news is more money. The bad news? The company is open to a tender offer or an acquisition from a hostile or non-social investor. The members of the board of directors, as fiduciaries representing the shareholders, can be sued by fellow shareholders if they do not seriously review any offer to purchase the company and have an airtight case for not accepting a legitimate buyout offer that benefits shareholders. There is no way out. Once a private company goes public, falling under the guidance of the SEC, securities laws, many, many lawyers, and case law, it is a whole new ball game. The big winners are the investment bankers and lawyers who line their own pockets after convincing the owners to go public, raise lots of money, and give shareholders liquidity.

Business Ethics correctly pointed out that there are stakeholder laws in some states that allow boards of publicly traded companies, when considering a buy-out or merger offer, to take other factors into account, such as the well being of company employees and the community where the company is located.[15] The problem is one of continual litigation and cost. The follow-up question becomes: Who has deep enough pockets to fight litigation to protect the mission?

The law does not require a private social business to be acquired by a publicly traded or private business based upon maximizing shareholder value. This is especially the case if it is a closely held (owned) company, and there are protections written into the company's bylaws, articles of incorporation, and/or shareholder agreements. If the founders of a private business wish to retain control among the original founding shareholder community, buy-sell agreements—such as those written by the founders of Working Assets—work well. Buy-sell agreements simply require original investors to provide the right of first refusal to purchase shares of other founders of the company when a shareholder desires to sell. If the other founders for whatever reason can't purchase the shares, then the company itself can buy them. If the company can't buy them, then the founding shareholder can sell to an outside party. This is only one protection—many more are needed.

At WaterHealth International, a limited protection for preferred shareholders was a redemption provision or "put" feature that forced the company to buy back the first investors shares after a specified period of time for a specific price—or allow the preferred shareholders to convert to common stock on a non-diluted basis. This was to ensure that the original investors, who had taken the most risk, would have a locked-in and reasonable return and the ability to exit the investment at some point in time. This was also an incentive for the original founding common stockholders to succeed, share success with the folks that took the most risk with them, or buy back the stock and increase their ownership in the business.

Unfortunately, in the case of WaterHealth International the majority of directors attempted to sell to Monsanto, against the wishes of the original investors, then reduced overall shareholder rights, placing all power in the board of directors, thus alienating the SRI community of investors. This was the nail in the coffin, which eventually drove the company into bankruptcy. In retrospect, a better protection for investors would have been a shareholder agreement restricting the sale of the company, based upon its original social mission of assisting the rural poor to gain access to clean water. This, as well as requiring a supermajority vote of the preferred shareholders before any management change, merger, or acquisition could occur, would have made it much more difficult for the company to have been sold to Monsanto or surreptitiously taken over by a Johnson & Johnson insider. Certainly, WaterHealth International should have required Addy to disclose all of his financial interests to shareholders, thus avoiding a clear conflict of interest. When Addy was the acting CEO of WaterHealth International, and employed by Johnson & Johnson, to whom did he owe his loyalty and fiduciary duty? The shareholders of Johnson & Johnson, the shareholders and owners of WaterHealth International, or his own company, Plebys (which ultimately gained control of WHI when Addy and his attorneys filed for Chapter 11 bankruptcy)?

HEALTHY SIGNS

Michael Kieschnick, a colleague and one of my partners in founding Working Assets, often said that what we need most is to encourage progressives to attend business schools, earn MBAs and then go out and create socially conscious business enterprises. Many folks, including Will Rosenzweig, who founded the Republic of Tea, have written extensively on social entrepreneurship. He currently teaches MBA students at the Center for Responsible Business at the University of California Berkeley Haas School of Business, is a Partner of Great Spirit Ventures, and recently founded Brand New Brands—a $15 million venture fund to finance small companies that develop healthy foods. He certainly shares Michael's belief and has done much personally to advance this goal.

Leslie Christian and Carsten Henningsen of Portfolio 21 are working with other individuals to create a holding company, similar to the structure of Warren Buffet's Berkshire Hathaway, called Upstream 21. This company, initially raising $15 to $20 million from accredited investors, will purchase private socially responsible companies to serve the common good.

Upstream 21 will be committed to sustaining communities, the natural environment, and enhancing the long-term viability of the enterprises it acquired, under a new stakeholder mandate. At some point, this innovative private company may go public, but it pledges a corporate charter and stakeholder mandate that is much different than traditional, exclusively profit-oriented corporate enterprises. This newly created structure will be organized to redefine, redistribute, and renew wealth, as well as operate under an entirely different multi-owner structure, created for sustainability and community.

Upstream 21's Articles of Incorporation, unlike traditional corporate structures, require that management run the day-to-day operation of the business in the best interests of the company's stakeholder community with due consideration of the firm's "... social, legal, and economic effects on their employees, customers and suppliers and on the communities and geographical areas in which the company and its subsidiaries operate; the long-term as well as short-term interests of the company and its shareholders; and the company's and its subsidiaries' effects on the environment."[16]

Similar goals have been advanced by Jed Emerson for training managers of nonprofit business enterprises. Emerson is the co-author of *Enterprising Nonprofits: A Toolkit for Social Entrepreneurs* (John Wiley & Sons, 2001) and co-author of *Strategic Tools for Social Entrepreneurs: Enhancing the Performance of Your Enterprising Nonprofit* (John Wiley & Sons, 2002). This groundbreaking work has been of great assistance in providing the guidance and tools that many nonprofit professionals need to hone their entrepreneurship and reinforce their organization's mission. Global Exchange (GX), as an example, has managed two fair trade retail stores in Berkeley and San Francisco, California and has recently opened a third store in Portland, Oregon.

Emerson's concept of applying business skills and techniques to nonprofits has caught on across the country. The Yale School of Management, the Goldman Sachs Foundation, and the Pew Charitable Trusts have joined together to form The Partnership on Nonprofit Ventures, which runs a National Business Plan Competition for Nonprofit Organizations to expand successful profit-making ventures. The business plan competition includes several rounds of evaluation, and the four winners receive $100,000 each and hours of technical business planning assistance. In the San Francisco Bay Area in September and November 2003, the Social Fusion Nonprofit Venture Series provided seven weeks of intense business training, networking, and access to funders for social entrepreneurs. Social Fusion is a program of the Women's Technology Cluster (www.info@wtc-sf.org), funded by the Three Guineas Fund, a foundation dedicated to social justice for women and girls.

The Goldman Sachs Foundation made an initial $1.5 million grant to help launch the Partnership, and another $1.5 million to continue its mission of fostering business growth among nonprofits. Out of this effort has come the creation of the Social Enterprise Alliance, a nonprofit membership organization designed to mobilize nonprofit practitioners and assist them in gaining access to information, technical assistance, and capital. The idea is to strengthen nonprofit organizations' ability to create revenue-generating enterprises that will supplement grants and charitable donations to maximize the opportunities for nonprofits to become fully sustainable.

In 1999, Haas School of Business students at the University of California, Berkeley developed a Global Social Venture Competition (www.socialvc.net) to allow budding entrepreneurs in business schools to submit business plans to a group of judges for a $100,000 prize offered by the Goldman Sachs Foundation. Haas was joined by the Columbia Business School and the London Business School in sponsoring the competition. In 2004, 129 business plans were submitted and winners were selected in April at the London Business School. I was honored to have been one of the judges participating at University of California at Berkeley.

4

SRI Mutual Funds: Making It Easy

The beginning of contemporary socially responsible investing was modest. At first it was scarcely known to the public. The media gave little or no attention to the introduction of Pax World and Dreyfus Third Century Funds, created by Protestant ministers and anti-war activists, respectively. Mutual funds were in their infancy in the early 1970s, and socially screened stock and bond portfolios were almost unheard of by the investing public. SRI mutual funds, successfully launched a decade later in the early 1980s, were based on a more broad range of social, economic, and political issues.

The launching of the Calvert Social Money Market Fund on the East Coast, and Working Assets Money Fund on the West Coast, attracted more publicity than the earlier funds primarily due to the strong and vocal anti-apartheid movement across the United States. While founders Wayne Silby and John Guffrey were entrepreneurial in starting Calvert's first social fund, the founders of San Francisco-based Working Assets were progressive and committed political activists, having a background and professional standing in the anti-Vietnam War movement with strong ties to the anti-apartheid movement.

Needless to say, the early pioneers of SRI were not always successful, but they took risks and had the courage of their convictions. One such individual, Robert Schwartz, whom I consider the grandfather of the movement, was the first to coin the phrase "socially responsible investing." As an early congressional candidate in New York, he was against the Vietnam War, and as a financial professional, he tirelessly campaigned against South African apartheid. Throughout the 1970s, Schwartz worked as a financial consultant for Shearson/American Express, Inc., helping his clients avoid investing in companies that benefited from the Vietnam War and South African apartheid. While he found it deplorable that the "American system was run by corporations and by the military-industrial complex,"[1] he nonetheless hung in there, attempting through Shearson to launch the Trust for Balanced Investment Mutual Fund in 1983.

This mutual fund offering was unique, utilizing inclusionary and exclusionary criteria, including labor-management relations, human rights and equal job opportunities, environmental protection, and preservation of natural resources. The fund would have excluded investing in companies that actively supported South Africa but encouraged investments in companies that promoted employment of the handicapped, affirmative action, and that established day care centers for employees. Schwartz's Herculean task of raising capital for such an unprecedented SRI mutual fund was made more difficult when Shearson demanded that he raise a minimum of $75 million in four months (later extended to seven months) with a minimum investment of $100,000, thus primarily limiting the investment to wealthy individuals and institutional investors.

Schwartz's trust offering so enraged the National Right-to-Work Committee that the anti-labor group launched a campaign against Shearson and other financial firms for supporting "compulsory unionism."[2] The committee was particularly upset because the former president of the United Auto Workers' union, Leonard Woodcock, was to be the trust's chairman. He was also the former U.S. ambassador to the People's Republic of China, so the right wing anti-union group saw "red" in more ways than one.

Despite Schwartz's great investment track record, Woodcock's leadership, and the unique opportunity it afforded organized labor to participate in a non-union fund, the trust failed to attract sufficient assets by the end of 1983 and the fund never opened.

But there was a silver lining: the SRI community gained insight from Schwartz's groundbreaking work. By the end of 1983, both Calvert and Working Asset's money market funds were launched and immediately received national media attention and union support. Both funds utilized and advocated comprehensive inclusionary and exclusionary investment portfolio social screening. The contemporary SRI mutual fund game was afoot. The timing couldn't have been better—American investors clearly had, and continue to have, a love affair with mutual funds.

According to the Investment Company Institute, mutual fund assets totaled $6.39 trillion in December 2002 and the number of mutual funds totaled 8,269. By August 2004, mutual fund assets had increased to over $7.6 trillion. The number of American households owning mutual funds has more than doubled since 1990 to about 54.8 million, encompassing over half of all households (93.3 million individual shareholders).[3]

There are also about six thousand hedge funds worth almost $1 trillion (in 1990 assets totaled $50 billion), which are private, non-liquid, high-risk funds that cater to the wealthy. Analysts and traders estimate that they often make short-term "bets" which account for 35 to 40 percent of all stock trading.[4]

In June 2003 Catholic Healthcare West announced that upon SEC approval its fund and four others would launch the Good Steward Hedge Fund, which utilizes a social screen as well as engages in shareholder advocacy. I talked to Bill Mills of Highland Associates who oversees this "fund of funds" from Birmingham, Alabama. As of June 30, 2004, the fund had about $200 million in assets and was managed by AIG. The hedge fund is socially screened, and excludes about 180 companies, such as those involved in providing products or services related to abortion, weapons, gambling, alcohol, and tobacco. It also has inclusionary criteria covering environmental and labor issues. Mills indicated that they hope to expand the fund's assets to $500 million. The minimum institutional investment is $5 million.

Traditional socially screened funds have abounded as well, due in large part to the growing demand for socially responsible investing as well as the convenience of one-stop shopping at financial factory outlets such as Charles Schwab and Fidelity Investments, which have created discount broker supermarkets for mutual funds. About 5 percent of mutual funds sold in 2001 were purchased through these supermarkets.[5] Such giants offer a potpourri of mutual funds to meet every investor's need, including access to a wide offering of socially screened funds.

When I wrote *Investing With Your Conscience* in 1992, I attempted to define socially responsible investing and presented the debate within the SRI movement at that time. As did several prior SRI books, I also discussed how investors could set their social goals, build securities or mutual fund portfolios, and select a responsible financial professional. I concluded my book by predicting a future of increased environmental investing, the creation of innovative new mutual funds, determined shareholder advocacy, the growing power of pension and retirement funds in the economy, and the inevitable shift in political power, moving from garnering votes to leveraging capital.

I was partially right. At that time, SRI was a $625 billion movement of capital, and by 2003 it was a $2.16 trillion movement of capital equaling over 11 percent of the $19.2 trillion in total assets under management.[6] The SRI movement has come of age.

In the past thirty years, socially responsible screened mutual funds jumped from a half dozen to over two hundred, including new innovative sector funds as well as screened funds added to traditional "families" such as Vanguard, Fidelity, and Neuberger Berman. This assortment of SRI funds meet just about every need, offering a wide variety of investment management styles and strategies to address a vast array of financial, social, and environmental objectives.

In 2002 SRI mutual funds had a net inflow of $1.5 billion, while diversified equity funds had a nearly $10.5 billion outflow, according to Lipper Inc., the mutual fund-tracking unit of Reuters. In the first quarter of 2003, SRI mutual funds pulled in a net of $185.3 million, compared to a net outflow of $13.2 billion for all diversified non-SRI U.S. equity funds.[7] The ICI says that about two hundred mutual funds are socially screened, totaling approximately $151 billion in assets in 2003. This is an 11 percent growth since 2001.

By the end of 2003, the number of screened mutual funds remained constant, but after the three-year bear market, while non-screened funds struggled to grow and acquire assets, SRI funds' growth blossomed. In early 2003, it was already apparent that socially screened mutual fund assets were catching the public's eye.

SOCIALLY RESPONSIBLE SCREENING

Undeniably, even in the three years of the bear market, SRI has gained strength from the increased flow of investors' dollars. Retirement assets held in mutual funds alone represent $2.662 trillion, while total retirement-plan assets amount to $12.1 trillion.[8] SRI has gained credibility in the eye of investors because of: (1) competitive risk adjusted performance; (2) increasingly accessible SRI products and services; (3) increasing disillusionment with traditional corporate management because of excessive CEO and director compensation, fraud, neglect, mismanagement, incompetence, and corruption; (4) increasing skepticism with traditional mutual funds and portfolio managers' support of the Wall Street Rule which opposes corporate transparency and progressive corporate governance; and (5) SRI's support for increased corporate governance, shareholder advocacy, overall ethical philosophy, and action on behalf of global human, labor, and environmental rights.

SRI practitioners and fund managers have been marginally successful in raising governance, environmental and social justice issues at the shareholder levels; voting stock; communicating and dialoguing with corporate management; and screening portfolio secondary market securities. Some have suggested that SRI firms, as well as mutual funds, should screen companies for greed, corruption, deceitful accounting practices, and excessive CEO compensation, and screen investment banking firms that participate in "spinning," or giving IPO offerings to executives of companies in exchange for their investment banking business. Others have suggested that SRI folks screen companies that refuse to respond to shareholders when a majority votes for a change in corporate policy, or screen companies that refuse to expense stock options, thus artificially inflating stock valuations. Other suggestions include screening for companies that are involved in mergers or acquisitions, since most fail. This usually creates inflated valuations and unholy alliances between investment bankers and corporate management, leading to ridiculously high investment banking fees and sweet golden parachutes for retiring executives.

Screening has become big business. Institutional Shareholder Services (www.iss.proxy.com) now has its own Social Investment Research Service that provides investors over eighty screens and recently purchased a major social research firm, the Investor Responsibility Research Center (IRRC). Web sites for screening services will be found at www.socialinvest.org, www.socialfunds.com, and www.SRI-adviser.com. The Ethical Investment Research Service (EIRIS) has a partnership agreement with a Japanese research company, Good Bankers, to provide environmental, social, governance, and ethical behavior information on over four hundred Japanese companies. *Morningstar* Japan, a leading provider of independent investment research, has also launched its first index covering the Japanese market which exclusively screens companies based on their performance in corporate governance, employment, consumer services, the environment, and social issues. The Center for Public Resource Development (www.public. or.jp/english.html), a nonprofit organization that assisted in the development of the index, reported that only about 150 companies remained after *Morningstar* cut its list of acceptable companies down based on liquidity and tradability.

Passive screening, however, should not be seen as a panacea.

Stephen Viederman, co-founder of the Initiative for Fiduciary Responsibility, has been an outspoken advocate of mission-related investing both during and after his tenure as president of the Jessie Smith Noyes Foundation. He has spoken and written extensively on the subject of passive social screening: "Passivity is not a virtue in the face of assaults that confront us. Thus, screening portfolios may be a necessary beginning, but it is not sufficient. I say may because screening is such a blunt instrument for change. Institutional investors may get more bang for the buck by not screening and being active shareholders among a field of more egregious companies."[9]

Perhaps he's right in the sense that portfolio screening's effectiveness as a tool to change corporate behavior is difficult to understand or quantify. Obviously, it is not directly confrontational, and corporate management does not like to be challenged on social, environmental, or governance issues. It also depends upon the strength or liquidity of national or global capital markets. Obviously, in a healthy economic environment, there will be less impact, where the reverse may be true in a recessionary environment. Depending upon the particular security, and especially if it is an

IPO or new bond issue, the lack of demand will have an impact on security pricing or the interest rate required to be paid to investors.

In most liquid secondary securities' markets, passive screening will probably have little impact on securities' prices but could have some impact on corporate management if investors divest in large numbers while receiving national publicity. This would certainly have a negative impact on corporate management, reduce credibility in the marketplace, and possibly damage a company's reputation. Over time, passive portfolio screening by a growing SRI community on a particular issue—let's say excluding nuclear power producers—compounds its legitimacy and lends additional credibility to anti-nuclear activists and environmental organizations that are questioning plant safety, the disposal of dangerous waste, and the health of surrounding communities.

Of course, exclusionary screening appeals to individual investors, offering a means to overcome guilt. It appeals to institutional investors that want to avoid securities of specific companies that directly contradict the organization's purpose or mission, e.g., church/weapons or health clinic/tobacco. Less passive inclusionary screening appeals to both institutional and individual investors if they support an organization's mission financially as well as socially or environmentally; i.e. an environmental group investing in alternative energy.

Some institutional investor spokespersons, such as Viederman and Lance Lindblom, president and CEO of the Nathan Cummings Foundation, have suggested that screening has far less impact than the exercise of shareholder rights and advocacy. Certainly there is no reason that both cannot be utilized.

Generally, based upon traditional social and environmental criteria, the overwhelming majority of most secondary market stocks fall in a middle group, i.e., those that adhere to minimal inclusionary standards but whose negative conduct is not substantive enough for exclusion. The top tier of social and environmental performers usually represent about the same number of companies that fall out due to an SRI exclusionary screen, so SRI investors are left with a large spectrum of companies suitable for investment, which are well suited for improvement through shareholder advocacy and/or other strategies.

Increasingly, SRI mutual funds and individual and institutional investors are focusing at least a portion of their portfolios on community investments. According to the Social Investment Forum, SRI funds flowing into community investing increased 84 percent between 2001 and 2003, from $7.6 billion in 2001 to $14 billion in 2003. These investments are primarily in Community Development Financial Institutions (CDFIs), which include community banks and credit unions, domestic and foreign global loan funds, and microcredit enterprises.

According to an analysis of 442 CDFIs, these institutions transacted $2.6 billion in financing. They assisted 7,800 businesses, and created or maintained over thirty-four thousand jobs.[10] Privately managed clients are committing assets to private placements, social venture funds, and other alternative investment vehicles. However, this is only a small portion of total SRI funds. The overwhelming majority of SRI money is still in passively screened assets. This is the main reason why four years ago the SIF and Co-op America launched a community investing campaign to Forum members to increase their commitment to CDFIs. Since the initial launch, over $1 billion of new money has been committed to CDFIs by the SRI community. Harrington Investments, for example, has about $14 million or 8 percent of its clients' portfolios invested in direct community investments, including CDFIs, private placements, and social venture funds.

There is recognition by many in the labor and the SRI communities that direct capital investments, or new money in primary markets, have much more impact than secondary market investing, even though inclusionary screening is accepted as a more "active" screening. Harrington Investments, Inc. attempts to pick stocks that meet certain social or environmental characteristics that are consistent with criteria designed in consultation with the client. For example, working with our client ACLU Northern California Foundation, Harrington Investments, Inc. has developed unique civil rights criteria to guide the organization's asset management and social investment strategy. This portfolio is unique, in the sense that it is designed to meet the individual client's mission, but portfolio companies are still secondary market instruments which add no new assets to the companies' balance sheet to support any new products or services.

There is no doubt, however, that more than thirty years of SRI exclusionary screening has raised investor awareness of serious economic, social, political, and environmental issues. The same is true for inclusionary screening which continues to educate investors about the positive products and services provided by companies whose stocks comprise many SRI portfolios.

Producing evidence of U.S. corporate complicity in supporting apartheid in South Africa or in the Vietnam War was the focus of much SRI activity in the 1970s and 1980s. The generation of baby boomer activists came of age during the Vietnam conflict and matured in the struggle against South African apartheid. Much of this maturation process included linking corporate conduct with atrocities abroad. SRI screening did not become the ultimate solution, but it was the hallway leading to the closed door. For socially responsible investors, the solution to Vietnam was absolution and divestment. There was no middle ground. Military contractors were not going to stop selling weapons and Dow and Monsanto were not going to give up their lucrative defense business of providing the means to burn people to death and poison successive generations of Vietnamese and U.S. servicemen and women. If money was not the root of all evil, it was evil's handmaiden. The sole reason these corporations exist is to make as much money as possible, regardless of the consequences. Self-interest rules.

Socially responsible screening has helped investors understand the connection between their money and the real world of the global economy. Charitable giving and consuming connects one to the community. The same is true for investing. Investing completes the triangle; it is the third leg of the metaphorical stool that represents the options for a citizen to maximize his or her social, economic and political impact through the use of money—by giving, consuming, and investing. Social screening is an evolving and ongoing process. It has led SRI investors the first few steps down a road that leads to significant social change, away from the corporate oligarchy and towards increased public power. As screening evolves, it will raise new issues. At this point, it can only be improved and enriched.

Generally, socially and environmentally screened mutual funds have performed pretty well. On average, most of them outperformed other stock funds in the 1990s, mainly because of the high allocation of technology stocks. According to a fund analyst at *Morningstar*, from 1998 to 2003 the average SRI equity fund allocated 23 percent of its portfolio to the tech and telecom sector versus an average of 14.5 percent for all other equity funds.[11] According to Lipper, Inc., the SRI funds produced an average gain of 15.5 percent in the second quarter of 2003, slightly outperforming the 15.4 percent of S&P 500 for total return.[12] This single quarter performance comparison is similar to that of the socially screened Domini 400 Social Index, which tracked the S&P 500 for a ten-year period ending April 30, 2003. Domini produced a 9.64 percent annualized return vs. 9.66 percent for the S&P 500 Index.[13] This review is also consistent with a 2003 Lipper study indicating that SRI funds ". . . performed about in line with regular diversified equity funds over the past three-year and five-year periods."[14] (If you want to look at lots of numbers and conduct mind-numbing analysis, go to Lloyd Kurtz's www.sristudies.org. If you want to discuss SRI performance, you can even visit http://srinotes.blogspot.com.)

While performance comparisons are important, they are all relative. In other words, today's money management or mutual fund's guru may be tomorrow's fool, or vice-versa. Measurement of a mutual fund's performance is only relevant when it is compared to similar mutual funds with the same management style or against indexes relevant to that style. It is also true that past performance is no indication of future performance.

It is important for an investor to stay focused on an investment objective, be it income, capital appreciation, or both. Too many people end up chasing performance, investing in funds that have gone up or had spectacular performance, only to pull out when the fund goes down. Often mutual funds launch advertising campaigns right after they've had a terrific year, or several quarters. Dollar cost averaging is a more important and disciplined approach for most investors, since an equal amount of money can be invested on a regular basis (monthly or quarterly) when fund shares are low as well as high, depending upon the market. This smoothes out the peaks and troughs and takes advantage of market cycles.

Most investors can't time the market and shouldn't even try. According to a study by Dalbar, Inc., a Boston-based financial services market-research firm, for the eighteen-year period from 1984 through 2002, the S&P 500 index of large-cap stocks had a cumulative return of over 793 percent and an annualized return of 12.22 percent. The annual return of the average stock fund investor was just 2.57 percent, which is less than inflation.[15]

Most mutual funds offered are called "open-ended," meaning an investment manager can buy and/or sell securities in the mutual fund daily. The value of all of the securities in the portfolio changes every day based upon the close of the market, as does the value of the fund's shares, which are priced at net asset value (N.A.V.). The N.A.V. is simply the total market value of the mutual fund portfolio of securities divided by the total number of shares comprising the mutual fund sold to investors in the fund.

Open-ended mutual funds are a convenient vehicle for investors to put a relatively small amount of money in a diversified, professionally-managed portfolio of securities which are designed to meet specific investment goals and/or objectives. Mutual funds set limitations on initial minimum investment deposits and minimal additional investments. They also charge fees, including what are called 12(b) (1) fees, which cover marketing and other expenses. Some funds may have "loads," or additional charges when initially investing in a fund or charge fees when funds are withdrawn. It pays to look at the expense ratio, which indicates annual expenses of the fund, contained in the fund's prospectus. Always ask for the Prospectus, Statement of Additional Information, and a copy of the latest portfolio appraisal or schedule of investments (which may appear in the fund's last annual or quarterly report). If the SEC has its way, mutual funds may soon be required to publish a list of all portfolio securities on a quarterly basis.

Most mutual funds spend large amounts of money marketing and advertising their performance numbers. Numerous academic studies have shown that investors are attracted to funds that advertise more or are heavily promoted by commission-paid brokers and financial planners. Investors should always compare performance with both mutual fund peers (apples with apples) and with the relevant index.

Also, investors should beware of hot stock funds with big performance numbers in short periods of time. Remember the Internet rage? Many large mutual fund families rolled out and heavily advertised their new specialized Internet funds in late 1999 and early 2000, just before the bubble burst. In early 2004 many fund families were adding funds investing in China, even though the managers investing such funds had no experience investing in volatile and risky Chinese markets. When Vietnam became hot, large mutual funds were added to "families" of funds to take advantage of the rush to Vietnamese markets. Many of these funds closed when the fund manager couldn't find enough companies to fill up the portfolio. Not only should investors avoid chasing hot or trendy mutual funds with big returns, they should also beware of funds that add names to their funds, or simply change names. One academic study even found that mutual funds that changed their names attracted 22 percent more new money than funds of similar size and investment style, but did not have a name makeover. For example, AIM Small Cap Equity Fund changed its name to AIM Small Cap Growth Fund and over the next year drew in $189 million in new investments.

THE LEARNING CURVE

The 1990s bull market created a gold rush for growing mutual fund families. This rapid growth, however, came at a price. While mutual fund assets grew, along with management fees to portfolio advisers, it fed investor expectations, and created sophisticated appetites for specialty and sector mutual funds of all sorts. We now have sector funds, geographic funds, foreign funds, environmental funds, and shareholder advocacy funds. Traditional investment advisers and financial planners have also gotten into the act of creating multiple funds in their newly organized fund families. There is now an industry of financial specialists and consultants whose job it is to open, close, maintain, and service hundreds of mutual funds, many which were created in the "decade of the bull."

For example, since 1969, U.S. Bancorp Fund Services, LLC, has provided numerous one-stop shopping services to the mutual fund industry. As of 2003, it was serving over nine hundred mutual funds for 212 fund groups that represent over 1.5 million shareholders and over $130 billion in assets.[16] The service is through a multiple series trust which allows a new fund to be registered within seventy-five days, providing a new fund's staff the services of reviewing registration statements, coordinating artwork and a logo, printing a preliminary prospectus, and developing a marketing and distribution strategy.

The U.S. Bancorp Fund Services may be an expedited and inexpensive approach for mutual fund creation, but it has drawn even more SEC attention to the fact that the same board of trustees in a multiple series trust oversees so many funds. This raises issues of competent oversight, fiduciary responsibility, and outside trustee independence. The same potential problems arise for large fund families such as Fidelity, which manages almost three hundred portfolios, or MSDW (Morgan Stanley) managing 358 portfolios. A *New York Times* article of September 14, 2003 reported that Joseph S. DiMartino, the chairman of the board of Dreyfus Funds, a unit of Mellon Financial Corporation, monitored 191 funds and earned $816,000 in 2002 for serving as a multiple fiduciary. Another Dreyfus director, and the company's chief administrative officer from 1990 to 1994, made $258,250 in 2002 for serving as a director of sixty Dreyfus funds. The fifty-two Dreyfus directors collectively earned $3.5 million in compensation for 2002, the *Times* said. These are nice earnings, but what kind of oversight and monitoring can you provide for sixty funds at a time?

Serving on a mutual fund board is seen as a part-time job, usually involving four to twelve meetings a year that run two days a piece, and often two or three years may go by before fund trustees go face-to-face with specific portfolio managers.[17] Some directors make as much as $250,000 a year, while Marvin Mann, sitting on 292 Fidelity boards collected $324,000 in compensation in 2003.[18]

Mutual funds have lately not only run into trouble with regulators over illicit trading practices, but the SEC has been spending a great deal of time investigating a host of conflicts. About 80 percent of mutual fund boards of trustees are chaired by the management company president or CEO. In June 2004, on a three to two vote, the SEC required mutual fund companies to have individual chairmen and said that 75 percent of fund boards be comprised of independent directors who have a fiduciary responsibility to fund shareholders, not to the management company. The Investment Company Institute opposed the move, as did Fidelity Investments and Vanguard Group.

In September 2004 the U.S. Chamber of Commerce filed suit against the SEC on the ruling, claiming that the Commission ignored costs of implementation and ". . . didn't give enough credence to evidence that an independent chair is likely to harm rather than help fund performance."[19]

Thanks to Fidelity Investments, other mutual fund companies, and financial industry lobbyists, Congress tacked on language in an SEC funding bill that required the agency to "analyze whether mutual funds chaired by disinterested directors perform better, have lower expenses, or have better compliance records than mutual funds chaired by interested directors." The SEC was be required to report and "act upon the recommendations" no later than January 2006. This is an obvious attempt to dismantle very limited mutual fund "reforms."

Many small mutual funds encountered increasing financial difficulties in the bear market from 2000 to 2003, and many were consolidated into larger funds, while some simply disappeared. The number of mutual funds decreased from 8,307 to 8,269 in 2002, while mutual fund assets dropped 2.6 percent. Many management companies that struggled with reduced assets needed to "break even" from a cash flow perspective. That is, the management fees earned by the investment adviser did not cover the costs of managing the fund. This is especially true of many new fund advisers who subsidize management fees to compete with other funds, and thus the management company earns less money in the early years of a fund's life. Social funds have not been spared.

The Shareholder Advocacy Fund, created in September 2000, had $1.87 million and went out of business. Two others—Bridgeway Ultra Large 35 Index, created in July 1997, which has $7.8 million, and the Light Revolution Fund, which has been open for six years and has less than $5 million—were constantly under pressure from the SEC to grow their assets or close down.

John Waggoner reported in *USA Today* on September 9, 2002 that since the bear market began in April 2000, 414 stock and 158 bond mutual funds had been liquidated. And the *San Francisco Chronicle* reported on December 28, 2003 that about one thousand funds were liquidated or merged out of existence in 2003. If a bear market reappears, there is little doubt that small mutual funds will struggle to survive. Most experts agree that the absolute minimum a mutual fund must have in assets to break even is $10 to $20 million. I think the true number is closer to $30 million to cover normal operational, administrative, and marketing costs. Some funds, like the Light Revolution Fund, have been able to limp by on less revenue only because the portfolio manager has deferred all management fee income. This fund, however, is being purchased by John Hancock.

Small struggling SRI funds have also failed. For example, in August 2002, the Humane Equity Fund launched by Salomon Brothers Asset Management for the Humane Society of the United States (HSUS), announced that it had closed its doors after thirty months, stating: "The fund was a great idea, but many funds suffered in the recent economic conditions. Still, HSUS is committed to the concept of animal-friendly investing, and we will continue to look for similar opportunities."[20] The fund sought to avoid pharmaceutical, cosmetics, meatpacking, and other companies that produced items adverse to the humane treatment of animals, such as manufacturers of hunting and trapping equipment. Conversely, the fund attempted to only invest in companies that promoted the humane treatment of animals.[21]

In March 2002, the Friends Ivory European Social Awareness Fund, which invested at least 65 percent of its assets in large-cap European companies, was liquidated after its performance suffered in the bear market. The fund excluded companies involved in military contracting, environmental damage or pollution, nuclear power, tobacco, alcohol, or gambling, and purchased companies that were proactive in improving human rights. The fund had about $16 million in assets when it was liquidated.[22] Six months later, the portfolio manager, Friends Ivory & Sime, announced its merger with Royal & Sun Alliance Investments to form ISIS Asset Management, currently one of the largest British-owned fund management companies which provide investors with socially screened investment funds.

Some SRI funds that fail are simply merged with other funds in the mutual fund family. For example, the Calvert South Africa Fund, which opened October 1999 and was valued at $1.8 million, merged with the Calvert World Values International Equity Fund.

The SEC now requires mutual funds to report how its shares are voted at annual shareholder meetings. Such information, made available to shareholders beginning August 2004, is especially important to SRI mutual fund shareholders, to determine if their fund votes in a manner consistent with its environmental and social policy as described in the prospectus. This transparency will also be important for non-screened mutual funds shareholders to determine whether their fund manager is representing shareholders' interests or is supporting corporate management in an effort to gain access to lucrative 401(k) corporate-controlled pension plans.

According to a September 5, 2003 analysis in the *Boston Globe* of thirty-two thousand votes cast by fifteen major funds at three investment firms—Fidelity, Putnam and MFS—which manage a combined $268 billion in stocks, fund managers voted with management 86 percent of the time. It will be interesting to see if increased transparency has any impact on such voting patterns. Peter Kinder, president of KLD Research and Analytics, Inc., a Boston-based social research firm, told the *Globe* that, "It's really not in their DNA to vote against management."

A recent study by the Coalition for Environmentally Responsible Economies (CERES) showed that of the one hundred largest mutual funds in America, a mere 2 percent of the assets of these funds supported shareholder resolutions calling for more corporate disclosure on the financial impacts from global warming. The study, entitled "Unexamined Risk: How Mutual Funds Vote on Global Warming Shareholder Resolutions," found that Fidelity, Vanguard, and America Funds, which alone manage about 70 percent of the assets held in the nation's one hundred largest mutual funds, are among the twenty-five investment management companies that either voted against or abstained on all global warming proposals in 2004. Pension funds, on the other hand, are voting in increasing numbers for such resolutions, often adding to supporting shareholder votes of as high as 37 percent at some 2004 annual meetings.[23] Obviously, pension fund trustees see their fiduciary obligations differently than mutual fund managers, who often solicit corporate 401(k) retirement plan business. No conflict of interest here.

Morningstar has identified 194 open-ended mutual funds promoted as "Socially Conscious" as of November 30, 2004, but the list includes all classes of mutual funds, including funds sold only through financial professionals, those sold only to institutional clients, and those mutual funds with varying fees and loads sold to retail customers. Depending upon the definition of "socially conscious," "socially screened," or "SRI," the number of funds available to investors currently ranges from 200 to 250. I first pared the *Morningstar* list down to ninety-one funds with performance records of five years or more, eventually narrowing the list of covered funds to twenty-two for "socially conscious" funds with performance records of ten years or more, from mid-1994 through mid-2004 (see the table on pages 138–139). This includes the oldest of the social funds, such as Dreyfus Premier Third Century and Pax World Balanced, along with four Calvert funds, Citizens Income, Domini Social Equity, New Alternatives, four Parnassus funds, two Ariel funds, Green Century Balanced, and three Smith Barney funds.

Funds covered in this chapter include the Amana Income Fund, a mutual fund operated consistent with Islamic principles. Three funds listed in the following table, Smith Barney Growth & Income, GMO Tobacco Free Core, and PIMCO Total Return Institutional, will be discussed separately as a group of Odd Ducks.

From a purely financial performance standpoint, John Roger's two Ariel funds, Ariel and Ariel Appreciation, led the pack with a ten-year annualized return of 15.44 percent and 14.75 percent, respectively, followed by Jerry Dodson's Parnassus Equity Income Fund at 12.39 percent. The Ariel Fund also beat all the SRI mutual funds covered herein for performance, returning an annualized 13.09 percent for five years and 12.90 percent for three years.

It cannot be overstated, however, that the funds listed in the table and throughout this chapter have different management styles and investment goals. For example, the Ariel Fund is a small value fund, while Parnassus Equity Income is a large cap blend, and the Parnassus Fund is a large cap growth stock fund, whose manager considers himself an investment "contrarian." The Ariel funds and the Parnassus Fund approach investing differently to grow or provide capital appreciation, while the Parnassus Equity Income Fund is designed to provide income and capital appreciation. All mutual funds may employ portfolio managers either in house or as outside sub-advisers—who are hired by the principal portfolio manager to manage a specific mutual fund within a family of mutual fund portfolios.

Much has been written on social screening. Today's mutual fund managers have greatly expanded areas of exclusionary and inclusionary issues of social and environmental concern. Some of the improved criteria will be discussed throughout the remaining chapters of the book. To serve as a useful historical guide, I've included the original 1983 Working Assets criteria as Appendix B. I believe this criteria still reflects the heart and core of contemporary screening.

The technology, research methodology, organizational sources, nonprofit social databases, and the Internet have improved remarkably over the last twenty years and provide immediate access to social screening information in usable formats. (One good resource on the web is www.socialfunds.com).

Socially responsible mutual funds and social researchers in Europe are already working on guidelines to keep consumers well informed. In July 2003, the European Sustainable and Responsible Investment Forum (Eurosif) released a pilot version of its Transparency Guidelines, a voluntary initiative for the retail SRI sector in Europe. Questions on the research process ask whether research teams are in-house or if managers use outside consultants, if external verification is required, if such social research includes outside stakeholder input, how managers make divestment decisions, and how they communicate these decision to clients, investors, and affected companies.

Social and environmental screens can be exclusionary, inclusionary, or both. Companies can be excluded for involvement with nuclear power, weapons, tobacco, alcohol, or gambling. Inclusionary screening criteria is much more subjective in that managers add a company to the portfolio for an attribute such as adopting employment policies that are nondiscriminatory to lesbian or gay couples, or for their positive products or services, such as alternative energy, organic and health foods, childcare, education, or transportation.

Socially Screened, Open-Ended Mutual Funds
Ten Years or More — 6-30-94 to 6-30-04

Fund Name	Ticker	Phone Number	Manager Name	Manager Tenure
Amana Income	AMANX	800-728-8762	Kaiser, Nicholas	15
Ariel	ARGFX	800-292-7435	Rogers Jr., John W.	18
Ariel Appreciation	CAAPX	800-292-7435	Rogers Jr., John W.	2
Calvert Soc Inv Bal A	CSIFX	800-368-2748	Holmes/Habeeb/ Alexander, III/ Nottingham	3
Calvert Soc Inv Bond A	CSIBX	800-368-2748	Habeeb/Nottingham	6
Calvert Soc Inv Equity A	CSIEX	800-368-2748	Boone, III, Daniel W.	6
Calvert World Val Intl A	CWVGX	800-368-2748	Darnell/Hancock	2
Citizens Income	WAIMX	800-223-7010	Kelly, Susan	4
Domini Social Equity	DSEFX	800-762-6814	Management Team	0
Dreyfus Prem Thrd Cent Z	DRTHX	800-373-9387	Tuttle/Hilton	2
GMO Tobacco FreeCore III	GMTCX	617-330-7500	Management Team	0
Green Century Balanced	GCBLX	800-934-7336	Robinson, Jackson	9
New Alternatives	NALFX	800-423-8383	Schoenwald/ Schoenwald	22
Parnassus	PARNX	800-999-3505	Dodson, Jerome L.	20
Parnassus CA Tax-Ex	PRCLX	800-999-3505	Dodson, Jerome L.	6
Parnassus Equity Inc	PRBLX	800-999-3505	Ahlsten, Todd	3
Parnassus Fixed-Inc	PRFIX	800-999-3505	Dodson, Jerome L.	12
Pax World Balanced	PAXWX	800-767-1729	Brown, Christopher H.	6
PIMCO Total Ret III Inst	PTSAX	800-927-4648	Gross, William H.	13
SB Growth & Inc 1	CGINX	800-451-2010	Kagan, Michael A.	4
Smith Barney Soc Aware A	SSIAX	800-347-1123	Cammer/Graves, III	6
Smith Barney Soc Aware B	SESIX	800-347-1123	Cammer/Graves, III	6

SOURCE: MORNINGSTAR, INC.

The information contained in this chapter and in Appendix C on SRI mutual funds simply provides a starting point for investors. It is especially important for the investor to use relatively objective mutual fund resources, such as *Morningstar*, to determine if the fund manager's investment style is stable and doesn't drift. In other words, you want to make sure that if you

Incept Date	Morningstar Category	Assets ($ Mil)	Expense Ratio	Annualized Performance (%)		
				3 Year	5 Year	10 Year
1986-06	Large Value	24.30	1.89	1.33	0.43	8.54
1986-11	Small Value	2980.80	1.10	12.90	13.09	15.44
1989-12	Mid-Cap Blend	2902.30	1.20	8.53	8.52	14.75
1982-10	Moderate Allocation	492.10	1.24	0.31	0.03	7.17
1987-08	Intermediate-term Bond	162.90	1.17	5.91	7.11	7.03
1987-08	Large Blend	707.70	1.29	1.78	4.75	10.46
1992-07	Foreign Large Blend	211.70	2.05	1.54	-1.82	3.57
1992-06	Intermediate-term Bond	59.60	1.37	3.11	4.09	5.67
1991-06	Large Blend	1312.60	0.92	-0.33	-3.11	11.43
1972-03	Large Growth	478.10	1.14	-6.40	-6.72	8.51
1991-10	Large Value	453.50	0.48	-0.43	0.17	13.10
1992-03	Moderate Allocation	55.40	2.44	-3.05	10.87	10.82
1982-09	Small Blend	36.53	1.39	-7.23	3.27	5.99
1984-12	Large Growth	346.70	0.99	-3.90	3.65	8.89
1992-09	Muni California Int/Sh	24.90	0.62	4.85	5.21	6.07
1992-09	Large Blend	712.20	0.95	6.42	8.04	12.39
1992-09	Intermediate-term Bond	36.30	0.62	6.96	6.39	7.09
1971-11	Moderate Allocation	1302.90	0.99	2.18	2.92	11.43
1991-05	Intermediate-term Bond	1349.70	0.50	8.03	7.45	8.03
1987-04	Large Blend	546.00	1.00	-0.63	-2.42	9.04
1992-11	Large Blend	271.00	1.20	0.36	0.04	9.06
1987-02	Large Blend	105.10	2.00	-0.49	-0.77	8.22

purchase shares of a fund whose objective is growth, your manager doesn't start buying value stocks or all of a sudden become a blend manager or balanced manager, buying stocks and bonds which clearly violate the objectives listed in the prospectus.

Other information provided in fund disclosure material should include whether the mutual fund uses passive exclusionary or inclusionary screens, participates in shareholder voting and advocacy, files or co-files shareholder resolutions, engages in dialogue with corporate management or invests a portion of the mutual fund portfolio in direct community investments. Be aware that the information provided here may be dated by the time you've consulted this book.

EQUITY FUNDS

More information on each of these funds, including their Expense Ratio, Assets, ten-year performance, criteria for screening and background on the fund managers is provided in Appendix C.

Ariel and Ariel Appreciation Funds

Ariel and Ariel Appreciation funds were launched in 1986 and 1989, respectively. Since 1983, as the founder of Ariel Capital Management, Inc., John W. Rogers, Jr., has overseen the growth of Ariel Capital Management's assets. As of January 31, 2005, the two Ariel socially screened funds had assets of over $7 billion and, annualized over ten years, had outperformed all other SRI funds profiled in this chapter. The Ariel Mutual Funds do not invest in companies which are involved in the manufacture of weapons, the production of nuclear energy, or whose primary source of revenue comes from the production of tobacco products.

Domini Social Equity Fund

The closest thing you'll get to a socially screened S&P 500 Stock Index is the Domini Social Equity Fund, which has grown to over $1.3 billion. This fund is comprised of four hundred stocks, of which about one-half are S&P 500 companies that are socially qualified for Domini. Another 150 are added to insure that Domini's portfolio is comprised of a broad representation of S&P 500 industry sectors. This means that Domini's sector weighting is as close as possible to the S&P 500 Stock Index. Domini invests 100 percent of the assets of the fund in equities. In every year since its inception, and

certainly for the past ten years, the Domini Social Equity Fund's performance has been closely aligned to the S&P 500 Stock Index's performance.
Domini screens companies involved with tobacco and alcohol, gambling,
nuclear power, and weapons.

Dreyfus Premier Third Century Fund

A screened fund that has been around since 1972 is the Dreyfus Premier
Third Century Fund, which has more than $426 million in assets with
about 98 percent of the portfolio invested in equities. Dreyfus does not
have a rigid exclusionary screen (other than excluding tobacco), but
instead focuses on companies that enhance the quality of life in America
by considering their record in different areas, including the environment
and natural resources, occupational health and safety, consumer protection and equal employment opportunity.

New Alternatives Fund

New Alternatives is the oldest of the environmental funds, founded by
Maurice Schoenwald and his son, David, in 1982. Originally named the
Solar Fund, it was incorporated as a limited partnership in 1978. New
Alternatives is best identified with its investments in alternative energy
and related new technologies. Obviously, the fund's portfolio does not
include oil, coal, or nuclear energy. Products and technologies the fund
does include are batteries for solar energy, natural gas, resource conservation (including biomass), recycling, photovoltaic cells, and fuel cells. New
Alternatives Fund is a small cap blend, and as of June 30, 2004, it had over
$36 million in assets, increasing to over $51 million by January 31, 2005.

Parnassus and Parnassus Equity Income

Jerry Dodson's Parnassus family of funds has been around for more than
ten years, and until recently, he had managed all of the funds personally.
Now he manages only the original Parnassus Fund, as he has very successfully done for twenty years. Parnassus is labeled a large cap growth
fund, but its $346 million as of June 2004 still had 25 percent invested in
cash; in January 2004 that number was about 82 percent. Of the stocks in

Parnassus, most are invested in financials and health care. The Parnassus equity funds avoid companies involved with alcohol, tobacco, or gambling and screen out weapons contractors and nuclear power producers.

Calvert Social Investment Equity Fund

Founded in 1976, Calvert Group, Ltd. operates twenty-seven funds with over $10 billion in assets and has one of the largest socially responsible fund families in the country. It is owned by Ameritas Acacia Mutual Holding Company. One of Calvert's many socially screened funds, the Calvert Social Investment Equity Fund, with assets of $790 million has been managed by Daniel W. Boone, III, for over five years. Most of the portfolio is invested in stocks. The portfolio had almost 20 percent invested in health care, over 18 percent in consumer services and 13 percent in financial services as of June 30, 2004. Calvert Social Investment Funds are very proactive shareholders, engaging in dialogue with corporate management, filing and co-filing shareholder resolutions, and voting their stock in a manner consistent with their overall social guidelines. It avoids companies involved with repressive regimes, nuclear energy, gambling, weapons, and tobacco.

Calvert World Values International Fund

In September 2002, Calvert's $1.8 million South Africa Fund was merged into World Values, and as of June 30, 2004, total assets of the fund were almost $212 million. The social criteria for the World Values Fund is similar to Calvert's other socially screened funds, but its standards are less stringent, primarily due to the lack of adequate corporate disclosure, different regulatory structures, environmental standards, and differing national and cultural priorities. The fund, however, has inclusionary criteria and attempts to invest in companies that are proactive in the environmental area, labor rights, and women and minority rights.

Smith Barney Social Awareness Funds

Smith Barney Equity Funds, a Massachusetts business trust, and Salomon Smith Barney, a subsidiary of Citigroup, manage Smith Barney Social Awareness A and B. The primary difference between the Social Awareness

A and B is that the Class A fund is a front end loaded 5 percent and the Class B fund is a 5 percent deferred loaded fund. Smith Barney manages sixty mutual funds altogether with $200 billion in assets. Social Awareness excludes companies involved in tobacco, weapons, and nuclear power. It attempts to invest in companies that exhibit the positive attributes of fairness in employment policies and labor relations, involvement in community causes, and fairness of marketing and advertising practices.

Amana Income Fund

The Amana Income Fund opened in 1986 and currently has about $35 million invested in large value companies that are operated consistent with Islamic principles, including companies that share in profit and loss and receive no usury or interest. It screens out businesses involved in alcohol, gambling, pornography, insurance, pork processing, and Internet-based banks or finance associations. Also excluded are bonds, debentures, or other interest-paying obligations of indebtedness.

SOCIALLY SCREENED BALANCED FUNDS

More information on each of these funds, including their Expense Ratio, Assets, ten-year performance, criteria for screening and background on the fund managers is provided in Appendix C.

These are considered "balanced" funds, that is, a significant portion of their assets are allocated to fixed-income securities.

Pax World Balanced Fund

Founded in 1971, Pax World Balanced is the elder statesman of socially responsible mutual funds in the country and has the best ten-year performance track record of the three balanced funds. Given the deep religious roots of two of the fund's founders, Jack Corbett and Dr. Luther Tyson, and the fact that the fund was created at the height of the Vietnam War, the social criteria is wedded to an anti-weapons, anti-defense department exclusionary approach and also excludes companies that derive revenue from the manufacture of liquors, tobacco, or gambling products. As of June 30, 2004, Pax World's total assets were over $1.3 billion; by January 31, 2005, assets reached $1.47 billion.

Green Century Balanced Fund

Green Century is an interesting socially screened mutual fund that was created in the early 1990s. Green Century Capital Management is owned and was founded by Paradigm Partners, a California general partnership, the partners of which are all nonprofit environmental advocacy organizations, including California Public Interest Research Group (CALPIRG), Citizen Lobby of New Jersey, Colorado Citizen Lobby, ConnPIRG Citizen Lobby, Fund for Pubic Interest Research, Massachusetts Public Interest Research Group (MASSPIRG), MOPIRG Citizen Organization, PIRGIM Public Interest Lobby, and Washington Sate Public Interest Research group (WASHPIRG). The $66 million Green Century Balanced Fund invests in smaller growth companies that protect the environment, minimize environmental impact, and promote a healthier environment, and a sustainable future. According to *Morningstar*, more than 68 percent of Green Century Balanced was invested in stocks, and over 27 percent was in fixed-income as of June 30, 2004.

Calvert Social Investment Balanced Fund

The Calvert Group's family of socially screened funds was launched in 1982. One of the founders, Wayne Silby, remains board chairman of Calvert Social Investment Fund. The Balanced Fund's $502 million is currently managed by a team of portfolio managers, including Brown Capital Management, SSqA Funds Management, Profit Investment Management, and Calvert Asset Management Company, Inc. As of June 30, 2004, the fund's assets were allocated 60 percent stocks and almost 28 percent in bonds. More heavily weighted stock sectors included financial services (22 percent), and health care (14 percent).

Bond Funds

More information on each of these funds, including their Expense Ratio, Assets, ten-year performance, criteria for screening and background on the fund managers is provided in Appendix C.

Taxable Bond Funds

Calvert Social Investment Bond Fund
The Calvert Social Investment Bond Fund was opened in 1987 and is the largest of the fixed-income funds profiled in this chapter. It invests in U.S. government agency debt obligations that are generally compatible with Calvert's overall social criteria, which require the avoidance of major polluters, nuclear power and weapons producers, companies involved in gambling operations or the manufacture of tobacco and alcohol, and companies that have a record of employment discrimination, aggressive anti-union activities or unsafe workplaces.

Citizens Income Fund
Citizens Income Portfolio is comprised of government agency and treasury securities, as well as corporate bonds, of which up to 35 percent may be invested in lower grade issues. Citizens avoids companies involved in manufacturing alcohol and tobacco products, in nuclear power and weaponry, companies that lack diversity on their boards or in senior management, and companies that test on animals beyond what is required by law. Citizens focuses on protecting human rights and on companies that have a history of environmental stewardship and strong employee and community relations.

Parnassus Fixed-Income Fund
Parnassus Fixed-Income Fund invests most of its portfolio in cash, but also invests in short-term corporate bonds, of which at least one-half are rated AAA. Parnassus excludes companies that manufacture alcohol, tobacco products, weapons and nuclear power or are involved in gambling.

Parnassus uses its best judgment, on the other hand, to find and include companies that treat employees fairly; adopt sound environmental protection policies; have a good equal employment opportunity program; produce quality products and services; have a record of civic commitment; and have ethical business practices.

Parnassus California Tax-Exempt Muni Bond Fund
This fund has had positive investment return for eight of ten years and for at least five of the last ten years has outperformed either the Lehman Brothers Muni Bond Index or the Lehman Brothers California Muni Bond Index. It also has the distinction of being the only socially screened California tax-exempt bond fund in the United States. The $25 million fund invests in California intermediate-term municipals bonds, about 8 percent in housing, almost 14 percent in public transportation, 11 percent in education, almost 15 percent in environmental bonds (primarily waste water and water projects), 3 percent in health care, and about 13 percent in California General Obligation bonds.

ODD DUCKS

Three funds that appear in the table as *Morningstar* "Socially Conscious" that have not been profiled include the SB Growth and Income Fund, GMO Tobacco Free Core, and the PIMCO Total Return Institutional. The SB Growth and Income is a large cap blend fund that only passively screens tobacco and alcohol. The GMO Tobacco Free Core Fund only passively screens for tobacco and is available for investors with a $1 million minimum amount.

PIMCO is the largest of the socially screened bond funds with over $1.3 billion in assets. The fund's minimum investment is $5 million; therefore, it is available only for institutional investors. Similar to Dodson's Parnassus Fixed Income Fund, PIMCO has lots of cash (51 percent) to guard against declining bond prices as interest rates increase.

The social screening appears to be totally exclusionary and passive.

PIMCO does not invest in companies principally engaged in health care services, in the manufacture of alcoholic beverages, tobacco products, pornography, pharmaceuticals, military equipment, or in the operation of gambling casinos. PIMCO defines "principally engaged" as a company that derives more than 10 percent of its gross revenues from such activities.

Over the past 10 years, PIMCO Total Return Fund's investment performance has mostly matched or exceeded the Lehman Brothers Aggregate Bond Index.[24]

PIMCO's portfolio is managed by the founder and managing director of Pacific Investment Management Company, Bill Gross, who manages about $250 billion in bond funds. Gross, a Vietnam vet, was one of the first portfolio managers to oppose the war in Iraq and one of the few, if not the only, traditional investment advisers to take on General Electric (GE) for misleading investors about the company's debt and selling most of PIMCO's $1 billion in GE bonds.[25] He said he "picked on GE because [he] wanted to alert the investment universe that it wasn't just Enron, Tyco, or WorldCom pulling some fast ones, but GE – the biggest guy on the block – and probably everyone in between."[26]

WHEAT FROM CHAFF

Increasingly, it is harder for determined financial activists and SRI proponents to separate the wheat from the chaff. Mutual funds that screen out for one criterion (tobacco) or for two criteria (tobacco and alcohol) will inevitably be lumped in with all socially screened or "socially conscious" mutual funds. The good news for mutual funds utilizing single or double screens is that they get the best of all possible worlds; they get categorized as "socially conscious," and their advisers may invest in weapons of mass destruction.

Caveat emptor! The SRI-screened mutual fund investor still needs to be able to critically evaluate each mutual fund and be able to distinguish the difference between simple passive exclusionary screening, and comprehensive exclusionary and inclusionary screening, coupled with a commitment to shareholder advocacy and community investing. Not only must the reader and prospective investor be fully cognizant of the mutual fund's published criteria, he or she must also be able to overlay the portfolio appraisal or schedule of investments with the criteria to determine if there's a match. The prospective investor must also turn a critical eye to vague or generalized social and environmental criteria to determine if it represents purposeful obfuscation. The end result may be to confuse the investor, so the adviser can invest in anything available in the market.

Paul Hawken, an activist, environmentalist, and author of *Natural Capitalism*, has also been raising the issue of transparency relating to SRI mutual fund screening. He is concerned that most of the SRI portfolios look identical to the S&P 500 Index and over 90 percent of the Fortune 500 companies are included in SRI portfolios. He states that the term "socially responsible investing" is so broad it is meaningless.[27] He feels that the most important factor in determining a company's social responsibility is whether the company should exist at all. Hawken argues that few SRI mutual funds screen for environmental responsibility, pointing out that the Sierra Club Stock Fund has only one company that addresses the environment in a proactive way (Starbucks) and there are no alternative energy companies, but the fund includes companies that make surge protectors, fastening screws, steakhouses, anti-wrinkle creams, and candy bars.[28]

At the 2004 Bioneers Conference, Hawken distributed a Natural Capital Institute publication entitled "Socially Responsible Investing: How the SRI Industry Has Failed to Respond to People Who Want to Change It." He calls for SRI mutual funds to change screening criteria; improve and modify fund language descriptions; moderate investor expectations; become transparent and specific with respect to how companies are chosen; and maintain constant online disclosure of portfolios with full commentary on why a company has been selected or deleted.

To address some of the issues he raises, Hawken's Natural Capital Institute has partnered with Michael Baldwin, Baldwin Brothers, Inc. (investment advisory firm), and the Marion Institute, to develop a database of SRI mutual funds worldwide. He has also created High Water Capital, LP, as an alternative investment vehicle for socially responsible investors.

Proxy Voting

Compared to non-screened mutual funds, SRI funds tend to be more active shareholders, especially relating to the introduction and co-filing of shareholder resolutions. Most traditional mutual funds are also reluctant to engage in proxy battles. According to the *Wall Street Journal*: "Mutual funds also generally refuse to defy management teams because gaining a reputation for siding with dissidents can harm their ability to get business managing the 401(k) plans of employees in companies whose stock they own."[29]

Institutional investors control close to $7 trillion in mutual funds, 45 percent of all equities,[30] and according to Amy Domini, 19 percent of all publicly traded securities.[31] These mutual funds vote 22 percent of all proxies voted each year at annual corporate shareholder meetings.[32]

All mutual funds are responsible for disclosing their proxy voting record, much like CALPERS, the Calvert Social Investment Funds, Pax World Growth Fund, and Domini Social Equity Fund currently report on their Web sites.

Many SRI funds introduce shareholder resolutions, some only vote their stock by proxy, while several funds do both. Parnassus votes stock proxies on a regular basis, supporting many SRI colleagues' shareholder initiatives, but does not introduce resolutions of its own. New Alternatives Fund has co-filed several resolutions, including one at IdaCorp. According to David Schoenwald, New Alternatives has engaged in dialogue with a few companies, but "generally divested from uncomfortable situations," primarily because its fund is focused on a small group of companies in a particular sector. The fund always votes its proxies.

In June 2003, I talked with Monem Salam, Director of Islamic Investing at the Amana Income Fund and was informed that the fund does not introduce shareholder resolutions; it does vote its stock, but rarely against management. The most notable exception was voting against management on the AOL/Time Warner merger. Talk about the correct vote on that one!

Pax World not only keeps records on its shareholder votes on its Web site, it also discloses its own fund's annual meeting votes, as well as a video of its annual meeting. Pax World has also co-filed two shareholder resolutions in the last five years, one which was withdrawn—Bemis in 2002 regarding Equal Opportunity disclosure—and a resolution at EMC on board diversity.

For a quick, abbreviated list of social screens used by SRI mutual funds, see www.socialinvestmentforum.org.

Responsibility demands that the investor always request and read a prospectus, statement of additional information, a current proxy voting record of the mutual fund, the most recent schedule of investments, or a description of the securities comprising the mutual fund's portfolio. The investor can *never* ask a stupid question or receive too much information. I've included publicly disclosed information about each manager or management team in Appendix C. There is no reason, however, that a prospective investor cannot contact the manager directly and request additional information about the portfolio manager's education, or SRI history, including nonprofit, educational, charitable, environmental, or other organizations in which the manager has participated. This is indeed the kind of information that will assist the social investor in determining the social and environmental commitment held by the portfolio manager.

5

The Power of Nonprofits

I f Americans are having a difficult time putting their faith in government, the privatized public sector, politicians, democracy, and the electoral system, what about the nonprofit sector? Not unlike the corporate scandals of Enron, WorldCom and the rest, the nonprofit sector has had its own share of problems. Have Americans lost faith in all of their hallowed institutions?

Speaking of faith, let's look at the Catholic Church, one of the largest nonprofits around. Most Catholics applauded the Catholic bishops' moral challenge to George W. Bush's pre-emptive war against Iraq in November 2002. On the other hand, Catholics were somewhat embarrassed that the chairman of the bishops' committee on war and peace was none other than Cardinal Bernard Law of Boston, who resigned a month later after failing to crack down on known pedophile priests.

Two studies commissioned by the American Catholic bishops in 2002 and released in late February 2004, found that the church suffered an epidemic of child sexual abuse that involved 10,667 children allegedly victimized by 4,392 priests (4 percent of total) from 1950 to 2002.[1] After the scandal, Cardinal Bernard Law was rewarded by the late Pope John Paul II to head a basilica in Rome, whose predecessor earned about $12,000 per month in the position, as well to live in a "palatial apartment alongside the right flank of the basilica ..."[2] After Law left Boston, his successor helped broker a settlement wherein the church paid out $85 million to more than 550 victims of pedophile priests.[3]

In California, the Diocese of Orange County reached a record settlement of at least $100 million with eighty-seven victims of abuse by priests and lay employees over several decades. In addition, the Archdiocese of Los Angeles faces five hundred claims of abuse.[4]

Unfortunately, the ongoing revelations over the sexual proclivities of priests are compounded by publications of books such as *Vatican Exposed: Money, Murder and the Mafia* (Prometheus Books) and films such as "Gods Bankers"—directed by Giuseppe Ferrara—which claims that the Vatican was at the center of a conspiracy involving drug-dealing Mafiosi, corrupt bankers and politicians, arms dealers, and Freemasons. The Roman Catholic Church is now even attacked for its reliance on Opus Dei, a secretive and authoritarian group that lobbies governments all over the world on behalf of the Vatican. Maybe some of the negative news coming out of Vatican City is simply history's payback for the Spanish inquisition.

NONPROFITS GONE AWRY

The Roman Catholic Church, however, doesn't hold a candle to the corporate-sponsored and ubiquitous United Way for getting into financial trouble.

Remember Bill Aramony, who headed United Way for twenty-two years? He was fired in March 1992 and convicted in 1995 on twenty-five counts, including conspiracy to defraud, mail fraud, wire fraud, transportation of fraudulently acquired property, engaging in monetary transactions of unlawful activity, filing false tax returns, and aiding in the filing of false tax returns.[5] He defrauded United Way out of $600,000. When he "retired" from United Way, Aramony was receiving an annual salary of $390,000 and $73,000 in additional compensation—including contributions to his pension funds.[6]

United Way can't seem to stay out of trouble. In 1993 it created PipeVine, a $100 million back office clearinghouse operation for nonprofits, spinning it off as an independent entity in 2000. It still provides clearinghouse work for United Way, and many of PipeVine's top employees and board members are former United Way employees. PipeVine closed its office after admitting it improperly used donations earmarked for charity for its own salaries and operating expenses.[7]

Of course, we'll probably never forget, or forgive, Christian business executive John G. Bennett, Jr., head of the bankrupt Foundation for New Era Philanthropy who was sentenced to twelve years in federal prison for eighty-two counts of defrauding charities and individuals out of about $354 million. He ran a pyramid scheme which promised to double the amount of a donor's gift in six months with funds from anonymous wealthy benefactors. In reality, he used incoming donations to pay off outstanding pledges while diverting substantial amounts for personal use and to his for-profit companies.[8] New Era reportedly fraudulently obtained $517,000 from Fidelity stockpicker Peter Lynch, $3.2 million from former Treasury Secretary William Simon, and at least $3.5 million from philanthropists Lawrence and Mary Rockefeller.[9]

In the San Francisco Bay Area, between 1979 and 1987, Goodwill of Santa Clara County lost as much as $25 million. For the seventeen years prior to 1994, Andrew Liersch ran the Goodwill operation in Santa Clara, allegedly diverting and laundering money through an unrelated business, transferring hundreds of thousands of dollars between banks in Switzerland, Austria, Arizona, and the Isle of Man. In May 2003 he was expelled from Guatemala and returned to the United States to face money laundering and fraud charges.[10]

Trustees of the James Beard Foundation, a leading promoter of the American culinary arts, alleged in December, 2004 that Leonard Pickell, former foundation president, stole over $1 million from the organization. Pickell was indicted by a grand jury on charges of grand larceny and forgery, and arrested and released on $800,000 bail in New York.[11] Talk about indigestion.

California law requires commercial fundraisers to register and file annual financial disclosure reports with the Attorney General's Registry of Charitable Trusts. Records show that commercial fundraisers (telemarketing firms, thrift stores, and vehicle donation programs), on average, return less than 50 percent of the contributions to charities, and in 2001 the average was 38.03 percent.[12] Commercial solicitors for nonprofit organizations can return as much as 100 percent to the charity (Egrants.org, Working Assets Online) to as little as zero (National Gay & Lesbian Task Force, Share Group, Inc.).[13]

California has 85,455 registered charities, which hold over $200 billion in assets and receive over $70 billion in annual revenues.[14] In 2004 the California Legislature enacted "The Nonprofit Integrity Act," which will strengthen disclosure laws regarding commercial fundraisers as well as require nonprofit organizations with gross revenues of over $2 million to prepare annual audits and strengthen internal financial controls.[15]

The New York Times reported that the nonprofit International Narcotic Enforcement Officers Association based in Albany, New York, used a fundraiser in 2002 to gather over $428,000 to support the children of slain police officers. The Association cleared $57,000, or 13 percent. Commercial fundraisers collected $184 million in New York in 2002.[16]

In an effort to raise more and more money for their nonprofit organizations, many executive directors solicit, or are in turn solicited by, major corporations to serve as "independent" or "outside" directors on corporate boards. Often it is a symbiotic relationship. The nonprofit gains access to corporate charitable dollars as well as other wealthy board members, while the corporate CEO and management gain the credibility of new independent board members. The problem is that once a nonprofit professional takes money from the corporation, corporate affiliate, or other board members, independence is compromised. This is especially the case when independent directors serve on audit and compensation committees and are asked to approve enormous pay packages.

The SEC and the stock exchanges are attempting to define independence, and the NASDAQ stock market has proposed that companies disqualify as independent any director who is the executive officer of a nonprofit to which the company gives $200,000 or 5 percent of the nonprofit's annual revenue, whichever is greater. According to a *Wall Street Journal* article, Enron's chief executive and affiliated foundations directed millions of dollars in donations during the 1990s to a Houston cancer center headed by Enron director John Mendelsohn, who served on Enron's now famously inattentive audit committee.

The conflict also works the other way. Should a corporation be unduly influenced by a board member who is also an executive of a nonprofit? Should that nonprofit be more deserving than another? Automatic Data

Processing, Inc. (ADP) is one of the few companies that has adopted the guidelines advocated by the Council of Institutional Investors, a Washington, DC-based trade group representing more than 130 pension funds (assets: $3 trillion). ADP capped its annual donation to a nonprofit of which a board member is an employee, officer, or director at the lesser of $100,000 or 1 percent of the total contributions the nonprofit receives per year.[17]

This undue corporate influence is disturbing, but we have to remember that the majority of contributions to nonprofit, charitable organizations [IRS Code 501(c)3], are made by individuals (83 percent). It is also important to note the distinction between charitable giving and philanthropy. According to author Julie Salamon (*Rambam's Ladder: A Meditation on Generosity and Why It Is Necessary to Give*), charity responds to the "immediate need," while philanthropy "addresses the problem that causes the need."[18]

Americans gave an estimated $240.92 billion to charities in 2002, a 0.5 percent decrease on an inflation-adjusted basis from the previous year, or an estimated 2.3 percent of U.S. gross domestic product.[19] Many nonprofits have reported lower corporate giving, and human services suffered the steepest decline in contributions, falling 11.4 percent.[20] Charitable giving reached $241 billion in 2003, of which individuals contributed $179 billion. Only 5 percent went to social change causes.[21] According to Tracy Gary of the nonprofit philanthropic organization Changemakers: "The gap between the rich and poor grows daily. The wealthiest 1 percent of Americans now has more assets than the bottom 90 percent combined. Meanwhile, the gap between small and large nonprofits is also increasing. While many universities construct a new building every year, grass roots social change organizations struggle to pay a single staff person."[22]

The latest rounds of corporate scandals have revealed that corporate executives took personal credit for charitable donations when the cash actually came out of the shareholders' pockets. For instance, Tyco International's philanthropic tycoon, Dennis Kozlowski, personally took credit for more than $43 million in donations which was really Tyco's.[23] The National Committee for Responsible Philanthropy had the same problem in separating and identifying contributions by Ken Lay and Enron. According to Rich Cohen, president of the National Committee: "We're pretty sure that less than 40 percent of corporate philanthropy is being disclosed to the public."[24]

Even when a corporate charitable contribution is disclosed, you wonder what the true political story behind the donation is all about. This was the case when it was revealed that Jack Grubman, a former Salomon Smith Barney analyst "confided in an email that he changed his AT&T rating in part because Mr. [Citigroup CEO Sanford] Weill agreed to use his influence to help Mr. Grubman's twins get into an exclusive nursery school in New York . . ."[25] Mr. Grubman's children were admitted to the 92nd Street Y School, and the Citigroup Foundation did pledge $1 million over five years.[26] This gives a new meaning to vouchers, i.e., corporate vouchers. It is no wonder that every year shareholder resolutions are introduced at major corporations calling for a halt to all corporate charitable giving.

THE LACK OF SRI INVESTMENT POLICIES

Spending priorities for the public sector are no more skewed than investment priorities for many social change and environmental organizations. At a time when foundations and nonprofits need to make every dollar count, many nonprofits have resisted adopting an investment philosophy and strategy to align their investment goals with their organization's mission. Only about one-half of groups Changemakers defines as "community-based public foundations" maintain an SRI investment policy.[27]

In an appendix to *American Foundations: An Investigative History* (2001), Mark Dowie briefly discussed the reluctance of foundations to invest in a manner consistent with their mission, saying "Historically, mainstream philanthropy has resisted portfolio screening." That's certainly true, but many big name environmental, conservation, liberal, and human services organizations are not aware of SRI, and most of their staff is not knowledgeable enough to enlighten donors of the groups' investment policy, or even know how to obtain such information.

All nonprofit organizations, including those considered public and private foundations, private trusts, and tax-exempt charities, are required to file an IRS Form 990. Copies of the forms are available to the public online at www.guidestar.org. Unfortunately, a lot of nonprofits report investment information generically as "mutual funds," "equity securities," and "U.S. Government and Agency," as opposed to identifying individual corporate securities or mutual funds by name.

In 1992, for my book *Investing With Your Conscience*, I surveyed twenty-seven national environmental organizations, which then formed a coalition called the Environmental Federation of America (now called Earth Share). The survey was to determine if these organizations would provide me with a copy of their investment policy relating to social and environmental criteria and a copy of a list of securities (schedule of investments) comprising the groups' investment portfolios. Only eleven of the twenty-seven responded to my survey, and only two indicated they had developed general environmental or social investment guidelines, while no respondent had developed comprehensive written social or environmental investment criteria. Ten years later, in 2002, I again surveyed Earth Share members. In addition to requesting a copy of the schedule of investments and investment policy, I also asked for a copy of any social or environmental criteria, proxy and shareholder voting policy, and a record of the organization's shareholder voting record for 2000 and 2001. Only four organizations responded.

Three of the four had an investment policy. One exclusively invested in money market funds, and the other three invested in stock and bond mutual funds. Only one organization had an investment policy that included a comprehensive social and environmental policy. The respondents that identified mutual funds in their portfolios listed three socially screened funds: Citizens Money Market, Citizens Core Growth, and Domini Social Equity Fund. Only one respondent had a proxy and shareholder voting policy, but none had voted in 2000 or 2001, because they held only mutual funds in their portfolios. One purpose behind the survey was not only to identify organizations that had adopted a social or environmental investment policy, but to determine if, in fact, the group was correctly implementing such policy by identifying specific securities in the organization's schedule of investments.

About the same time, my wife and I initiated an unscientific experiment related to nonprofit solicitations we received at home and at my office for a period of about nine months. As everyone knows, once you've contributed to a nonprofit organization, there's a more than even chance you'll be solicited again and again, and that your name will be sold to direct mail brokers. Each time we were solicited, we did not make an immediate donation, but instead wrote the soliciting nonprofit a letter requesting a copy of the organization's goals and objectives, how the organization planned to meet them, a copy of its investment policy, and a copy of its schedule of investments.

Of the twenty-two soliciting organizations with which we corresponded, over half (twelve) did not respond to our request for information or material, but continued to bombard us with bulk rate mailers; one group even personalized a request for funding.

Here are the responses we received:

In the case of Ralph Nader's Citizen Works, we received two more solicitations, and then a personal letter from President Theresa Amato, stating that the organization was newly formed and did "not have nor intend to have an investment portfolio." She enclosed "Citizen Works at a Glance" which included an overview of the organization's mission, project, and staff.

The American Association of University Women (AAUW) responded to my wife's initial request for more material by sending a voluminous packet on AAUW programs, but never responded to her follow up letter requesting specific investment information.

The Sierra Club responded by sending out thirteen direct mail pieces to my home, eventually sending me the group's Statement of Purpose, the 1999 Financial Report, and a copy of their 2000 IRS Form 990. The only relevant information regarding its investment portfolio was the record of seventy-five securities sold in two accounts in the year 2000. Among sold securities I found the names of WorldCom, Citigroup, Qwest, Morgan Stanley, AT&T, Time Warner, and Ingersol Rand, among others. In the two accounts, they recorded gains of over $2.7 million. When I wrote to Sierra Club president, Carl Pope, a seventh time, in January 2002, again requesting a copy of the group's investment policy and current schedule of investments, I received a letter from Yolanda Anderson, member services manager, stating that Pope had asked her to respond. "Unfortunately, I am not able to provide you with the information you are requesting as we do not disclose this proprietary information," Anderson wrote. It was hard for me to understand how the information requested was proprietary, since it is required to be at least broadly reported in the IRS Form 990, and they had already sent me a copy of the group's 2000 IRS Form 990. Not wanting to give up, I obtained a copy of not only the 2001 Form 990, but also the Sierra Club Foundation's 2001 Form 990. Again, I could only find a list of 102 securities sold in 2001. The most notable of the securities sold included The Gap, Citigroup, Coca-Cola, Texas Instruments, WorldCom, Qwest, Morgan Stanley, and Goldman Sachs. In their two accounts, the Sierra Club recorded losses of over $1.1 million.

In the 2001 and 2002 Sierra Club Foundation IRS Form 990s, I found only a listing of the Foundation's investment portfolio by security types:

	2001	2002
Corporate Bonds	$26,411,127	$9,675,093
Mutual Funds	30,682,485	33,997,825
Equity Securities	187,523	90,223
U.S. Government & Agency	46,209,129	45,417,069

I wrote a total of four letters to the Nature Conservancy after receiving additional solicitations. We did receive two copies of the Financial Summary for FY 2000, but no investment policy and no schedule of investments. I find the lack of response by the $3.3 billion, 3,200-employee Nature Conservancy particularly vexing, since the organization's internal activities were publicly exposed in a three-part series in the *Washington Post* in early May 2003. Among other issues, the articles revealed that the Nature Conservancy now boasts 1,900 corporate sponsors, and includes major corporate executives on its Board of Governors and advisory council which represent oil and chemical producers, auto manufacturers, mining, logging, and utility companies, many of which have numerous conflicts of interest, including examples of self-dealing. Since the scandal surfaced, it has made some changes and eliminated some conflicts.

After three letters to the Natural Resources Defense Council (NRDC), I did receive a nice personal letter from a volunteer, Yvonne Vulliemoz, a copy of NRDC's 2000 Annual Report and publication "In Profile," which included NRDC's latest financial statement, but no investment policy and no portfolio schedule of investments.

Following nine personal letters to Greenpeace and eleven more solicitations from them, I finally received a copy of Greenpeace's 1999 and 2000 Financial Statement and a Certificate of Appreciation, but alas, no investment policy and no schedule of investments.

Action Against Hunger sent me its IRS Form 990, and a beautiful 1999/2000 Activity Report. In two separate letters, Shirley Eng informed me that 91 percent of all funds are allocated directly to field programs and that "Action Against Hunger does not have an investment policy, as we do not invest in any securities."

Common Cause responded immediately to my request for information by sending me its December 31, 2000 and 1999 Consolidated Financial Statements, but never responded to my follow-up letter requesting the organization's investment policy or list of portfolio securities.

Amnesty International, on the other hand, following lots of back and forth correspondence, sent me a copy of both its audited financial statements for 2000 and 2001, a copy of its 1999 IRS Form 990, and its June 2000 Annual Report of the Investment Committee to the Board of Directors AIUSA, which included Amnesty's investment policy as well as its "Social Investment Policy." Unfortunately, however, no portfolio was included to determine Amnesty International's compliance with its stated investment policy.

Lastly, the Humane Society of the United States sent me its 2000 annual report, December 31, 2000 Consolidated Financial Statements and a copy of the Humane Equity Fund Prospectus dated January 28, 2003, including the "Social Responsibility" investment policy of the fund. The fund, however, closed and I never did see a copy of its portfolio schedule of investments.

There are several conclusions to be reached from the results of my survey. Most staff members of nonprofit organizations are unable or unwilling to respond to requests for information of more than the most rudimentary kind. Even when some material was received, it was not what was requested or it was incomplete. Most of the groups that responded had no social or environmental investment mission statement, and when they did, it could not be determined whether it was being implemented.

The Missing Link Between Mission and Investments

While foundation support for nonprofit organizations adds up to only about 13 percent of total charitable donations, private, corporate, and community foundation assets total almost $600 billion, most of which is invested in stocks, bonds, mutual funds, and cash equivalents, as well as real estate and other investments.

The Prudent Man Rule as stated by Judge Samuel Putnum in 1830 says: "Those with responsibility to invest money for others should act with prudence, discretion, intelligence, and regard for the safety of capital as well as income." The Prudent Expert Rule, required by the federal Employee Retirement Income Security Act of 1974 (ERISA) which governs private pensions and profit-sharing plans, adds that the manager must act as someone with familiarity with matters relating to the management of money, not just prudence. ERISA also required diversification, investing for the exclusive benefit of the beneficiaries, established personal liability for certain actions by trustees, prohibited self dealing and conflicts of interest, and created the Pension Benefit Guarantee Corporation to insure private plans. It also says the fiduciary is required to act "with the care, skill, prudence, and diligence under the circumstances then prevailing that a prudent man acting in a like capacity and familiar with such matters would use in the conduct of an enterprise of a like character and with like aims."

The traditional Prudent Man Rule implied that a fiduciary/trustee may invest in a security only if it is one that a prudent man of discretion and intelligence would buy. Another definition of the Prudent Man Rule is: A legal maximum that restricts the discretion in a client's account to investments only in those securities that a prudent person seeking reasonable income and preservation of capital might buy for his or her own investment.

Private trust law, however, also requires prudence, "in light of the purposes, terms, distribution requirements, and other circumstances of the trust."[28] William McKeown, a nonprofit attorney for Patterson, Belknap, Webb & Tyler in New York, believes that directors have a fiduciary duty to consider the social impacts of their investment decision making because foundations and nonprofits are by law devoted to charitable purposes.[29]

The Uniform Management of Institutional Funds Act, which has been enacted in the overwhelming majority of states, and the District of Columbia, stipulates that:

> In the administration of the powers to appropriate appreciation, to make and retain investments and to delegate investment management of institutional funds, members of a governing board shall exercise ordinary business care and prudence under the factors and circumstances prevailing at the time of the action or decision. When exercising ordinary business care and prudence, they shall consider long-term and short-term needs of the institution in carrying out its educational, religious, philanthropic or other charitable purposes; its present and anticipated financial requirements; expected total return on its investments; price-level trends; and general economic conditions.[30]

The Internal Revenue Code states that no corporation that is a private foundation as defined by Section 509 of the Code shall "make an investment which would jeopardize the carrying out of any of its exempt purposes, within the meaning of Section 4944 of the Internal Revenue Code so as to give rise to any liability for any tax imposed by Section 4944 of the Internal Revenue Code."

According to the Council on Foundations, only one in ten foundations invest utilizing social criteria (1996 Foundation Management Report). Apparently, most U.S. nonprofit, charitable organizations have not embraced investment policies to advance their organization's mission. Most large foundations are not even willing to restrict investments in the securities of companies that actually resist, harm, or otherwise work to thwart or oppose the nonprofit sector's social or public mission. This issue is at least getting some recent attention in the United Kingdom. According to the Winter, 2002 edition of the Ethical Investment Research Service (EIRS)'s *Ethical Investor*, the government's report entitled "Private Actions, Public Benefit" recommended that charities with an annual income over £1 million declare their ethical investment stance in annual reports. If the report is adopted, it will bring charities in line with pension funds which, since July 2000, have been required to tell plan members whether they consider social, environmental, or ethical matters when making investment decisions.

Some scholars have long held the belief that nonprofit organizations have credibility and influence because they are granted tax-exempt status to ". . . pursue the welfare of their members or those they affect within the scope of their declared purposes . . ." which is justified because ". . . they bear burdens that would otherwise either have to be met by general taxation or be left undone to the detriment of the community."[31] In addition, according to Charles W. Powers, each group in the nonprofit sector ". . . contributes to the diversity of association, viewpoint, and enterprise essential to vigorous pluralistic society."[32]

Powers also notes that nonprofit organizations participate in the economy by purchasing goods and services as well as investing in the private sector. He believes, with justification, that nonprofit organizations should be leading other investors in ". . . longer-range ways" and should: (1) use their wealth to obtain social ends; (2) utilize their tax-exempt credibility to serve the public good, having ". . . a greater responsibility than the business sector to utilize its total resources"; and (3) nonprofits ". . . are better prepared to know what is required to ameliorate social ills than are corporations . . ."[33]

Only within the last decade have U.S. social justice and environmental organizations become directly involved in "mission related investing" (MRI) and become more active shareholders. Many small family trusts, social justice foundations, and environmental nonprofits have adopted comprehensive, socially responsible investment policies, as well as proxy voting guidelines. One of the early pioneers is the twenty-five-year-old

Funding Exchange (FEX) , a New York-based national membership organization of seventeen publicly supported, regionally based community foundations. FEX is a unique partnership of activists and donors dedicated to building a permanent institutional and financial base for progressive social change.

In October 1994, FEX adopted a mission-based investment policy challenging traditional investment practices and criteria by defining "the investment of capital as a political, as well as a financial relationship," and therefore developed social and political investment objectives. In addition to seeking the achievement of a high rate of financial return on the investment portfolio, FEX set as a goal the ". . . support of financial institutions and community development efforts which help to redistribute capital and strengthen the economic base of low-income communities and communities of color."

FEX adopted a social screening investment policy, which incorporates exclusionary and inclusionary criteria, as well as shareholder advocacy. FEX also included a "High Social Impact/Alternative Investments" approach and allocated a percentage of its assets to support community development and housing through investment in CDFIs and other financial intermediaries.

FEX has introduced and co-filed several shareholder resolutions, including one with the Jessie Smith Noyes Foundation at Intel in 1994, and again in 1995 after one of Noyes' grantees, the SouthWest Organizing Project (SWOP) in Albuquerque, New Mexico, was unable to obtain information from Intel on the environmental and social impacts of the company's microchip manufacturing plant expansion which could severely impact air and ground water resources. Noyes and FEX's resolution called for Intel to adopt a policy that would make information available to the public to allow assessment of potential environmental and safety hazards that would affect local communities. The resolution was withdrawn when Intel amended its environmental policy, which included a commitment to consult and share information with communities where the company operated. Unfortunately, a 2003 study by Corrales Residents for Clean Air and Water and SWOP alleges that air emissions from Intel's two large manufacturing facilities are causing illness in some residents.[34] According to SWOP, residents have been complaining to state and local official for years, which finally resulted in the New Mexico Environment Department spending $171,000 on a five-week air monitoring study.[35]

In 1995, FEX co-filed a resolution at Microsoft asking for a report on equal employment and affirmative action policies, and in 1999 the organization filed a shareholder resolution with U.S. Airways requesting that the company adopt the Coalition for Environmental Responsible Economies (CERES) Principles.

Other foundations, including the Nathan Cummings Foundation, focus almost entirely on shareholder proxy voting and activism. According to Lance Lindblom, the president of Cummings: "The real leverage for change is found in neither socially responsible investment nor seeking a 'blended value' of philanthropic and financial investments. Rather, it lies in acting like responsible shareholders—like owners instead of stock traders. Utilizing the shareholder proxy and related public awareness will bring about sustainable change and thus further foundation values, missions, and goals."[36]

The Cummings Foundation also joined Amalgamated Bank and the Sierra Club in filing a shareholder resolution with Smithfield Foods asking the meat company to examine the environmental, financial, and reputational risks of managing hog factories that generate millions of gallons of animal waste. The resolution received over 20 percent of the shareholder vote in 2004. In a joint press release issued on May 1, 2003, Lindblom said: "This is a convergence of two issues: environmental and social impacts and investment values. We hope that this resolution will be the first step in a constructive, on-going dialogue between the company and shareholders concerned about the impacts of current business practices on these long-term considerations."[37]

From 1994 to 2000 the Oakland, California-based Rose Foundation for Communities and the Environment developed and led a national campaign to preserve Northern California's ancient redwood Headwaters Forest, which was owned by corporate raider Charles Hurwitz and his Maxxam Corporation. Rose, led by the husband and wife team of Jill Ratner and

Tim Little, worked in collaboration with other environmental groups to encourage Maxxam to trade large tracts of the two-thousand-year-old redwood forest in exchange for relief from federal banking liabilities of $1.5 billion. The Rose Foundation generated a series of legal briefs leading to federal prosecution in 1995, seeking over $800 million in penalties from Maxxam.

Beginning in 1997, Rose and Harrington Investments, Inc., (HII) introduced corporate governance shareholder resolutions at Maxxam calling for a majority of independent board members and cumulative voting (allowing a minority of shareholders to be represented on the board of directors). About 15 percent of the shares were voted in favor of the resolutions, representing about half of the shares not controlled by Hurwitz. On the HII cumulative voting resolution, approximately 75 percent of the votes not controlled by Hurwitz supported cumulative voting.

The corporate governance resolutions were co-filed by the California Public Employees Retirement System (CALPERS) and led to a divestment of Maxxam shares by the California State Teachers Retirement System (CALSTRS). CALPERS also supported the Rose Foundation's nominees to the Maxxam board in 1999 and 2000. In 1999, Rose ran Abner Mikva, a former Illinois congressman, federal appellate judge, and counsel to President Bill Clinton and former U.S. Senator Howard Metzenbaum of Ohio, for the board of directors. In 2000, the candidates were Mikva and the late former U.S. Senator Paul Simon of Illinois. Because Hurwitz controlled 72 percent of the voting shares (41.9 percent of common and 99.2 percent of preferred), his candidates were elected.

This shareholder activism by Rose, however, did help to persuade Maxxam to compromise and sell a portion of the most sensitive area of the Headwaters Forest to the state and federal governments and significantly increased state oversight over Maxxam's forest practices. Unfortunately, when George W. Bush came to power in Washington, DC, the feds dropped federal banking charges against Hurwitz and Maxxam.

Since 1982 the SEC has required corporations to disclose environmental liabilities as part of their broad financial disclosure. Unfortunately, such disclosure has been very general, usually relating to broad health and safety issues. Following the accounting disclosure practices of Enron, WorldCom, and Tyco, Congress enacted the Sarbanes-Oxley Act of 2002, requiring more corporate disclosure and certification, and adding major felony liability with relatively minimal evidence of criminal intent on behalf of corporate management.

Pursuant to "Generally Accepted Accounting Principles," disclosure of corporate environmental liability was the subject of specific SEC rules setting out mandatory disclosure requirements:

> Regulation S-K101 requires disclosure of material costs associated with compliance with existing federal, state and local environmental laws. S-K103 requires disclosure of material pending legal actions. S-K303 requires disclosure of anticipated material changes in financial conditions due to any known trends, demands, or commitments. Sarbanes-Oxley overlays these detailed disclosure requirements with mandatory, criminally enforceable CEO/CFO certification requirements not only going to the accuracy and adequacy of the disclosures themselves, but also to the effectiveness of the internal controls designed to assure adequate disclosure. Thus, the law has radically altered the context in which Regulation S-K will be interpreted and applied, and the consequences of failure to disclose accurately and in a timely manner. Diligent inquiry and assessment will be required in order to confidently certify that environmental disclosure is accurate and defensible, and, by so doing, to protect the certifying officers against criminal liability.[38]

Unfortunately, the threshold of "material costs" and "anticipated material changes in financial conditions" are not quantified or well defined, while "disclosure of material pending legal actions" are considered non-enforcement proceedings when claims for damages potentially exceed 10 percent of a company's current assets and are only "material" if there is a reasonable potential for sanctions exceeding $100,000.[39] Prior to the enactment of Sarbanes-Oxley, this left corporate management and its paid CPAs lots of wiggle room. Sarbanes-Oxley has now tightened things up a bit by requiring increased accuracy and reliability of SEC disclosure statements and corporate certification. Criminal penalties and fines for up to $5 million or imprisonment of up to twenty years will be levied against corporate management for untrue statements, misrepresentation, or omission of material facts in SEC disclosure statements.

In the past, many companies have hidden, downplayed, or understated environmental-related costs, fines, or other liabilities that shareholders should have known about. In July 2004, the Government Accountability Office (formerly the Government Accounting Office) published a seventy-five-page report, finding that the SEC did not systematically track environmental liabilities in company filings and did ". . . not have the information it needed to analyze the frequency of problems involving environmental disclosure, compared with other types of disclosure problems . . . that, if undisclosed, could impair the public's ability to make sound investment decisions."[40]

The Rose Foundation has led the way in raising the issue of the lack of corporate environmental disclosure and the increased risk to investors due to the absence of transparency and environmental accountability. In its report "The Environmental Fiduciary: The Case for Incorporating Environmental Factors into Investment Management Policies," Rose found that a corporation's ability to profit from environmental innovations and prepare for future environmental risks and exposures could have a significant impact on corporate earnings, potential cash flow, and growth opportunities. Rose argued that fiduciaries, including foundations, charitable trusts, and pension funds, needed to institute financially sound policies to encourage strong corporate environmental performance in corporations held in their portfolios.

Rose's groundbreaking study and the possible "off balance sheet" land mines, including the hidden risks associated with global climate change, have begun to get attention. Munich Re, a large German insurance company, estimated that global warming could cost $300 billion annually by 2050 due to weather damage, pollution, industrial and agricultural losses, and other expenses[41] and in 2003 AIG's American General Life Insurance Company, a large insurance holding company, called for more corporate environmental insurance to manage increasing corporate environmental liabilities.

The Rose Foundation has launched the Environmental Fiduciary Project and petitioned the SEC to enforce corporate environmental liability disclosure. The petition includes a reporting standard from guidelines developed over six years conducted by the American Society for Testing and Materials, a leading U.S. engineering organization. Currently these guidelines are voluntary; but if the SEC adopts Rose's proposal, companies could be required to aggregate environmental liabilities before determining whether corporate data exceeds SEC's materiality threshold. Currently, corporations themselves are allowed to determine what environmental costs (liability) will have a "material" effect on a corporation's finances.

Rose's two year "Workplan" calls for the creation of binding federal standards for environmental transparency, activation of the $2.5 trillion public pension fund industry campaign to support such standards, and challenging the philanthropic community to recognize that the connection between its mission and its investment goals and objectives is "mission-related investing."

In July 2004, the Rose Foundation released a new report, "Fooling Investors and Fooling Themselves," which identified aggressive accounting and asset management tactics that lead to environmental accounting fraud. The report examined how companies keep information about expensive environmental liabilities like toxic pollution, product health hazards, worker exposure, and global warming away from shareholder scrutiny, and named Halliburton, Dow Chemical, and Kaiser Aluminum as companies that failed to estimate or disclose billions of dollars of asbestos liabilities and related worker health claims.

NONPROFITS UNDER ATTACK

The corporate-financed American Enterprise Institute (AEI) would clearly accuse the Rose Foundation and others discussed in this book as pursuing a leftist or liberal agenda, favoring "global governance, and trying to use the multilateral system to try to regulate corporations and governments." That is what Cornell University Professor Jeremy Rabkin said at an AEI-sponsored conference in June 2003 in Washington, DC entitled: "Nongovernmental Organizations: The Growing Power of an Unelected Few."[42] Others attending the conference accused international NGOs of "pursuing a new and pervasive form of conflict against corporations," and that the social investing movement was a "wolf in sheep's clothing."[43] One participant, an AEI adjunct fellow and long a right wing critic of SRI, John Entine, said: "Anti-free market NGOs under the guise of corporate reform are extending their reach into board-rooms of corporations. In many cases, naïve corporate reformers, within corporations and in government, are welcoming them."[44]

The attack on NGOs by the extreme right is not unlike its attack on "activist" pension funds, such as CALPERS. Texas A&M scholar Tracie Woidtke claims CALPERS' behavior "often represents a clear conflict of interest for managers who are responsible for improving funds' returns and, at the same time, want to realize political goals." She recommends that states work to de-politicize pension funds by turning their adminis-tration over to "professional" governing boards.[45] It's safe to assume that by "professional" she means investment bankers and brokers, the same cast of characters who sit on corporate boards and for years have controlled the New York Stock Exchange. Woidtke also wants shareholder proposals to be harder to submit if they don't draw significant support and for groups submitting them to pay some of the costs to re-submit them after they have failed twice.[46] I'm surprised Woidtke didn't call for an end to all share-holder meetings, so corporate management wouldn't have to put up with shareholders for two hours a year, and for a total prohibition of advisory shareholder resolutions.

The exact opposite argument is being made by Judith Richter, author of *We the People or We the Corporations? Critical Reflections on UN-business partnerships.* She posits that corporations, through public private part-nerships, are restructuring the United Nations and its agencies, which are trading away public interests in the hope of receiving large-scale corporate and private foundation funding.[47] Indeed, Richter claims that the United Nations is at risk of selling itself off by allowing corporations to cherry pick public health interventions that focus on technical solutions which provide class benefits to corporations while more complex problems are left to cash-strapped governments.[48] I think we still call that externalizing corporate costs and sticking it to the taxpayer. It is also called the privatization of the public sector.

AEI is not the only conservative nonprofit organization attacking social justice and other NGOs. In June 2001, the tobacco and oil industry-supported Frontiers of Freedom group asked the IRS to revoke the tax exempt status of Rainforest Action Network (RAN), an environmental organization known for its protests against logging companies and Citigroup's lending practices. Frontiers of Freedom was founded by former Republican U.S. Senator Malcolm Wallop, a friend of Dick Cheney. Frontiers' biggest donors include Philip Morris, ExxonMobil, and R.J. Reynolds Tobacco Holdings, Inc.[49]

Another right-wing organization, the Center for the Defense of Free Enterprise, has questioned the tax-exempt status of People for the Ethical Treatment of Animals (PETA) based upon the IRS Ruling 75-384 related to acts of violence by demonstrators. I went to the Washington secretary of state's Web site and found that the Center for the Defense of Free Enterprise in its fiscal year report ending December 31, 2002 reported revenue of $76,899 and expenses of $100,702. It seems they could use a lesson in "free enterprise."

SOCIAL JUSTICE GROUPS THAT GET IT

Some social justice, environmental and conservation organizations, family and public foundations, church, labor, and professional associations managed by SRI portfolio managers are socially screened and relatively passive. Many are mission-oriented specific to each organization's particular goals or objectives.

In addition to the previously mentioned groups (FEX, Rose Foundation, and Nathan Cummings Foundation), here are some others that are actively relating their investments to their organizational mission:

The Land Trust of Napa County in California (http://napalandtrust.org), a nonprofit organization dedicated to saving land in the Napa Valley, excludes securities of companies that consistently and flagrantly violate EPA regulations; manufacture or distribute tobacco products; develop publicly traded real estate investment trusts (REITs); genetically engineer food, plants, or seeds produced or grown for human or animal consumption.

In addition to supporting companies that maximize corporate charitable giving, the Land Trust encourages investments in companies that enhance and preserve the natural environment, agriculture, and open space lands, including companies that reduce the use of hazardous or toxic chemicals; utilize recycled materials; employ state-of-the-art pollution control equipment; promote alterative energy and clean sources of fuels, including wind solar, biomass, natural gas, or cogeneration; have written environmental guidelines or policies, including the endorsement of an environmental code of conduct utilizing outside or non-company monitoring and reporting; promote sustainable agriculture, with an emphasis on organically grown products and small scale farming practices.

Civil liberties organizations, such as the ACLU Northern California Foundation (www.aclunc.org), avoid investments in companies which have policies that violate the goals of the organization including the denial of equal employment opportunities based on gender, race, disability, national origin, religion, political beliefs, or sexual orientation; violation of privacy rights of employees through drug testing, pre-employment psychological screening, and illegal monitoring of employees' conduct on or off the job; the construction, management, or development of private or public correctional facilities.

The San Francisco-based Women's Foundation of California (www.womensfoundca.org) prioritizes both exclusionary and inclusionary social screens by primarily avoiding companies that manufacture weapons; that have been fined or penalized for affirmative action; that are involved in life-threatening liability cases, or in controversies relating to advertising, marketing, price fixing, anti-trust, or consumer fraud; that lack a written policy forbidding discrimination on the basis of sexual orientation (Lavender Screen); that are in the tobacco industry.

The foundation also excludes companies for environmental and employee relations concerns as well as avoiding alcohol and nuclear power producers. Positive screens include investing in companies with exemplary records of retaining, hiring, and promoting women, ethnic minorities, the disabled, gays and lesbians, and persons with HIV/AIDS. The foundation also supports companies which promote family benefits and community relations, unions, alternative energy, quality products, the environment, and quality in the workplace. Another investment priority for the foundation is a commitment to economic development, low-income housing, and shareholder activism.

The Vanguard Public Fund (www.vanguardsf.org), a San Francisco-based community foundation, which is a member of the FEX family, has a proactive social investment policy which includes traditional exclusionary and inclusionary criteria as well as shareholder activism and a commitment to high social impact investing, initially investing in 1996 in the Northern California Community Loan Fund. As an active shareholder, in 2002 and 2003, Vanguard filed a resolution with Oracle Corporation requesting the company to endorse human and labor rights in China.

Global Exchange (GX) (www.globalexchange.org), a San Francisco-based human rights organization, is committed to shareholder advocacy, incorporating inclusionary and exclusionary social and environmental screening with a global human and labor rights campaign, including fair trade. Global Exchange sets aside up to 20 percent of its portfolio for proactive shareholder work as well as up to 20 percent of the portfolio for investment in CDFIs including community banks, credit unions, domestic and international loan funds, and socially responsible venture funds.

Global Exchange bases much of its work around corporate campaigns, shareholder democracy, fair trade and challenging policies of the World Bank, the WTO, NAFTA, the IMF and the proposed Free Trade Area of the Americas. Global Exchange has fair trade stores in Berkeley and San Francisco, California as well as in Portland, Oregon where alternative products, including food, coffee, chocolate, and other goods are sold. Global Exchange also has an on-line Fair Trade store. The Fair Trade system benefits over eight hundred thousand farmers organized into cooperatives and unions in forty-eight countries. Fair Trade has helped farmers provide for their families' basic needs and invest in community development.

Global Exchange has attended shareholder meetings and has been responsible for resolutions at Nike, Disney, and Gap (sweatshops); Proctor & Gamble and Starbucks (fair trade coffee); Ford (SUVs); Unocal (Burma); Hershey (fair trade chocolate); and numerous other companies regarding the China Human and Labor Rights Principles.

Global Exchange co-founder and activist, Medea Benjamin, held the stock proxy for the company and was to attend the Halliburton shareholders meeting in Houston Texas in 2004. The corporation's security force prevented her from entering the meeting, searching her belongings before turning her away from the meeting. She had planned on asking company executives about the firm's "work" in Iraq. This is another example of how corporate management treats the legal owners of its empires. But in 2005, she returned to Halliburton's annual meeting and management could not prevent her from entering and asking some embarrassing questions.

PROGRAM-RELATED INVESTMENTS

Very few foundations, whether they are large, mainstream foundations or small social justice, community-based organizations, do much in the way of program-related investments, or PRIs. Even though PRIs can be booked as grants and credited toward the minimum 5 percent of asset value that foundations must pay out annually, very few (the major exceptions being Ford Foundation and the John D. and Catherine T. MacArthur Foundation) pay any attention at all to this innovative approach. Most PRIs have been low interest loans to nonprofits who were also grant recipients in which the loan complimented the grantee's program.

The New York-based F. B. Heron Foundation devotes 18 percent of its $230 million portfolio, or $42 million, to mission-related investments, and $14 million are invested in a variety of community development organizations.[50] The foundation provides grants that build the capacity of community development credit unions to meet the credit needs of their low-income members, but it also provides market-rate and below-market rate deposits and secondary capital to the credit unions themselves to increase their capacity to lend. It distributes grants to nonprofit housing groups that seek to make home ownership affordable to larger numbers of low-income people, and also purchases asset-backed securities issued by Habitat for Humanity to expand its self-help housing programs and AAA-rated taxable municipal bonds that provide "soft-second mortgages" for low-income, first-time homebuyers. The foundation is making a concerted effort to focus on mission-related investing, and it is paying off both financially and for local communities.

In December 1992, Harrington Investments, Inc. (HII) was hired by the Seattle-based Program for Appropriate Technology in Health (PATH) to evaluate its Fund for Technology Transfer (FTT) and make recommendations concerning its capitalization. PATH is a global nonprofit organization working to improve health, especially the wellness of women in developing countries. HII's contract was part of an ongoing review and assistance provided by the Ford Foundation's PRI. In 1981, Ford had loaned $1.5 million to PATH to develop the FTT "to increase the availability and quality of primary health care and family planning products and services in developing countries through program support and loan financing." Ford's PRI combined technical assistance and grants with a loan to fulfill the Ford Foundation's mission of providing funding for women's worldwide health care services. My report to PATH was presented in late April 1993, and shortly thereafter the Ford Foundation "rolled over" and increased its PRI and grants to PATH and FTT. PATH recently celebrated its twenty-fifth anniversary working in the area of global health.

My experience in working with Ford's PRI staff reinforces Mark Dowie's comments as to why PRI's remain very limited in the philanthropic world today:

> For one thing, prospective recipients often prefer outright grants. PRIs can be labor-intensive for foundation staffs—though a number of capable firms will package the investments or conduct due diligence for short-staffed funders. And PRIs are vulnerable to

the classic bureaucratic imperatives that define grantmaking's staff-board relationships. 'Failure is more visible with PRIs,' one foundation director told the authors of a 1989 Council on Foundations study. 'If a grant goes wrong, it's the grantee's fault. If it's a loan, you've both goofed. It is clearer that you've screwed up.' There's also a broader zone of success for a grant. With a loan, trustees tend to look only at the bottom line: Did the money come back on time?[51]

It is not clear yet that nonprofit organizations have recognized their investment or ownership responsibilities. Too few social change organizations and environmental groups have adopted a mission-based investment policy.

Mission-related investing has been a major focus of the Jessie Smith Noyes Foundation and its former president, Stephen Viederman, since 1994. The foundation utilizes social and environmental screens, votes its shares, and engages in shareholder advocacy and dialogue with corporate management. The foundation believes that fiduciaries have a duty to consider whether investment decisions further their charitable purposes, or at least don't run counter to them. According to the Noyes Web site: "The philosopher, Schopenhauer, believed that all truth passes through three stages: first, it is ridiculed; second, it is violently opposed; third, it is accepted as being self-evident. We mission-related investors are at, or are close to, stage three in our beliefs that social, environmental, and financial values must be linked."

Viederman, who retired from the presidency of the Noyes Foundation in March 2000 and co-founded the Initiative for Fiduciary Responsibility, is a tireless crusader. He is a prolific writer and speaker who has won many friends, and not a few enemies, by strongly advocating that fiduciary responsibility for foundations requires them to inexorably link their philanthropic mission with their investment goals and objectives. Changing institutional behavior is Viederman's long-term goal. While president of Noyes Foundation, he instituted a three-pronged approach to SRI, including screening, shareholder advocacy, and mission-related venture capital investing. His Foundation Partnership on Corporate Responsibility Web site at www.foundationpartnership.org is one of the most comprehensive resources available on foundation mission-related investing.

PENSION FUNDS AND LABOR

Institutional investors are only now beginning to recognize that their portfolios include stocks of companies operating in "terrorist states," as defined by the U.S. State Department, and only recently have human and labor rights and sweatshops in China become a topic of conversation in pension fund boardrooms. The issue of environmental liabilities relative to global climate change, genetic engineering, chemical dumping, pesticide exposure, and dangerous animal factory farms are slowly starting to enter public and private pension funds trustees' consciousness.

With a few notable exceptions, most of organized labor was not thrilled about venturing into the pension fund debate on issues of South Africa, weapons, or tobacco. Gradually, many local unions and some international union executives responded to the SRI call. Most, however, saw it as either a giant headache or a legal nightmare and hoped to avoid it altogether. It was a major policy decision for the unions to decide to bargain for joint administration of the pension fund with corporate management. Most of the time it was a throw-away item for union representatives in the collective bargaining process.

Today, with global pension funds totaling over $10 trillion ($7 trillion-plus in the United States alone), with the public pension funds in the United States total $2 trillion, with the Taft-Hartley law, and with nearly 1,500 pension funds with $370 billion in assets, organized labor has focused much of its energy on gaining control of public pension funds and Taft-Hartley assets. (Among other things, the Taft-Hartley Act, passed over the veto of President Harry S. Truman in 1947, allows for equal management and union representation on pension fund boards of trustees.)

The AFL-CIO has begun a trustee education program, Center for Working Capital, which will encourage labor and public fund trustees throughout the country to make long-term direct private investments. One such investment is $3 to $4 billion in new Taft-Hartley pension assets in over a dozen U.S. based private capital funds, called Labor–Sponsored Investment Funds (LSIF). Canadian LSIFs have amassed almost $10 billion.[52] The job of LSIFs is to invest in small, private, worker-friendly businesses. The AFL-CIO has also launched the Capital Stewardship Program to coordinate shareholder action. Unions doubled the number of resolutions they introduced in 2003 from two hundred to four hundred.[53]

The challenge for labor unions is to first bargain successfully to gain joint administration of Taft-Hartley-covered pension funds, and then to convince their fellow trustees (the management half) that investing in worker-friendly small businesses is in their beneficiaries' best interests. Tom Croft, a labor rights activist, argues that Taft-Hartley and other union-influenced pension funds especially need to commit more to private capital for financial return as well as supporting union-friendly business ventures: "Since 1999 Taft-Hartley pension funds have invested over $3 billion of new money in private capital, and that was two years ago; maybe it's now closer to $5 billion," Croft told me in 2003. "Our goal is 5 percent of Taft-Hartley funds to be invested in private capital."

Public employee unions, including the Service Employees International Union (SEIU) and the American Federation of State, County, and Municipal Employees (AFSCME) in California, New York, and Ohio, have adopted policies against using their retirement funds to privatize education and prisons. In California, the California School Employees Association (CSEA) has started to pressure CALPERS, which through its private equity program owns 6 percent of Student Transportation of America (STA), to cease STA's privatization and elimination of public sector jobs in the Lucia Mar Unified School District, north of Santa Barbara.[54] Increasingly, public employee pension funds hold ownership in both private and publicly–traded companies that are rapidly privatizing public sector jobs at the state, local government, and school district level.

In May 2003, Los Angeles County followed the Ohio Public Employees Retirement System and the New York City Employees Retirement System's adoption of an anti-privatization policy. Ian Lanoff, an attorney and the former head of the U.S. Department of Labor's Benefit Administration Division, provided the Los Angeles County Employees Retirement Association with the opinion that pension trustees could factor in loss of contributions from laid-off employees and weigh how that would affect the overall health of the fund when considering whether or not to invest in companies that privatized public sector jobs.[55] In Florida, SEIU has been raising a ruckus over the fact that the $94 billion Florida Retirement System, representing public school employees, teachers, and retirees, bought over 96 percent of the stock and used $70 million of Florida money to own education-privatizing Edison Schools, Inc. and pay off its debt.[56] The use of public employee capital to destroy public sector jobs is a major organizing issue whose time has come.

For organized labor gaining access to capital may be a do-or-die proposition. Certainly, having a say in how capital is directed or invested is important, as is making sure that private and public sector unions participate at the shareholder level on not only corporate governance issues, but on longer-term social, environmental, and economic issues that are important to its membership base. One can imagine no greater threat to union retail employees than Wal-Mart. It is certainly in beneficiaries' interest to encourage competition and oppose the oligopolistic takeover of towns and villages by Wal-Mart Super Centers.

The late Jesse Unruh, the former Speaker of the California State Assembly and former California treasurer, recognized the power of pension funds. Unruh, seeing dollars as power, pushed through legislation adding the treasurer to both the CALPERS and CALSTRS boards. He then was the major impetus for the creation of the Council of Institutional Investors (CII), now representing 130 pension fund members, with total assets presently exceeding $2 trillion.

Since 1985, CII has represented large pension funds which address investment issues that affect the size and security of plan assets. Much of CII's attention has recently been focused on corporate governance, and many of these issues addressed are the results of years of corporate management abuse and corruption, including self-dealing, excessive director compensation and perks, as well as influence peddling at home and abroad. CII has no choice but to weigh in and influence members to represent their beneficiaries. If this rash of corruption and scandal is not a social issue, nothing is.

The CII board includes representatives from SEIU, the Carpenters Union, and CALSTRS as well as five other public employee pension plans, while the Council Board is represented by the United Food and Commercial Workers (UFCW), the Communications Workers of America (CWA), and three public employee retirement systems. This membership represents a significant portion of the Gross Domestic Product of the United States as the deferred wages of American public and private sector employees and beneficiaries.

Today public employee pension funds are clearly the dominant players managing socially screened assets for their beneficiaries, and are generally more active than their private sector colleagues in the quest for more corporate management accountability to shareholders. That has not always been the case, and it has only been within the last few years, following the great bear market of 2000–2002 and a couple of years of massive corporate abuse and fraud, that many public employee plans, endowments, foundations and charitable trusts have seriously questioned corporate management and paid attention to corporate governance issues. Of the twenty-five largest pension plans in the country, nineteen are public plans.

The Center for Security Policy, a group composed of former Reagan administration officials and conservative business interests, has raised questions about pension funds investing $188 billion in foreign companies that do business with "terrorist-sponsoring" nations of Iran, Syria, North Korea, Sudan, Libya, and pre-war Iraq.[57] The same group conveniently ignores U.S.-based companies that do the same thing but use a loophole of an offshore subsidiary to get around U.S. law. Halliburton immediately comes to mind. Perhaps U.S. companies should lose their corporate charter protection, and both U.S. and foreign companies should be prohibited from doing business anywhere in the United States when they also do business with "terrorist nations." Of course, that would include nations like China, which sponsors terrorist actions against Tibet and its own population.

Of the more than $6.7 trillion in qualified pension assets, private sector

Top 25 Pension Funds/Sponsors *January 2005*	
Sponsor	Assets (in millions)
California Public Employees	$168,320
Federal Retirement Thrift	141,026
New York State Common	117,450
California State Teachers	116,695
General Motors	107,039
Florida State Board	102,517
New York City Retirement	95,801
Texas Teachers	84,855
New York State Teachers	79,609
New Jersey	67,133
General Electric	66,495
Wisconsin Investment Board	65,946
IBM	64,806
Boeing	61,002
North Carolina	60,736
Ohio Public Employees	59,892
Ohio State Teachers	54,177
Verizon	51,815
Michigan Retirement	50,743
Ford Motor	49,667
Pennsylvania School Employees	47,889
University of California	47,060
Washington State Board	46,810
Oregon Public Employees	46,110
Georgia Teachers	42,313

SOURCE: PENSIONS AND INVESTMENTS ONLINE (WWW.PIONLINE.COM)

plans (of which 90 percent are controlled exclusively by corporate management) hold more than $4 trillion.[58] According to Hawley and Williams in their book *Fiduciary Capitalism*, the decline in private pension funds is due to a shift from defined-benefit plans to defined-contribution plans and corporate restructuring. On the other hand, public pension fund assets have been increasing along with state and local government employees.

In the 1996–1997 fiscal year, state and local government public employee pension plans held about $1.5 trillion in assets, the bulk of them (82.7 percent) held by state funds, and about 35 percent of the total funds ($528 billion) were invested in corporate equities. In 1999 public pension plans alone represented 45 percent of the Gross Domestic Product and 33 percent of market capitalization.[59]

The California Public Employees Retirement System (CALPERS) is the largest of the state pension plans engaged in shareholder advocacy. One of the more active members is California State Treasurer Phil Angelides, who makes no bones about exercising his fiduciary oversight to protect state beneficiaries by constantly engaging in public and private dialogue with corporate management on a variety of corporate governance, social, and environmental issues. His leadership at CALPERS has been an inspiration to many other pension trustees across the country.

Recently, CALPERS has been under siege by corporations and big business organizations because of the pension fund's advocacy on behalf of beneficiaries. With the help of Governor Arnold Schwarzenegger, the U.S. Chamber of Commerce and the Business Roundtable were able to coerce the State Personnel Board to vote 3 to 2 to replace Sean Harrigan as president of CALPERS. Harrigan, an ally of Angelides, was one of the strongest voices on the board for corporate reform and shareholder advocacy. But CALPERS and other pension plans immediately responded that their shareholder advocacy would not falter. Angelides certainly shows no signs of changing his stance as he is an active candidate for his party's nomination for California governor, and stands head and shoulders above other candidates on responsible investment issues.

Most importantly, in the long run, the key stakeholders of progressive nonprofits, foundations, pension funds and labor must come to grips with how they will control their own destiny with the capital that is in their control.

Within the SRI movement, there is a spirited debate on the question of the appropriate direction and flow of responsible capital. Many of my colleagues have developed their skills for secondary market penetration, while others work tirelessly to move capital to the primary market where jobs and community wealth are created.

In the next chapter, we will explore this debate within the SRI community, as well as discuss SRI portfolio performance and the impact of investing in Community Development Financial Institutions (CDFIs) and others, including fair trade enterprises and microfinance opportunities. We'll also look at the growing corporate use of such terms as sustainability, corporate social responsibility, and the adoption of corporate codes of conduct and how this affects SRI strategies.

6

Substance or Illusion?

The socially responsible investment community has created problems for itself, and the problems grow more serious as SRI professionals become more successful, assets under management increase, and the global marketplace for SRI products and services expands. Similar to the traditional financial services industry, the growing SRI professional cadre is creating an increasing array of secondary market products for ethically concerned investors that make money and increase employment for the financial services industry, but do little to advance the goals of social and environmental investing. These secondary market instruments do not add a single new dollar to fund non-financial service business enterprises or jobs, nor do they build new housing, rehabilitate existing housing, or create alternative energy opportunities. The community is also creating a vocabulary of increasingly useless "corporate speak" that exacerbates confusion among SRI practitioners, investors, and the public at large.

The growth of socially responsible investing, and the increasing number of professionals participating in SRI trade and professional organizations is important. The question is, however, whether these organizations are agents of social change, forums for ideas, and networks for raising capital, or simply a cadre of New Age marketing professionals and consultants. I believe it may be all of the above.

A PROLIFERATION OF INDEXES

SRI products are springing up all over the globe, especially esoteric indexes such as the Dow Jones Sustainability Index (DJSI), DJSI STOXX, and

FTSE4 Good. Launched in 1999, the DJSI includes over three hundred corporations from twenty-three countries, while the Pan-European sustainability benchmark, DJSI STOXX, includes more than 180 companies from fourteen countries. FTSE4 Good, created in 2001 by the London Stock Exchange and the *Financial Times*, has four indexes that separately cover U.K. companies, European companies, U.S. companies, and a global universe of companies: FTSE4 Good UK 50, FTSE4 Good Europe 50, FTSE4 Good US 100, and FTSE4 Good Global 100.

FTSE4 GOOD and DJSI base their indexes on companies that have voluntarily adopted environmental and business principles, an equal opportunity policy, and have signed voluntary human rights initiatives. DJSI generally defines "sustainability" as creating long-term shareholder value and integrating economic, environmental, and social criteria. Sustainability was also defined by the United Nations Environmental Program and the World Commission on Environment and Development in the 1980s and further refined in American terminology thanks to Armory Lovins, Hunter Lovins, and Paul Hawken in *Natural Capitalism*, (Little, Brown and Company, Boston 1999); but like many concepts, visions, ideals, and goals regurgitated again and again in the media and through corporate spokespeople, it has become so gray that it is, in fact, unrecognizable.

The DJSI corporate sustainability index is based on looking for the best company in a sector and subsectors (best in a class). The premise is that DJSI builds a portfolio or index of the best companies that meet its sustainability criteria to produce an above average performance that will eventually form the basis of a retail product. This product is then sold to unsuspecting and naïve investors who believe the "sustainability" public relations propaganda. The term "sustainable corporation" may even be an oxymoron.

According to Russell Sparkes, author of *Socially Responsible Investment: A Global Revolution*, by April 2001 the DJSI had been licensed to thirty-four leading investment management groups across Europe, Japan, and Australia, and by the end of April 2002, the total assets invested in DJSI funds were $2.1 billion. The largest investor in this potpourri of global "sustainable" corporations was none other than the Swiss Federal Social

Security Fund through U.S.-based State Street Global Advisers. There are about twenty investment products in Europe that have been linked to the FTSE4 Good indexes. Assets linked to those indexes in Europe total about $1.5 billion.[1]

In early November 2002, FTSE and the American Stock Exchange indicated that they planned to introduce exchange-traded funds (ETFs) based on the FTSE4 Good Indexes. Dow Jones also indicated that it has a license for an ETF based on the DJSI. ETFs are like closed-end mutual funds that are traded on exchanges just like stocks, and represent a basket of securities of companies including the FTSE4 GOOD and DJSI. Another ETF recently launched is iShares KLD Select Social Index Fund representing a basket of company stocks that have positive social and environmental characteristics while maintaining risk and return characteristics similar to the Russell 1000 Index.

These are examples of secondary market instruments that are created to spin money out of money. Their only purpose is to create financial services products that are then marketed by the industry to undiscriminating investment customers for a fee or commission to make investors think they're having a positive social and environmental impact. All an investor truly purchases is a packaged product in the secondary market, even further removed from ownership than a standard fund, that will provide the investor with far less control and will have absolutely no impact on corporate management to improve their governance or global conduct.

"Sustainability" sounds terrific until you identify some of the companies that have appeared in these indexes. Among companies included in FTSE4 GOOD U.S. are Anheuser-Busch, Coca-Cola, Disney, DuPont, GAP, Georgia-Pacific, Harrah's, Merrill Lynch, Nike and WorldCom. And among the companies included in the DJSI are Dow Chemical, AstraZeneca, Boeing, BP (LLC), British American Tobacco, Duke Energy, Harrah's, Nestle, Nike and Royal Dutch Petroleum.

So, without even conducting an elaborate review of FTSE4 GOOD US, we find alcohol, sugar, water, hazardous chemicals and pesticides, excessive CEO compensation, unsafe theme parks, sweatshops, gambling, corporations that cook the books, fraud, and accounting and analyst irregularities.

Reviewing DJSI we find hazardous chemicals and pesticides, gambling, environmental damage, sweatshops, genetic engineering, tobacco, defense contractors, and nuclear energy. The definition of "sustainability" has become meaningless.

The SRI community's financial professionals have now come up with the Johannesburg Securities Exchange (JSE), an "SRI Index based on triple bottom line performances. . . including social, environmental and economic sustainability, as well as corporate governance, best practice."[2] The Index will be based on the results of a tabulated questionnaire returned by respondents. As of August 17, 2004, only 74 of 155 companies listed on the FTSE/JSE all share indexes applied for inclusion in the JSE SRI index, of which fifty-one actually made it into the index.[3] All in all, if it is anything like FTSE4 GOOD, it will represent "best in class" and represent a group of company stocks trading on the secondary market.

If this isn't enough to make a skeptic out of you, the JSE is thinking about creating a derivative instrument so that the index can be traded. I wonder how many SRI investors will be hoodwinked into pouring money into this useless secondary market vehicle.

I'd much prefer honesty when it comes to investing in useless indexes by shorting the KarmabanQue Index 2004, which is wholly composed of corporations with "bad karma." This U.K.-developed index is comprised of stocks of companies currently being boycotted by a variety of different organizations throughout the world. The index is not "real" unless you make it so. However, according to an email I received from Max Keiser of karmabanque.com, they are in the process of listing the index with a major spread-betting company in the United Kingdom. The index goes up when the price of the basket of stocks goes down, so as the companies listed below are boycotted, or get into legal or regulatory trouble, the investor makes money, because the index goes up in value. Here are the KarmabanQue Index Top Ten: McDonald's, Coca-Cola, Microsoft, ExxonMobil, Citigroup, GlaxoSmithKline, Pfizer, Procter and Gamble, Ryanair Holdings, and Starbucks.

THE HOSTILE TAKEOVER OF SUSTAINABILITY AND CSR

"Sustainability" and "corporate social responsibility (CSR)" have become captives of "corporate-speak," now completely devoid of meaning, used primarily by marketers and public relations firms working for large corporations. We now even have sustainability and CSR consultants, people who sell themselves to corporate management to teach executives how to appear "sustainable" or "socially responsible."

Agricultural, chemical and pesticide corporations such as Monsanto, refer to themselves as "life science" companies, and corporate health care companies running dementia units for seniors call them "remembrance centers." Governments use words like "youth center" for juvenile halls, and state fish and game departments when killing mountain lions, say they "dispatch" them. The Bush administration calls for "modernizing" Social Security when it wants to privatize it.

The Conference Board, a business membership organization with over 3,300 corporate and business members, holds annual sustainability conferences. Participants include such lofty "sustainable" and "socially responsible" businesses as Rio Tinto, PLC, Ford Motor Company, DuPont, Dow Chemical, Boeing, ExxonMobil, General Motors, Lockheed Martin, Shell Oil, and Philip Morris.

Not to be outdone by the Conference Board, the SoL Forum on Business Innovation for Sustainability was held at the Ford Motor Center in Dearborn, Michigan in October 2004, sponsored by major American corporations, including Coca-Cola, Shell, United Technologies, McDonald's, Unilever, and BP. A month earlier, another conference was held in Seattle, Washington, called "Profitable Sustainability: The Future of Business," where participants included "sustainable" companies such as Boeing, Starbucks, Russell, and US Bank. CSR was high on the agenda at a November 2001 global summit of public relations advisers in San Francisco. At least CSR was described as it should be—as public relations.

At the first Asian Pacific CSR Seminar Series and Social Venture Network Asia Conference in Singapore in 2004, many participants were highly skeptical of contemporary CSR as currently defined by corporate management.

Among most attendees ". . . there was a desire not to simply transport foreign models to the region, as they don't appear to be working overseas."[4] CSR was difficult to define, although some defined it narrowly as "corporate governance" or "corporate reporting," while most attendees believed that CSR was PR and that it was ". . . effectively impossible to measure corporate social responsibility from an accounting point of view."[5]

Well, think again, because the International Organization for Standardization (ISO) is about to say that's all there is to CSR—another corporate marketing tool to be standardized. At its senior management meeting in Stockholm, Sweden in June 2004, ISO decided to develop an international standard for social responsibility. ISO develops voluntary technical agreements between countries, and ISO standards-setting bodies have ". . . a strategic partnership with the WTO."[6] Of course, ISO is also market driven to facilitate free trade and make it easy for large corporations to dominate world markets. If you loved "CSR" and "sustainability," you'll just adore the homogenizing ISO "social responsibility" standards.

CEO Lord John Browne took corporate speak to new heights when he took over British Petroleum and soon bought Amoco Corporation for $57 billion and recently invested $7 billion in a joint venture with Russian oil producer TNK. British Petroleum is now the world's second-largest oil company after ExxonMobil, with revenues of about $240 billion. In 2002, Lord Browne decided to end the oil company's political contributions and rename the company "BP," adding a green and yellow sun logo and the slogan "Beyond Petroleum."[7] Of course, he will help out with its multinational lobbying effort and its employees' Political Action Committee (PAC) to develop government policies and purchase politicians. BP isn't getting out of the oil business anytime soon, either. The first words out of Lord Browne's mouth when discussing "Beyond Petroleum" were ". . .let's build fifty nuclear reactors."[8] Lord Browne has gone so far "beyond petroleum" that he now wants to invest in dangerous nuclear power. So far, BP hasn't said what percentage of its research-and-development budget actually goes to develop alternative fuels if BP excludes nuclear power.

Another international business strategy and sustainable development "consultant" by the cute name of SustainAbility has been created for the purpose of attacking NGOs. Obviously, the world is not privatized enough for them. SustainAbility "studied" more than two hundred NGOs in twenty-two countries and is raising "some questions about their independence and integrity" and warns that "the greatest threat to the not-for-profit sector is the betrayal of public trust."[9]

Business for Social Responsibility (BSR) touted "sustainability" and CSR at its "Building and Sustaining Solutions" conference in Los Angeles in November 2003, which was kicked off by Carly Fiorina, former CEO and chairman of Hewlett-Packard (HP) and a major donor to Bush's reelection campaign, and was sponsored by HP, Disney, and McDonald's. Since 1992 BSR has evolved from a group of primarily small, private, socially responsible businesses to a large nonprofit organization controlled by multinational corporations. The BSR board of directors includes representatives of Coca-Cola, Stride Rite, Southern California Edison, Liz Claiborne, Phillip-Van Heusen, Ford, Nordisk, and Chiquita Brands.

Adding prestige and corporate power to the annual EnvironDesign Conference in Washington, DC, in 2003, were the Big Five automakers General Motors, Ford, Daimler-Chrysler, Honda, and Toyota, which were showing off their "environmentally friendly" vehicles. Presidential candidate John Kerry was also there complaining that Washington lobbyists spent $100 million or more a month to influence government decisions, labeling the U.S. Senate as "nearly dysfunctional for its inability to move the nation forward in solving our environmental problems such as oil dependence, downstream pollution, air quality, waste, and global warming."[10] His answer: provide more marketplace incentives to industry, such as subsidies, tax credits, partnerships with industry, and joint ventures with universities.[11] In other words, provide more taxpayer money to corporations and share more public taxpayer-supported university research with corporate management to give them the proper "incentives" to do the right thing. That's a very innovative idea, John. I'm sure it has never been thought of before.

CSR is purposely being immersed in gray thanks to the obfuscates of the world. For example, in March 2003, a Corporate Responsibility Index was launched by Business in the Community (BITC), a British consortium of

seven hundred companies. BITC released its benchmark for CSR performance, indicating that the 122 companies that *volunteered* to be assessed
were included in the index, such as British Petroleum, Dow Chemical, Shell
Oil, and Unilever, which scored in the top quintile. Dow scored 90.14 percent because of its corporate strategy and environmental performance.
I wonder if that score included an accurate tabulation of chemical pollutants, dangerous spills, hazardous waste sites, Union Carbide's Bhopal
disaster, and persistent organic pollutants supplied by Dow's team of
environmental leaders. The Union Carbide 1984 chemical leak in Bhopal,
India killed thousands overnight and left as many as 150,000 people permanently disabled. It makes me especially proud to hear Scott Nocson,
Dow's director of sustainable development, declare: "We are proud of our
accomplishments to date but realize we still have much to do to reach the
Triple Bottom Line objectives of economic prosperity, environmental
stewardship, and corporate social responsibility."[12]

There is nothing inherently wrong with indexes which represent stocks in
companies that have been socially and environmentally screened, as long as
such screening is based on comprehensive social and environmental criteria
and is not exclusively a "best in class." So-called SRI indexes also need to be
explained to investors. These indexes represent a basket of stocks; they do not
represent ownership and have absolutely no influence on the management
of corporations in the indexes. These indexes are sold to spin money out of
money, to make money for commissioned salespeople, and, possibly, for the
investors in the indexes *if* the value of the basket of securities represented by
the index increases and the index is sold for a realized gain.

Indexes are secondary market instruments which remove progressive
investors from their money, responsibility, and control. They represent a
highly impersonal financial relationship to capital. It is like investing by-the-
numbers on a computer screen, evading the responsibility of ownership and
accountability. The rubber never meets the road. There is nothing inherently
wrong with secondary markets where investors buy and sell stocks, bonds,
indexes, mutual fund shares, and other securities. The secondary market
is important to the liquidity of capital markets, but it does not add one
dollar to a business balance sheet or provide money to a plant, equipment,

or manufacturing facility, or add one job to the economy. It is simply the trading of already existing securities between buyers and sellers.

While many of the original founders of SRI firms and progressive non-profit organizations have retired or moved on to other endeavors, others remain active and committed to the policy of fighting corporate dominance over the political and global economic system. Many twenty- and thirty-year veterans of responsible investing have been joined by a new cast of characters, some eager to capitalize on a growing social market niche and some environmentally or socially motivated to combine professional talents with political, social and environmental advocacy.

Currently, SRI casts a very large net, including, not only new mutual funds, financial planners, bankers, brokers, and investment advisers, but also, for better or worse, consultants, media, and PR professionals. In many ways SRI is a victim of its own success. Everyone wants to emulate it, by creating new screened mutual funds, new indexes, and new esoteric products. Of the participants at the "SRI in the Rockies" conferences in 2003 and 2004, many were new attendees sent by their traditional Wall Street employers. Some are seeking the SRI market-niche and "The Money." Many are dedicated and committed to the concept of SRI, but few new advocates appear to be seeking a profession or career that will challenge the corporate-dominated economic structure as we know it today.

Corporate management loves to recruit public opinion to its cause and has adopted a strategy of buying its critics. George Monbiot of *The Guardian* has called it "image transfer," or absorbing other people's credibility.[13] Many environmentalists and social activists are now corporate consultants, playing right into corporate management's belief that CSR equals self-regulation. As Monbiot explains: "So the environmentalists taking the corporate buck in the name of cleaning up companies' performance are, in truth, helping them stay dirty by bypassing democratic constraints. But because corporations have invested so heavily in avoiding democracy, CSR has become big business for greens."[14]

The SRI asset and financial base has been enlarged by social screening and product diversification. More mutual funds, asset managers, SRI financial professionals, and consultants grow the business and increase its exposure and credibility. Wall Street firms and the Vanguard and Fidelity mutual fund companies of the world have acknowledged the growing demand and legitimacy of socially responsible and even "ethical" investing. Why not, there's money to be made.

Sorely lacking in all of this growing SRI power is an overriding political philosophy or vision as to where this should take our society. SRI can be a progressive force of change. That is part of the vision. The goal is not simply to maximize financial return and feel good about it, or to have less guilt, but to understand that capital is a major source of power and authority in American culture. Making money is not an end in itself. Investment capital is not a neutral force. It has been utilized politically for years by corporations to empower management and funnel society's capital to those wealthy interests that have less need for more access. Wealthy corporate management has plenty of access to the global political levers of power, the politicians, government bureaucrats, and regulators.

Corporate Codes of Conduct

If you almost choked on "sustainability," and "CSR," you'll need emergency medical attention when you attempt to digest all of the voluntary corporate codes of conduct, principles, and initiatives created to give large corporations additional cover. The United Nations Secretary-General Kofi Annan even proposed his own Global Compact in an address to the World Economic Forum in January 1999, in Davos, Switzerland. The United Nations had plans to work with a dozen financial institutions to develop global guidelines for responsible investment by September 2005. Of course, these will also be voluntary and unenforceable.

The concept of a corporate code of conduct was first discussed in 1972, when the U.N. Economic and Social Council asked the secretary-general to appoint a group to study the impact of corporate activity on economic development. While the process of writing a code had been ongoing at the United Nations, sweeping political unrest in apartheid South Africa and the growing strength of a U.S. divestment campaign to force corporate dis-engagement necessitated the emergence of a compromise solution.

The Reverend Leon H. Sullivan, a black civil rights activist who had been appointed to the General Motors board of directors in 1971, after failing in his attempt to convince GM to withdraw from South Africa, publicly introduced an American business code of conduct, later iden-tified as the seven Sullivan Principles. In March 1977, after eighteen months of hard campaigning, Sullivan announced formulation of the code, endorsed by twelve of approximately 350 U.S. corporations oper-ating in South Africa. The initial six principles called for desegregation of the workplace, fair employment practices, equal pay for equal work, job training, and advancement and improvement in the quality of workers' lives. In 1984, the seventh principle was added, calling on companies to work to eliminate laws and customs that impede social, economic, and political justice.

The principles received praise from business leaders and the U.S. State Department. Challenged by the growing divestment movement, seventy-five colleges and universities, along with several trade unions, promoted the Sullivan Principles in their investment programs, stating they would divest their holdings in corporations that had not signed them. Not even the South African government protested the implementation of the fair employment code.

Naturally, the principles were voluntary, self-monitored, and there were no penalties or sanctions for non-cooperation or for non-compliance. Arthur D. Little, a Cambridge consulting firm, was contracted to send companies questionnaires and compile summary reports on company progress as to how well they were moving toward equal pay for equal work, and desegregating company rest rooms and dining facilities.

In 1986, after ten years of brutal apartheid, internal uprisings, global economic sanctions, a cessation of bank lending, a national U.S. divest-ment campaign, and the beginning of a mass corporate exodus, Reverend Sullivan repudiated his principles as unworkable and a failure in abolishing apartheid in South Africa and demanded immediate U.S. corporate with-drawal. What had *not* failed was corporate management's recognition of a great cover for business-as-usual. Voluntary corporate codes of conduct became an intrinsic part of corporate speak.

In the twenty-first century, this voluntary non-binding corporate code bandwagon has been boarded by corporations, advocacy groups, NGOs, the SRI community, and just about everybody's mother, as the panacea for a non-governmental, non-regulatory, non-statutory, voluntary and unenforceable private sector solution to environmental, human, and labor rights violations around the globe. The decade of "the Code" is now upon us.

Seeing that history can be rewritten, the 290 endorsers of the 1997 Global Sullivan Principles of Social Responsibility (GSP) are now crediting the original South African Sullivan Principles with dismantling apartheid. Many of the 189 corporate supporters laud these "new" global principles for encouraging businesses to work with their communities toward common goals of human rights, social justice, and economic opportunity. The GSP endorsers include a long list of sterling human rights activists such as Coca-Cola, Chevron Texaco, Freeport McMoRan Cooper & Gold, Occidental Petroleum, Shell Oil, Tyco International, and Unocal. According to the July 2002 GSP President's Report, an Eminent Advisory Council was formed, including former Ambassador Andrew Young (remember his whitewashed paid report on Nike's sweatshops?), former Republican Congressman Jack Kemp (who serves on the Oracle Corporation board along with founder Larry Ellison, who opposes a voluntary China Business Principles code for Oracle), and John F. Smith, chairman of General Motors. "Eminent" is arguably the right word to describe this group.

A sophisticated international ambiance was added to the corporate code mystique when the Caux Round Table (CRT) came up with its Principles for Business, launched in 1994 and presented to the U.N. World Summit on Social Development in 1995. CRT was founded by Frederick Philips, former president of Philips Electronics, and an elite group of senior business executives from Japan, the United States, and Europe. The CRT Principles support three values: shared prosperity, justice, and civic responsibility. Who can argue with those illustrious values?

In 1998 I presented a resolution on behalf of a shareholder in Portland, Oregon at the Nike Annual Shareholder's Meeting in Memphis, Tennessee,

which linked executive compensation more closely to financial performance, and to a reasonable ratio between executives and the lowest wages
for factory workers in the United States and overseas. Due to lower corporate earnings, Phil Knight, Nike's CEO, had his wages drastically reduced
(40 percent) in 1998 making only $1.6 million. His hourly pay of $769 per
hour was somewhat above Nike's minimum wage of eighty-five cents an
hour paid to Indonesian factory workers. The response to Nike's problem
was—you guessed it—a code of conduct.

Sweatshops and Nike are now almost synonymous in the public's view,
the result of so much media attention being focused on Nike and Phil
Knight in the late 1990s. As an outgrowth of the sweatshop controversy,
several codes were developed, including the American Apparel & Footwear
Association's (AAFA) Worldwide Responsible Apparel Production (WRAP),
Principles and Certification Program, and the Fair Labor Association's
(FLA) Workplace Code of Conduct. The FLA was a successor to the White
House Apparel Industry Partnership, created by the apparel industry and
the Clinton administration. WRAP and FLA were both established in 1998
to promote basic standards for labor practices, factory conditions, environmental and customs compliance, and to promote brand certification
for garments and sports shoes marketed by corporations in compliance
with the FLA Workplace Code of Conduct. Confused yet?

In 2000, the Workers Rights Consortium (WRC) was created by college and university administrations, students, and human and labor rights
activists following the successful organizing efforts of the United Students
Against Sweatshops (USAS) movement on campuses across the country.
WRC is a nonprofit organization whose purpose is to assist in the enforcement of manufacturing Codes of Conduct adopted by colleges and universities, designed to insure that clothing and other goods produced by
corporations which bear school logos respect basic rights of workers. The
primary motivating force behind USAS and WRC was based on sweatshop
abuses perpetrated by Nike and other textile manufacturers operating in
Asia when students, faculty, college, and university administrations recognized their logos on apparel manufactured by these companies in Southeast
Asia, Indonesia, and China and were not convinced that AAFA and FLA

would be effective in enforcing voluntary corporate codes and industry standards.

About the same time as Leon Sullivan was releasing his new global principles, Alice Tepper Marlin's (now defunct) New York-based Council on Economic Priorities (CEP) established Social Accountability 8000 (SA8000), a cross-industry standard for workplace conditions and a verification and certification system based on the six basic conventions of the International Labor Organization as well as the U.N. Declaration of Human Rights and the U.N. Convention on the Rights of the Child. Social Accountability International (SAI) is the nonprofit organization that is responsible for development, implementation, and oversight of voluntary verifiable social accountability standards. SAI accredits organizations that pay a fee to verify corporate compliance with its standards.

Unfortunately, according to Heather White, the executive director and founder of Verité, an international nonprofit human rights monitoring organization, SAI has only certified for-profit entities, such as PricewaterhouseCoopers. SAI-USA Advisory Board members include Toys 'R Us, Dole Food Company, and Chiquita Brands. Avon Products and Toys 'R Us are among a small number of companies that had adopted SA8000 standards. By December 2002, 183 factories and facilities had obtained SA8000 certification.

Obviously, it's good that factories are receiving certification, but it's much more important that NGOs are authorized to certify facilities. Private auditing firms normally work for corporations and have a history of listening to management and not workers.

In 1989 the Coalition for Environmentally Responsible Economies (CERES) developed an environmental code of conduct—originally the ten Valdez Principles—which challenged corporate America to address serious environmental concerns. Over seventy companies have endorsed CERES. The group also works in a coalition with SRI portfolio managers (including Harrington Investments, Inc.), mutual funds, and other financial professionals to sponsor annual conferences, introduce shareholder resolutions, and dialogue with corporate management to implement environmental goals. The voluntary principles include protection of the biosphere, the sustainable use of natural resources, a commitment to reduce and dispose of waste, energy conservation, risk reduction, safe products and services, environmental restoration, public disclosure, management commitment to the principles, and annual audits and progress reports.

In 1997 the Global Reporting Initiative (GRI) became a project of CERES and the United Nations Environmental Programme and began to work with U.N. Secretary-General Kofi Annan's Global Compact. In June 2002, GRI became an independent nonprofit organization, and an expanded version of the organization's Sustainability Reporting Guidelines was issued that year prior to the World Summit on Sustainable Development in Johannesburg, South Africa. These guidelines represent a framework for comprehensive sustainability reporting, encompassing the triple bottom line of economic, environmental, and social issues.

More than 250 companies in twenty-five countries are reported to be using the GRI reporting standards, including Nike, Ford, General Motors, Nokia, Volkswagen, Bristol-Myers Squibb, KLM, and British Telecom. Since September 2003, companies listed on the Johannesburg Securities Exchange in South Africa have voluntarily abided by the GRI.

Not to be outdone, the Interfaith Center on Corporate Responsibility (ICCR), which coordinates the work of 275 Protestant, Roman Catholic, and Jewish religious institutions and represents over $100 billion in investment portfolios, has devised its own Global Principles. Called "The Principle for Global Corporate Responsibility: Benchmarks for Measuring Business Performance" they were written with the assistance of the Ecumenical Council for Corporate Responsibility in Great Britain and the Taskforce on the Churches and Corporate Responsibility in Canada. The eight Global Principles call for a sustainable living wage; workers' rights to freedom of association, including collective bargaining and the right to strike; corporate standards for subcontractors; NGO monitoring; public transparency; public reporting; and consequences for noncompliance. In May 2003, ICCR released its corporate code's "Benchmarks" report, highlighting three major issues: labor rights, bio-diversity, and access to pharmaceuticals.

The crescendo of corporate speak revolving around the development of voluntary codes has reached such a fever pitch that a corporate-dominated nonprofit organization, Future 500, is releasing a new version of the software used by corporations to consolidate their corporate accountability performance standards. The software, called the Corporate Accountability Gap Audit, combines twelve leading standards including GRI, the New York Stock Exchange Governance Standards, Dow Jones Sustainability Initiative, and Domini social investment criteria. The membership of Future 500 includes Coca-Cola, Coors, ERM, General Motors, Matsushita, Mitsubishi Electric, WSP, Weyerhauser, Hewlett-Packard, Nike, Deloitte & Touche, Shell Oil, and many others.

The proliferation of corporate codes has clearly taken on a global perspective with Kofi Annan's Global Compact, initially signed by nearly fifty corporations in August 2000. The nine voluntary principles were so broad and open-ended that PR-minded companies such as BP Amoco, Bayer, Dupont, Novartis, Shell, Nike, and Rio Tinto quickly came on board. There are now over 1,700 corporations on-board Annan's U.N. Global Compact and ten voluntary principles. It has become meaningless. An international coalition of human rights and environmental groups denounced the new collaboration, charging that the compact was "threatening the mission and integrity of the United Nations."[15] John Cavanaugh, director of the Washington, DC-based Institute for Policy Studies, even said "The first three words of the U.N. Charter are 'We the People.' Private corporations are accountable only to their shareholders, often in flagrant disregard of the rights of people who work for them, live near them, or suffer the consequences of their decisions."[16]

The Global Compact's signatories flaunt it at will, because there are no follow-up reviews and the agreement is non-binding. Bayer signed the pact and yet continues to oppose the Kyoto Protocol for protection of the climate as well as European Union laws regulating chemicals. According to the Coalition Against Bayer-Dangers, the company uses its involvement with the United Nations to "bolster its integrity. . . on the company's homepage," and even uses its annual report to compliment Kofi Annan with his picture and the U.N. logo.

French President Jacques Chirac, who hosted the 2003 summit of the Group of Eight (G8) most industrialized nations in Evian, France, even proposed that the G8 leaders endorse a Charter of Principles for a Responsible Market Economy. According to Friends of the Earth International he withdrew the proposal because of the U.S. and British governments' opposition.

In February 1999 Global Exchange, the San Francisco, California-based human rights organization, issued a report on Walt Disney Company's use of sweatshop labor in China, based on research by the Hong Kong Christian Industrial Committee. In conjunction with Amnesty International and the International Labor Rights Fund, Global Exchange launched the U.S. Business Principles for Human Rights of Workers in China based upon basic labor standards as defined by the International Labor Organization (ILO) and basic human rights as defined by the U.N. Covenants on Economic, Social and Cultural Rights, and Civil and Political Rights. These principles were signed by the Chinese government, as well as included in China's national laws.

The initial ten China Business Principles (CBP) were endorsed by twenty-one global human rights groups and nonprofit organizations, as well as five SRI firms, and Harrington Investments, Inc. (HII). Three corporations originally signed the CBP, including Levi Strauss, Mattel, and Reebok.

In cooperation with Global Exchange, in August 1999, HII began communicating with primarily HII-owned high tech companies located in California and on the West Coast, requesting information on existing corporate codes, introducing the CBP, and urging endorsement. The first three companies we contacted were Hewlett Packard, Intel, and Cisco Systems. Hewlett Packard simply did not respond. Intel and Cisco immediately responded and offered to meet with representatives of Global Exchange, HII, and Amnesty International. Intel and Cisco brought together all of the relevant personnel from China as well as the United States, and spent several hours openly disclosing their China operations and responding to our questions.

Our positive experiences with Intel and Cisco, being ignored by Hewlett Packard, experiencing evasiveness with Microsoft, and going head-to-head with an uncooperative Larry Ellison at Oracle Corporation, fit an all too familiar historical pattern of what happens when shareholders attempt to converse with corporate management. (For more on shareholder advocacy, see Chapter 7.)

Unfortunately, many of us in the SRI community are quick to disclose too much to corporate management at an initial dialogue conference: goals, strategy, shareholder information, and so on. Sometimes to gain another meeting or a promise of further dialogue we're happy with a friendly pat on the shoulder, a lunch, or simply a conversation. Often a resolution is dropped for a promise to meet again, or attend a conference, or talk to "higher ups." Occasionally, these conferences do lead to a change in corporate policy (Wal-Mart gay rights endorsement is one example). Most of the time, however, they lead to more meetings, more wasted time, and little else.

Verité has operated in China since 1995, conducting over two hundred factory audits. What it has been finding leads one to believe that little has changed, thanks to voluntary corporate codes. Verité found that China's own Work Safety administration reported one hundred forty thousand deaths in 2002, an increase of 7 percent over 2001; Chinese media reported two hundred fifty thousand injuries and more than thirty thousand industrial accidents in the first quarter of 2003; the ILO ranks China as the world leader in industrial accidents; about 2.5 million Chinese workers are exposed to toxins annually; a majority of factories do not pay legal overtime; there's limited enforcement of labor laws; and harassment and lengthy imprisonment for those who report violations, peacefully demonstrate and who try to associate freely.[17]

When asked to comment at a congressional hearing regarding voluntary corporate codes adopted by global corporations, Verité Director of Policy Mil Niepold said:

> Codes are squarely in the camp of voluntarism and while they are a useful starting point for improving labor rights compliance, they alone are simply not enough to right the 'imbalance of power' that exists today between major multinational corporations (MNC) and most governments. Governments do not have the resources that MNCs do—resources that are in many places including China— greatly eroded by endemic corruption . . . Violations of human and labor rights thrive in cultures of impunity . . . strengthening the

rule of law in any given country is not a task merely for MNCs and their voluntary initiatives. This is a task for governments.[18]

Verité not only monitors corporate operations in China, but has conducted over one thousand factory evaluations in more than sixty-five countries, interviewing more than eighteen thousand workers. Verité also works with CALPERS to develop a quantitative assessment of country performance on several labor issues in order for the pension fund to determine whether or not to invest in country equity markets. Verité is also exploring the system in Asian labor markets where women work as migrant employees in the garment industry, where their families borrow funds to pay placement fees for eighteen-month employment contracts. Usually these women work long hours in unsafe working environments, suffer sexual harassment, verbal abuse, and discrimination. The Verité research, which is turning into a human rights campaign, is funded by the Sigrid Rausing Trust (SRT), a U.K. humanitarian foundation.

According to Robert Rosoff, labor rights violations are so widespread in China that human rights violations can be presumed to exist in every factory until proven otherwise.[19] A 2004 ICCR report indicated that Chinese labor law ". . . is inadequately enforced and doesn't contain sufficient incentives or penalties to induce compliance," and the ". . . lack of truly independent, worker-run trade unions in China impedes the attainment of better terms of employment through collective bargaining."[20] In other words, nothing will change in China until human rights protection, freedom of association, and collective bargaining rights are enforced by its government.

In early 2003, four European and U.S. banks, in collaboration with the International Finance Corporation (IFC) and the private sector arm of the World Bank, drafted guidelines for funding projects in emerging markets. According to an April 6, 2003 article in the *Financial Times*, the banks consulted with U.S. and European environmental NGOs to develop social and environmental rules on a host of issues—from preservation of natural habitats to respect for indigenous cultures and support for child care and condemnation of forced labor. This agreement is called the "Equator Principle: An Industry Approach for Financial Institutions in Determining, Assessing and Managing Environmental and Social Risk in Project Financing." According to the April 21, 2003 BSR *News Monitor*, an electronic newsletter published weekly, "Under the principles, the banks agree 'not to provide financing to projects where the borrower will not or is unable to comply with our environmental and social policies and processes.'" The Equator Principles are now endorsed by twenty-one banks from seven countries, including ABN Amro, Barclays, Citigroup, Credit Lyonnais, Credit Suisse Group, HVB Group, Rabobank, Royal Bank of Scotland, West LB, Westpac Banking Corporation, and Bank of America.

These principles certainly sound good, but are they effective? Elizabeth McGeveran, vice president of governance and socially responsible investment at ISIS Asset Management, said: "Banks love to take credit for all the good that providing capital does, especially in developing countries, but they've not been willing to date, to take responsibility for the many negative repercussions of their role in financing globalization."[21] ISIS has been in dialogue with Citigroup, one of the Equator signatories since 1999, concerning the environmentally disastrous Three Gorges Dam project in China.

In addition to saying that "the principles are very weak on social issues," Ilyse Hogue, a global finance campaigner for Rainforest Action Network, also said: "Some banks will be best practice implementers, and other banks could just sign and do nothing. Because the principles don't have clear enforcement or review mechanisms, how are the best practitioners going to police the system to ensure that free riders don't undermine it? . . . There's not enough in the principles that recognize and assure indigenous communities' right to prior and informed consent for development on their land, much less a straight-out right to veto like you or I would have if these companies came into our homes."[22]

In a June 2004 report, the Dutch nonprofit organization BankTrack conducted the first review of the Equator Principles, titled "Principles, Profits or Just PR? Triple P Investments Under the Equator Principles." BankTrack found it hard to adequately evaluate the implementation of the principles. One project in particular, the Baku-Tbilisi-Ceyhan pipeline, which was approved for financing was opposed by the public interest community and lacked adequate transparency. BankTrack also stated that participating

204 — The Challenge to Power

banks did not implement the principles consistently and the banks were still reluctant to engage stakeholders in project discussions.

The World Bank's IFC is also concerned that the Equator Principles are seen has unenforceable. Peter Woicke, executive vice-president of IFC, has indicated he wants to include "human rights" in the principles, according to a November 4, 2003 article in the *Financial Times*. Woicke, however, wants to make sure that IFC is not moving too fast for commercial banks in upgrading the principles to include "human rights," and that IFC is holding informal discussions on the issue which would be "very delicate" for a non-political institution. Obviously, we wouldn't want to move too fast by including something as insignificant as human rights in a voluntary code.

Besides dealing with the World Bank and the IMF, nothing stops the SRI community from targeting individual private sector financial institutions. Citigroup came under attack by the Rainforest Acton Network (RAN), which sponsored television ads by Hollywood celebrities asking Citigroup credit card holders to destroy their cards to protest the bank's policy of funding extractive and fossil fuel industries that contribute to global warming. According to RAN, Citigroup helped finance the controversial Camisea pipeline project that will ship natural gas from the Amazon region of Peru to the Pacific Coast; oil drilling in Papua, New Guinea, and Colombia; oil pipelines in Chad, Cameroon, Ecuador, and Venezuela; and giant power plants in Thailand and the Philippines.[23] Until recently, many critics of corporate projects, such as logging and releasing more carbon-based gasses into the air, focused on the World Bank or IMF financing instead of targeting major private sector lending institutions.

At the 2003 World Economic Forum in Davos, over one hundred environmental and human rights organizations signed the Colleveccio Declaration which called for financial institutions to implement more socially and environmentally responsible lending policies. Most NGOs recognize that this is only a small step and are not directly endorsing the Equator Principles. Instead they are calling for mandatory lending guidelines, categorical lending prohibitions, and allowing affected communities to have recourse with a bank when standards are not being met or implemented. In other words, what is needed relative to lending standards is no different than what is needed for a labor and human rights code: enforceable standards with penalties and sanctions for abusive lending practices.

At the September 2002 Johannesburg World Summit on Sustainable Development, British Prime Minister Tony Blair announced the Extractive Industries Transparency Initiative (EITI), yet another voluntary corporate effort to stall, limit, or prevent governments from enacting meaningful legislation to force mandatory codes, monitoring, compliance, and sanctions. EITI's purpose is to increase voluntary disclosure of revenues from oil, gas, and mining companies in the form of taxes, royalties, or other payments to the governments in over fifty developing countries. Blair claims the current lack of transparency leads to corruption, conflict, and poverty.

Historically, governments in developing countries have required extractive corporations to conceal payments to government bureaucrats, politicians, and military leaders. EITI was initially supported by BP (British Petroleum), Shell, Rio Tinto, and Anglo-American among others. Under its Governance of Natural Resources Project, the World Bank will provide research and advice to the United Kingdom.

In June 2003, a coalition of thirty-six institutional investors (including CALPERS, Fidelity Investments, and Merrill Lynch Investment Managers) which collectively manage over $3 trillion in assets announced support for EITI. BP disclosed its $100 million "signature bonus" payment to Angola, and in June 2003, Shell Oil disclosed $900 million worth of payments the company made last year to the Nigerian government for oil extraction.[24] Most corporations are barred from disclosing payments to governments, since contracts with governments often force confidentiality. The EITI efforts and others seem to be aimed at obtaining voluntary disclosure from corporations, as well as convincing developing country governments to voluntarily eliminate confidentiality requirements.

In late August 2003, the United Nations began discussing "Norms on the Responsibilities of Transnational Corporations," a set of requirements to regulate human rights standards at global corporations—similar to standards previously only required of U.N. member nations. The requirements subject companies to periodic monitoring and verification to ensure compliance and, according to the *Financial Times*, have already attracted business opposition.[25] According to a representative of the Paris-based International Chamber of Commerce, global human rights standards would "move away from the realm of voluntary initiatives . . . conflicting with the approach taken by other parts of the U.N.," as evidenced by the United Nation's non-binding Global Compact.[26]

Currently about 25 million people in seventy countries are dependent on the $35 billion-a-year retail coffee market for jobs. The producers, competing against each other in developing countries, barely survive when coffee prices fall. As a result, growers go out of business, subsistence wages are lowered, children are employed, and environmental standards are eliminated. In an effort to address coffee "fair trade," in September 2004, another voluntary code was announced. The voluntary Common Code for the Coffee Community (CCCC) was endorsed by Nestlé's, Sara Lee, Kraft Foods (Philip Morris Tobacco), and Tchibo of Germany. To date the code has been adopted by 80 percent of the international coffee market. CCCC will require voluntary compliance and press producers and traders to pay minimum wages, eliminate child labor, permit collective bargaining, and comply with international environmental standards.

CCCC was not supported by the German-based Transfair group because the organization doesn't believe the code protects small producers. Oxfam, in supporting CCCC, doubted that it solicited small producer input or guaranteed that small producers would have a strong presence in the CCCC. Oxfam believes that CCCC should complement, not substitute, other solutions to the coffee crisis, including the Sustainable Coffee Partnerships, the International Coffee Organization, and Fair Trade certification.

If you don't drink coffee, perhaps you drink tea. We now have the Ethical Tea Partnership, launched by the U.K. House of Commons, which includes Sara Lee, Tetley, Twinings, and Unilever. The Tea Partnership promotes social responsibility by monitoring labor conditions in the seven countries that produce 65 percent of the world tea exports, including Kenya, Malawi, Sri Lanka, Tanzania, Zimbabwe, and later in 2005, China. If you believe that this partnership will produce more than lots of PR and "noise," you may be drinking something a lot stronger than tea or coffee.

Electricity seeks the path of least resistance, and so too may the voluntary

Electronic Industry Code of Conduct prepared by a number of companies that are engaged in the manufacture of electronic products. The code, created between June and October 2004, was developed by Hewlett Packard, IBM, Dell, Solectron, Sanmina SCI, Jabil, Celestica, and Flextronics. The voluntary code includes seven labor standards (also covering freedom of association), seven health and safety standards, six environmental standards, and company management commitments and ethics responsibilities.

Voluntary codes are just that: voluntary. Even with the most comprehensive corporate voluntary human and labor rights code of conduct, it is essential that an impartial, financially independent entity monitors compliance on a regular basis, whether it is an NGO in the country where the corporation operates or a non-corrupt government agency. Such monitoring must include open and unannounced inspections, not unlike current SEC examinations of registered investment advisors. And like the SEC, upon a finding of noncompliance, such monitoring must include mandatory sanctions. Without a comprehensive code enacted into law and enforced by national and international laws, and an international judicial system with the authority to levy penalties and mandatory sanctions, voluntary codes are a great waste of everyone's time, including the SRI community.

Not unlike the lessons we learned from the Sullivan Principles, voluntary codes allow both global corporations and governments to get off the hook. They encourage corporations, governments, activists, NGOs, and the SRI community to spend thousands of hours—meeting, holding hearings, conferences, seminars, workshops, and dialogues—where the end result is the same: corporate business as usual; corporations moving from country to country, following the cheapest labor, natural resources and cost of production; buying politicians at home to ward off U.S. laws; and corrupting government bureaucrats and politicians in foreign countries through direct and indirect bribes.

Corporate management's embrace of codes of conduct and sustainability leads an unsuspecting investor to assume that corporate social responsibility (CSR) is an integral part of the corporation's articles of incorporation, by-laws, and overall management philosophy. Well, guess again. CSR is PR and little else. According to an Ernst and Young 2002 global survey of senior executives from 147 global corporations, 94 percent believed that the development of a CSR strategy could deliver real business benefits, but only 11 percent made significant progress in implementing such a strategy.[27]

One of the great pioneers of CSR promotion is Milton Moskowitz, author of *The 100 Best Companies to Work for in America*, a prolific editorial writer for Trillium Asset Management, and a contributor to *Business Ethics* magazine as well as many other publications. Moskowitz once lauded both Levi Strauss and Hewlett Packard (HP) as "icons of social responsibility." However, in a 2002 op-ed piece for *Business Ethics*, Moskowitz had second thoughts: "Job security was a given at the old HP, but today the company is absorbing Compaq Computer and cutting its workforce by fifteen thousand. Levi Strauss once swore it would not move its production overseas, but now it is closing all of its U.S. factories. Morale at both companies is now at an all-time low."

Levi Strauss has continued to cut both domestic and foreign jobs, eliminating another 1,180 employees in Edmonton, Alberta; Stoney Creek, Ontario; and Brantford, Ontario. Levi's debt currently tops $2.3 billion. Standard & Poor's downgraded its debt from BB- to B and spurred speculation that bankruptcy for the company is right around the corner.[28]

I am sure Moskowitz is equally unhappy that this once great socially responsible company is also cutting health benefits for its retirees and eliminating future retirement health benefits for new employees as it exits the Americas and heads for sweatshop Asia.

In 1999 Global Exchange, Sweatshop Watch, the Asian Law Caucus, and the garment workers' union, UNITE, filed a class action law suit on behalf of workers in Saipan, a U.S. commonwealth, against over two dozen major U.S. retailers. The list included Levi Strauss because of sweatshop conditions in Saipan. In September 2002, twenty-six companies agreed to settle the lawsuit, halt sweatshop abuses, and pay $20 million into a fund for back wages and to create an independent monitoring system to prevent future abuses. Only one company, Levi Strauss, refused to halt its abuses and settle.

Moskowitz was so depressed after the Enron scandal and learning that

Alice Tepper Marlin, founder of the Council on Economic Priorities (CEP), had closed CEP's office, he said: "What have we accomplished if things are as bad as ever? It appears that much of the corporate social responsibility movement has dealt in peripheral matters, in language, in mechanical social screens. Behind the scenes, the dirty work went on as usual. I am sorry to be so cynical, but you have to admit it is depressing."[29]

HAS INCLUSIVENESS CHANGED CORPORATE BEHAVIOR?

The only positive accomplishment of CSR, Moskowitz observes, was being able to push corporate America to nominate African-Americans to corporate boards of directors, but he remains skeptical if that has really changed corporate management's behavior. In 2002, the Interfaith Center on Corporate Responsibility (ICCR) surveyed seventy-three companies to ascertain whether any progress had been made since 1991, when the federal Glass Ceiling Commission released its report indicating that women and minorities made up a very small fraction of the members on the boards of directors of Fortune 500 companies. The results of the ICCR study showed that America's corporate boards still suffered from a lack of diversity.

According to the September 13, 2002 *Corporate Examiner*:

> The [ICCR] survey showed that non-inclusiveness at top corporate levels reaches 90%, with white men occupying the majority of senior executive and corporate board positions. While the average size of the board of the 73 companies surveyed was 12 persons, the average number of women per board was only two. Ten companies – Affiliated, American Power, Deere, Devon, EMC, Polaris, Robert Half, Sicor, Unilever, and Werner had no female board members at all. Overall, women constituted 15.2% of surveyed board members.

According to Diane White, a senior diversity consultant at Calvert Group, Ltd. who presented the Calvert's Women's Principles to the 2004 SRI in the Rockies Conference, women held 5.2 percent of the top earning positions in the Fortune 500 in 2002, 10 percent of those companies had women corporate officers who were top earners in 2002, 13.6 percent of all board seats and five chief executive positions in Fortune 500 companies were occupied by women, and 7.1 percent of CFO and 1.6 percent of CEO positions at the largest companies were held by women.

White also pointed out that 70 percent of the 1.5 billion people living on $1 per day or less are women, 86 million of the 140 million illiterate young people are women, and only 14 percent of the world's parliaments are women.

Columnist Arianna Huffington raised the same issue regarding women's attempt to bust through the corporate glass ceiling, including the few women that have successfully taken over CEO spots at major corporations. As an example, she points out Anne Mulcahy, CEO of Xerox, who received a 48 percent increase in salary and bonuses while the company paid a $10 million penalty to the SEC and "restated" its earnings by 36 percent."[30] She wrote:

> Clearly, the mere presence of more women in positions of power will not by itself be enough to guarantee a change in corporate behavior. Given the current business culture, the temptation for piggish behavior is far too great in both genders. And in any case, we can't wait twenty years to find out if an infusion of estrogen would clean up the corporate muck, so we've got to get out the hoses today and wash down the entire corporate establishment without fear or favor. If something better—more ethical, more honest, less narcissistic—can rise in its place, then I, for one, wouldn't care if it were dominated by men, women, or chimpanzees of either sex.[31]

STILL PERFORMING AFTER ALL THESE YEARS

Socially responsible mutual fund assets are growing, or at least in the recent three-year bear market, not being withdrawn as rapidly as from many non-screened mutual fund assets. In fact in 2002, while investors in non-socially screened assets pulled $10.5 billion out of U.S. diversified equity mutual funds, social investors added $1.5 billion. SRI investors are more patient, loyal, and committed. Thanks to the likes of Enron, WorldCom, Tyco, and Arthur Anderson, assets are not fleeing socially-screened funds, but looking for diversification and social and environmental responsibility. Many SRI investment firms, however, still suffered thanks to Enron and WorldCom. Even the most comprehensive of social screens could not guard against fraud, cooking the books, and outright criminal activity.

According to a study by portfolio manager Marc J. Lane, investors can express their preference for social justice and environmental values through stock selection without giving up portfolio diversification or long-term performance. From January 1995 through December 2003, " . . . the most rigorously screened subsets of companies' behavior in Social Justice and the Environment achieved gross compound annual return of 14.62 percent and 15.58 percent, respectively," versus 13.05 percent for the benchmark universe, consisting of the 2,884 stocks for which data could be complied within the Russell 3000 Index.[32]

Socially-screened portfolio managers have also had competitive performance numbers when compared to unrestricted portfolios. In fact, looking back to the debate over South Africa Free (SAF) versus South Africa Invested (SAI) portfolios, it was assumed that anytime a manager was restricted in any way to a smaller universe of securities, underperformance inevitably was the result.

Pension administrators and their in-house portfolio managers hated to have their judgment questioned, and primarily reacted to calls for a SAF portfolio in a defensive and insecure manner. Questioning investment policy simply wasn't allowed at that time. When the political heat finally forced a more objective debate, the public quickly learned that not only could SAF portfolios provide competitive returns, other social and environmental issues could be considered without harming performance and increasing risk.

As early as April 1982, Daniel and Bell Capital Management submitted a study to the Connecticut state treasurer which found that the SAF portfolio outperformed the SAI by an average annual basis of 6.3 percent and the overall market for the five years analyzed. United States Trust Company Boston, The Boston Company, Robert Schwartz of Shearson/Lehman/

American Express, and studies by Ted Brown and Favia Hill Associates, an affiliate of Chemical Bank, all reinforced prior studies in finding that even when limiting investment choices, SAF portfolios returns were competitive based on relative risk and liquidity. In a similar study by Nobel Prize winner William F. Sharpe and a colleague, Blake R. Grossman, they found that "Even after adjustment for risk, such a strategy (excluding companies in South Africa) would have outperformed the New York Stock Exchange index, a fortiori, the S&P 500, and the majority of actively managed institutional portfolios. Moreover, it is not unreasonable to expect such performance to continue."[33] Guess what? It did!

Studies have consistently pointed out that portfolio restrictions, in and of themselves, do not limit portfolio performance since all management styles limit the universe of securities purchased. As the Sharpe and Grossman study pointed out, however, in the case of SAF portfolio limitations, large capitalized global companies were excluded and replaced by smaller capitalized companies that historically result in out-performance. The difficulty in beating indexes with multiple screened portfolios is that entire sectors are excluded. The performance results of a particular portfolio have more to do with management style and the historical time frame studied. Various industry sectors perform differently depending on the underlying economy and where we are in an economic or business cycle. Performance is also dependent on what particular industry sector is partially or totally excluded, e.g., defense, chemicals, tobacco.

More recent studies also indicate that there has been little statistical difference in performance between screened and unscreened portfolio stocks measured from 1987 through 1996. In regard to specific environmental screening criteria, in a 1997 study entitled "Linking Financial and Environmental Performance," Roger Adams found there was no adverse impact on share price performance or company profitability due to improved environmental performance. Richard Read Clough at Duke University, in his research paper entitled "Impact of an Environmental Screen on Portfolio Performance: A Comparative Analysis of S&P 500 Stock Returns," found that the mere existence of an environmental screen actually enhanced financial performance.

Recent performance studies covering 2001–2003, were published in the 2003 Report on Socially Responsible Investing Trends in the United States, by the Social Investment Forum as well as in *The SRI Advantage: Why Socially Responsible Investing Has Outperformed Financially* by Peter Camejo. Thanks to Lloyd Kurtz, a portfolio manager at Nelson Capital Management, I received information on another important study, linking social responsibility with superior financial results, which won the Moskowitz Prize at the "SRI in the Rockies" conference. For a peek at this study, go to http://business.auckland.ac.nz.

INVESTING IN THE COMMUNITY

For socially responsible investors requiring a diversified portfolio, rates of return, liquidity, and safety are not the only factors to consider. Global investing should include secondary market securities such as stocks, bonds, and mutual funds, but also be diversified with high social impact investments, including community development banks, loan funds, micro-lending enterprises, credit unions, community development venture capital funds, social venture funds, low-income housing tax credit programs, private placements, partnerships, and limited liability companies that have a direct and quantitative social or environmental impact. These "community" investment opportunities include U.S. domestic communities, as well as investments in local communities throughout the world.

The Coalition of Community Development Financial Institutions describes CDFIs as "private-sector, financial intermediaries with community development as their primary mission. While CDFIs share a common mission, they have a variety of structures and development lending goals. There are six basic types of CDFIs: community development banks, community development loan funds, community development credit unions, microenterprise funds, community development corporation-based lenders and investors, and community development venture funds. All are market-driven, locally-controlled, private-sector organizations."

As I admonish my colleagues in the financial services sector who create those esoteric investment instruments that simply spin money out of money, I admire those innovative, socially motivated professionals who dedicate their lives to creating investment vehicles that focus on meeting capital needs in underdeveloped and neglected neighborhoods in America and third world communities. Most of these investments are in the primary market, but a few are now emerging which provide secondary market liquidity for traditional investors. One such Wall Street product, providing 100 percent FDIC insurance protection is a certificate of deposit (CD) in ShoreBank, the oldest and one of the most successful community financial intermediaries in the country. It can now be purchased and custodied in brokerage accounts in Wall Street favorites such as Charles Schwab. ShoreBank was the first successful community development bank to serve the needs of a largely low- and moderate-income minority population on the Southside in Chicago. ShoreBank, the leader and most successful of the community financial institutions in the United States, is now one of hundreds of emerging CDFIs.

ShoreBank, with $1.3 billion in assets, has sponsored ShoreCap International and an affiliated nonprofit advisory service, ShoreCap Exchange, to develop, microfinance, and invest in small financial institutions in Asia, Africa, and Eastern Europe that provide financial services to local micro and small enterprises. ShoreBank invested $2.5 million in ShoreCap International, and committed two senior ShoreBank managers to run the company under the direction of Mary Houghton, President of ShoreBank, while the company's Investment Committee will be chaired by Frank Kennedy, the former president and CEO of HSBC Equator Bank in South Africa.

There are currently between eight hundred and one thousand CDFIs in low-income communities across the country, including Puerto Rico. CDFIs provide traditional banking services as well as loans to small businesses, for low-income housing, and to nonprofit organizations.

According to the CDFI Data Project, a collaborative initiative, the 512 CDFIs surveyed had over $5.7 billion of financing outstanding at the end of 2001. That same year, these 512 CDFIs financed 7,484 businesses, constructed or rehabilitated 43,428 homes for low-income families, built or renovated 501 community facilities, and created 52,798 jobs.

Community development banks and credit unions are federally insured financial institutions that provide all the services available at conventional banks and credit unions, including savings and checking accounts, lines of consumer and mortgage credit, debit cards, etc. Community development banks, such as ShoreBank in Chicago, Community Capital Bank in Brooklyn, and Community Bank of the Bay in Oakland, supply capital to build in low-income neighborhoods by providing minority small business loans and loans for housing construction and rehabilitation. The over two hundred member-owned and controlled Community Development Credit Unions have combined assets of $1.8 billion, and include the new People's Community Partnership Federal Credit Union in Oakland. Both community banks and credit unions have a lending tradition of maximizing employment, economic leverage, and keeping money in its local neighborhood or regional community.

With about $2.3 billion in assets nationally, community loan funds operate in specific geographic areas, acting as financial intermediaries by pooling investments and loans that are provided to individual, for-profit, and non-profit organizations, generally at or below market interest rates. These financial intermediaries are not federally insured, but have few if any loan defaults and generally return a specific annual percentage rate of return to investors. Similar to community banks and credit unions, loans are targeted to small business owners and low-income housing, and many loan funds specifically fund nonprofit corporations. The Northern California Community Loan Fund (NCCLF) located in San Francisco is one such fund.

Incorporated in 1987, NCCLF has committed almost $25 million to over 170 community organizations, and has experienced no defaults. Investors can buy NCCLF notes ranging from 0 to 3 percent from one to ten years. NCCLF primarily funds affordable housing, human services, and nonprofit and employee-owned businesses. For instance, NCCLF loaned $150,000 to Berkeley-based Inkworks Press, a collectively-owned and operated union shop, to refinance debt, fund an operating reserve, and purchase four new color presses that enabled the company to complete all its printing jobs in-house. Thanks to its new press, Harrington Investments, Inc., has a very attractive promotional brochure.

NCCLF has recently issued a new prospectus for raising an additional $3 million for loan capital, structured as unsecured promissory notes to expand lending in Northern California. Two NCCLF programs that have enjoyed wide community support are the Fiscal Fitness Program, which builds capacity for organizations by offering technical assistance on critical financial management issues, and the Nonprofit Space Capital Fund to fund and provide technical assistance so that nonprofit organizations can purchase permanently affordable space.

Another loan fund, or CDFI, is Cascadia Revolving Fund in Seattle, Washington, which specializes in loans to small emerging businesses. Cascadia has had great success in making 379 loans since 1985 totaling almost $24 million, many to minority and women entrepreneurs in the Pacific Northwest.

More socially responsible primary market vehicles are being created to cater to investors through investments in short and intermediate term notes similar to NCCLF. On a much larger scale, there are Calvert Community Investment (CCI) notes, now surpassing $75 million, which invests in a global portfolio lending money to over 180 organizations, including ten thousand micro and small businesses employing over fifteen thousand people. Investors can invest personal funds, and now retirement accounts, in CCI notes available at a 3 percent interest rate with a rolling one-year term. Funds are globally diversified into community banks, credit unions, domestic and international loan funds, and other financial intermediaries that finance everything from housing, health care, agriculture, and education to cooperatives and nonprofit human service organizations. CCI is administered by the Calvert Foundation, now holding over $100 million in assets which includes donor advised funds of over $10 million.

In January 2005, the Calvert Foundation made a historic breakthrough in community investing by creating a method in which brokers and investment advisors can purchase CCIs directly for their clients and have such investments appear directly on their brokerage account statements. This will greatly increase the availability of capital for CDFIs across the globe.

Not only do international loan funds such as Oikocredit (formerly the Ecumenical Development Cooperative Society) utilize CCI notes for a portion of their U.S. capitalization for third world cooperative loans and lend to over four hundred microcredit banks in sixty-seven countries, but Fair Trade organizations, such as Newcastle upon Tyne, England-based Shared Interest, offer interest and non-interest bearing notes to fund alternative trade lending programs. In April 2003, Shared Interest closed a five-year, £1 million zero coupon bond offering to fund microcredit loans to third world farmers, shopkeepers, and artisans. According to Managing Director Stephanie Sturrock, Shared Interest finances fifty thousand individual artisans and farmers comprising about 10 percent of the world's fair trade.[34]

Unlike "free trade," fair trade is committed to an equitable trade relationship, where the producer, generally a farmer or artisan, is guaranteed a minimum price and a larger portion of the final price of the marketed product, traditionally reserved for the "middle man" or distributor. One of my clients who lives in Tagbilaran City, Bohol, in the Philippines, recently introduced me to Southern Partners and Fair Trade Corporation (SPFTC). Like many, SPFTC is a fair trade organization established by small producers, farmers, fisher folk, and NGOs that provide services to the islands, bringing more profits home to producers.

Thanks to long-time South African anti-apartheid activists Donna Katzin and Mary Tiseo, as well as pro-majority rule portfolio managers such as Robert Zevin and Sam Folin, new lending organizations have been created in South Africa, with U.S. ties, that allow progressive investors to support the rebirth of the South African economy.

Shared Interest USA is a nonprofit organization based in New York, created in 1996 by South African activists and financial professionals. It accepts grants and investments from individuals and institutions in the United States to partially collateralize loan guarantees made though the South Africa-based Themboni International Guarantee Fund (TIGF) so that South African banks can fund community development financial institutions. Shared Interest invests funds from investors in the United States and invests in socially screened debt securities and insured CDs through the issue of promissory notes to investors.

Shared Interest has funded more than forty thousand low-income housing units in South Africa. Through TIGF it has secured loans to support low-cost housing, microenterprises, and rural development, including clinics, roads, drinking water, and sewage systems. As of December 31, 2002, Shared Interest had increased its loan capital to almost $6.4 million. It was particularly proud of a loan guarantee to the Bee Foundation (yes, and packaging honey) to provide livelihoods for ten thousand families for three years in remote rural areas of Mpumalanga and Limpopo Provinces.

Reinvest In South Africa (RISA) Charitable Trust, a nonprofit group based in Philadelphia, raises investor funds and donations to support small, medium, and microenterprise businesses along with low-income housing. Sam Folin, RISA president, is the president and CEO of Benchmark Asset Managers, LLC, and managed South Africa-free portfolios during the apartheid era. Elena Thandive Pullen-Venema is the current executive director, taking over from Bob Schminkey in May 2003.

RISA Charitable Trust provides loan guarantees for a woman-owned housing finance company and Peulwana Financial Services to provide small loans for employed low-income people to expand or build new homes in the Johannesburg area. RISA supports its program through grants and Reinvestment Notes, which provide 3 to 5 percent interest depending upon the extent of the maturity and note amount. The minimum investment is $10,000.

Microfinance is a growing business model, especially in developing countries. As of December 31, 2003, according to the State of the Microcredit Summit Campaign Report 2004, 2,931 microcredit institutions loaned small amounts of money to over 80 million poor people in developing countries to create sustainable employment and wealth creation. Over 80 percent of loan recipients were women. This success has attracted western financial specialists to provide investment opportunities for social-oriented investors. Just over $500 million is committed to microcredit loans worldwide. According to the Association for Enterprise Opportunity, providing funding to low-income entrepreneurs would result in $16.5 billion in income to the new business owners, $10.3 billion in income for employees, $3.3 billion in increased net worth for new business owners, and $416 million in total welfare savings.

The Dexia Micro-Credit Fund (DMCF), Blue Orchard Finance s.a., was created in Geneva, Switzerland, in September 1998 as the first microfinance loan obligation project. As of early 2005, its net asset value was about $55 million. Dexia is a diversified fund financing forty-four banks and financial intermediaries, which in turn invest in microenterprises operating in twenty countries.[35] The Dexia portfolio is diversified; the five largest financial intermediaries are located in Ecuador (8.02 percent), Bolivia (5.01 percent), Dominican Republic (4.81 percent), Cambodia (4.01 percent), and India (4.01percent).[36] Investments can be made in U.S. dollars, Swiss francs, or Euros. About 40 percent of the fund is held by institutional investors, pension funds, and insurance companies, while about seventy investors have just less than $100,000 using over twenty commercial depository banks and several asset managers.[37] Fund composition is 41.59 percent institutional clients, 55.06 percent private clients, and 2.68 percent SRI funds.[38] The fund seems to be growing in popularity, especially in Europe. The foreign exchange risk is hedged on a monthly basis for the Swiss and Euro share classes against the U.S. dollar.

Blue Orchard is open to retail investors for a minimum investment of $10,000. The fund has returned 6.8 percent net of fees in 2001 and 4.1 percent in 2002, according to Alexandre de Lesseps, co-owner of Blue Orchard.[39] Blue Orchard was founded by the former United Nations microfinance specialists Cedric Lombard and Jean-Philippe de Schrevel.

Developing World Markets, an investment advisory group based in Washington, DC, recently closed a $40 million securitization of loans by microfinance institutions for Blue Orchard Finance. The proceeds were lent to nine microfinance institutions in Bolivia, Cambodia, Ecuador, Nicaragua, Peru, and Russia which will be used to make new loans to an estimated forty thousand low-income small business owners, of which about half will be women.[40] Blue Orchard expects to close another $40 million securitization of microfinance loans by mid-2005.

Other interesting opportunities occasionally come up for social investors. For example, I was recently able to review an offering memorandum to capitalize Fonkoze Capital, LLC, in New York, which plans to purchase Bank Fonkoze S.A. in Haiti. The bank will then provide microcredit for small merchants in Haiti. One of the initial investors is the Calvert Foundation.

Another example of a social-oriented investment opportunity is Equal Exchange, a seventeen-year-old fair trade coffee collective offered by Financial West Group, which owns 40 percent of PAM. Equal Exchange, a $10 million dealer in coffee, tea, and cocoa, not only pays farmers a fair price for their products, but also provides advance credit for crop production, and trades directly with developing country democratic farmer cooperatives. Equal Exchange's revenues have grown an average of 35 percent annually, and it is owned by forty worker-owners.[41]

An investment in Equal Exchange will primarily finance the purchase of organic coffee (85 percent of total) carrying the Transfair USA seal, meaning that Equal Exchange will be paying producers a guaranteed minimum of $1.26 per pound. The rest of the approximately $500,000 offering will finance employee salaries, marketing, and working capital. The largest loan to support Equal Exchange came from Shared Interest, the British fair trade financial intermediary, which has been financed, in turn, by Oikocredit.

Linda Pei, founder of the Women's Equity Mutual Fund and Pro-Conscience Funds, Inc., is currently working on the development of a Community Investment Income Fund to increase capital access to disadvantaged communities in the United States, and minority and women-owned businesses. Pei's fund, a Delaware Business Trust, plans to invest in securities that provide a secondary market and financing vehicle for community development and small business loan originators. It will provide leverage and appropriate diversification to make it worthwhile for large institutional investors to participate. Nothing is easy, especially coming out of a three-year bear market; but if anybody can make it work, Linda Pei is the person.

Social venture investing through venture funds and individual private placements has been gaining momentum among investors who are attempting to put money directly in the hands of local community entrepreneurs, as well as target investments to specific environmental or "clean technologies." According to Cleantech Venture Network, LLC, nearly one in ten venture deals is now in clean technologies. Just over $325 million was invested in fifty-seven emerging Cleantech companies in the first quarter of 2003. According to Cleantech Venture Monitor, this was an increase of nearly 50 percent over the fourth quarter of 2002 and almost double the amount invested in the first quarter of 2002.

Unlike esoteric secondary market indexes and corporate PR driven "sustainability" and "corporate social responsibility," community and primary market investments create real jobs, housing, small businesses, economic development, and wealth. The community is where we begin to create a new economy.

7

Shareholder Revenge

About 100 million Americans don't vote and have pretty much ignored the electoral process and democratic participation. About the same number of individual investors in this country treat their shareholder voting rights in an identical fashion; they don't vote their shares. Historically this has been the case, and it probably won't change anytime soon.

Only about one-half of American households own stocks, and most of that stock is held through a retirement or pension plan, or an IRA or profit-sharing plan, largely out of sight and out of mind for most Americans. The distant investor may not even have voting rights, having delegated them to someone else, such as a retirement or investment board, an elected or appointed board, or to a broker, financial planner, or God forbid, an investment advisor.

Investors may also buy bonds or certificates of deposit (CDs) or be the beneficial owners of mutual funds that only invest in bonds or CDs, generally called "income funds," "bond funds," or "fixed-income funds." None of these assets provide voting rights to investors. Even if an investor holds shares of a stock mutual fund, the investor is the beneficial owner and doesn't vote the shares; the portfolio manager or investment advisor votes company shares on behalf of the mutual fund investor. Thanks to the SEC, mutual funds and investment advisors will now have to disclose how they vote at annual shareholder meetings.

Common stock shares are the results of buying equity in a publicly or privately traded company or corporation. For our purposes, we'll discuss only publicly traded securities, or common stock of companies traded on stock exchanges in the United States. These shares represent ownership. Even if you have only one share, you are entitled to vote that share and attend an annual shareholders meeting, voting on matters of ordinary business—usually to elect the board of directors, approve the annual selection of auditors, or on any other matter that comes before the shareholders meeting. Corporations only hold these annual meetings because they are required to do so by law. Most corporate CEOs and directors don't like shareholders, unless that shareholder is Warren Buffet (Governor Schwarzenegger's finance guru) or someone with whom they play golf in the Bahamas or spend time with on Martha's Vineyard. They think all shareholders only want their free coffee, donuts, or Big Macs every year and should restrain their remarks to questions about where to park or where to hold the next annual meeting. They don't mind too much if you come to the meeting to praise them, or to wish them or their wives happy birthday, or to tell corporate management how much you enjoyed the handsome photo display in the annual report. (I've actually heard all of these comments at annual meetings.)

At Harrington Investments, Inc., we've always believed that corporations ignore us because we are so obnoxious and "uppity" in wanting to exercise our shareholder rights and freedom of speech. More often than not, companies don't answer our telephone calls, don't respond to our correspondence, and often "lose" our shareholder resolutions. It turns out we don't have to take it personally; it is not just we who are being ignored.

Corporate management, with the help of mainstream media, usually disparages shareholder advocates, using pejorative references to those introducing resolutions or speaking at annual shareholder meetings. The late John and Lewis Gilbert, who introduced hundreds of resolutions and were an important part of the landmark 1947 case *SEC v. TransAmerica*, which defined shareholder rights, were dismissed as gadflies for over sixty years. Corporate management used the term in an attempt to ridicule the Lewis brothers' important groundbreaking advocacy.

The American Heritage dictionary defines a gadfly as "one habitually engaged in provocative criticism of existing institutions, typically as an individual citizen." More importantly, Socrates referred to himself as a gadfly in *The Apology* before the Court of Justice in Athens:

> God has sent me to attack the city, as if it were a great and noble
> house, to use a quaint simile, which was rather sluggish from its
> size, and which needed to be aroused by a gadfly: and I think that
> I am the gadfly that God has sent to the city to attack it; for I never
> cease from setting upon you, as it were, at every point, and rousing,
> and extorting, and reproaching each man of you all day long.

John and Lewis Gilbert were truly gadflies in the tradition of Socrates, as their lives were committed to raising important corporate governance issues. The last shareholder resolution introduced by John Gilbert, predeceased by his brother Lewis, was in 2001. He received almost 20 percent of the shareholder vote on a resolution to limit executive compensation.

According to a November 2002 study by WhisperNumber.com, a research firm that studies investor sentiment, 80 percent of respondents said corporate investor-relations offices aren't individual-investor friendly.[1] After receiving the results of the study, the staff of the *Wall Street Journal* sent email questionnaires to the investor relations offices of Time Warner, Microsoft, Altria, Coca-Cola, Verizon, Berkshire Hathaway, Eastman Kodak, American Express, and Disney. Most offices failed to respond, and those which did neglected to answer the reporters' questions.

Institutional investors—including mutual funds, private and public pension systems, colleges and universities, environmental and religious organizations, and public interest nonprofits and foundations—hold the largest percentages of common stock and thus are more likely to occasionally receive corporate responses. For example, as of January 2005, CALPERS had assets totaling $168 billion. It votes its stock proxies at annual corporate shareholder meetings. Institutions hold more than 50 percent of the equity in 71.3 percent of the largest one thousand corporations and more than 90 percent of the equity in forty of them.[2] Institutional ownership of U.S. corporations has grown and is mostly concentrated in large corporations. Institutional fund managers control about 19 percent of the stock in American corporations on behalf of almost 100 million individual investors.

Individual shareholders should not continue to ignore the opportunity of voting their stock proxies at annual meetings. It is simply a fact of life in corporate-dominated America that individual shareholders have been marginalized because they have remained silent and non-attentive for decades. It is even been reported that people who buy individual stocks read annual reports less than 18 percent of the time.[3] At least I hope they look at the pretty pictures.

Corporate princes so dislike shareholders that they are leading the charge to change state corporation codes to permit companies to conduct "online" shareholder meetings. Delaware has been joined by Michigan, Maryland, California, and Oklahoma in amending statutes to allow "remote communication." Now corporate executives won't have to face many of us in person anymore, when they hold their meetings in "remote" locations. I'll bet the coming trend is satellite remote communication from board and shareholder meetings in the Bahamas, and other resort locations.

SHAREHOLDER RIGHTS

Corporate management controls the nomination of directors, the proxy solicitation process, and has exclusive access to shareholders, unless someone, generally a large institutional investor, has deep enough pockets to hire a proxy solicitation service to gain access to all other corporate owners at a cost of about $2 per shareholder. Unfortunately, because most individuals and many smaller institutional shareholders are only identified under a "street name" in corporate shareholder records, the broker dealer must "pass through" solicitation material to individual shareholders, identified as "beneficial owners." This not only delays the formal communication process but also adds another layer of impersonal bureaucracy.

Even in small companies, it is expensive for dissident shareholders to challenge corporate management's nominated directors. James Mitarotonda, a New York investor who won election to the board of Liquid Audio, said the proxy fight cost him at least $500,000 in legal fees, postage, and travel on top of the roughly $3 million spent to solicit the vote.[4] The battle can cost more if, as is often the case, management litigates to slow down the process.

In 2003 the SEC solicited public comment on a proposal to allow limited shareholder access to the corporate director nominating process, but only if 35 percent of shares in the prior year were withheld for any company-nominated director or a majority of shares had been voted in favor of a shareholder resolution, opposed by management. The proposed rule has been denounced by corporations, and the U.S. Chamber of Commerce has threatened to sue the SEC if it is adopted. Many corporate CEOs say that the rule would undermine their ability to run *their* companies as they see fit and giving shareholders limited power to nominate directors would corrupt the board process and open companies to the whims of special interests.[5]

Of over nine thousand letters to the SEC commenting on the nominating proposal, most corporations and trade groups opposed the idea, including the Investment Company Institute, the mutual fund industry trade group.

The overwhelming majority of corporate director nominees are selected by the chairman or CEO, often one and the same person, since few corporations have an independent nominating committee. Even if the SEC allows limited opportunities for non-board controlled nominees to be submitted to a shareholder vote, it will take many years to implement and have no immediate impact. According to Sarah Teslik, former executive director of the Council of Institutional Investors, which represents more than 130 pension funds and over $3 trillion in assets: "If fifth-graders picked their teachers, fifth-graders would get A's. As long as boards are chosen by the people they're supposed to oversee, oversight won't happen. It's that simple."[6]

Even before the mutual fund disclosure law took effect, the AFL-CIO supported an alternative slate of directors at El Paso Corporation, which received 47.5 percent of the vote. Mutual funds refused to disclose their vote, even after Richard L. Trumka, secretary-treasurer of the AFL-CIO, asked the fifty largest mutual fund companies to voluntarily disclose how they voted in the 2003 proxy season.[7] Bill Patterson, director of investment for the AFL-CIO, says that big mutual fund managers like Fidelity do not want to anger companies that are current or prospective clients for mutual fund services, such as employee retirement plan management.[8]

Numerous SRI portfolio managers, including Harrington Investments, Inc., have addressed the SEC rule change regarding nominating directors by calling for a series of changes:

- Greater access to the ballot by allowing investors holding an aggregate of 1 percent of the outstanding shares to nominate a candidate or candidates to the board of directors;
- Banning broker votes or unsolicited share voting;
- Annually electing all directors to prevent corporate management from staggering board terms, so a change of the board would take only one year not several years;
- Cumulative voting, so minority shareholders could pool their votes and have some representation (so that not all directors are elected by 50 percent plus one share);
- Full nominee personal and financial disclosure in the proxy material to shareholders;
- Elimination of the "for" and "withhold" options, replaced on the proxy card with "for," "against," and "abstain" for the election of directors, which is what is currently required for voting on shareholder resolutions;
- Equal space on the proxy card for all candidates for election to the board;
- Annual attendance required to the shareholders meeting for all directors.

In his letter to the SEC regarding shareholder nominations of corporate directors, Stephen Davis, president of Davis Global Advisors, Inc., indicated that even if an overwhelming majority of shareholders under the current system vote to "withhold" their votes, it has no legal effect and the director with a minority of votes can still be elected. Sara Teslik was more direct. She said: "The direct result of a withhold vote is nothing."[9] Of course this contradicts the public relations campaign created by mutual fund managers in 2002 when corporate governance pressure was mounting and mutual fund voting transparency was being questioned. A *Wall Street Journal* article from June 11, 2002, reported that Bill Miller, manager of $13 billion in two mutual funds at Less Mason, was taking credit for "withholding" his vote from directors at six companies in the 2002 proxy season. What a brave stand about nothing. Stephen Davis also called for an end to broker votes without instructions from shareholders because such votes are always in favor of management's recommendations. In his letter to the SEC, he said: ". . . the current system has become an outmoded management entrenchment device that serves to undermine rather than spur corporate performance."

Current SEC rules require companies to put proposed stock option plans to shareholder votes and prohibit brokerage firms from voting non-instructed shares in management's favor. The rules, however, do not prohibit brokers from voting on the election of auditors and directors, proposals to increase the number of shares (which dilutes shareholders), and cash compensation for CEOs. ADP Corporation, the big processor of proxy votes, reported that 23 percent of the votes in the 2002 proxy season were cast by brokerage firms that lacked instructions from shareholders, and that *every vote* by the firms supported management.[10] ADP also reported that small investors are the least likely to vote, saying that only 41.5 percent of ballots from holders of one thousand or fewer shares were returned.

Regardless of any rule changes the SEC makes in the future, investors must vote, even if such a vote is "advisory" or simply represents disgruntlement and will not oust management. Investor indifference is no less debilitating for corporate democracy as voter apathy is debilitating for participatory democracy.

The current shareholder resolution process needs drastic and revolutionary attention and change. Almost all shareholder resolutions, even those with large approving majorities, are advisory only, and can be—and often are—totally ignored by corporate management. SEC Rule 14a-8(i)(1) allows corporate management to exclude most mandatory proposals as "not a proper subject for action by shareholders" under the corporate law of the company's state of incorporation, or both the board of directors and the shareholders would have to approve a mandatory proposal. The rules of the game have been rigged in their favor, as have most of our laws at the state and federal level, including judicial rulings.

What are considered pure "corporate governance" issues, such as resolutions calling for the elimination of staggered board terms for corporate directors ("Classified Board"), have received majority shareholder votes, often several years in a row. As of early August, a record 139 shareholder resolutions received majority votes in 2003, according to Institutional Shareholder Services.[11]

Corporate management has a long record of ignoring shareholders. At Intel, Hewlett-Packard, Apple Computer and IBM, shareholders have voted against management in favor of expensing stock options. In 2004, 68 percent of Gillette shares supported a resolution asking the company to repeal its classified (staggered) board elections in favor of annual elections. In 2003 the vote was 64 percent in favor and in 2002, it was 56 percent in favor. Gillette continues to ignore the majority of its owners.

The good news: A recent study found that firms with the strongest shareholder rights significantly outperform companies with weaker shareholder rights. A 2001 study of 1,500 firms conducted by researchers at Harvard University and the University of Pennsylvania's Wharton School found a significant positive relationship between greater shareholder rights, including annual election of directors as measured by a governance index, and both firm valuation and performance from 1990 to 1999.

In addition, a recent report found that there is a positive correlation between corporate social performance and corporate financial performance. Every year the Social Investment Forum (SIF) and Co-op America sponsor the Moskowitz Prize, based upon outstanding research in the field of socially responsible investing. In December 2004, the award went to Marc Orlitzky, Frank Schmidt and Sara Rynes for their research paper entitled: *Corporate Social and Financial Performance: A Meta-Analysis.* The paper examined over fifty academic reports, concluding that "there was a positive association between corporate social performance and financial performance across industries and across study contexts." The authors reported that the link "varies (from highly positive to modestly positive) because of contingencies, such as reputation effects, market measures of financial performance, or corporate social performance disclosures." The study also found that corporate social performance was a better predictor of financial performance using accounting measures than market-based ones.

The better news: While most of the approved resolutions are considered corporate governance and supported by large institutional investors, most of those votes were also aided by SRI mutual fund and SRI portfolio managers. Under pressure from Calvert Group and other SRI managers, Dell Computer agreed to set goals and measure progress in the recycling of its computers and pledged to do what it could to stop exporting computer work to developing countries. Occasionally, companies will see the handwriting on the wall and respond. For example, in a confrontation at the annual shareholder meeting of Safeway, the company announced that it would name three new independent directors and begin expensing options in 2005.[12]

Larger votes for social and environmental resolutions began appearing in 2002. A campaign by Responsible Wealth, a group of wealthy donors and shareholders supported by Shareholder Action Network (SAN), and three lawsuits against Household International, led 27 percent of the shareholders to vote for a resolution linking executive pay to measures to prevent predatory lending. The resolution was introduced by NorthStar Asset Management and Domini Social Investments.

At ExxonMobil, 29 percent of shareholders voted in 2003 to adopt a policy prohibiting discrimination on the basis of sexual orientation (the vote was 24 percent in 2002), and more than 20% of shareholders supported two resolutions: one requiring the company to report on how it would increase investments in renewable energy and another on how it would respond to the risks of global warming. While ExxonMobil has pledged $10 million per year for ten years to Stanford University for climate research, it also funds numerous Washington, DC-based groups that question the human role in global warming and argue that proposed government policies to limit carbon dioxide emissions are excessive. ExxonMobil largely supports such groups as the Competitive Enterprise Institute, Frontiers of Freedom, The George C. Marshall Institute, the American Council of Capital Formation, Center for Policy Research, and the American Legislative Exchange Council (ALEC).

According to the Investor Responsibility Research Center (IRRC), more than 1,053 shareholder resolutions were introduced in 2003, up from 802 in 2002. SocialFunds.com reported there have been 760 corporate governance resolutions filed in 2003 (about half by labor unions), up from 529 in 2002. Over 40 percent dealt with executive compensation, which is not surprising, considering that the highest-paid CEOs over a three-year period received $219 million (Steve Jobs at Apple), $87 million (John Chambers at Cisco), and $51 million (John Blystone, now retired, of SPX Corp.).[13] In March 2003 the AFL-CIO resolution at Tyco to limit executive severance packages received almost 51 percent of the shareholder vote.

One of the most significant civil rights victories of the 2003 shareholder season was Wal-Mart's agreement to prohibit discrimination based on sexual orientation in its company policy. Unlike ExxonMobil, which is the only one among the top seventy-one companies in the Fortune 500 to not have a gay and lesbian workers' rights policy, Wal-Mart worked with the Pride Foundation and other organizations to adopt a non-discrimination policy. Ironically, Wal-Mart is currently being sued in a class action suit for discriminating against 1.6 million female employees. There are 318 Fortune 500 companies that have similar gay rights policies, and 197 that offer benefits to same-sex partners.[14]

In December 2002, the state of New York enacted the Sexual Orientation Non-Discrimination Act, prohibiting companies from discriminating on the basis of sexual orientation. Dover Corporation is one of the largest New York employers, and in 2003, over 42 percent of the shares voted by shareholders were in favor of amending the company's non-discrimination policy to explicitly include sexual orientation. According to Human Rights Campaign, major companies headquartered in New York which explicitly prohibit this form of discrimination in their written policies include AIG, Time Warner, Citigroup, Goldman Sachs, IBM, International Paper, Merrill Lynch, MetLife, J. P. Morgan Chase, Morgan Stanley, PepsiCo, Pfizer, Philip Morris, and Verizon.

Some shareholder advocates believe the SRI community is overly concerned with passive securities screening and not enough with shareholder action. Lance Lindblom, president and CEO of the New York-based Nathan Cummings Foundation, says that "the real leverage for change is acting like

owners instead of stock traders."[15] He argues that all too often foundations delegate investment decisions to portfolio managers and only evaluate them on the basis of quarterly returns. And most managers, Lindblom
believes, have no concept of corporate ownership or stewardship and are
only trading to maximize short-term financial returns. By delegating voting
power to portfolio managers, he says, foundations abrogate their ownership responsibility, because portfolio managers do not have a commitment
to the foundation's mission, nor know how to implement a comprehensive
investment strategy to fulfill that mission.

I believe that there is a disconnect between the trading nature of investment management, which is impersonal, short-term and only aimed
at maximizing performance numbers and the idea of responsible long-
term ownership—there is currently no relationship between the owners
of capital and the managers of a corporation. Sixty-five years ago, Berle
and Means, in their book *The Modern Corporation and Private Property*,
claimed that the concentration of economic powers that are separate from
owners creates economic empires, and relegates owners "to the position of
those who supply the means whereby the new princes may exercise their
power." They went on to say shareholders have ". . . exchanged control for
liquidity."

Occasionally, organizations will buy stock in an attempt to gain access
to corporate management as a shareholder, as well as use the media to
capture attention. In 1999, the Reverend Jesse Jackson announced that his
nonprofit group, Rainbow/PUSH Coalition, bought $51,000 of shares in
fifty-one technology companies specifically to gain access to shareholders'
meetings so it could pressure management to add minorities to corporate
boards of directors and staff, and to urge large corporations to do more
business with minority firms. Other than receiving some media attention,
obtaining a $100,000 contribution from Intel and Cisco, and picking up
a few minority internship positions, the Rainbow/PUSH Coalition made
little headway in meeting its main objective.

No matter how good the personal relationship is between shareholders
(individual or institutional) and corporate management's representatives,
the fact remains that resolutions are advisory only and mostly ignored

by management. This will lead us to another discussion later in the book on alternative strategies to check the almost unlimited power of corporate management. One strategy discussed by Hawley and Williams in *The Rise of Fiduciary Capitalism* reminds us that ". . . in addition to submitting proxies, some institutions have begun to submit amendments to the corporation bylaws. The important distinction is that bylaw amendments are binding changes in the constitution of a corporation while proxies are only advisory."[16]

On the other hand, many shareholder advocates recognize that there is power in simply confronting corporate management through the resolution process and that, in effect, is leverage. As one advocate said: "Shareholder resolutions on a number of topics have presented the issue in a forceful and public way. Whether it's effective or not, it's perceived as effective, which means it is effective."

Some companies have opposed shareholder resolutions, only to later adopt the substance of a resolution. Carol Bowie, director of governance research at the IRRC, an independent research organization that sells information to institutional investors on corporate governance and CSR issues, witnesses many companies reversing course on expensing stock options because there is a political price to be paid otherwise. "It would be very shortsighted to discount the impact of shareholder activists on corporate change. It may be slow, subtle, and difficult to measure, but I doubt we would see any change at all if not for that activity."[17]

Individual investors can introduce shareholder resolutions if they have held the stock one year and the market value is no less than $2,000. Normally, a company will attempt to convince the shareholder to drop the resolution, and management's attorneys will file a "no action" letter to request that the SEC allow the company to omit the resolution from the proxy material on a technical SEC Rules violation, usually claiming that the resolution submitted relates to "ordinary business" and should be excluded from the shareholders' view. For example, at least twenty-nine corporate governance proposals out of more the 552 submitted in 2001 were thrown out on grounds that they related to a company's "ordinary business."[18] Harvey Pitt, the former Chairman of the SEC, when speaking before six hundred members of the Council of Institutional Investors in Manhattan in 2002 said: "It is my hope that we can eliminate this exception, making shareholder suffrage a reality."[19] Well, we're still a long way from suffrage, and the SEC isn't likely to make this quantum leap anytime soon.

SEC Rule 14a-8(i)(7) gives corporate management the authority to exclude a proposal from its proxy material because the resolution relates to an ordinary business operation. An exception would be allowed under Exchange Act Release No. 40018 if the proposal focuses on "sufficiently significant social policy issues," because as such they would "transcend the day-to-day business matters." Obviously, this is a gray issue, still left to the SEC to determine on a case-by-case basis.

On September 15, 2004, the SEC released Staff Legal Bulletin No. 14 B (CF) clarifying the guidelines it will use when reviewing statements by corporate management in proxy materials. Basically, it limited the technical reasons that management can use to ask the SEC to exclude shareholder resolutions. This will, in all probability, result in more shareholder resolutions being included in corporate shareholder proxy materials in the years to come, thus allowing owners to voice their opinion on a growing number of issues.

The Social Investment Forum produced a report in 1997 entitled: "Shareholder Rights Analysis: The Impact of Proposed SEC Rules on the Submission of Shareholder Resolutions," which found that from 1986 to 1995, an average of 226 companies, or 15 percent out of the largest 1,500 companies, actually faced votes on shareholder resolutions. The report cited an SEC study showing that an average company spends $36,603 per shareholder proposal.

The most famous—or infamous—case of a company attempting to exclude a resolution on "ordinary business" grounds was in 1992 when Cracker Barrel was alleged to have a discriminatory policy of not employing gays and lesbians. The New York City Employees Retirement System attempted to introduce a shareholder resolution pushing for a non-discrimination policy, but the SEC ruled that it was a personnel issue and therefore "ordinary business." The SEC staff issued a "no action" letter, meaning that if the company excluded the resolution from the proxy material, the SEC would take no action. Predictably, the company excluded the resolution and was promptly challenged by the Interfaith Center on Corporate Responsibility (ICCR), New York and other SRI investors. Eventually, the Cracker Barrel SEC ruling was reversed, and the company changed its policy.

Shareholder resolutions are designed to get management's attention on an important issue that may have a financial impact on the company. Many issues may be seen as social or environmental, but all such issues eventually involve financial and public relations risks.

In the case of Cracker Barrel, it was a domestic employment discrimination issue. Most of the time, however, shareholder issues reach across national boundaries, impacting large populations and markets. When human rights are at stake and a U.S.-based company is involved, shareholders have a responsibility to act.

THE CHINA CONUNDRUM

The People's Republic of China has adopted the U.N. Declaration of Human Rights and other U.N. covenants into Chinese law. These laws prohibit racial or sexual discrimination, arbitrary arrest, torture, and extrajudicial executions. Chinese laws also assert citizens' freedom of speech and association, as well as freedom to join a trade union. Unfortunately none of these laws are enforced by the government, and China is considered one of the most repressive governments in the world, calculated on the basis of extrajudicial executions or disappearances, torture, prisoners of conscience, and official violence against citizens.

The country, ruled by a communist party dictatorship, has been an economic powerhouse based on cheap natural resources, cheap labor, and a large and growing consumer market. While business booms, labor, human rights, and environmental laws go unenforced. China is also a major exporter of raw material, agricultural products, manufactured goods, electronics, toys, textiles, and weapons. The strong Chinese economy is the main reason that the United States runs a monthly multi-billion dollar trade deficit.

China is well suited for manufacturing technology, a reflection of its $19 billion market for semiconductors.[20] A 2003 World Bank International Finance Corporation report had predicted that, by 2005, the country would be making more electronics than all of Western Europe, thanks primarily to an abundance of cheap labor.[21]

But China's record on human rights issues, to put it mildly, is sorely lacking. In his book *Socially Responsible Investment: A Global Revolution,* Russell Sparkes writes: "China is the most important oppressive regime in terms of the sheer number of Western companies operating there."[22]

Global Exchange, Amnesty International, and the International Labor Rights Fund developed a voluntary code of conduct for companies operating in China following a 1999 report on labor abuses in factories which produced clothing for Disney. Initially, Reebok, Levi Strauss, and Mattel signed on to the principles.

China currently leads the race to the bottom in regard to wages, as factories relentlessly cut costs, and require 18-hour days with minimal training. Often the starting salary is 40 percent below China's official minimum wage, or about $32 a month.[23]

Writing in the *Third World Quarterly* in 2003, Anita Chan and Robert Ross pointed out that the issue of minimum wages in China is much more complex:

> In China the setting of a minimum wage is extremely decentralized. Each city, or even a district in a city, can set its own minimum wage based on a formula provided by the central government that takes into account factors such as the cost of living in the locality, the prevailing wage, and the rate of inflation. The minimum wage is adjusted each year. On paper, local governments comply with the central government's decrees about raising minimum wage level annually to keep up with inflation. In reality, the wages of migrant industrial workers are often considerably lower than the official legal standards. Moreover, according to a survey Anita Chan conducted of China's footwear industry, the average number of work hours each day came to 11, often with no days off. Nor do the official statis-

tics take into consideration the staggering amount of wages owed but not paid to migrant workers. Local governments in Guangdong province periodically launch campaigns, especially just before Chinese New Year, to collect unpaid wages and/or unpaid overtime wages. When the illegally long work hours and the unpaid wages are taken into account, a sizeable proportion of the workers are making considerably less than the legal minimum wage.

In China, subsistent wages and overtime go together. According to Verité, overtime is defined as work hours exceeding 60 hours per week. It is so widespread that 93 percent of the factories it audited for International Brands in 2002 and 2003 had instances of excessive overtime.[24]

China also ranks high worldwide when it comes to corruption. In a 2002 study entitled "Corruption and International Valuation: Does Virtue Pay?" authors Charles M.C. Lee and David T. Ng of Cornell University discovered that China ranked forty-second out of forty-six for corruption, which was correlated with lower valuations for Chinese companies. The study sought to determine if corruption had an impact on shareholder valuation. It did indeed! Pakistan scored the lowest for shareholder valuation and highest for corruption, while Denmark with the lowest amount of corruption was valued at the top.

China's repressive government has everything corporate management wants and needs to maximize profits. Just about every major corporation is stampeding into China. With China's entry into the WTO, the stage is set for unbridled growth—assuming, of course, that the state banks and corporations do not collapse, unemployment in the major population centers doesn't get out of hand, inflation doesn't take off, the Chinese currency doesn't implode, China's large poor rural population doesn't rebel, and pollution, industrial growth and vehicle traffic doesn't destroy the environment.

In the past, China, unlike other communist countries such as North Korea, Vietnam, and Cuba, annually received congressional approval for Most Favored Nation (MFN) status, which exacerbated our country's trade deficit by making it cheaper and easier to import goods from China. From a human and labor rights standpoint, the benefit was an annual congressional review of progress, if any, that the Chinese government was making, including other issues related to political and economic policies. This was always an opportunity for rights advocates to inform Congress, and to perhaps apply pressure to the Chinese government to release dissidents or democracy advocates in China and improve its human rights record.

In 2000, President Clinton pressed Congress to enact Permanent Normal Trade Relations (PNTR) for China which eliminated the annual review of China's trade status. It also eliminated any leverage the United States had to pressure the communist dictatorship to improve human rights or advance democracy. According to the U.S. State Department, as China has received more Western investment and trade, the Chinese government has increased human rights abuses. Things have gotten worse, not better.

This result is no different than the suppression of the non-white majority by the white minority under apartheid in South Africa. As Western investments and trade increased, so did the violation of human rights. A stronger economy and a stronger authoritarian government do not weaken the resolve of the oppressor, but tighten the grip and provide the government more tools to force its will on the population. In South Africa, it was only after the majority of that nation's population took to the streets, and forces outside the country worked together to reduce capital transfers, limit trade, ban new bank loans and investments, and enforce mandatory economic sanctions, that apartheid collapsed from within.

Compared to China, workers in the textile industry in Bangladesh must be on easy street. Many workers (mostly young women) work seventy hours a week and average about twenty cents an hour with overtime. The Multi-Fiber Arrangement, an international trade pact that uses quotas to regulate about $450 billion in garment trade, expired at the end of 2004, and most of the Bangladesh textile jobs are expected to move to China.[25] This will make large retailers like Wal-Mart happy, since, as the *Wall Street Journal* reports: "With its economies of scale, cheap labor and integrated cotton, textile and garment industries, China probably will beat any other exporter on price. The World Bank estimates that China will control nearly half of the world's clothing exports by 2010, up from 20 percent today."[26]

Since the enactment of PNTR, the Chinese government has continued to repress the population, including terrorizing ethnic minorities in the country, and harassing, imprisoning, and torturing Falun Gong members, a peaceful and nonviolent organization practicing its religion. The government also continues to provide nuclear weapons technology to Pakistan and at one time supplied fiber optic technology to the Hussein government in Iraq to shoot down U.S. aircraft over the "no fly" zone. While Chinese law prohibits human rights abuse, it is not enforced, and foreign and domestic companies, including government industries, regularly violate labor rights, including physical abuse, forced labor, child labor, and dangerous working conditions. The Chinese government does not permit the existence of any group that could potentially challenge its authority, including religious organizations and independent trade unions.

According to *China's Golden Shield: Corporations and the Development of Surveillance Technology in the People's Republic of China* (International Center for Human Rights and Democratic Development, 2001), U.S. and Canadian technology and telecommunications companies are providing strategic and sensitive advanced technology to the Chinese government: "China's Golden Shield project threatens the protection of human rights—in particular the right to privacy—a right that underpins other essential elements of democracy activism such as freedom of association and freedom of expression. It positions the alliance of government and business in opposition to those standing on the cyber-frontline of the human rights movement in China today."

Some of this technology is specifically being used by the military and police to spy on the Chinese population and identify dissidents. Companies identified by name include Cisco Systems and Sun Microsystems. Harrington Investments, Inc. discussions with staff at Microsoft and Oracle clearly revealed business links with Chinese military authorities and police. Microsoft, for example, signed an agreement with the Chinese Information Technology Security Certification Center so that it could participate in Microsoft's Government Security Program. Microsoft Chairman Bill Gates said in part: "As a government customer and trusted partner, we are committed to providing the Chinese government with information that will help them deploy and maintain secure computing infrastructures."[27]

In an effort to tighten media control ahead of a major Communist Party Congress, China blocked Google—a U.S. Internet search engine—in September 2003. Given China's estimated 45 million Internet users, it is clear that technology can either be a tool to advance access to information and free expression or an instrument of authoritarian rule and censorship. In January 2001, Human Rights Watch reported that a new Chinese government regulation made it a capital crime to send "secret" or "reactionary" information over the Internet. Chinese regulations limit news postings on U.S.-based company Web sites operating in China. The English chat room of SOHU.com, partly owned by Dow Jones, posts a list of issues prohibited on the Internet by Chinese law, including criticism of the Chinese constitution, topics which damage China's reputation, discussion that undermines China's religious policy, and "any discussion and promotion of content which PRC laws prohibit."

Some American companies seem to be ethically challenged and have no qualms about doing business in China and providing the government with censorship and surveillance technologies and creating what Ethan Gutmann, author of *Losing the New China*, calls "the world's greatest Big Brother Internet." The reason, he says, of course, is money. "Building China's Internet meant making lots of it for some of the big players such as Cisco, Eriksson, Motorola, Nokia, and Nortel." China has become a money-making machine for information technology companies.

U.S. technology companies, such as IBM, were of strategic importance to the maintenance of the pass system in apartheid South Africa. Long before apartheid, however, IBM's punch card and card sorting system was used in 1933 to automate human destruction by identifying and moving Jews to concentration camps under Adolf Hitler's "final solution." Hitler also targeted gypsies, homosexuals, the mentally ill, and prisoners. As Edwin Block described in his book *IBM and the Holocaust*, "IBM's subsidiary, with the knowledge of its New York headquarters, enthusiastically custom-designed the complex devices and specialized applications as an official corporate undertaking. . . IBM NY always understood—from the outset in 1933—that it was courting and doing business with the upper echelon of the Nazi Party."

IBM never lost its taste for authoritarian governments or the corporation's love of money and provided key services for the South African government. In Germany, technology was invaluable to the Nazis to control and murder large population groups. In South Africa, technology was invaluable in eliminating a skilled labor bottleneck when not enough whites were available to keep the apartheid wheels greased. Technology helped the government run efficiently without the need to educate and train non-whites. Technology was also utilized, not unlike the case in Germany, to identify, monitor, and control the movements of potential opponents of apartheid in South Africa. In China, technology is again rearing its dark side to assist an authoritarian government in identifying, monitoring, controlling and in this case, assisting in the apprehension of pro-democracy advocates.

IBM had a love affair with Nazi Germany and South Africa's apartheid rulers, and now finds itself in bed with the Chinese authoritarian government, compounding the problem by outsourcing thousands of U.S. technology jobs to India and China. As many as 4,730 IBM programmers or "programming jobs" will move to India and China, and American IBM employees in the Application Management Services Group, comprising more than one-half of IBM's 315,000 employees, will be training their replacements, reported the *Wall Street Journal* in its December 15, 2003 edition. "By the end of the coming year (2004), one out of every ten jobs with U.S.-based computer services companies will move to emerging markets, as will one of every twenty technology jobs in other corporations, according to tech-industry researcher Gartner Inc.," the paper said. "Another research firm, International Data Corp., recently estimated that by 2007, 23 percent of all information-technology services jobs will be off-shore, up from 5 percent this year (2003)."

Manufacturing jobs were the first to leave the United States, now it's information technology jobs. What's next? In December, 2003, Linda Buyer, president of Alliance@IBM, a union that has been organizing IBM employees, predicted that about 40,000 of IBM's 160,000 jobs would be transferred overseas by 2005.[28] IBM claimed the number would be closer to 12,000. Other companies, such as Microsoft and AT&T Wireless, are joining IBM's exodus. Morgan Stanley estimated the number of jobs outsourced to

India would reach 150,000 in three years, and some analysts predicted that as many as 2 million U.S. white collar jobs, such as programmers, software engineers, and applications designers, will leave by 2014.[29]

Harrington Investments, Inc. (HII) located in Napa wine country in California, is not far from Silicon Valley. Like most social investors in the 1990s, HII invested in major global technology companies. California's high-tech industry is generally perceived to be more responsive than corporations in the rest of the nation when it comes to listening to shareholders and promoting policies that address social and environmental issues. This industry is also known for its wage and fringe benefit programs, positive response to employee concerns, leadership in affirmative action, and donations to community organizations. HII knew that technology companies were moving into China in a big way to gain a foothold on consumer and business markets, lured by the access to cheap labor for new manufacturing facilities. We initially wrote letters to Cisco Systems, Intel, and Hewlett-Packard, requesting copies of their human and labor rights policy in China as well as for their global operations. We received no response from any of the companies until we filed shareholder resolutions.

After some delay and after we showed proof that the resolution was indeed filed with the SEC, Cisco immediately arranged a meeting. Six Cisco management personnel participated and representatives from HII, Global Exchange, and Amnesty International met with them, receiving an agreement from the company to join the China Working Group (CWG), which had been created to work with companies and NGOs to share "best practices" and other information on China's unique working and business environment. Cisco pledged to work with the CWG to ensure that the principles were incorporated into Cisco's Global Human Resource Policies and Practices. Cisco representatives repeatedly and excitedly expressed the view that the Internet would break down all forms of authoritarian rule and spread democratic values throughout China. Even though we didn't agree with this widely optimistic view, we withdrew our resolution.

I doubt if the Chinese Communist Party sees things as Cisco representatives do. Actually, Cisco has helped the government close down Internet sites that post articles on political or constitutional reform. Cisco has been identified as being ". . . at the forefront of the development of firewalls in China."[30] Network firewalls are used by the Chinese government to block, monitor, and inhibit the use of Internet technology.

In 2003, a shareholder resolution was submitted to Cisco Systems, requesting a China report on the company's sales of "all hardware and software to all government agencies or information technology entities which allow monitoring, interception, keyword searches, and recording of the Internet, or which acts as a 'firewall.'" Not surprisingly, Cisco's management opposed the resolution, issuing a statement that the company and its competitors sell this equipment to many governments, including our own, which use the technology "for law enforcement, national security purposes and to protect their citizens against the threat of terrorism." In its argument against the resolution, the company also stated that the report would be time-consuming, costly, difficult, and impact its relationships with customers. Suffice it to say, the resolution failed. It did, however, confirm that companies, in their pursuit of profits, will sell technology to authoritarian governments, police, and security agents to spy on its citizens, to identify dissidents, and to repress human and individual rights.

At Intel, following several telephone conversations, a meeting was set up between the company's top China personnel and HII, and Global Exchange. Intel agreed to participate as an "observer" to the CWG and arrange for a tour of the company's Shanghai facility.

Hewlett-Packard (HP), on the other hand, was simply not concerned about human rights issues in China. HP was the first high-tech firm to operate in China, launching its first joint venture in 1985. Total HP China sales growth annualized at around 29 percent, and HP was the first foreign-invested information technology company to exceed sales of $1 billion. Now that HP has swallowed up Compaq, the extent of its investment in China and involvement with the military, police, and Internet security is unknown.

HII and the CWG staff repeatedly attempted to meet with HP's management, but it refused and only communicated in formal letters, including its Letter of Opposition to our reintroduced proposal in 2000. Melanie Vinson, corporate counsel of HP, indicated that a decision was made at the "highest level" of the corporation not to join the CWG. It became apparent to HII that something was going on in China with HP, or at least with Compaq China. According to the *Golden Shield* report: "Journalists reported that company representatives at Security China 2000 'refused to answer questions about the firm's involvement in the Golden Shield project . . .' Qin Li of Compaq China was equally evasive, claiming: 'We are not the only company [in China]; everybody's doing it. Go and ask Sun!'"[31]

The resolution to HP was presented in 2001 by Medea Benjamin, co-founder and corporate accountability director of Global Exchange. I presented the resolution in 2002, and it was resubmitted and voted upon again in 2003. In all three years it received about 8 percent of the shareholder vote, falling short of the 10 percent threshold in the third year, and could no longer be re-introduced. In 2003, HII totally divested stock in HP.

Global Exchange, Amnesty International, and HII continue to introduce resolutions that urge high tech and other firms to endorse the China Principles, or at the very least, join the CWG to share best practices and other experiences operating in China with other corporations. Companies are asked to work in a cooperative spirit with NGOs in China, to share information regarding government policies, including the implementation of company policies regarding labor and human rights. If companies cannot endorse the principles, we request that they incorporate the principles in their company's code of conduct. Several companies where we presented resolutions, such as 3Com, have agreed to participate in the CWG. Other companies, when approached, agreed to participate. Besides 3Com, Cisco and Intel, these companies include KLA-Tencor, Gap, Nike, Palm, and Target.

And besides HP, companies which refused to participate in the CWG or, in some cases, to meet or talk on the telephone with us, include Time Warner, Coca-Cola, Disney, McDonalds, Microsoft, IBM, Oracle, and Sun Microsystems.

After failing to get a "no action" letter to get the SEC to omit the resolution, some companies, such as Microsoft, reluctantly agreed to talk with us on the telephone, corralling the investor relations folks, along with their human resources staff and General Counsel. Microsoft staff tried to get us to withdraw the resolution, offering nothing in return. We were amazed at how unorganized, ill prepared, and uninformed these key staff members were about the specifics of the company's policy, and the resolution itself. In a September 20, 2000 telephone conversation with Microsoft representatives, none of them knew whether or not the company had a corporate policy for workers in China. They admitted that the company did not have a "specific labor code," and that it "never felt a pressing need to have one." They did say, however, that Microsoft had an employee handbook.

HII presented the China Business Principles three years in a row, requesting that Microsoft, at the very least, join the CWG and share best practices. The Microsoft resolution gained 8.2 percent the first year, 9.47 percent the second year and 7.47 percent the third year.

At Coca-Cola, the resolution was presented in both 2002 and 2003 by B. Wardlaw, an heir of one of the original Coke family founders, receiving 4.45 percent and 6.04 percent votes, respectively. In 2000 and 2001, Wardlaw had also introduced a shareholder resolution asking Coke to phase-out its use of genetically engineered corn used in the company's corn syrup.

The Walt Disney Company, which manufactures clothing and toys in China that allegedly utilize child labor, was the subject of an HII China Business Principles resolution in both 2002 and 2003. The resolution received 5.77 percent and 9.37 percent of the shareholder vote, respectively. It was re-filed in 2004 but did not receive 10 percent of the vote. It was presented on our behalf in 2002 by Responsible Wealth, which was presenting its own resolution on executive compensation. In presenting the resolutions, Harriet Denison and Nancy van Schoenderwoert explained: "The company lost money last year and laid off four thousand workers. Over the last five fiscal years, Disney's stock price declined 9 percent compared to an 86 percent increase in the S&P 500. Over the same period, Disney's chairman, Michael Eisner's total compensation exceeded $650 million. After Eisner announced that the resolution had been supported by 7 percent of the shareholders and therefore failed, about three people clapped. Eisner looked into the audience and joked: 'Thanks, Mother.'"[32] For $650 million, I bet you'd have a great sense of humor, too, and probably never take your Mickey Mouse ears off.

Perhaps it is a problem with technology companies or the fact that their staff has less experience fielding shareholder communications, but when HII began writing Sun Microsystems in February 2000 about its operations in China, we received no response. We wrote again in October 2000, and still received no response. In May of 2001, we filed our proposal and still heard nothing from the company. HII became convinced that Sun Microsystems did not want to talk to us about its operations in China when the *Golden Shield* report stated: "Sun Microsystems is indeed involved in transferring high-tech expertise to the Chinese security apparatus. Working with the Changchun's Hongda Group, market leaders in fingerprint recognition technology, Sun Microsystems developed a computer network linking all thirty-three provincial level police bureaus, forming one layer of the Golden Shield, allowing the PBS instant comparison of fingerprints with a nationwide database."

In August 2001, we sent yet another letter to Sun Microsystems. Finally, in mid-August, our telephone calls were answered and we were told that Sun Microsystems never received our proposal. What?

We then sent them our proof of delivery, which had also been sent to the SEC. On August 29, Sun mailed us its Statement of Opposition. The sad "saga" doesn't end here. After HII presented the resolution on November 7, 2001, garnering 14 percent of the shareholder vote, little dialogue ensued, even though at the meeting, Mike Morris, Sun's general counsel, expressed a desire to do so. Moreover, when Alana Smith Johnk of HII filed the resolution again in 2002, we again received the company's Statement of Opposition. Sun misstated the vote against the resolution and had to restate the numbers after we corrected them. When the resolution was filed again in 2003, it received only 9 percent in 2003 (compared to 10 percent in 2002); therefore, it could not be re-introduced again in 2004. HII has since sold all of its Sun stock.

While attorneys for some companies, such as Hewlett-Packard, do everything they can to get a "no action" letter from the SEC to omit a resolution on a technicality, other companies go to extremes to keep shareholders in the dark and resolutions off the ballot.

In early February 2000, HII corresponded with Oracle Corporation regarding the China Business Principles, also requesting a copy of the company's code of conduct. Two months later we received a response and a copy of "Oracle Corporation's Business Code of Conduct." In May we sent a letter, explaining major differences between Oracle's code and the China Principles and offered to meet with management, suggesting it consider incorporating the China Principles into its company code. In two weeks we received an Oracle letter requesting "proof of ownership" and a letter to withdraw the resolution that only needed our signature. What? And no offer to dialogue.

About a month later, Oracle filed a "no action" request with the SEC on three technicalities: (1) the premise that Oracle's business in China represented less than 5 percent of its total activities; (2) that it was "ordinary business" and not subject to shareholder vote; and (3) the principles had already been substantially implemented. HII submitted a formal response to Oracle's "no-action" request. On August 15, 2000 the SEC ruled in our favor. On August 29, Robert Rosoff, staff of the CWG, Medea Benjamin of Global Exchange, and I met with Oracle's management representatives, which included corporate attorneys and the company's China personnel, including the Senior VP of its Asia Pacific Division.

The meeting was subdued and professional, and we did learn something. Upon questioning, Oracle representatives admitted that the company provided products and services to China's military and police. This substantiated earlier reports of U.S. corporate technology being used by Chinese security forces to identify, apprehend, and eventually imprison, torture, and murder dissidents who advocated for democratic freedom and reforms.

Not unlike a national ID program that former Attorney General John Ashcroft and Oracle CEO Larry Ellison have discussed for American citizens' use, the Chinese government has introduced an electronic ID card which is accessible to its Ministry of Public Security. This database will store vital information on 960 million Chinese citizens. Activists are worried that it will be easier for the government to monitor political and religious dissidents using a smart card with a chip, but not to worry, says Public Security Official Guo Xing: "The ID card and the ID number are mainly going to be used to verify a resident's identity, safeguard people's rights, make it easier for people to organize activities and maintain law and order."[33]

Unfortunately, Oracle never agreed to participate in the CWG or continue its dialogue with us, so our resolution appeared on the shareholder ballot. In October, because of a major traffic tie up in the East Bay, I arrived a few minutes late to present the resolution, and the vote tally on the resolution was never provided. In the question-and-answer portion of the annual meeting, I asked Larry Ellison if he was interested in working with the CWG and other companies in China to develop best practices and learn more about government policies and conditions in China. In one curt word, in typical Larry Ellison fashion, he answered: "No."

Ellison does not seem to really care much about free enterprise, since twenty-five years ago Oracle got its start feeding at the public trough via a contract with the Central Intelligence Agency. He has certainly invested in the political system. Ellison and Oracle spent $2.3 million to lobby Congress and during the 2000 election cycle gave over $821,000 in campaign contributions. Oracle was a little embarrassed, however, when California's Governor Gray Davis had to return a $25,000 check to Oracle over "concerns" regarding a $95 million no-bid state contract with Ellison's company.

When we attempted to file our China Business Principles resolution the second year, it was rejected on a technicality. In April 2002, HII re-filed the resolution, and this time, however, the SEC ruled in our favor, and I presented the resolution on November 6, 2002, receiving over 7 percent of the vote. John of HII presented the resolution before shareholders in 2003, again receiving over 7 percent of the shareholder vote, as it did in 2004. Because it did not reach the 10 percent threshold, the resolution was not reintroduced in 2005.

According to Chinese law, Time Warner is legally obligated to report to the Public Security Bureau any Chinese citizen who breaks the law. And the company seems to have no qualms about complying. An internal Time Warner memo recommended that if the company was asked whether it would provide records on dissidents to the Chinese government, staff should respond: "It is our policy to abide by the laws of the country in which we offer services."[34] This corporate policy supporting an authoritarian government in China was not unlike U.S. corporate policy in South Africa three decades ago.

It is even more frightening what companies will do to "pro-actively" get in the door with Chinese government officials. According to a February 25, 2002 article in *The Daily Standard*: "AOL is quietly weighing the pros and cons of informing on dissidents if the Public Security Bureau so requests; the right decision would clearly speed Chinese approval for AOL to offer Internet services and perhaps get a foothold in the Chinese television market." Maybe this is why the chairman of the board and CEO of Time Warner wouldn't respond to HII's inquiry or dialogue with us about our shareholder resolutions.

GENETIC ENGINEERING

HII has filed over a dozen shareholder proposals requesting that food and food-related companies report on, label, or phase out the use of genetically engineered ingredients. We have also targeted the Scotts Company for special concern because of the company's development and distribution of genetically modified seeds to grow a species of grass that could have a substantial long-term negative impact on the environment. Now Scotts has purchased Smith & Hawken to capture the "environmentalist" side of its business. Scotts, by the way, is the major distributor for Monsanto's Roundup herbicide.

Representing our clients, HII has urged the state and federal regulatory agencies to require pre-release safety tests for consumer and animal food products that are genetically modified. We are concerned about the long-term public safety issue, but also, as a fiduciary, we are afraid that our investment in food companies may be endangered due to large liability claims against companies that sell products containing genetically engineered ingredients. We are especially mindful of the potential dangers of such foods being sold to the public when there are no accompanying consumer benefits: taste is not improved, nutrition is not enhanced, and prices are not reduced. What's more, food corporations have been adamantly opposed to labeling products so consumers know whether bio-engineering was involved.

According to Austin Sullivan, General Mills senior vice president for corporate relations: "Manufacturers, who currently receive no benefit or marketing advantage from bioengineered ingredients, do not want to present their products in a way that is negative to consumers. With no manufacturing or consumer benefit to offer and only downside risk of adverse consumer behavior, mandatory labeling would lead manufacturers to ask their suppliers for non-bioengineered ingredients only. The net result of this would be to eliminate choice and retard the development of a potentially beneficial technology."[35]

Genetic modification of seeds and plants, which are able to resist Monsanto's Roundup Ready spraying, appeals to farmers. Many have been sold on this product, and now U.S. farmers, unlike their European and many third world counterparts, are producing soy, corn and cotton crops, the majority of which are genetically modified. Many food companies in Europe abandoned foods with genetically-modified organisms (GMO), as well as Gerber Products Co., and Frito Lay in the United States, among others.

In 1999, HII began addressing our concerns over food safety to food companies held in our clients' portfolios. After corresponding with company representatives in 1999, we filed resolutions with General Mills and Sara Lee to phase out the purchase of bio-engineered ingredients. General Mills indicated that Monsanto was working on several genetic modifications of food products that will help consumers lower "bad" cholesterol and increase their intake of healthy omega-3 fatty acids.[36] In August 2000, Sara Lee informed us that it was still assessing its suppliers, GMO ingredients, and the feasibility of removing those ingredients, indicating that it was an overwhelming and complicated issue since Sara Lee had over 100 operating companies and over a dozen in meat processing alone. The process of evaluating whether or not to be committed to a GMO-free policy similar to McDonald's policy regarding potatoes was complicated even further by Sara Lee's decentralized management process.

While dialogue and discussion between HII and several food companies continued, our resolutions were opposed by management, and typically received 4 to 9 percent of the shareholder vote. Arguments were made, questions were asked and answered, issues were discussed, but little was resolved. Most of the resolutions remained on the ballot for two or three years. In the case of both General Mills and Sara Lee, after unsuccessfully attempting to convince management of our concerns of liability and our clients' financial exposure, HII divested its stock positions.

In several instances, HII asked a food company to label GMO ingredients, based upon consumer choice and polls that show upwards of 90 percent of consumers favoring GMO labeling. In the case of Procter & Gamble (PG), HII's labeling resolution received over 10 percent of the shareholder vote in 2002 but did not exceed 10 percent in 2003, its fourth consecutive year on the PG shareholder ballot. It could not be reintroduced in 2004.

When the issue of voluntary labeling was addressed by Whole Foods Market, management was already in the process of complying and our co-filed resolution was withdrawn. Several opponents of GMO ingredients have told HII that they are disappointed at Whole Foods' lack of follow through to implement its labeling plan, and another resolution is being considered. When HII approached Hain Celestial Group to request a report on the feasibility of phasing out GMO ingredients from its products, management initially resisted. It was only after the resolution won over 23 percent of the shareholder vote in its second year, that a compromise was reached and the resolution was withdrawn.

Requiring all genetically engineered foods sold in the United States to be labeled, as will be required of all U.S. food imports into the European Economic Community (EEC), would have severe repercussions on marketing and sales in this country. In discussions with food company representatives, they were unanimous in their opinion that based on surveys, American consumers would reject genetically modifidied foods or food with genetically modified ingredients. This is the primary reason Monsanto is putting pressure on U.S. trade representatives to force the EEC to back off its labeling requirement. Monsanto opposes full disclosure of GMO ingredients because, as Frank Dixon, one of the authors of the Innovest study entitled "Monsanto & Genetic Engineering: Risks for Investors" told me: "Labeling of GMO products in the United States would be the end of genetic engineering."

The Coalition for Environmentally Responsible Economies (CERES) and Joan Bavaria, of Trillium Asset Management, work with other SRI institutional investors to convince corporate management to endorse an environmental code of conduct. About seventy companies have signed the Principles and participate in CERES' conferences and educational programs, as well as providing annual CERES reports on the companies' compliance with the principles. CERES is building stakeholder teams, matching its members with endorsing companies to provide ongoing dialogue and feedback on corporate sustainability disclosure and performance. The organization is also reaching out to pension funds and other institutional investors to build the Investor Network on Climate Risk (INCR), following the 2003 Investor Summit on Climate Risk at the United Nations. INCR will work to educate corporate management on the long term financial risks of global warming.

Since 1997, HII has been corresponding with corporate management and introducing shareholder resolutions with over a dozen of our portfolio companies to convince them that it is in their best long-term interests to voluntarily endorse the CERES Principles and participate as CERES members, including filing annual reports on compliance with a code of environmental conduct. We have been marginally successful at entering into dialogue and bringing them to the CERES table.

MONSANTO: A VERY SPECIAL COMPANY

Here are some of Monsanto's claims to fame: Agent Orange; dioxin; NutraSweet; polychlorinated biphenyls (PCBs); and genetically engineered foods. Just about everything that the company produces injures, maims, or destroys human health and the planet's environment. Scientific studies of *Nutrasweet* since 1983 have shown a correlation between the artificial sweetener and an increase in brain cancer. PCBs, banned in the United States since 1976, are a potential carcinogen linked to a wide array of reproductive, developmental, and immune system disorders. The company was fined $700 million for one of its former chemical facilities in Anniston, Alabama, where PCBs are believed to have caused everything from severe brain damage among workers to cancer and death.[37]

Understanding only too well Monsanto's PCB and other toxic financial liabilities, the company's attorneys convinced management to spin off Solutia, Inc., the most dangerous part of the company's chemical business. Monsanto contributed $390 million to help Solutia settle two PCB suits around Anniston, and Solutia has been spending about $100 million a year to resolve other environmental problems, defend itself against lawsuits, and provide benefits to Monsanto retirees. These liabilities and other "legacy" obligations of about $755 million drove Solutia into Chapter 11 bankruptcy.[38] Solutia, with $2.85 billion in assets and $3.22 billion in liabilities, is, naturally, suing its former parent, Monsanto, "seeking to shift an estimated $475 million in health care benefits for 20,000 retirees back to the original company."[39]

Monsanto ($45 billion in sales in 2002) and its "environmental sustainability" friend Dow Chemical were the leading manufacturers of defoliants used in Vietnam including the infamous Agent Orange. Not only did these eleven million gallons of chemicals destroy Vietnamese rainforests during the war (the intended goal), the consequences of chemical warfare are still being endured by Vietnam veterans and successive generations of Vietnamese citizens who have developed various forms of cancer, dioxin-related deformities, and serious skin and liver disorders (the "collateral damage").

In fact, a study in the *Journal of Occupational and Environmental Medicine*, Volume 45, entitled: "Food as a Source of Dioxin Exposure in the Residents of Bien Hoa City, Vietnam," revealed that even after three decades of Agent Orange spraying (which began in 1962), heavy dioxin contamination continues to show up in food, soil, animals, fish, and humans. Chemicals manufactured by Monsanto and Dow cause an increased risk of cancer, immune deficiencies, reproductive and development changes, nervous system damage, liver injury, elevated blood lipids, skin damage, and death. Over 15 percent of Vietnam was sprayed with Agent Orange.

Vietnam veterans have suffered debilitating symptoms attributable to

Agent Orange, and in 1984, they won a $180 million settlement, of which over 45 percent was ordered by a judge to be paid by Monsanto.[40] In early 2003, the U.S. Veterans Affairs Department extended benefits to Vietnam veterans diagnosed with chronic lymphocytic leukemia (CLL) a disease linked to Agent Orange exposure; ten thousand Vietnam vets are currently receiving disability pay for other illnesses related to Agent Orange.[41]

Scientists at Monsanto also created a recombinant bovine growth hormone (rBGH—also known as Bovine Somatotropin, or BST) to get cows to produce more milk. While banned in Europe and Canada, it was declared "safe" by the U.S. Food and Drug Administration (FDA) in 1993, and Monsanto began selling brand name *Prosilac* to dairy farmers. Not only do many cows not produce more milk, those that do often lose weight, become infertile, and are more susceptible to diseases. Some farmers have lost up to 75 percent of their herds. The most serious problem, however, is the increased risk of mastitis, or inflammation of the cow's udder, which means the cow produces milk with pus in it. Sounds attractive, doesn't it? The problem is often treated with antibiotics, which end up in the milk consumed by humans, and then leads to the development of health problems caused by antibiotic resistance. Studies have also linked rBGH to cancer.

Monsanto attorneys have been very aggressive in protecting the company by trying to intimidate the media into firing reporters who write negative stories about the company's products. Monsanto sued Oakhurst Dairy of Portland, Maine, for labeling its milk "rBGH-free." This is in fact, consistent with earlier lawsuits against dairies labeling their milk as hormone-free. Monsanto claims such labeling implies that there's something wrong with milk if it comes from cows that have been injected with a growth hormone.

Monsanto's influence is especially strong within government, both under Democratic and Republican administrations. The FDA regulations that discourage labeling of milk as rBGH-free were written by Michael Taylor, an attorney who worked for Monsanto both before and after his tenure as an FDA official.

In order for the FDA to determine if Monsanto's growth hormones were safe, the company was required to submit data on rBGH. Margaret Miller, a Monsanto researcher, put the report together, but before it was even submitted, she left Monsanto and went to work for the FDA. Her first job at the FDA was to approve or reject the report she wrote for Monsanto. In short, Monsanto approved its own report. Assisting Miller at FDA was another former Monsanto researcher, Susan Sechen.[42]

The FDA's unethical favoritism extends to other Monsanto products as well. Consider the "safety tests" Monsanto conducts to prove that genetically modified soybeans, for example, are safe for animals and humans. In the case of a safety assessment application prepared by Monsanto for the Japanese Health Ministry for approval of *Roundup Ready* soybeans, a leading Japanese scientist called Monsanto's data "riddled with flaws, incomplete and manipulated."[43]

When Japan announced that if the U.S. government allows wheat to be genetically modified, Japan will discontinue importing about 2.5 million tons of U.S.-grown wheat, Monsanto responded by putting genetically-modified wheat on hold.[44]

Monsanto, however, has been able to convince farmers in India to buy more expensive genetically modified cotton seeds to produce better cotton with increased yields, but the reverse has actually occurred. Crop yields for modified cotton were actually five times less than conventional cotton and the income for farmers was seven times less thanks to Monsanto's cotton having lower quality and shorter fibers.[45]

Prior to being on the U.S. Supreme Court, Clarence Thomas was once Monsanto's lawyer. The former U.S. secretary of agriculture, Anne Veneman, was on Monsanto's Calgene Board of Directors, and Secretary of Defense Donald Rumsfeld was on Monsanto's Searle Pharmaceuticals board of directors. The former U.S. secretary of health, Tommy Thompson, received $50,000 in Monsanto campaign contributions when he ran for the governor's chair in Wisconsin, and the two congressmen receiving the most donations from Monsanto in the 2004 election were Larry Combest, chair of the House Agricultural Committee, and former U.S. Attorney General John Ashcroft.[46]

In March 2003, Ashcroft's Justice Department began a probe into possible antitrust practices in the glyphosate-herbicide industry, which is dominated by Monsanto's Roundup weed killer. In August 2004, it closed its inquiry "requiring no actions by the St. Louis company."[47]

But it isn't just Republicans that side with Monsanto. Taylor, Miller, and Sechen were all FDA officials during the Clinton administration, and John Gibbon, chair of the Congressional Office of Technological Assessment, has been a Monsanto consultant for more than a decade. Marcia Hale, former assistant to President Clinton, then went on to work for Monsanto in the United Kingdom, and former California Democratic Party political hack, Mickey Kantor, the former U.S. Trade Representative and U.S. secretary of commerce under Clinton, is now on the Monsanto Board of Directors.[48]

Besides its other flagship products like *Nutrasweet*, PCBs, Agent Orange, and r-BGH, Monsanto's biggest commercial success has been *Roundup*, a glyphosate-based herbicide farmers spray on food crops to kill all kinds of weeds, while allowing Monsanto-owned genetically engineered ("Roundup Ready") crops to flourish. These bio-engineered herbicide-tolerant food crops include cotton, soya, corn, and canola. In 2002, Monsanto products accounted for 91 percent of the total area sown with GMOs. In 2001, 26 percent of all corn in the United States was GMO, and 68 percent of all soybeans, 69 percent of all cotton, according to the International Service for the Acquisition of Agri-biotech Applications (ISAAA). Because corn, soya, and canola are the source of many ingredients in processed food, up to 70 percent of all packaged foods found on supermarket shelves could include genetically modified ingredients.

Farmers who use Monsanto's *Roundup Ready* Canola seed and other bio-engineered seeds must sign a contract with the company promising that they will buy new seeds from Monsanto every year. They cannot save, store, or trade their seeds. Monsanto has admitted that there is no way to prevent its seeds and pollen from being carried by wind and birds to non-genetically engineered fields. They can easily mix with other non-genetically engineered crops and that there is no guarantee of containment.

To intimidate and threaten farmers into using Monsanto seeds, the company has filed over 550 law suits against farmers for illegally using Monsanto seeds. The most famous case was against a third-generation Canadian canola farmer, seventy-two-year-old Percy Schmeiser, sued for

$200,000 by Monsanto for stealing its seeds after the company's private investigators found *Roundup Ready* canola on his farm. Monsanto didn't have to prove its case since the judge ruled that it didn't matter how the seeds came to be in Schmeiser's field, he was deemed to have infringed on the company's patent rights simply by growing and harvesting it without permission. It made no difference that he did not spray the crop with Monsanto's *Roundup* weedkiller and therefore did not benefit from the altered genetic structure of the plants. Schmeiser lost the case on appeal.

Monsanto must love Canada, since the company originally sought government approval to grow a variety of genetically modified wheat that's resistant to *Roundup*. Organic farmers in Saskatchewan (where Schmeiser lives) went so far as to prepare a class-action lawsuit to stop it. According to the Canadian Wheat Board, which markets the grain, Monsanto was urged to withdraw its application since 82 percent of its customers didn't want GM wheat because they feared it would contaminate nearby crops.[49]

One farmer who opposed the company's genetic seed licensing practices was sentenced in federal court to eight months in prison and a fine of over $165,000 for lying about a truckload of cotton seed he hid for a friend, saving GMO seed, and later burning the seeds.[50]

Monsanto has filed seventy-three civil lawsuits against farmers in the past five years, hoping that the cases would send a stern message.[51] One farmer receiving a prison sentence said: "Me and my brother talked about how rotten and lowdown Monsanto is. We're tired of being pushed around by Monsanto. We are being pushed around and drug down the road like a bunch of dogs. And we decided we'd burn them."[52]

GMO products have not been independently tested prior to release by the FDA or any health research organization. Some studies indicated that allergic reaction and other illnesses may occur depending upon one's sensitivity to different GMO foods. In Mississippi, more than sixty-one farmers who planted Roundup Ready cotton found that their yields were low and the cotton balls fell off or were malformed. Monsanto and the seed distributors reached an agreement with the affected farmers and settled privately for about $5 million.[53]

Under current FDA rules, if genetically modified crops are shown to be "substantially equivalent" to conventional crops, further review isn't needed before the crops can be marketed. The company is responsible for doing the safety review and the FDA relies on company data and information. From information obtained under the Freedom of Information Act, the Center for Science in the Public Interest (CSPI) found that Monsanto's data submitted to the FDA was lacking. When FDA sought more data, it was rebuffed by the company.[54] In general, an FDA review is limited to a "voluntary consultation" in which it examines a company's scientific information on potential allergic and toxic reactions, and the nutrient content of the foods. Science Director Doug Gurian-Sherman of CSPI said the review found that "biotech companies weren't always performing the right tests to look for potentially dangerous compounds, including allergens, and that there was a great deal of unevenness among different developer's submissions."[55]

There are some GMO products that are only approved by the U.S. Department of Agriculture for animal—not human—consumption (although it may eventually get into the food chain). In the Fall of 2001, Friends of the Earth analyzed grocery store food products and uncovered widespread contamination by a GMO corn variety known as *StarLink*, which contained an insecticidal protein that had not been approved for human consumption due to potential allergic reactions. Upwards of 10 percent of U.S. corn was contaminated and *StarLink* had to be recalled.

Another "snafu" occurred when ProdiGene, a small Texas-based genetic engineering firm, was found to have mishandled genetically-engineered pharmaceutical corn that produced pig vaccines in Iowa and Nebraska. Ordinary soybeans that were planted in the same field became contaminated by the genetically-engineered corn and mixed with five hundred thousand bushels of soybeans. Now there is opposition from the food industry to further development and commercialization of food crops genetically altered to contain industrial or pharmaceutical proteins ("Pharma-crops" or "biopharms").

Even major trade groups, such as the National Food Processors Association, the Grocery Manufacturers of America, General Mills, and PepsiCo's Frito-Lay, questioned Monsanto's genetically-modified wheat and opposed biopharm crops. In one of its 10K disclosure reports to the SEC, Monsanto admits that genetic drift from biotech and biopharm crops is unavoidable and that potential liabilities are unpredictable. This disclosure hasn't stopped Monsanto and other biotech companies from conducting three hundred secret field trials of pharma-crops, two-thirds of them utilizing corn, the crop noted for spreading its genetically-engineered pollen.[56]

Then there are those genetically-altered pigs. The FDA reported in 2003 that as many as 386 fast-growing genetically-engineered piglets *may* have been sold and entered the U.S. food supply. They were experimental swine, sold to livestock brokers, who sold them to slaughterhouses, who sold them to grocery stores, who sold them to consumers as chops, sausage, and bacon.[57] The World Health Organization (WHO) reportedly plans to recommend that nations phase out the use of antibiotic growth promoters in animal feed to help keep antibiotics effective for humans. Without hormones in animals and animal feed, how will little piggy get to market?

The FDA is currently reviewing ten applications from companies seeking to sell genetically-engineered animal products to consumers. In a 2002 National Academy of Sciences report on genetically-engineered animals, there were several food-safety issues that arose, including allergies, digestive disorders, and antibiotic resistance. The European Union banned U.S. biotech foods in 1998. This policy was naturally blasted by U.S. Trade Representative Robert Zoellick, a stalking horse for Monsanto and other agricultural chemical companies, who criticized the European Union for "Luddite" and "immoral" opposition to genetically-engineered foods.[58]

Even the Chinese government, which has been sucking up to the United States and the WTO in efforts to continue to gain access to export markets and import capital, has questioned GMOs. In January 2002, China issued new import regulations for genetically modified products, and the Chinese General Administration of Quality Supervision, Inspection, and Quarantine renewed a limited soybean-import ban, saying traces of harmful bacteria were found in soybean import shipments from Brazil, Argentina, and the United States. Seventy percent of U.S. soybeans are genetically modified.[59]

In a response to a Greenpeace China campaign, thirty-two local and overseas food producers that sell about fifty-three food brands in China have publicly announced that they will not sell GMO foods.[60] According to the *Xinhua News Agency*, a 2002 Greenpeace survey of one thousand residents in South China found that 56 percent would choose non-genetically-modified foods, and the *Environment News Service* reported 87 percent wanted genetically-modified food labeling. Labeling genetically-modified ingredients in food products has been mandatory in China since July 2002; the government conducted a nationwide inspection to enforce the legislation and plans to penalize violators.[61]

The Cartegena Protocol on Biosafety was ratified by the European Union and went into effect in September 2003, allowing countries to ban imports of genetically-engineered seeds, microbes, animals, or crops deemed a threat to their environment. It also requires international shipments of genetically-engineered grains to be labeled.[62] Shortly thereafter, the United States announced that it would request the WTO to convene a panel and act to end the European Union ban that farm groups say is "depriving agricultural businesses of hundreds of billions of dollars a year."[63]

In July 2003, the European Parliament adopted two proposals to allow European Union countries to drop the ban on importing genetically-engineered seeds and food as long as GMOs are labeled to say, "This product is produced from GMOs." In a related act, the U.N. food advisory body, the Codex Alimentaries Commission, adopted voluntary guidelines asking countries that produce GMO food to ensure the safety and traceability of the product for potential recalls and continued monitoring.[64] Since FDA standards do not require safety evaluations before genetically-modified products hit the market, it will be interesting to see how the United States responds, especially since Codex includes provisions for carrying out safety evaluations before food products are put on the market, which include "assessing unexpected allergic reactions, and implementing measures to ensure products can be traced back to their origins for recall purposes and post-market monitoring."[65]

Those European Luddites just won't give up. The Luxembourg-based European Court of Justice ruled in September 2003 that Italy could restrict genetically-modified products made by Monsanto, Syngenta AG, and Pioneer Hi-Bred International, Inc.[66] The court upheld Europe's precautionary principle which allows preventative measures and temporary restrictions of GMOs to be taken to protect public health. On the other hand, the European Union broadened an approval for Monsanto to import GMO corn in October 2004, but European food manufacturers continue to avoid GMO because of consumer resistance and labeling requirements.[67]

Monsanto desperately wants access to developing country markets to peddle its herbicides and GE seeds. It has used the Bush administration to hassle the European Union, the United Nations, and the WTO to allow more genetically-engineered crops to enter African markets. The U.S. government has been subsidizing U.S. cotton farmers with $3 billion over the last two years, which is more than the entire economic output of African nations like Burkina Faso, where more than two million people depend on cotton exports.[68] Over 70 percent of U.S. cotton is genetically modified and has become the most pesticide-intensive export crop.

Monsanto and two hundred other companies are involved in the production and marketing of hybrid cotton seeds in India. Other large companies such as Unilever, Bayer, Syngenta, Advanta, and Emergent Genetics hire local farm contractors to cultivate cotton seeds. These Indian farmers have hired nearly 450,000 children, mostly girls between the ages of six and fourteen, to work in the fields for agrochemical and agribusiness companies.[69] This issue of child labor and Monsanto was raised in a study commissioned by the India Committee of the Netherlands and written by Dr. Davuluri Venkateswarlu, director of the Hyderabad-based Global Research and Consultancy Services. In responding to a June 2003, letter from Harrington Investments, Inc. questioning Monsanto's role in using child labor for its cotton seed cultivation, Monsanto president and CEO Hugh Grant said: "We are minority owners of Maharashtra Hybrid Seed Company (Mahyco), which markets hybrid cotton seed. Mahyco assures us that they work to ensure that all their seed production contractors follow local labor laws and that they discourage the use of child labor by suppliers. With our vested interest in Mahyco, we in turn continue to encourage them to take appropriate actions to avoid the practice of child labor."

When the European Union approved rules replacing the ban on importing GMOs with a requirement to label genetically-engineered products, the Bush administration, Monsanto, and just about every agrochemical and biotech friend and financial contributor of Bush was critical, saying the rules would be "overly burdensome to producers" and that labeling does nothing to increase consumer choice.[70]

It took ten years of lobbying by organic food producers and consumers to finally convince the USDA to develop organic labeling standards that are much more complex and require a great deal more work and oversight by organic producers than a simple label identifying a GMO product. The USDA began certifying and labeling organic products in October 2002. To be deemed organic, meat, poultry, eggs, and dairy products must come from animals that are given no antibiotics or growth hormones. For a dairy to be certified organic, its cows must graze on grass that hasn't been subjected to pesticides, and organic vegetables must be grown "pesticide-free."

To receive a label, items must meet one of four categories: "100 percent Organic"; "Organic" (95 percent or more organic ingredients); "Made with Organic Ingredients" (70 percent or more of the product is organic); "Contains Organic Ingredients" ("organic" can't appear on the front of the package, since less than 70 percent of the item is organic).[71] According to the USDA, agricultural land that is certified organic increased on average 74 percent between 1997 and 2001.

In 2002, the biotech industries in Oregon spent about $5 million to defeat a ballot measure requiring GMO labeling, and at the biotech industry's 2003 annual convention in California, not one panel discussed GMO food labeling, because, as Gregory Jaffe of the Center for Science in the Public Interest said, they "felt it was too controversial a topic to have an open discussion about."[72]

Americans overwhelmingly, in poll after poll, support the labeling of GMOs. For example, an ABC News poll in July 2003, found that 55 percent of U.S. consumers are now opposed to genetically-engineered foods, while 92 percent support mandatory labeling. Sixty-two percent of American women would not feed genetically-engineered food to their children.[73] In a 2001 survey conducted by the Pew Initiative of Food and Biotechnology, 65 percent of respondents were concerned about eating bioengineered food, and 45 percent lacked confidence in the government's ability to ensure the safety of such food. While labeling—or some form of GMO ban— is required in at least a dozen countries as well as the European Union member states, big U.S. corporations have successfully opposed any form of labeling in the United States, even though these companies have been doing it for years in other countries.

On the other hand, Procter & Gamble Co., which opposed Harrington Investments, Inc.'s shareholder resolution to label GMO ingredients in its food products, successfully lobbied the FDA after seven years to remove a food label warning on Olestra chips of possible "abdominal cramping and loose stools." Olestra, which the company sells under the brand name Olean, also will no longer alert consumers that vitamins A, D, E, and K are added because some vitamins aren't absorbed when eating Olestra. Procter & Gamble has always said the "gastrointestinal disturbances" are common among Americans and shouldn't be blamed on Olestra.[74]

Harrington Investments, Inc., has introduced over a dozen shareholder resolutions banning, phasing out, or labeling GMOS, all opposed by corporate management. Every spokesperson we talked to admitted that the industry looked foolish opposing labeling and said that GMO food if labeled as such, would be avoided by consumers. Karil Kochenderfer, the biotechnology coordinator for the Grocery Manufacturers of America, which represents food companies such as Kraft and General Mills said: "To the extent that consumers want choice, they want to choose non-biotech."[75] That sort of says it all.

So what are the benefits for consumers of genetically-modified food? Does it decrease the cost? Does it improve the taste? Is it more nutritious? In fact, Monsanto conveniently failed to mention that its own studies have shown that genetically-engineered soybeans have a lesser nutritional value than conventional soybeans and actually inhibited growth in laboratory mice.[76]

Genetic engineering allows Monsanto and other agrochemical companies the ability to make more money by selling the seeds to farmers and selling *Roundup* to spray on their crops. It also allows Monsanto and other agrochemical companies to hook farmers on their patented products. The main ingredient of Monsanto's *Roundup* is glyphosate, which is commonly assumed to dissipate in the soil after being broken down by soil bacteria. Denmark uses eight hundred tons of glyphosate a year and according to tests conducted by the Denmark and Greenland Geological Institution, concentrations of 0.54 micrograms per liter are being found in the upper ground water of Denmark, about five times more than the allowed level for safe consumption.[77]

Meanwhile, Monsanto continues to swallow seed companies, recently spending $1.4 billion to buy a California company, Seminis, Inc., which controls more than 3,500 seed varieties in nearly sixty species.[78] This purchase followed some negative publicity involving Monsanto's admission of paying more than $700,000 in bribes to Indonesian government officials between 1992 and 2002.[79] Controlling food and bribing government officials; it all goes hand-in-hand in operating a global "life science" company.

AMUSEMENT PARK SAFETY AND WALT DISNEY

I have a friend in Napa who lost her wonderful seventeen-year-old daughter when she was killed when a Banzai Pipeline water slide collapsed at a WaterWorld USA theme park in 1997. She was the only person killed, while thirty-two other high school seniors were injured, a lot of them severely. The results of this accident so infuriated parents that, after years of lobbying, a new California law took effect in January 2001 requiring regular ride inspections and investigations of serious accidents. The rules or standards eventually adopted, however, are fraught with loopholes, thanks to the power of corporate attorneys that lobby and manipulate regulators at the state capital. It is not just a strong law that must be adopted; it also must have a strong regulatory and enforcement arm to make it effective. But nothing is easy when it comes to battling the power of corporations.

In reviewing reports of accidents as described in the media and court settlements, I thought it appropriate to review our clients' portfolios for companies that may have amusement park liabilities. The only company that popped up was Disney, which has parks in California, Florida, Paris, and Tokyo, with one under construction in Hong Kong.

From 1987 through mid-1997, there were forty-three fatalities on amusement rides in the United States, although no such figures are available for deaths at U.S. corporate-run parks in other countries. In writing to Disney in 2000, Harrington Investments, Inc. cited the U.S. Consumer Product Safety Commission (CPSC) report, which showed that more than ten thousand people were treated in hospital emergency rooms for amusement ride-related injuries in 1999, that such injuries increased 35 percent since 1993, and injuries associated with fixed rides (as opposed to rides of traveling carnivals or fairs) increased 59 percent. CPSC data released for 2000 indicated that park ride injuries had increased 95 percent in a four-year period, while overall park attendance was only up 7 percent. We requested information regarding Disney's policy on amusement park ride safety and asked if the company supports public disclosure of its policy.

Disney, unfortunately, didn't respond to our letter and only did when our shareholder resolution was filed. Naturally, Disney opposed it, which only gained 4.42 percent of the shareholder vote at the 2002 annual shareholders meeting, but was enough to allow us to reintroduce the resolution in 2003 in which we received 8.57 percent. In 2004 the resolution received over 10 percent.

We were alarmed at the increasing number of accidents occurring in 2001 at Disneyland, including a boy pinned underneath a car on the Roger Rabbit Cartoon ride and a report of a confidential settlement with a woman who claimed the Indiana Jones Adventure attraction caused a brain hemorrhage. These and other incidents at California amusement parks caused such a stir that a September 17, 2001 *Los Angeles Times* editorial headlined "Rattles, Rolls, and Risk" stated, in part: "Earlier this month a young woman died of a ruptured brain aneurysm, hours after losing consciousness on Montezuma's Revenge at Knott's Berry Farm. The ride takes a mere three seconds to accelerate to 60 mph and whips through loops up to seven stories high. In June, a woman died after riding the Goliath roller coaster at Six Flags Magic Mountain in Valencia. She had suffered from hypertension–related heart disease, and she too died from a ruptured brain aneurysm. A third brain injury-related death occurred in July at Six Flags Marine World in Vallejo."

In addition to protecting amusement park consumers and Disney, HII believes it is in everyone's interest to not only publish Disney safety policies and procedures and to disclose accidents and related company financial settlement information to investors, but also to inform riders of the potential risks of thrill riding.

Nancy van Schoenderwoert of Responsible Wealth presented our resolution in 2003 in Hartford, Connecticut. She closed her presentation by noting that accidents have resulted in cash settlements, and added: "Shouldn't our company's management be spending our money on making Disney theme parks safe, and adopt an open public policy on theme park safety instead of spending potentially millions of dollars on settlements? Without uniform reporting, disclosure and total corporate transparency, it is impossible to know how safe, or unsafe, amusement park rides are for visitors."

On September 5, 2003, one person was killed and ten injured, including two children, when a locomotive broke loose from a train on Disneyland's Big Thunder Mountain Railroad. Ten people have been killed in Disneyland since it opened in 1955. In 2004 Big Thunder Mountain Railroad was again shut down after a ten-year-old boy and his parents were injured after two trains collided. According to reports, twenty-four people have claimed injuries from the ride since 2001.[80]

Amusement park accidents are almost a daily event across America and the world. See www.rideaccidents.com for an eye-opening review of accidents, injuries, and fatalities since 1972.

BANK OF AMERICA

Bank of America Corporation (BAC) announced in October 2003 that it was acquiring FleetBoston Financial Corp. for $47 billion. About the same time, receiving slightly less publicity was an announcement that the Charlotte, North Carolina-based banking giant was setting up a subsidiary in India and outsourcing more than one thousand technology jobs. A stock market analyst said that the outsourcing was "a way to manage the overhead" for BAC,[81] while David Lazarus, a reporter for the *San Francisco Chronicle,* said that for customers "that means an ever-increasing risk of personal data slipping beyond the bank's grasp."[82] He added: "The simple fact is that your records—your credit history, financial data, medical files and all other personal information—are far better protected within the United States than anywhere else on the planet."

Lazarus had earlier reported on the danger of "offshoring" after a woman in Pakistan, doing cheap clerical work for the University of California, San Francisco (UCSF) Medical Center, threatened to post patient's confidential files on the Internet.

Naturally, BAC public relations people provided assurances that customers' confidential financial information will not fall into the wrong hands. Confidential customer information is more sensitive than information that has been outsourced previously, as is confidential personal tax information, which is now also being outsourced to India. Access to confidential information is the golden goose for identity theft, one of the largest and fastest growing forms of white collar crime in the world.

Holding stock with over $2 million in BAC, Harrington Investments, Inc. introduced a shareholder resolution requesting the bank to "report to the shareholders no later than June 2004 on the company's policies and procedures for ensuring that all personal and private information pertaining to all Bank of America customers will remain confidential in all business operations 'outsourced' to India or any other offshore location. This report should also cover policies relating to those employees of contractors and sub-contractors hired by the company."

The resolution received over 9 percent of the shareholder vote and we planned to reintroduce it in 2005, but it was omitted from the proxy material by the SEC on the grounds of "ordinary business."

Despite Bank of America's assurances and promises, the bank announced at the end of February 2005 it had lost computer data tapes in late December 2004 containing personal information (names, Social Security numbers and addresses) on 1.2 million federal employees, including most members of the U.S. Senate, making them potentially vulnerable to identity theft.[83] The U.S.

Marine Corps immediately issued a press release alerting its members that they were subject to identity theft. This followed another disclosure, this time by ChoicePoint Inc., a data warehouser, that as many as one hundred forty-five thousand consumers may have had their personal confidential information released to identification criminals posing as ChoicePoint customers.[84] ChoicePoint and six of the largest sellers of private consumer data spent at least $2.4 million in 2004 to lobby Congress and federal regulatory agencies to prevent federal oversight of the data collection industry.[85]

THE HARRINGTON INVESTMENTS APPROACH

Harrington Investments, Inc. (HII) works in coalition with other SRI investment advisors, mutual funds, and shareholder advocacy organizations such as Shareholder Action Network, which is part of the Social Investment Forum, and the Interfaith Center on Corporate Responsibility. Since I'm also on the board of Global Exchange, I work with Global Exchange and other human rights, environmental and economic justice organizations to raise mission-oriented concerns. This is also consistent with HII's fiduciary duty to maximize financial, as well as social and environmental, performance on behalf of our clients.

HII's social and environmental criteria, as well as our proxy voting procedures and guidelines, are identified on our website (www.harringtoninvestments.com). Our shareholder advocacy record, including our voting record, is available upon request.

HII surveys its clients and sets shareholder advocacy goals annually. The majority of our clients consistently put human rights as their top priority, with environmental issues as a close second. This is consistent with a 2003 MMA Praxis Mutual Funds report entitled *The Ethical Issues Report: What Matters to Religious Investors*, which found that the top five ethical concerns for religious investors were operation of sweatshops, product safety, excessive executive compensation, environment, and adult entertainment.

It is interesting to note that "faith-based" mutual fund assets have grown from $3.3 billion at the end of 2002, to $4.7 billion through October 2004, according to an informal survey by Lipper Inc. in New York.[86]

As an ongoing process, HII corresponds with the management of companies that are included in our clients' and HII's portfolio based upon our goals for the annual proxy season. Our communication may span several years, and much of our dialogue with companies is in conjunction and cooperation with other SRI investors and SRI investor coalitions. Because we are "buy and hold" managers, and not market timers, our fiduciary relationship to companies HII owns for clients is generally regarded as long-term ownership. We feel it is in our clients' interests to follow through on our ownership obligation.

As a shareholder, HII has a responsibility to marry its duty as an owner of capital with its fiduciary duties as an investment advisor. The responsibility of a corporation is to maximize sustainable value for shareholders consistent with minimizing damage to society and the environment. It must not only remediate damage it has caused, but implement sustainable policies that will avoid causing social or environmental harm in the first place.

In addition to working on numerous corporate governance issues, HII has communicated, met, and dialogued with corporate management on a variety of other issues including health and safety, pesticides, genetic engineering, and the enactment of human, labor, and environmental codes of conduct. From 1999 through 2004, HII has introduced about fifty shareholder resolutions, reintroduced twenty-five resolutions and co-filed dozens of additional ones with shareholder coalition members.

After discovering a social or environmental injury, Harrington Investments, Inc., attempts to communicate directly with corporate management by written and verbal communication including telephone, letters, email and faxed documents. Often, management does not respond, leading to more attempts to communicate. Unfortunately, more often than not, management does not respond until a second and third round of attempts by HII, or we introduce a shareholder resolution with an accompanying statement of support. This will usually get management's attention. Sometimes, however, it does not, and management only responds through legal counsel or not until the annual shareholders meeting when we "face off." Normally, this does not result in any real communication.

"For every rule, there is an exception and for every exception there is a rule." More often than not, however, I'm a firm believer in a quote by Emerson: "A foolish consistency is the hobgoblin of little minds, adored by little statesmen and philosophers and divines." This speaks succinctly of the SRI advisor in the sense that HII's Shareholder Agenda and the setting of priorities occasionally is circumvented by "special circumstances."

One such special circumstance was mentioned above, when a close friend who had lost her daughter caused HII to examine our fiduciary responsibility, incorporating our financial duties with our code of ethics and sense of morality. There is no inconsistency here, but rather a deviation of our normal process of determining within our own company how shareholder advocacy priorities would be set. In this case, because Disney did not even bother to respond to our letter, and when they did respond it was inappropriate and incomplete, we eventually filed a shareholder resolution.

In the case of Disney and the amusement park safety issue, Disney stock was a portfolio holding, both personally (both within my retirement account and the HII corporate investment account) and within my client's original portfolio. Like many advisors, HII when managing a new client's portfolio may "inherit" particular securities that, for a variety of reasons, must continue to be held for some length of time. Often it is because the security has an extremely low cost basis and selling the security would significantly increase our client's capital gains tax liability. Because most of our clients are major donors to nonprofit organizations, the appreciated security may be donated as a charitable contribution. Because an "inherited" stock position may be significant in the number of shares and value, it may need to be held in the account for several years. HII will hold the stock in the client's account, "cover" the stock as we would an ordinary HII holding (meaning it would receive an analyst's coverage and investment review), and HII would exercise shareholder advocacy and proxy voting rights.

In the case of Anheuser Busch, HII "inherited" the stock and exercised our shareholder responsibility by introducing a shareholder resolution for two consecutive years, attempting to convince the company management to phase out the use of GMOs in its products or at the very least label its beer as a GMO product.

Occasionally, we witness such an egregious and harmful corporate act, that a "sin of omission," or failure to act, becomes a "sin of commission." This was the situation when we discovered that Monsanto was dumping cancer-causing and other dangerous, banned-in-the-U.S.A. pesticides on third world countries. As is usually the case with Monsanto, there was little dialogue, but lots of legal maneuvering when HII introduced its resolution.

8

A New Beginning

I want you to take a moment to imagine a world where corporate power is unchecked. A dark future may behold a world of the predominately white and wealthy living in the West and North, pitted against the non-white poor in the South and East. This will be the new apartheid. A minority of educated white people will have already been cloned to have advanced IQs and will be stronger and taller than any generation before them. Thanks to science, technology, and wealth, the white West will be reaching for physical immortality and mental superiority. Cloning and eugenics will bring us closer to a new master race envisioned by the Nazis in the 1930's.

Governments will be totally subservient to corporate power, which will be held by those who are wealthy, educated, and connected enough to have stepped into positions of power. Corporate democracy shall be the rule of law, and all decisions shall be made by corporate princes who have sacrificed ideals, honesty, and integrity, who have lost any resemblance of humanity, and who have joined the ruling class, exempt from all worldly laws and morality. Their true God will be money and power. Their codes of conduct and ethics will be voluntary.

The mass of Western society will be tracked electronically, more for corporations' ability to predict consumer behavior than for police surveillance to detect criminal or other deviant social behavior. Political ideology and ethics will have been overpowered by consumerism. All personal identification will be implanted on a chip at birth and will be continually updated throughout an individual's life. Everything about the individual will be known and recorded; from DNA to what one buys for dinner. Government will be owned by corporations and it will prescribe and predict. There will be no surprises. There will be nowhere to hide; nowhere to run.

Conventional military battles and skirmishes, not wars, will be fought between developing countries based on political or military power grabs for natural resources, including mineral wealth, timber, natural gas, agricultural products and, most of all, potable water and oil. Developing countries' governments will change hands rapidly; in those countries, government will represent the only access to wealth and power, thanks primarily to the spoils of the national government being sold to the highest corporate bidder. American's military power will be used preemptively when needed to protect corporate interests and assets, including oil and other resources necessary for corporate economic dominance and to keep consumers happy.

Of course, corporate management will be obliged to maintain political control of the U.S. government and the economy, and over an increasingly privatized police and military, as rising expectations from the working poor, primarily people of color, will periodically boil over into desperate civil disobedience and will have to be squelched by the state. There will be a tremendous gap between the rich and the poor, those in prison and "free," white and non-white, and the educated and the uneducated. All manufacturing will be overseas, while some assembly of finished goods will be done in Mexico, America's fifty-first state. The largest government budget items will be for privatized law enforcement, prisons, the military, and interest on the national debt. Education and a few other public services will be the responsibility of state and local governments, funded predominately by regressive local taxes, mostly sales and value-added taxes, as well as gambling taxes, borne primarily by the working poor and those fortunate enough to have been able to make it to the "middle class". U.S. citizens will have no access to employer health care or Social Security. Unions will become voluntary employee associations. Corporations and people of wealth will not be taxed. Fiscal and monetary policies will be aligned with the needs of corporations, the wealthy, and will conform to globally enforced "free" trade policies.

America will continue to be dependent on capital from abroad, and the country will continue to import more than it exports. Most of the U.S. Treasury will be held hostage by foreign lenders and Americans will borrow and consume more than any other country on earth. The principal economic power bases in the world will be the European Community, the United States, and the East, comprised primarily of Japan and China. National sovereignty, however, will continue to be held at bay by the ubiquitous corporate-controlled World Trade Organization. Democracy, as we know it, will be dead.

This surreal future may not be that distant.

As we saw in chapter 1, with the exception of a more competitive 2004 presidential election between almost identical candidates, most Americans have grown weary of democracy, shedding the responsibilities of voting in ever-greater numbers. Most voters, or potential voters, are disgusted with politics and believe the system is driven by money, and it is. Money rules in corporate democracy, turning campaigns into mudslinging entertainment for distribution by media conglomerates, consumed by a sitcom-anesthetized public. Corporate money that doesn't get into the pockets of candidates ends up in the coffers of political parties at convention time—often evenly divided between the two major parties—resulting in our present day plutocracy. Some people would even say that after they've both been bought off, only one party, the Republicrats, rule. Michael Moore calls voters' choices "the evil of lessers." Jim Hightower says he doesn't necessarily want a third party; he'd be just as happy with a second party.

Former President Clinton's ability to raise campaign money by the bucket-full, and his mimicking of the Republican Party platform, finally made the Democratic Party competitive in fundraising. It also homogenized the traditional Democratic political base to make the party ideology, if that's the word, no different than that of the Republican Party: to simply win elections, rule, and take money from special interests—mostly corporations. This, coupled with the lack of contested elections at the congressional level, has totally turned off the American voter and has made politics in America meaningless. In 2004, many Democrats were convinced to vote for Kerry, even though Kerry wanted more troops in Iraq, supported "free" trade, and believed, as George W. does, that we need preemptive military strikes to make the world safe for democracy.

We must admit that those elected to Congress and to state legislatures don't represent the majority of the population in their districts, but probably do represent a slimmed down electorate, consisting mainly of white, older, middle-class property owners. Today the founders of our constitution would feel right at home if only women and people of color couldn't vote. The American population is increasingly becoming a majority of minorities, but elects old white men. This political disconnect becomes more pronounced as the gap between the rich and the working poor grows ever larger.

The corporate money spigot does not stop when politicians are not campaigning. It continues to flow into lobbyists' pockets to keep politicians, bureaucrats, and government regulators in line. Companies receive handsome returns on their investments in the government, obtaining enormous tax breaks or loopholes (also called tax expenditures), contracts from government agencies, regulations and laws favoring their particular industry or business, and lots of upper-crust government jobs. One result of this is to shift the burden of the cost of government from corporations to individual taxpayers and consumers. Thus, inevitably, the voter will rebel and vote against further tax increases, including bond issues. The lack of funds leads to budget cuts, which will inevitably lead to a decline in state and federal regulation and oversight of corporate activities. This further erodes public control of corporate behavior. What a vicious cycle it becomes.

The booming U.S. economy in the 1990s camouflaged the greed and misdeeds of corporate management, its accountants, and attorneys—only to be exposed in the following three years of a bear market. The WorldCom, Enron, and Arthur Andersen "busts," and Wall Street excesses, forced the SEC and state attorney generals to pay more attention to white collar crime to placate public and investor outrage. Corporate and financial services industry conduct has come under increasing scrutiny and hardly a day passes that another misadventure is not reported in the national media.

Despite the recent horrific corporate crime spree, corporations have continued to grow in financial and political strength and now symbolize America's culture of greed, obesity, big SUVs, oil consumption, and materialism to the global community. French and Italian culture is represented by art, architecture, and music—while America's culture is represented by corporate branding of fast food, sugar water, coffee, clothes, and the construction of prisons and gambling casinos. Ironically, America's traditional pastime, competitive sporting events—including baseball, football, and basketball—have fallen victim to corporate branding and the "horse-trading" of players (the new contractual slavery or voluntary servitude for big bucks). Almost every coliseum, ballpark, and stadium housing professional sporting teams is branded by a corporate name: PetCo Park, SBC Park, Arco Arena, Nationwide Arena, FedEx Field, Miller Park, Reliant Stadium, Minute Maid Park (formerly Enron Field in Houston), and many more.[1]

How often do we see a professional or college sports figure *without* a corporate logo on their clothing? The symbol of America has become the corporate logo and a potpourri of corporate symbols has become the many "flags" of America.

Taxpayers are constantly dishing out money to protect themselves against crime, terrorism, North Korea, Iraq, natural disasters (earthquakes and tsunamis), high blood pressure, obesity, pain, and allergies, among other things. We even subsidize foreign and domestic corporations with cheap, taxpayer-guaranteed bank loans. In an effort to subsidize every corporation on earth, public employee pension fund money is utilized to capitalize companies that are destroying public employee jobs. According to *Downsizing Democracy*: "privatization is not just a way to get the most for the taxpayers' dollar. It is also an instrument for achieving privileged access to 'power', and once achieved, that power is sometimes exercised to impose additional costs on American taxpayers."[2]

Federal, state, and local governments and even school and special districts are privatizing like there's no tomorrow. Everything from providing water and sewage at the local level to defense at the national level is getting privatized. Defense contractors and the U.S. Defense Department might as well consolidate all of their offices in the Pentagon, as should the U.S. Treasury and the U.S. Department of Labor locate their offices on K Street in Washington, DC along with pension actuaries, consultants, corporations, and financial institutions representing employer pension plans. With the privatization of Social Security, the Social Security Administration can be run out of the offices of Fidelity and Vanguard mutual fund families.

It is time for citizens to utilize their investment dollars and act as responsible shareholders and confront corporate management directly. Citizens don't have to sacrifice voting rights to exercise their ownership rights. We can do both. We can act as responsible fiduciaries as well as responsible public-minded citizens in a democracy. The power of our dollars is as close as our wallets, our credit cards and our proxies.

Fighting Back: What works and What Doesn't

Socially responsible investment professionals have been around for over thirty years and are responsible for expanding a multitude of financial and investment vehicles and instruments which are available for investors of all stripes, shapes, and sizes, requiring various and sundry investment strategies. With over two hundred mutual funds, as well as stocks, bonds, cash equivalents, CDFIs, private placements, social venture funds, limited liability companies, tax credit programs, and community bank and credit union CDs, SRI has come a long way since the days when Pax World and Dreyfus Third Century were the only mutual fund kids on the block. The SRI universe has expanded astronomically.

In growing the SRI movement we have stumbled; some of the wounds have been critical, but most of them were only superficial. Among the major success stories are Working Assets, Citizens Trust, Calvert Social Investment Funds, Domini, KLD, Trillium, Walden Asset Management, and Parnassus among others, but we lost publicly traded Ben & Jerry's Homemade, Inc., along the way, as well as a few screened mutual funds. Unlike the rest of the herd in the financial services industry, the top echelon of SRI leadership belongs to three strong, determined and progressive women: Amy Domini (Domini Social Fund and KLD), Sophia Collier (Citizens Trust Mutual Funds), and Joan Bavaria (Trillium and CERES).

Through trial and error we have learned that SRI private businesses should approach the public capital markets with a skeptical eye, understanding that IPOs may be more beneficial for investment bankers, attorneys, and accountants than for social entrepreneurs or investors. When companies go from IPO to Chapter 11, the same financial leeches call the shots. Chapter 11 bankruptcies is a cash cow for attorneys which short-changes shareholders, as the courts increasingly have allowed corporate management to retain control of company assets, duping new investors to fund "their" corporations. Poison pill defense strategies may not be appropriate for socially responsible businesses, but offering documents, buy-sell agreements, partner contractual agreements, and by-law amendments articulating the company's social commitment and mission are in order.

A two-thirds vote requirement for any major change in corporate structure or ownership, including joint ventures, would also be appropriate, and would have been beneficial for many companies, including WaterHealth. It is certainly high time for some major structural changes in the private sector along the lines of Upstream 21. I believe that this new structure is the first step in changing the way we think about business development or "capitalism," creating a culture where business is committed to stakeholders and the environment. We might even discover free enterprise again, revive competition, and re-create a market economy not dominated by oligopolies.

The SRI journey has produced a distinguished list of mutual funds and fund families that provide competitive returns, often beating non-screened colleagues and indexes. The ten-year performance records of funds such as Ariel, Ariel Appreciation, Parnassus Equity Income, and others provide not only practical guidance for social investors, but justify SRI claims of competitive portfolio performance. From a social and environmental performance standpoint, most SRI mutual funds vote their stock proxies, and several have an outstanding record of shareholder advocacy, dialogue, and filing resolutions. Some of the funds also have a history of innovative primary market investing; directing capital into community-based loan funds, credit unions, and local banks; and funding third world lenders through the Calvert Foundation. Most mutual fund inclusionary screens would be considered "best in class," with strong exclusionary criteria that primarily excludes gambling, tobacco, alcohol, nuclear power, and weapons stocks. We should not be under any illusion that screening alone will result in changes in the corporate culture or corporate activities. Yet, while it does not cure all ills, screening is still a valuable tool for social change. SRI mutual funds provide competitive performance with non-screened funds, and they narrow the liquid secondary market capital base for company stocks which do not meet minimum social criteria.

SRI mutual funds and private asset managers, while focused primarily on screening, are increasingly raising their primary market allocations by investing in Community Development Financial Institutions (CDFIs). These CDFIs include community banks and credit unions, domestic and global loan funds, and microcredit enterprises. Community investing grew 84 percent between 2001 and 2003, totaling over $14 billion.[3]

Thanks to corporate scandals, accounting frauds, and recent SEC actions, we have seen SRI mutual funds, private equity managers, and institutional portfolio managers increasingly focus on shareholder advocacy. Most of this activity centers around basic corporate management governance issues.

Independent company and mutual fund researcher *Morningstar* now has a new grading system for mutual funds, based upon five categories of corporate governance: regulatory issues, board quality, manager incentives, fees, and corporate culture.

Despite recent scandals, thousands of lay-offs, and public discontent, management salaries are still skyrocketing—and CEOs are ignoring shareholders, even when confronted by (non-binding) resolutions that have gained a supermajority of the vote (often over 70 to 80 percent). Present day corporate princes will resist shareholder demands until forced by law to relent, and there is a precedent for this type of legal action. In 1999, the Oklahoma Supreme Court ruled against Fleming Company and in favor of the International Brotherhood of Teamsters, ruling that shareholders could propose by-laws that restrict board implementation of shareholder rights plans. According to Hawley and Williams in *The Rise of Fiduciary Capitalism*: "The rise of mandatory proposals is fueled by institutional investor anger over the number of shareholder resolutions that have been approved by a majority of shareholders but ignored by management." Shareholder resolutions are "precatory," they express entreaty or supplication. Entreaty is an earnest request, petition or plea. Supplication is to ask humbly, or, as the American Heritage dictionary defines it, "To make a humble and earnest petition; beg." The only action not yet taken by shareholders introducing non-binding resolutions before an omnipotent corporate management is to "beg" on their knees.

Shareholders, the legal owners of corporations, gave up "control for liquidity" as Berle and Means found as early as 1939. Owners can't even afford to nominate outside corporate directors and can't vote "against" corporate board-nominated directors. The most shareholders can do is to "withhold" a vote, which legally means absolutely nothing. In essence, the owners can't nominate a director and can't defeat one either. Stalin would have loved "corporate democracy"; it is no different than one-party communism.

Shareholders submitting binding amendments to bylaws, the constitution of a corporation, is an important development. Unfortunately, it is effective only in states in which corporate codes permit such an action. In California, pursuant to Section 902.(a) of the Corporations Code, amendments to the corporate articles can only be "approved by the board and approved by the outstanding shares (Section 152), either before or after the approval by the board." So unless shareholders effectively nominate and then can elect a majority of directors, and, by a majority vote, adopt a shareholder resolution amending the articles, then, and only then, are the results binding on California corporations.

Corporations can roam at will, playing off one state or city against another for reduced taxes or subsidized local services. They can also manipulate local government planning commissions and city councils to lower development and other real estate-related costs, as well as receive special exemptions from local planning ordinances. James Surowiecki, writing in the December 13, 2004 issue of *The New Yorker* magazine, claims that "With tax breaks, cheap loans, and outright giveaways, states and local communities hand out almost fifty billion dollars in incentives every year."

Corporations have the choice to incorporate in states, such as Delaware, which has historically provided the most liberal corporate statutes for management flexibility and limiting shareholder rights. With the exception of litigation, boycotts, corporate campaigns, and a few other tactics which will be discussed later in this chapter, advocates of shareholder democracy are left with begging corporate management for reforms, voluntary codes, and good corporate governance, while relying on captive state legislatures, Congress, and regulators, including the SEC, to police corporate conduct. Much of the shareholder begging takes the form of letter writing, going to the media (also dominated by corporations), and introducing non-binding shareholder resolutions. The SRI community, ignoring much of its activists roots, has become increasingly comfortable with dialogue, often withdrawing a non-binding shareholder resolution in exchange for the chance to talk to mid-level corporate bureaucrats, public relations personnel, or corporate attorneys who are willing to spend an hour or two in their office or conference room. Receiving a response to a written communication from corporate management is a big deal for many investors. The only time management is *required* to respond to a shareholder is when a resolution is introduced.

I'm reminded of a shareholder-coordinated meeting with representatives of Monsanto to discuss a shareholder resolution on genetic engineering. There were representatives of SRI shareholder groups as well as five Monsanto participants. Most of the talking was by shareholders. Monsanto's concluding and only statement was that the questions presented so much depth and substance that another meeting would have to be scheduled to discuss them. In other words, we achieved a lengthy and one-sided "dialogue" in which shareholder representatives were allowed to sound off, providing Monsanto representatives a great deal of information about shareholder concerns, and questioning Monsanto GMO policies, while Monsanto said nothing. Monsanto was represented by its communications (public relations) personnel and a CSR consultant among others. The principle reason Monsanto participated in this discussion was to give its PR specialists an opportunity to learn shareholder advocacy strategies first hand, so that the company would have access to a wealth of information to improve company propaganda instead of making corporate policy changes. These so-called dialogues fundamentally play into the hands of corporate management. My belief is that many SRI shareholder advocates see dialogue as an end in itself, not a means to an end. Shareholder dialogue is almost always a one-way street, traveling a path that exclusively benefits corporate management. Shareholder advocates should no longer approach management with hat in hand, hoping that a PR person will talk to them.

Monsanto's Robert Shapiro is a natural dialogue expert, putting a happy, well-educated "sincere" face forward, as he did when he addressed the Greenpeace Business Conference in London in 1999. "We are now publicly committed to dialogue with people and groups who have a stake in this issue," he said, adding that a dialogue was a "search for answers, a search for constructive solutions that work for a wide range of people."[4] While Shapiro was uttering this rhetoric, Monsanto continued to spread GMO crops and pesticides around the world. This is just one example of the classic corporate strategy of appearing reasonable and open to change, while carrying on business as usual. Andy Rowell in *Battling Big Business*, claims that many stakeholder dialogues are fundamentally undemocratic, and have no public input. Rowell quoted Mark Dowie in his book *Losing Ground* who criticizes "third wave environmentalists" who shift the battle for the environment from the courtroom to the boardroom as "institutionalized compromise." Dowie is further quoted as saying that "the closer mainstream environmentalists get to corporations and regulators, the more difficult it becomes to maintain their independence and identify as adversaries . . . they can do a lot of damage by helping corporate polluters create the public impression that they are a lot greener than they really are."[5]

This is not much different than the dilemma facing the SRI community. Are we part of the problem or part of the solution? Are we too close to the beast and do we have too much to lose (financially, of course) if we truly challenge corporate power? Corporations are so powerful they can even litigate against and attempt to intimidate Tim Smith of Walden Asset Management (owned by the Royal Bank of Scotland), to prevent him and other active shareholders from speaking at shareholder meetings—even though the resolutions presented are non-binding.

SLEEPING WITH THE ENEMY

The SRI community must avoid being wined and dined by corporate management, as well as avoid personal "relationships" with paid PR and CSR consultants. Too often, we view these as relationships between equals as friendships inevitably develop. Allowing these friendships to develop is exactly the goal of corporate management. Corporations are not "people," they are non-living economic entities created by government and given special privileges. Corporate representatives, as real people, are paid by the elites in corporate management and are hired and fired by them. It is their job to befriend the SRI community. That is why corporate lobbyists are so powerful in Washington, DC and at the state and local government levels—influencing decision makers with money and with personal, friendly relationships. Most lobbyists are former elected officials and staff; everybody knows everybody, everyone is everyone's best friend. The purpose of corporate inspired "friendships" is to infiltrate the SRI community and influence its goals and policies.

You cannot dance with the devil and not be burned. As a former California state senator said: "If you lie down with dogs, you'll wake up with fleas." It is more like waking up with tics, because corporate management is intent on sucking the life-blood out of the SRI community. Their purpose is to eliminate the SRI community altogether, or to strategically manipulate the relationship so that it seems symbiotic.

The Interfaith Center on Corporate Responsibility (ICCR) has a remarkable, thirty-year record of confronting corporations on a wide variety of social, environmental, human rights, and corporate governance issues. ICCR, however, also raises money from these very same corporations. Is this any different than politicians raising money from the special interests they are responsible for overseeing? When corporations such as Citigroup/ Smith Barney, Coca-Cola, Time Warner, Abbott Labs, Disney, Ford, General Motors, Merrill Lynch, Schering Plough, BP, and Anheuser-Busch donate money to ICCR, doesn't this have influence on ICCR, or at the very least, on ICCR's attitude toward corporate donors? This is a corporate investment, like any other. Corporations invest in the legislative and the shareholder process. They seek a return on their investment.

Corporations have a history of hiding behind meaningless voluntary corporate codes, while litigating so that they can continue to ignore human and labor rights and environmental laws. Asserting that the Alien Tort Claims Act (ATCA)—which prohibits companies from supporting slavery, extra-judicial killings, torture, and human rights violations—puts

U.S. corporations at a competitive disadvantage against foreign companies which are not "hindered" by ATCA proves that their voluntary codes are nothing more than propaganda and PR. Time and time again, U.S. corporations operating in apartheid-ruled South Africa hid behind the Sullivan Principles—one of the first voluntary, non-enforceable corporate codes of conduct—to legitimize their economic support of the murderous and illegal white-minority government.

It is my contention that many in the SRI community may have already abandoned long-held social, environmental, and political goals in search for the "legitimacy" of larger shareholder votes on the recently popular corporate governance issues. Unfortunately they believe that bigger, *nonbinding* shareholder votes will result in gaining credibility and, ultimately, gaining access to the boardroom. Many of the new SRI entrants come out of the larger, broker-dealer network, where commitment to core social and environmental policies may be lacking. Others see SRI as simply a niche marketing opportunity. When reviewing social criteria of many of the funds *Morningstar* identifies as "socially conscious," it is clear that there is little pro-active commitment by many SRI screened fund managers to reach social and environmental goals. There is much more reliance on passive exclusionary screens.

As early as 1939, Berle and Means, authors of *The Modern Corporation and Private Property*, claimed that power was so vested in management that stockholders simply supplied capital and were no longer considered "quasi-partners" in the enterprise. They also claimed that the only reason management didn't abuse the suppliers of capital was that the company was in constant need of such capital. Not much has changed in sixty-five years.

The most potent weapon an investor has is to deny capital to a business or substantially increase the cost of such capital. By the same token, the most important consumer weapon against a company is a coordinated strategy to deny market share through actions such as consumer boycotts.

The lesson of the divestment campaign in South Africa is that only when actions affect the bottom line do they impact corporate conduct. SRI will only have an impact on corporate management if it costs a corporation money, as a negative, or proves that good corporate conduct is profitable, as a positive. Unfortunately, as the SRI community legitimizes "corporate social responsibility" we may be playing into the hands of our corporate princes. According to Sheldon Rampton, in a 2002 article in PR Watch entitled *Corporate Social Responsibility and the Crisis of Globalization:* "From the point of view of 'anti-globalization' protestors, these issues [child labor, climate change, ozone depletion, GMOs, urban air quality, etc.] demonstrate why corporations cannot be trusted to oversee the emerging new global order. From the point of view of corporate leaders, however, corporate social responsibility is important precisely as a vehicle for reassuring the public that corporate globalization is a good thing."

In March 2002, Sustainability, a British company, and Ketchum PR produced a report calling for activist dialogue with corporations that are embroiled in environmental and human rights controversies. Rampton also reported that earlier, at a November 2001 summit organized by the International Communications Consultancy Organization, Ketchum chairman David Drobis declared that the "new global imperative for public relations" was "confidence building to save globalization" by targeting three groups: "The private sector, non-governmental organizations, and international institutions." Drobis said that the best way to disprove that "international capitalism is nothing but a byword for oppression, exploitation and injustice . . . was to demonstrate that there is a positive correlation between social responsibility and profitability." In other words, as the SRI community legitimizes good corporate governance, CSR, "sustainability" and other PR gimmicks of corporate management, we reinforce as well the concentration of corporate oligopolies over our global economy and political system. It further legitimizes corporate self-regulation and voluntarism, as opposed to mandating statutory conduct.

There are those in the SRI community that want to step even closer to the "evil empire" and believe they can be everything for everybody. U.K.-based ISIS Asset Management claims that it has "decoupled" shareholder engagement from asset management with its Responsible Engagement Overlay (REO), first introduced in 1999, when it was known as Friends Ivory & Sime. ISIS has a twelve-member REO team that dialogues with corporate management and engages in shareholder advocacy, but does not exclude any company from the investment portfolio. Investors can be owners of every detestable corporation engaged in egregious activity around the globe and still feel good, because the REO team is advocating on their behalf. This is a marketer's dream come true, and the ultimate insult to the SRI community.

Elizabeth McGeveran, vice-president of governance and socially responsible investment at ISIS, explains the program: "What's so attractive to institutional investors such as universities or pension funds that want to address social and environmental issues is that this work doesn't in any way impact stock selection. REO allows them to have their cake and eat it, too: they still have the whole universe of stocks to pick from while we're out there working for productive change in the marketplace. With screening, you avoid the ownership position, but REO is a completely unscreened option that works directly with companies to get them to alter corporate practice: it is totally focused on change.[6]

This irony, or perhaps you could say, absurdity, plays very well from a marketing standpoint, but only if you believe that dialogue and shareholder advocacy are effective in *changing* corporate behavior. (Let's keep in mind that shareholder votes are advisory only, and it is almost impossible for shareholders to nominate directors or defeat management's slate of directors.) Otherwise, it can be seen by critics and skeptics alike as political face-saving and an SRI marketing triumph. This allows the SRI community and corporate management to put a serious dialogue and shareholder engagement public relations effort forward, forever linking them in a symbiotic relationship. SRI professionals can continue to take money from clients while attempting to convince them that they are in serious dialogue with corporate leadership, ultimately prevailing in changing corporate behavior. Everybody wins—or do they? Does anything really change? Isn't this somewhat similar to Vanguard Group's propaganda campaign to convince its mutual fund clients and the public that it is advocating for corporate governance changes?

Vanguard, which voted last year with corporate management 90 percent of the time, is now approving only 29 percent of the full slates of directors proposed by corporate management.[7] It may be more PR than good corporate governance, since Vanguard is now required by the SEC to disclose its shareholder voting record. Vanguard and Fidelity were both adamantly against the SEC rule mandating full disclosure and transparency of mutual fund voting records. Vanguard makes it appear that it has reformed by only approving about a third of director nominee slates, while in actuality, withholding its vote has no impact on corporate governance.

The latest action by the SEC is the use of "shame." According to a Dow Jones news story, the SEC has approved rules that will "shame" a company by requiring it to disclose why it doesn't have a nominating committee comprised of independent directors, whether or not the company has a process for shareholders to communicate with management, information on how a corporate board goes about identifying and selecting directors, and lastly, why the company never considers director candidates proposed by shareholders.[8]

I question the effectiveness of this tactic. History has shown us that corporations such as IBM (which sold technology to the Third Reich and South Africa's apartheid government) or Monsanto (which makes profits from cancer-causing products), are unlikely to respond to "shame."

Since the SEC shies away from its job, it is up to investors to advocate for change. Certainly one route that remains limited, but open, is shareholder action. Introducing resolutions does get *some* attention. The Reverend Jesse Jackson's nonprofit organization made an idealistic (if not realistic) attempt to influence technology companies and raise the banner for affirmative action, which received media attention when the Rainbow Coalition bought stock and threatened shareholder action. More important, and effective, have been the ongoing attempts by Global Exchange, Amnesty International, Rainforest Action Network, the Sierra Club, the Jessie Smith Noyes Foundation, and others, to institutionalize shareholder advocacy as part of mission-related investing.

Mission-related investing by public interest organizations, environmental groups, foundations, and family trusts are allied with what Robert Monks and Nell Minow describe in their book *Corporate Governance* as "universal owners," mostly played by large retirement funds, such as TIAA-CREF or

CALPERS. These institutional investors are universal owners because their portfolios encompassing the entire diversified market of stocks, bonds, real estate, and other holdings representing the country's economy, align fiduciary interests with stakeholders' interests and the public interest. Universal owners cannot be "one -company oriented" because if that company profits at the expense of others and the public (by externalizing costs such as the cost of pollution), higher taxes and burdensome regulations will be imposed that will reduce the performance of other investments in the portfolio. This is especially true for universal owners such as public employee pension funds when such external costs are borne by their beneficiaries. For example, universal owners/institutional investors that index their stock portfolio to the broad overall market and economy become universal "citizens" and are faced with difficult economic trade-offs when it comes to making money off tobacco stocks, while paying for long-term health care and the quality of life for their beneficiaries.

While shareholder advocate Stephen Viederman insists that screening alone is a blunt instrument approach to impacting corporate conduct, he is adamant in calling for shareholder advocacy and community investing. Certainly shareholder advocacy over the last 30 years has raised social, environmental, and corporate governance issues. With the SEC requiring mutual fund managers to disclose their votes, the result will clearly be more mutual fund shareholder scrutiny.

As early as May 2003, ISIS—the United Kingdom's biggest global money management firm, (with £58.5 billion in assets)—publicly reported how it voted on fourteen thousand resolutions in 2002, siding with management 93 percent of the time.[9] While transparency and voting records are important instruments of full disclosure of mutual funds, managers, and private client managers, we need to realize that manager attention still remains focused on quarter-to-quarter performance. Stock trading and ownership responsibilities are rarely compatible.

As Lance Lindblom, president and CEO of the Nathan Cummings Foundation, said: "Not surprisingly, they [portfolio managers] have no concept of corporate ownership or stewardship, only buy and sell recommendations."[10] According to the Motley Fool: "The average holding time of a stock by an actively managed mutual fund is 354 days—less than one year. They don't care what happens to the companies long term—they'll be gone."[11] Therein lies one of the greatest hurdles for socially responsible investors: the disconnect between ownership and constantly trading securities, which are meaningless and intangible to many portfolio managers, who see numbers and names on a screen and have no formal or informal relationship to corporate management, much less carry on written or verbal communication with them. I wonder if new managers have even seen or held a stock certificate. Many portfolios managers are totally removed from the life of the business, may not have any experience running a business, and may have never interacted with corporate employees and management. They are not only separated by physical distance but their overall objectives are quite different.

The objective of the manager or registered investment advisor is to produce income and/or capital gains for her clients at a performance level at or above the established indexes and at or above the performance of her colleagues in the profession. The pressure on a manager to perform is applied both quarterly and annually. Regardless of what anyone says, a manager is judged for both short-term and long-term performance. It may have little to do with companies' day-to-day operations simply because stock trading can be quarter-by-quarter, day-by-day, or minute-by-minute. The ability of the manager to take trading profits for the client often has little correlation with the company's ability, or lack thereof, to produce earnings or make a profit. Some managers' performances may be solely based on short-term changes in stock prices or based on technical market movements, which could be the result of rumors, speculation, insider trading, large institutions rotating out of a sector and into a new one, or changes required in manager sector weighting to an index.

The objective of corporate management is to make money for itself first, shareholders second. It is also under pressure to perform by increasing earnings quarterly and annually, but unlike a portfolio manager, corporate management cannot sell for a short-term capital gain and move onto another company stock in a manner of minutes. For the CEO, making money for himself first and shareholders second is one that ebbs and flows depending upon the economy, the industry, or a business cycle. While both corporate management and the portfolio manager may have long- or short-term performance objectives, they operate at a different level, and on an entirely different path. The CEO's eye is on his own self-aggrandizement while the manager's eye is on maximizing short-term financial return for her clients. Lindblom is correct in saying that most portfolio managers have no concept of corporate ownership or stewardship. Unfortunately, neither does corporate management.

If we follow this logic to the next level it is even more distressing. If portfolio managers are removed from ownership responsibilities, think about the other levels of bureaucracy that remove us from our money and our ownership responsibility. For example, if my 401(k) retirement plan is in a mutual fund it is managed by a portfolio manager who buys and sells stocks day to day. Or, let's say I am a participant in a retirement plan through CALPERS: board members are partially elected by members, appointed by the governor, or are elected officials. The board works with paid staff and consultants to hire portfolio managers, and the managers buy and sell stocks. You get the picture—the levels of ownership responsibilities are delegated which is further removed from the ultimate beneficiaries: retirees and employees.

If you think that the ownership relationship is distant between a retiree or employee in a large pension fund and company management, think about how much further one is removed if the portfolio manager is trading stock options—which represent no ownership in a company or companies—but are contracts to sell or buy stocks or baskets of securities (index options) within a certain period of time for a certain price. The relationship becomes even more confusing if the manager holds an option to purchase a stock (call option) and it is "assigned," requiring him to buy the stock, which then represents ownership. What about electronically traded funds? Or stock indexes such as those representing the S&P 500 Index or FTSE4GOOD? These esoteric instruments are legitimate investments to make money for a portfolio manager or a broker's clients, but they only represent a basket of stocks or securities, not real ownership. There is no stewardship by investors that have no legal ownership and for only a brief period of time hold a "representation" of ownership. How distorted capitalism has become; how impersonal and abstract.

Obviously, defining what constitutes true ownership would be a first step, but largely an academic one. Corporations have many stakeholders, including shareholders, management, employees, vendors, communities, customers, taxpayers, and global citizens. The real world demands real solutions, or at least an attempt at a real solution. The legal relationship of a common stockholder as the owner of the corporation cannot change overnight. Ownership responsibility cannot be forced, but it can certainly be encouraged. The SEC and the U.S. Department of Labor, by requiring mutual fund and manager shareholder voting and disclosure to be tied to ERISA fiduciary responsibility, have taken a good first step. Most important is the encouragement of shareholder responsibility, both institutional and individual. Voting stock proxies is another helpful action, especially if resolutions were binding on corporate management.

As early as 1978, organized labor found that its member-invested pension funds were not only *not* being used to benefit workers and retirees; they were often being used *against* them. This took the form of investments in anti-union companies, runaway shops, contracting out and privatizing public employee union jobs, and outsourcing private sector jobs overseas. Labor has been particularly adamant about speaking its mind at annual shareholder meetings and through its proxy votes. Labor sided with Amy Domini and the SRI community in successfully convincing the SEC to require mutual funds to disclose how they vote their shares on behalf of mutual fund shareholders. Richard Trumka, Secretary-Treasurer of the AFL-CIO, declared that 38 percent of the federation's 13 million union members are in defined contribution plans and that mutual funds are members' primary investment choice.[12]

Currently, about 20 percent of companies with defined benefit plans (the total number is 32,500) have either frozen or canceled their plans in the last three years, causing Congress to allow corporations to reduce their contributions by 10 percent in 2004 and 2005.[13] Corporations have moved rapidly to replace defined benefit plans with defined contribution plans for their employees because, unlike defined benefit plans, there is no contractual obligation on behalf of the corporation to meet a set benefit schedule for employees, and the employees are "on the hook" for any risky investments they make (primarily investments in mutual funds) in their defined contribution plans. The level of employees' future benefits depends on how well their investments perform. Think about what will happen to future benefits if the Bush administration is successful in partially privatizing Social Security (Republican propagandists are calling it "modernization"). Current and future Social Security beneficiaries will be rolling the dice to invest in mutual funds hyped by big Wall Street marketing firms. Social Security recipients and future beneficiaries will be subjected to a barrage of marketing gimmicks by Wall Street promising high returns and low risk. Beneficiaries will be stuck with just the opposite—low returns and high risk.

POLITICS AND "FREE" TRADE

Senator Hillary Clinton (D-NY) talked about a "vast right-wing conspiracy," but her husband Bill, who served two terms as president of the United States, gave corporate America and conservatives just about everything they wanted. Bill and his Democratic Leadership Council (DLC) abandoned traditional long-held core Democratic Party positions and constituencies on welfare reform, criminal justice, and world trade. He was basically a Republican in Democratic clothing. Clinton also proved that Democrats could represent corporations as easily as Republicans. As Matt Bai wrote in the July 25, 2004 article in *The New York Times Magazine*: "Under Clinton, who became the most powerful money magnet the Oval Office had ever seen, the Democratic Party and its various committees began sucking up mountainous contributors from what are known in politics as access donors—corporations."

The greatest damage, long-term, was Clinton's adoption of George Bush Sr.'s NAFTA, GATT, and WTO proposals to eliminate national sovereignty and place all power in corporate–dominated trade organizations. As Crensen and Ginsberg suggest in *Downsizing Democracy*: "President Clinton's tactic of 'triangulation,' or capturing the middle, indicated that the Democratic Party had turned its face from economically vulnerable factory workers and the poor and uneducated. Over the protests of organized labor, the Clinton administration promoted trade deregulation that threatened the jobs of American workers."

Where George Bush Sr. was unsuccessful in obtaining congressional approval of the GATT/WTO treaty, Clinton was successful in the final days of his first four-year term. The thirty-thousand-page agreement basically created a corporate controlled world government without fair representation for the United States and an international court system without due process. It includes fifty committees, boards, and panels. The WTO Dispute Settlement Body Panels are secret, and decisions are rendered anonymously by unaccountable bureaucrats.

In 1972, after twenty-five years of work by the Humane Society of the United States, Congress adopted its Marine Mammal Protection Act, which prohibited U.S. tuna fishermen from using purse seine nets that kill dolphins. Under the WTO, Mexico, supported by the Clinton administration, challenged the Act claiming it was a violation of free trade and won. It is now legal to catch and import into the U.S. purse seine-netted tuna from anywhere in the world, thus continuing the global practice of killing hundreds of thousands of dolphins caught in those nets.

According to Noreena Hertz of Cambridge University, in every environmental or species dispute that has come before the WTO, it "has ruled in favor of corporate interests against the wishes of democratically elected governments."[14]

If the WTO rules that a law is a barrier to trade, the offending government must change the law, pay heavy fines, or suffer severe trade sanctions. This result is a disaster for democracy, and for laws designed to protect labor, human rights, and the environment. National sovereignty has vanished.

The WTO uses "dispute settlement body panels" to review challenges by countries against other countries' safety, consumer, and environmental laws that are considered a barrier to "free trade." It is called "harmonizing" by the WTO. According to Thom Hartmann, the panels' "largest effect has been to put corporations on a level ground with national governments. Corporations can sue countries under WTO, and many have successfully won tens of millions of dollars for 'unfair restraint of trade' because of laws designed to protect the environment or workers. So far, no countries have sued a corporation under WTO."[15]

The amazing thing is that these panels have the force of law, violating democratic sovereignty while meeting in private. The public is forbidden to watch, listen, or participate in meetings and no information on documentation or testimony upon which a decision may be based is ever made available to the public. According to Hartmann, "Under NAFTA and WTO, a corporation can sue a foreign government and can also force the taxpayers of the dependent nation to pay the corporation for any profits it might have earned if the nation had not passed laws that restricted free trade."[16]

The European Union compromised somewhat by allowing the importation of genetically modified food, but only if it is labeled. The Bush administration is still fighting this, and the battle, much less the GMO war, is far from over.

California became the first state in the United States to ban the sale of genetically engineered, glow-in-the-dark zebrafish, and in March 2004, Mendocino County voters decided to prohibit GMO crops from being grown in the county. In August 2004, Trinity County's board of supervisors was the second county in California to ban the growing of GMO crops and animals, followed by the approval of a similar proposal by 61 percent of Marin County voters in the 2004 general election.

Many of the GMO battles are being fought in and around the WTO, but in Cancun, Mexico, with so much disagreement between wealthy and developing countries over U.S. and European Union farm subsidies (about $320 billion per year), trade discussions ended in failure. One Geneva-based diplomatic analyst said: "It certainly looks like the end of the World Trade Organization as we know it."[17] Don't bet on it. Of course, the United States blamed the failure on those greedy poor countries that wanted to unfairly compete with our publicly funded corporate conglomerate farmers. Actually, former U.S. Trade Representative Robert Zoellick said, "poorer countries—which demanded that the United States and the European Union end all farm subsidies and drop barriers to agricultural imports—had rejected good offers."[18]

Never to be outdone with outdated rules and regulations, European Union Trade Commissioner Pascal Lamy suggested that the size and disparity of the WTO, where the smallest member can block any action, had confirmed his view that the WTO was a "medieval organization" and needed streamlined decision making.[19] This means that if the big, wealthy countries can't get their way with developing countries, they'll just change the rules—it is now called "streamlined decision making." It will probably be modeled after the U.N. Security Council, where the richest and most powerful countries comprise the membership of an Executive Board, able to make decisions for the "uninformed rabble" of developing countries. There's even better news. Lamy now runs the WTO. Doesn't that make you sleep well at night?

The latest battle for corporate "free" trade advocates is to extend the North American Free Trade Agreement (NAFTA) to every country in Central America, South America, and the Caribbean, except Cuba (they're communist, but not in the good way like corporate-dominated communist China). The Free Trade Area of the Americas (FTAA)—which was also negotiated behind closed doors—further continues the race to the bottom for labor and environmental protection, similar to NAFTA. Negotiations began shortly after the completion of the NAFTA agreement in 1994 and were scheduled to be completed by 2005. Massive demonstrations erupted in Miami when the latest talks were held, as corporations were again accused by labor, civil, and human rights organizations of eliminating national sovereignty by creating an agreement that ignores transparency, international cooperation, cultural diversity, environmental sustainability, and social equality, relegating all human conduct to economic transactions.

Never to be deterred by democratic institutions, sovereign nations, or failed FTAA negotiations, Zoellick is cutting deals with Central American countries (Central American Free Trade Agreement or CAFTA) and hopes to include Costa Rica and the Dominican Republic. CAFTA will be presented to Congress for approval and will also include the original CAFTA members, El Salvador, Guatemala, Honduras, and Nicaragua.[20] This new "deal" regulates trades jobs, environmental protection, and health for corporate exports, including a requirement to strengthen intellectual property rights, which would further weaken generic drug manufacturers in Central America, limiting access by poor people to inexpensive medicine.

Within the U.S., farmers are overproducing agricultural commodities thanks to increased productivity, while giant food companies and the fast food folks stuff us with more twenty-ounce Cokes and super-size meals. U.S. agricultural policy was changed under Nixon's secretary of agriculture. Farmers were paid cash for overproduction, allowing them to flood the market regardless of price. Overproduction has been assisted by increased mechanization, hybrid seed, agrochemicals, and genetically modified crops.

So agribusiness produces too much food, subsidized by the U.S. taxpayer, who is destroying his health by eating lots of junk food, while supporting a government that is dumping cheap excess food on starving, developing countries, driving third world farmers out of business. All the while, food companies, agri-chemical corporations, and fast food chains stuff money in the pockets of politicians, lobbyists, and regulators to keep the system going.

Of course, most of the federal farm subsidies go to the largest corporate farmers, while small farmers continue to decrease in numbers. From 1999 to 2000, thirty-three thousand farms with annual sales of less than $100,000 disappeared, while farms generating more than $500,000 use 20.3 percent of farmland and account for 61.9 percent of all sales. The ten largest food companies account for more than 50 percent of all products on supermarket shelves.[21]

In a *New York Times Magazine* article, Michael Pollan added a cute political note to this tragedy: "It doesn't hurt that those lightly populated farm states exert a disproportionate influence in Washington, since it takes far fewer votes to elect a senator in Kansas than in California. That means agribusiness can presumably 'buy' a senator from one of these under-populated states for a fraction of what a big-state senator costs."

Now that's a smart, targeted, and cost effective corporate political strategy if I ever saw one. That's why corporate lobbyists and political hacks get those big bucks.

As much as the United States government talks about free trade—never fair trade—it still provides U.S. farmers with about $2 billion in annual subsidies and spends $2.6 billion to buy and ship U.S. commodities for food aid programs overseas.[22] Corporate farmers rake in lots of taxpayer money as do commodity-processing conglomerates such as Archer-Daniels-Midland and Cargill, Inc. In fact, the whole giant U.S. food industry benefits from U.S. policies, while poor third world country farmers get the short end of the stick.

African cotton farmers are forced to compete with U.S. agribusiness, which received as much as $3 billion in annual subsidies.[23] According to the October, 2003 *Africa Recovery*: "Despite pledges by industrial nations to reduce state subsidies paid out to their farmers, these have continued to grow and now average $300 billion annually—more than five times greater than official development assistance to poor countries."

The New York Times also reports that the Philippines, which have suffered economically since joining the WTO in 1995, "increasingly view the much-promoted globalization as a new imperialism." China also joined the WTO amidst much fanfare, and now Bush, his corporate buddies, and big agribusiness are upset that the authoritarian U.S.-supported government is blocking U.S. agricultural imports such as soybeans and cotton.[24]

"Free trade," as defined by the WTO and corporate management, puts to the test not only national sovereignty, but a traditional American economic philosophy of continuing to build a strong diversified economy which is not dependent exclusively on exports. If a nation's wealth, health, and economic success are dependent upon an export strategy alone, the economy will be subject to uncontrollable oligopolistic corporate forces that could destroy a domestic economy and put national security at risk. Just ask governments and nation-states that are dependent on a few natural resource exports, such as perishable agricultural food crops, timber, or extractive industries.

The criticism of Chinese government actions, especially within the context of the WTO, by Bush, agribusiness, and corporate oligarchies is ludicrous. On the one hand, they greedily rub their palms together in anticipation of a large consumer market; cheap labor to replace American, Mexican, and Southeast Asian workers; access to Chinese natural resources with no environmental, human, or labor rights restrictions; and a government only too eager to buy American corporate technology to spy on and suppress subversive democracy advocates within the country. Only when the strength of Chinese currency, state corporations, farmers, and overall Chinese exports threaten U.S. economic hegemony, does our government and large corporations whine about being placed at a competitive disadvantage to Chinese economic forces. The hypocrisy is revealed when these same entities—which have done everything in their power to pump U.S. capital and technology into the country and build up China's ability to become an exporting power—criticize the competition.

Corporate management so owns U.S. policy makers in Washington that they will always do their bidding for it. Companies play off city against city, county against county, state against state, and nation against nation to get the best deal. When corporations tire of buying local, state, and national governments and politicians, they can go to the WTO since now governments have delivered their people's sovereignty to the WTO where decisions are made by a small group of people meeting in private, answerable to no one. Politicians and government have been effectively replaced by corporations. Politicians and government have made themselves irrelevant!

SRI Under Attack

Non-governmental organizations (NGOs), such as Amnesty International, Global Exchange, Greenpeace, Rainforest Action Network (RAN), and others, have been able to work internationally to provide some support and protection for activists and environmentalists working to free citizens from corporate and authoritarian government control. RAN's tax-exempt status is being challenged by a conservative think tank that claims that the organization is pursuing a "utopian, pollution-free socialist world."[25]

Environmental groups and other NGOs are being attacked by right-wing corporate-sponsored nonprofits, such as the Institute of Public Affairs of Australia and the American Enterprise Institute (AEI), charging Amnesty, Greenpeace, and Oxfam with threatening U.S. sovereignty and free-market capitalism, and claiming that these "international NGOs are pursuing a leftist or 'liberal' agenda that favors 'global governance' and other notions that are also promoted by the United Nations and other multi-lateral agencies."[26] The fear of liberal "global governance" is particularly ironic when it comes from corporate-sponsored organizations, since corporations have been overwhelmingly in favor of "global governance" such as the WTO, and funding most of the politicians, including the two U.S. presidents, who signed "free trade" legislation. These same conservative organizations condemn international NGOs that led the fight for a ban on anti-personnel mines, the Kyoto Protocol—which called for a curb on greenhouse-gas emissions—and the treaty establishing the International Criminal Court (ICC).[27]

Not to be outdone by right-wing policy groups in attacking NGOs, the U.S. Attorney General's Office has filed suit against Greenpeace under an obscure 1872 law for an act of civil protest and disobedience. John Passacantando, executive director of Greenpeace in the United States, said this was a government attack on civil liberties, and that if Greenpeace were to lose this fight in court, "it would have a chilling effect on Greenpeace and on other groups that exercise their First Amendment right aggressively."[28] The nonprofit corporation Greenpeace couldn't go to jail, but a victory for the government could jeopardize the organization's tax-exempt status. This is certainly an attempt by the government to intimidate protestors, activists, nonprofits, and civil rights advocates.

Mission-related investing is a latent power available to NGOs, which includes the ability to move beyond simple screening—which has little impact on corporate management—to a broad range of ownership strategies. Besides the groups already mentioned—Amnesty International, Global Exchange, Rainforest Action Network, Greenpeace, and the Sierra Club—which are exercising ownership responsibilities, there are family trusts and foundations in the early stages of shareholder advocacy, coupled with more mature large institutional investors such as CALPERS, TIAA-CREF, and other public sector and union-trusteed pension and retirement funds. Leading the parade have been SRI mutual funds and private client asset managers, many of which have been shareholder advocates for more than thirty years.

Warnings from right-wing groups such as American Enterprise Institute have already been raised about SRI, declaring the movement "a wolf in sheep's clothing."[29] No doubt SRI is threatening to conservatives, since investors are owners of capital, supporters of "free enterprise," not oligopolies, and are demanding disclosure, corporate responsibility, and accountability.

Not surprisingly, HII has found that the investors with the most clout have the greatest access. Most of the time, publicly-traded companies do not even bother to respond to shareholder communications. A company is under no obligation or requirement to converse with shareholders other than at formal annual shareholders' meetings, which are occasionally held in foreign countries. Nike has been known to enjoy prohibitively distant venues such as Holland. It is also within management's discretion to restrict the annual meeting to two hours, limit shareholders' time at the microphone, or never call upon an aggrieved shareholder at all. Now several states allow companies to hold their meetings online. Thanks to the power of corporate lobbyists at the state legislative level, I'm sure there will be more states joining the crush to meet on-line and avoid facing shareholders in the flesh.

Lack of access not only frustrates shareholders who are the legal owners of corporations, but when a resolution actually receives a majority vote, it is only advisory and can legally be ignored by management, as it usually is. This inevitably leads shareholders, as well as other stakeholders, to look for alternative ways to influence corporate princes.

THE STRUGGLE FOR SHAREHOLDER POWER

We've seen how corporations have been able to ignore shareholders, and we've learned that corporate management spends time and money hiring and training corporate social responsibility (CSR) mouthpieces and developing voluntary codes of conduct and "sustainability" standards that can provide cover without any oversight or sanctions. These voluntary standards force the SRI community, NGO's, and investors to spend valuable time and money spinning their wheels, accomplishing little while continuing to delay effective code enforcement from legitimate rule-making government bodies or regulatory agencies, either domestic or global. Corporate management has been able to avoid enactment and enforcement of any statutory corporate codes of conduct, thanks to its ability to manipulate politicians and government regulators. Those corporate codes that do exist are voluntary, with no enforcement, and no sanctions for non-compliance. Basically, there are no rules other than those designed by and for corporate management. Marjorie Kelly summed it up nicely in the Summer, 2003 issue of *Business Ethics*:

> It is time we in CSR began studying these mechanisms, talking about system design, understanding why corporations behave so single-mindedly. And that means focusing on power. Because power is what it is all about, not good intentions or voluntary initiatives or toothless codes of conduct. Power.
>
> If the financial elite wield power, the CSR movement would talk. We put managers through ethics training, help them craft voluntary codes, applaud their environmental stewardship, or launch dialogues through shareholder resolutions—assuming that well-meaning managers can overcome the system-wide pressure to get the numbers. But they can't. To use an extreme analogy, it is like talking ethics to an S.S. officer in Weimar, Germany, while ignoring the system in which he must function.
>
> If CSR has been riveted on things colossally beside the point, it is because we haven't focused enough on system design—particularly on how the system lends power to the financial elite. We haven't fully advanced this issue of power. We haven't adequately studied how it is currently used or fully imagined how to craft new structures of power—structures where power is wielded not by the few but by the many. Structures that can turn stakeholder management from rhetoric into reality.

Kelly called for economic democracy and for the SRI community to create a new structure of justice with checks and balances to safeguard the common good.

Author and journalist William Greider also calls for major structural changes. He believes that the recent scandals and financial meltdown of the early twenty-first century have raised specific issues that need to be addressed. He believes that markets lack legitimacy and "that by their nature, are driven by self-interested profit objectives and serve other, larger clients (mainly corporations) in ways that directly conflict with the interests and values of the investors."[30]

Greider believes that the "shareholder value" doctrine needs to be replaced with a broader understanding of the corporation's purpose, including its obligations to its other constituencies, such as the employees, community, and society it serves.[31] He also believes that corporate behavior has been deformed by pressures to generate short-term gains which have often led to damaging society and destroying the very things people need in their lives, such as safe workplaces, stable communities, and a healthy environment. He questions the concept of who owns the corporation: Is it shareholders or is it really executive insiders exercising control, accompanied by a few financiers and large, institutional investors, i.e., universal owners defined by Hawley & Williams in *Fiduciary Capitalism*? He summarizes his concerns by stating: "So long as shareholders remain distant from the actual company and ready to dump their shares on short notice, it is illogical to imagine they will ever exercise wise and patient supervision. In fact, the destructiveness and inequalities generated by corporations are unlikely to be reduced until the steep pyramid of power is flattened, with the ownership distributed broadly among employees and other interested constituencies, including trustworthy community institutions."[32]

Therein lies one of the major obstacles to shareholders improving corporate conduct—shareholders have almost no power. Even if large institutional shareholders and other owners could effectively coordinate massive serious shareholder vote challenges to management; resolutions are "advisory," amounting to begging; non-management nominations of board members are prohibitively expensive; and "withhold" votes are worthless. As of the publication of this book, the illustrious SEC is already watering down its initial proposal to provide limited institutional shareholder access to board nominations, believing that such access "might disrupt boards."[33] And now, Christopher Cox, a conservative Republican from Orange County, California, has been appointed by George W. Bush as the new SEC chair.

Since a corporation is defined as a person, both the film "The Corporation" and Joel Bakan's book, *The Corporation: The Pathological Pursuit of Profit and Power*, decided to analyze what kind of "person" a corporation would be if it were composed of flesh and bone. Both found that corporations have a psychopathic personality with destructive behavior. The psychopathic corporation, if left uncontrolled, will do anything and everything to advance its own self-interest. Bakan believes that governments have freed corporations from almost all legal constraints and that they are now roaming the earth similar to the large prehistoric dinosaurs, eating and crushing everything in their path. Bakan argues that corporate rule is not inevitable and must be challenged. He sets forth numerous recommendations, including improving and strengthening regulatory oversight, increasing the role of trade unions, publicly financing political campaigns, restricting corporate lobbying and the revolving door between government and the private sector, improving and protecting "the commons" (publicly supported education, parks, water, health care, police and defense) and focusing more on people rather than "market fundamentalism."

One of the more positive results of the WorldCom and Enron "busts" is that to protect themselves, former directors took money out of their own pockets to settle shareholder suits. Ten former directors of WorldCom agreed to pay $18 million as part of a $54 million settlement and ten former directors of Enron agreed to pay $13 million of their own money as part of a similar $168 million settlement.[34]

Corporate directors usually hide behind a battery of attorneys, as well as liability insurance, to shield their personal assets from lawsuits. Directors, as fiduciaries, should be held personally responsible, go to jail, and have their assets seized when found guilty of a corporate crime.

CORPORATE CAMPAIGNS

Citizen, shareholder, and stakeholder frustration over corporate abuse and increasingly unchallenged economic and political power is leading many to call for a new round of "corporate campaigns," as well as other more aggressive strategies. A corporate campaign is a term that refers to a coordinated, often long-term, and wide-ranging program of economic, political, legal, psychological, and public relations efforts to influence corporate behavior. Jarol B. Manheim, in his book *Death of a Thousand Cuts*, describes such campaigns as coming from many directions "not merely from unions, but from religious, consumer rights, environmental, human rights, civil rights, and other groups and coalitions that are more or less closely allied with labor."

The first corporate campaign to receive major national attention was developed in 1976 by Ray Rogers and the Amalgamated Clothing and Textile Workers Union (ACTWU) to force the giant textile corporation J. P. Stevens to recognize ACTWU, settle strikes, and comply with several labor rulings of the National Labor Relations Board (NLRB). J. P. Stevens was the bad boy of employers, running southern textile mills with unsafe working conditions, paying low wages, and repeatedly violating labor, health, and safety rules, ignoring rulings by the NLRB, as well as being found guilty of racial discrimination. The movie *Norma Rae* was based on the J. P. Stevens unionization efforts.

Rogers researched and examined the corporation from top to bottom, evaluating corporate finances, large shareholders, vendors, lenders, corporate officers and board members, and their interlocking relationships. Rogers' "power analysis" identified the interlocks between J. P. Stevens' board and banks and insurance companies that provided corporate financing. "Rogers first targeted Manufacturers Hanover Trust, on whose board James Finley, Stevens' chairman, sat," writes Manheim. "Finley was forced to decline reelection to the board and also to resign from the board of New York Life. Shortly afterward, David Mitchell, chairman of Avon Products, resigned from both the Manufacturers Hanover board and the board of Stevens as well."

Rogers coordinated publicity through letter-writing campaigns focused on demanding that banks and insurance companies withdraw their support from Stevens, and ACTWU ran slates of directors for the board. Manufacturers Hanover Trust was threatened with the withdrawal of union pension funds, and citing a seldom-used New York law, Metropolitan Life was threatened with an election among its 23 million policyholders that could have cost millions of dollars. Other companies that supported Stevens were also under fire from other unions and consumer and religious groups. ACTWU was supported by SRI groups, including ICCR, which filed a pair of shareholder resolutions requesting corporate reports on labor practices and equal employment reporting.

The classic corporate campaign obviously involves a thorough analysis of the financial relationships of a company, but also an analysis of management and board and their relationship with stakeholders and others in the community. Often corporate campaigns get personal, as did J. P. Stevens, when directors' personal residences are picketed, and each director's relationship with his community is reviewed. Often outside board directors are not even aware of the social or environmental impact of a particular company operation, and a well-publicized corporate campaign may have immediate results. As John Vidal, environmental editor of *The Guardian*, reported: "In the United States, the head of a large Japanese corporation, which was responsible for much deforestation in the Far East, was reportedly so shocked about the scale of what his company was doing that he immediately changed the policy."[35]

Of course, not all corporate campaigns work, especially boycotts against large global companies. It is also true that few, if any, corporate executives will react favorably to criticism of corporate policy or a particularly harmful company operation. Civil actions against corporations and their top executives are becoming more personalized, much of it the result of the Internet and corporations themselves sharing confidential information.

Animal rights advocates are already targeting executives of companies conducting animal testing, publicly denouncing them in their local communities. For example, Stop Huntingdon Animal Cruelty papered a Los Angeles neighborhood with leaflets and gathered outside an executive's home, calling Huntingdon Life Sciences Company "puppy killers."[36] In a tactic adopted from anti-abortion activists, many groups are now posting targeted individuals' names and home addresses on the Internet, urging their supporters to contact corporate executives personally.

Huntingdon is Europe's largest independent animal testing operation, a

British-based laboratory which tests drugs, pesticides, and other products on about seventy thousand animals per year, killing nearly every animal they test "in order to study the animals' internal organs."[37] Because of animal rights protests, several financial institutions have severed their ties with the company, including Merrill Lynch, Citigroup, Barclays PLC, Royal Bank of Scotland PLC, and a half-dozen more.[38]

Some environmental organizations use unique legal approaches to effect change. One of these organizations is The Guardians, which leads a zero-grazing environmental movement based in New Mexico and seeks to eventually eliminate livestock grazing in the western United States. The Guardians identify ranchers that have grazing permits on federal lands and sue the government under the U.S. Endangered Species Act, accusing the feds of mismanaging the land by allowing overgrazing and other environmental harm to public resources.[39] About twenty-five thousand ranchers have grazing permits for three million head of cattle, while The Guardians have won or settled about eighteen lawsuits clearing five thousand head off two million acres of land.[40]

Corporate campaigns take various and sundry forms, and tactics differ depending upon the targeted company. Not all campaigns are labor-oriented, and some may be exclusively focused on media, attempting to draw consumer or public attention to serious corporate social injury or shameful conduct. Public attention, of course, may lead to litigation, legislative or regulatory action, consumer and investor boycotts, or all of the above. Consumer boycotts at the national or international level have limited impact on global corporations, unless the boycotted company product is an expensive impulse item or responsive to high-end discretionary spending where consumers can very well do without the product. Companies such as The Gap, Nike, Starbucks, and Levis may be more susceptible to consumer action than large corporate conglomerates such as Procter & Gamble, Nestle, or Ford Motors because of the companies' numerous diversified product lines, limited competition, and diverse global markets.

Coca-Cola is often the subject of boycotts and corporate campaigns, and is currently engaged in a nasty fight with human rights, labor, and church organizations over the issue of Coca-Cola officials allegedly collaborating with paramilitary terrorist groups in Colombia that utilize violence, murder, and torture to intimidate union officials at Coca-Cola bottling plants in that country. The International Labor Rights Fund, the United Steelworkers of America, and Sinaltrainal (the Colombian National Food Industry Workers' Union) have filed suit against Coca-Cola, charging that the company "contracted with or otherwise directed paramilitary security forces that utilize extreme violence and murdered, tortured, unlawfully detained, or otherwise silenced trade union leaders."[41]

Paramilitary groups—right-wing anti-guerrilla militia financed by landowners and the cocaine trade—have long targeted unions, particularly those which work for large multinational companies. Columbian landowner Rodrigo Tovar, one of the "terrorist" leaders of a five thousand member death squad in Columbia, said that union leaders have been "a disaster in Columbia for business" and that union activists are "the ones who sabotage, who hurt companies."[42]

Ray Rogers, of J. P. Stevens fame, is running the corporate campaign against Coca-Cola, utilizing his company's Corporate Campaign, Inc., media skills, contacts, and expertise (see Appendix D). This fight looks like a long and acrimonious one. At the 2004 Coke annual shareholders meeting in Wilmington, Delaware, Ray Rogers was dragged out of the meeting by security police after railing against the company's labor rights record in Columbia. Coke has been successful in the courts by separating itself from the bottlers, but the case is being appealed and it hasn't stopped the "Killer Coke" campaign (www.killercoke.org). Coke executives have reacted defensively. The company's public relations coordinator said, "I never thought I'd be in a position of trying to defend this company from murder."[43]

Corporate campaign strategies are not unique to the United States. The campaign model has been around for sometime in the United Kingdom and Nicholas Hildyard and Mark Mansley have written an excellent campaign guide focusing on U.K. financial institutions. This "how to" book for corporate campaigners is entitled *The Campaign Guide to Financial Markets: Effective Lobbying of Companies and Financial Institutions* and is a must read for activists attempting to change corporate behavior.

Socially responsible shareholders certainly have a major ownership role to play in corporate campaigns. This includes traditional civil dialogue with management, and an understanding that links have to be made to numerous diverse and divergent allied organizations, as well as with stakeholders, and all citizens impacted by global corporate conduct. Just as Edward Freeman defines a stakeholder to include "any group or individual who can affect or is affected by the achievement of the organizations objectives." According to his logic, corporate managers now have a fiduciary relationship with stakeholders.[44]

THE COSTS OF ENVIRONMENTAL PERFORMANCE

Just as managers have a fiduciary relationship with stakeholders, socially responsible investors have a fiduciary responsibility to consider social and environmental issues when making an investment decision. Almost every investment decision a fiduciary makes has an economic, social and environmental impact. To ignore or marginalize the importance of these possible impacts on financial return, market share, or corporate reputation violates fiduciary duty.

Perhaps at long last investors are waking up to their fiduciary duties. Environmental shareholder resolutions have been gaining larger votes at annual meetings, especially those that focus on the global warming responsibilities of auto, oil, and utility companies. According to the Hastings Group of Arlington, Virginia, auto company emissions comprise 20 percent of total U.S. emissions. The United States alone is responsible for 25 percent of world totals. General Motors' carbon burden grew 13 percent between 1990 and 2000, and Ford's grew 26 percent over the same decade thanks largely to the spread of SUVs, minivans, and large pickups. U.S. cars and trucks consume 11 percent of the world's total oil production and 40 percent of U.S. consumption.[45]

In 2003 the Interfaith Center on Corporate Responsibility (ICCR) and CERES members filed thirty-one shareholder resolutions on global warming with twenty-eight companies, targeting electric power companies, transportation, oil, gas, and manufacturing companies. One of the resolutions filed by the state of Connecticut with American Electric Power won 27 percent of the shareholder advisory vote, while 22 percent of the shareholders at Exxon Mobil supported a resolution on global warming, and 32 percent of Chevron Texaco shareholders supported a similar resolution.[46] ICCR withdrew a resolution at Ford based on a commitment by the company to address its contributions to greenhouse gas emissions and to review company efforts to increase fuel efficiency.

Over 1,100 governance and social shareholder resolutions have been filed in 2004 according to IRRC. Almost half of the fifty-seven proposals filed on environmental issues asked companies to report or reduce greenhouse gas emissions, to report how climate change may affect their operations, or to consider developing renewable energy alternatives.

Connecticut State Treasurer Denise L. Nappier, speaking at the Seventeenth Annual ICCR Fall Event in New York City on October 2, 2003, warned investors that global warming and other environmental risks needed serious attention and that corporations should not only disclose environmental risks, but mitigate them. In concluding her keynote address, she said: "So, on climate risk, and so many other so-called environmental issues, the potential for serious financial impact is becoming clearer, and the days of putting one's corporate head in the sand and waiting for the issue to pass is long gone. This issue is not going away, and neither are we."

Phil Angelides, the California state treasurer who is a trustee of both CALPERS and CALSTRS, has called for exploration of the need for screening portfolios for environmental performance. In November 2003, he was joined by the comptrollers from New York City and State, and the treasurers of Connecticut, Maine, New Mexico, Oregon, and Vermont, calling on publicly traded companies, federal regulators, and the financial community to begin assessing and disclosing financial risks posed by climate change. According to *The Wall Street Journal*, they argued that if the federal government caps emissions of carbon dioxide and other so-called greenhouse gases—something it has so far refused to do but that many corporate executives predict is only a matter of time—some of the nation's largest industrial companies could face costly changes, such as switching their power plants from coal to cleaner-burning natural gas."[47]

Insurance companies are starting to look at liabilities associated with global warming and greenhouse gas emissions. At least one company, Swiss Re, is considering denying insurance coverage to companies that are not seriously addressing climate change. A Swiss Re representative told a *Wall Street Journal* reporter in April 2003 that the company's decision came as the result of growing support of climate change shareholder resolutions. The president of the Reinsurance Association of America was quoted as saying in January 2003: "It is clear that global warming could bankrupt the [reinsurance] industry."[48]

The issue of corporate risk, and costs associated with future corporate environmental damage through a company's global operations, is continuing to draw attention from shareholders, regulators, and politicians. According to both CERES and Friends of the Earth, a national environmental organization, companies are not adequately disclosing their overall company environmental risk to investors. Friends of the Earth wrote a report in 2002 and found that only 15 percent of U.S. companies from carbon-intensive sectors discussed climate change risks in their 2001 SEC filings.[49]

In July 2003, the SRI community hosted a congressional symposium to consider the current state of public company disclosure of environmental and social risks in SEC filings. One of the presenters, Connecticut Treasurer Denise Nappier outlined several recommendations to the SEC including a CEO certification process to ensure that environmental and social disclosure requirements are met and enforced. She also suggested support for removing the "ordinary business" exception for resolutions seeking corporate environmental disclosure so that shareholders can obtain adequate information to make informed investment decisions.

Nappier was followed by Peter Lehner, assistant attorney general in charge of the environmental protection bureau of the office of New York State Attorney General Eliot Spitzer. Lehner invoked a 1998 EPA report that found 74 percent of companies under-disclosed their material environmental liabilities. "In other words, even with relatively well-known risks, such as the cost of cleaning up a superfund site or the cost of complying with existing clean air or clean water rules, most companies did not disclose in a manner that EPA believed compliant with the Securities and Exchange Commission and accounting requirements," said Lehner.

Exploring questions relating to adequate disclosure of environmental risks and financial liabilities has been a project of one of the symposium's participants, the Rose Foundation, since August 2002. The Rose Foundation published its findings in: "The Environmental Fiduciary: The Case for Incorporating Environmental Factors into Investment Management Policies." In that report, Tim Little, one of the lead authors at Rose, argued that fiduciaries of pension funds, foundations, and charitable trusts should encourage good environmental performance in corporations owned in institutional portfolios, and outlined a set of recommendations to control portfolio environmental risk and enhance environmental value. Among the recommendations, Little emphasized that fiduciaries should: Encourage and support both voluntary and mandatory corporate environmental disclosure; Proactively engage with companies to encourage best practices in environmental management; Integrate their fund's mission with portfolio management goals; Assess overall portfolio environmental performance and adopt a targeted corporate engagement strategy.

The report also recommended targeted engagement actions that fiduciaries could take as shareholders, including voting proxies, introducing shareholder resolutions, supporting the election of independent corporate directors, creating board-level environmental committees, creating an environmental watch list designed to improve the environmental performance of targeted portfolio companies, and to publicize fiduciary action— including a "clean and green" list of "best in a class" for companies with outstanding environmental performance and disclosure. The report went so far as to suggest that institutional investors underweight the portfolio with poor environmental performers, recommend that portfolio managers "capture the growth potential of emerging environmental technologies such as renewable energy," and consider community investment opportunities such as Community Development Financial Institutions (CDFI).

The Rose Foundation is one of several organizations seeking to influence the SEC to strengthen environmental reporting requirements, including the definition of "material risk" pertaining to environmental liabilities.

The SEC operates on the word "material," so that an issue must be deemed material to the financial life of a corporation in order to merit public disclosure. Unless challenged in court, corporate management determines what is material to the corporation's financial health. Even though what is considered material has been narrowly addressed by two Supreme Court cases, it is still up to the SEC to have the courage to determine if the potential costs of environmental risks are material to the financial health of the corporation and its shareholders.

The foundation is attempting to draw attention to the lack of public disclosure, at the SEC or elsewhere, of financial risk associated with potential environmental disasters. Environmental damage is due, in large part, to corporate management's short-term focus on "enhancing shareholder value" by taking shortcuts on environmental protection to save money or failing to recognize best practices to prevent egregious environmental corporate activity. As an example, the foundation points to Massey Energy Corporation, which ignored mine, health, and safety engineers' warnings, and its own experience with previous chemical spills and accidents, when a coal water dam collapsed, resulting in the release of 250 million gallons of toxic slurry that flowed into the Big Sandy and the Ohio rivers, killing wildlife and contaminating drinking water in much of eastern Kentucky. This little incident cost Massey shareholders $672 million (a 68 percent drop in share price) in market capitalization, as well as over $41 million in government fines.[50] Massey shareholders are suing top management for over $600 million in damages, charging board members with a breach of their fiduciary duty and, among other things, a refusal to comply with applicable environmental, labor, and securities laws.[51]

The Rose Foundation has launched an Environmental Fiduciary Project and the Corporate Sunshine Working Group, both of which challenge specific omissions or misleading statements found in company government filings as well as continue to encourage more comprehensive corporate, social, and environmental reporting. In December 2003, the foundation released "The Gap in GAAP: An Examination of Environmental Accounting Loopholes," written by staff members Susannah Goodman and Tim Little. The twenty-two-page report examined shortcomings in

Generally Accepted Accounting Principles (GAAP), summarizing ten years of research that exposed significant environmental liabilities which are misstated, under-reported, or unreported in corporate, SEC, and other regulatory filings and communications with shareholders. Rose revealed that these loopholes in financial reporting allow corporate management to hide, downplay, or disregard the financial significance of environmental problems such as toxic leaks, historic contamination, asbestos, compliance with environmental laws, response actions, defense and legal fees, property damage, business interruption, tort claims, and global climate change. Such obvious information discrepancies lead to dramatic unknown shareholder liability risks. The report also made several recommendations to plug the loopholes.

Long and short-term corporate financial risks associated with egregious environmental activity are not new. They are simply not required to be publicly disclosed by the SEC, state, or other federal regulatory agencies. There is no doubt that almost all corporate activities carry financial risks. Global warming, the results of the release of gas emissions from corporate manufacturing, electric power production, and the use of gasoline-powered vehicles, creates financial risk for corporations engaged in those activities. In September 2004, the conference board—a nonprofit organization known for its consumer confidence and economic indicators, and whose membership includes large corporations—concluded in a report on global warming that "businesses that ignore the debate over climate change do so at their peril."[52]

The same has been said of those corporate activities that may cause irreversible environmental damage, such as the release of genetically modified organisms (GMOs). Wendy Wendlandt, representing Green Century Capital Management and speaking before Kraft shareholders at the 2003 annual meeting, said: "Continued use of genetically engineered foods exposes investors to unnecessary financial risk. Another incident like the *StarLink* contamination could have devastating impacts on Kraft's bottom line and share value. The financial risks of genetically engineered foods became evident with contamination of the food supply by *StarLink* in 2000, which is estimated to have cost the food industry billions of dollars."

Wendlandt was referring to a September 2000 incident involving the company's Taco Bell taco shells that contained a genetically engineered protein pesticide Cry9C that had failed to receive EPA approval for human consumption because of concerns about allergic reactions. As a result, Kraft had to recall more than 2 million boxes of Taco Bell taco shells, costing Kraft and Aventis Cropscience USA Holding, Inc. (which engineered the pesticide) a significant amount of money.

In April 2003, the National Association of State Public Interest Research Groups (PIRGs) and the As You Sow Foundation released a report entitled: "Risky Business: Financial Risks That Genetically Engineered Foods Pose to Kraft Foods, Inc., and Shareholders," which outlined the numerous financial risks associated with the continued use of GMO products and food ingredients. These risks include product liability, biopharm contamination, consumer rejection, loss of competitive advantage, damage to reputation and brand image, increased insurance costs, security analysts and investor rejection, and sudden regulatory changes.

Also in April 2003, Innovest Strategic Value Advisors—a financial services firm based in New York, London, Paris, and Toronto—released a sixty-two-page analysis of Monsanto's genetic engineering strategy, giving the company its lowest environmental rating. Innovest's rating implies that there is an above average risk of exposure and projects that the company will likely under-perform in the stock market over the mid- to long-term. The report pointed out numerous publicly disclosed and undisclosed financial risks to investors that could ultimately bankrupt Monsanto. Primary among the findings were the increased risks associated with genetic food and environmental contamination, possible product rejection by U.S. consumers associated with suggested labeling, foreign market rejection or restrictions of genetically modified imported foods in as many as thirty-five countries, and an overall growing global consumer rejection of genetic engineering and genetically-engineered pharma crops.

The die has already been cast in the United Kingdom where insurance companies refuse to cover GMO farmers or to cover conventional farmers frightened about GMO contamination of their crops. The main farm underwriting firms in Britain have total exclusion clauses so that any damage associated with GMO crops, even arson of farm buildings, nullifies insurance claims. Firms such as NFU Mutual, Rural Insurance Group, and others "likened the idea of insuring against the dangers of GMOs to the situation with asbestos, thalidomide, and acts of terrorism."[53]

According to Frank Dixon, of Innovest, genetically-modified foods are unnatural life forms that cannot be recalled once released into nature and "pose the greatest environmental threat since, unlike any other environmental problem, there is no remedy." Dixon has advanced a model he calls Full Corporate Responsibility (FCR), based on interconnectedness, actualization, and posterity, which requires corporations to: (1) price into products and services all internal and external costs; (2) shift the focus of the business from maximizing short-term profits to maximizing the well-being of society; and (3) recognize that the primary obligation of the current generation is to preserve and enhance society for future generations.

Dixon's FCR is even more important to consider as the GMO industry and its public sector advocates look to modify other crops, including wheat, rice, and wine grapes. In the Napa Valley, California, discussions have already begun on how to genetically modify grape vines to ward off pests while not affecting the quality of the wine.

There are also financial losses to shareholders of companies that operate factory farms to produce meat products and confine thousands of animals which emit toxic gases from animal waste and pollute surface and ground water. The Adrian Dominican Sisters filed a resolution with Hormel Foods in 2004—similar to an earlier resolution introduced by Nathan Cummings Foundation with Smithfield Foods—requesting a report on the environmental impact of the company's factory farms. The resolution received over 20 percent of the shareholder vote. It doesn't take a financial analyst or CPA to imagine the financial and legal liabilities associated with environmental and health issues arising from factory farms.

Organizations such as the Sierra Club have been involved in raising awareness of corporate environmental risks for years, gaining media attention through litigation. A perfect example is its successful work to disclose Tyson Corporation's failure to report hazardous releases of dangerous ammonia from four animal factories under the company's supervision in

Kentucky. Ammonia, a toxic gas released from chicken production, can cause serious respiratory problems and can, in some cases, be fatal.

A key to fiduciary duty is to avoid undue risk, especially risk that can lead to large financial losses. Often portfolio managers are ignorant of risks associated with corporate environmental damage unless such risk is disclosed within regular SEC filings, or managers have access to independent third party sources, such as NGOs with particular environmental expertise or access to studies like those produced by Innovest. NGOs may include nonprofit organizations such as the Sierra Club, Pesticide Action Network North America, Friends of the Earth, the Natural Resource Defense Council, CERES, Rainforest Action Network, Greenpeace, or others with specific technical and scientific skills. Related information can also come from public documents, newspapers, periodicals, and journals, as well as from government sources including regulators or government agencies such as the EPA. It is the responsibility of the fiduciary to hunt out this information. Decades of lying about environmental risks have proven corporations will not volunteer the information themselves.

Since 1990 Kenny Ausubel and Nina Simon have been bringing thousands of scientists, economists, inventors, small business and venture fund entrepreneurs, ecologists, farmers, NGOs, and citizens together to provide information, data, and vision to enlighten fiduciaries and other policy makers. The annual Bioneers conference assembles some of the most knowledgeable people on the planet in an effort to educate fiduciaries, not only of future environmental and biological risks to business and society, but options to reduce, or eliminate costly problems before they occur.

Other corporate environmental risks are gaining increasing attention, thanks to nonprofit public interest organizations. One of these is Keep Antibiotics Working, which deals with the overuse of feeding antibiotics to healthy farm animals to promote growth. According to the Union of Concerned Scientists, 70 percent of all antibiotics in the United States are used on healthy pigs, poultry, and beef cattle. While pumping healthy animals with antibiotics increases profits for meat producers, humans who eat the meat build up antibiotic resistance, leading to increased numbers of people with bacterial infections who fail to respond to antibiotics. This has led the European Union and other countries to ban the import of antibiotic injected meat, and many medical organizations—including the World Health Organization (WHO), the American College of Preventative Medicine, the American Public Health Association, and the Council of State and Territorial Epidemiologists—to oppose the use of antibiotics in healthy farm animals.

The release of public health research studies obtained from environmental organizations points to a growing trend. Media attention of non-profit organizational studies are a helpful source of data and information for analysts and investment advisers to better assess overall financial risks of stocks of companies involved in meat processing, factory farms, food processing, and grocery store chains selling meat and other food products. These studies are helpful for analysts and portfolio managers to assess the financial risks of owning stocks, such as ConAgra, which is the second largest food company in the United States and twenty-four other countries, with labels recognizable by consumers, such as Armour, Butterball, Country Pride, Decker, Eckrich, Hebrew National, Oldham's Farms, Swift Premium, and Slim jerky snacks. It might even prompt legislators and regulators to re-evaluate ConAgra's contract under the School Lunch Program and other Federal Food Assistance programs.

Unfortunately, I don't think that the beltway captive FDA will be of much help in protecting us from antibiotic pumped up cattle, pigs, chickens, and turkeys. In October 2003, the FDA gave Monsanto approval for a Posilac powder-manufacturing facility to be built in Augusta, Georgia, "to meet increased demand for the artificial hormone that increases milk production in cows."[54] Monsanto says that Posilac increases a cow's milk production by eight to twelve pounds per day.[55]

Other than company sources, portfolio managers primarily rely on stock and bond analysts, financial data, and publicly filed SEC and related mandatory regulatory documents for information on corporate activity. Unfortunately, this can lead these delegated fiduciaries to miss, misinterpret, or completely ignore important information from nonprofit organizations and other sources, such as academic studies, that may lead to unexpected losses for corporate shareholders and stakeholders alike. Unless these non-traditional sources of information receive a great deal of media coverage on their research or studies, analysts and managers alike tend to pay little attention. With a media market that is owned by mega-corporations and reliant on corporate advertising dollars, there is little hope that there will be extensive coverage of studies and reports that could negatively impact corporate profits.

The financial fallout from long-term environmental, health, and safety aspects of the use of asbestos and tobacco is legendary. The same can be said for PCB exposure and the creation of Superfund sites. The costs have been astronomical. The public health and the environment have both suffered. Environmental damage has been enormous due to ozone-depleting chlorofluorocarbons manufactured by chemical companies, as well as the effects on health and society from water pollution, ground water contamination, smog and air pollution, acid rain, and global warming. Much of this overall cost to society and business is the result of unrestrained chemical and agrochemical manufacturing and use. Often the same companies that are responsible for polluting the water and the soil are also responsible for exposing the global environment to untested genetic engineering technologies that may forever change the world in which we live. Governments around the world are still trying to develop the technology and methodology to safely manage and dispose of hazardous and nuclear wastes. This cost to society, governments, and business may be insurmountable in the decades ahead. The immediate liability and financial risk to investors, including "universal investors" such as institutional shareholders, are of special concern when it comes specifically to chemical and agrochemical companies.

Recognizing the increased financial liability of chemical companies—especially those which produce pesticides—and the need for adequate disclosure to shareholders, stakeholders, and global citizens, the Rockefeller Brothers Fund brought a group of experts together at its Pocantico Conference Center in June 2002. This conference included pesticide reform campaigners, liability lawyers, corporate accountability specialists, and SRI professionals. Out of this brainstorming session, a thirty-page paper was produced entitled "Accountability in the Pesticide Industry," which found a clear disconnect between the increasing financial liability facing agrochemical companies and capital market support for this industry subsector.

In no uncertain terms, Peter Riggs, Program Officer at the Rockefeller Brothers Fund, said that the fund's long-term interest had always been to support sustainable agriculture, but that the work had been constrained because of "the aggressive presence of agrochemical interests, a presence characterized by strong-arm marketing tactics, the bribery of state officials, and a cavalier attitude toward public health and occupational safety standards. Frustrated by the limits of a 'positive approach' to influencing agricultural development, we concluded (along with many of our partners) that new tools for promoting accountability had to be developed. One clear way to promote accountability was to threaten its oxygen supply: access to capital. If capital markets could better reflect the potential liability of agrochemical companies and if corporate irresponsibility could be exposed as a 'material risk' to the business, then investments in this sector would be far less attractive."

The Rockefeller Brothers' report touched upon several issues dear to the hearts of many in the SRI community. It was suggested that SRI financial professionals should be encouraged to identify community development investment opportunities to support farmer-centered Integrated Pest Management and organic and sustainable agricultural production. The report also indicated that pesticide companies "crave recognition by international bodies," are actively pursuing partnerships with the World Bank and United Nations, and that the same agrochemical companies have been included in SRI and "best-in-class" indexes such as FTSE4Good and the Dow Jones Sustainability Index. The report concluded that agrochemical companies clearly manipulate definitions such as "sustainability" and that there was a need to broaden engagement to pursue social change through investments, and at the very least "we should not be complicit through our portfolios in funding activities that run counter to our beliefs and values. Nor should we ever be placed in the unfortunate position of being duped, watching our investments crash down around us, simply because a company that wasn't required to disclose certain information didn't do so."

Of course, it takes more than just avoiding nasty stuff. SRI demands proaction, both in committing to some form of shareholder advocacy, including actually purchasing stocks of companies violating SRI criteria in an effort to raise important social and economic issues, to direct primary market investing. At the 2003 Monsanto Annual Shareholders' Meeting, a representative of Greenpeace spoke on my behalf, after I had introduced a shareholder resolution requesting company information on its policies and procedures for exporting carcinogenic pesticides not registered in the United States to developing countries. Greenpeace not only questioned Monsanto about dumping cancer-causing pesticides in poor countries, but questioned the company about the dumping of unregistered, carcinogenic, and obsolete pesticides. The resolution won over 13 percent of the vote three years in a row and will be before shareholders again in 2006.

Dow Chemical, a company that has been included in the Dow Jones Sustainability Index (DJSI), owns Union Carbide, a company responsible for the Bhopal, India, disaster in which 20,000 people died and left an estimated 150,000 chronically ill. In November 2003, Boston Common Asset Management filed a resolution with Dow on behalf of its client, the Brethren Benefit Trust, asking the company for a report, describing the initiatives it has instituted to address the health, environmental, and social issues of Bhopal survivors, specifically requesting Dow to quantify and analyze the impacts that the Bhopal disaster may have had on the company's reputation, finances, and its expansion in Asia and elsewhere. Human exposure to dangerous chemicals and chemical impact on the environment is one of the major health and safety issues facing developing countries. The release of dangerous chemicals is still a problem in Bhopal, as well as ground water contamination from leaking containers remaining onsite at the Union Carbide plant. Dow Chemical and Union Carbide are considered criminals in India, while Dow and Monsanto are considered criminals by many throughout the world for the spraying of Agent Orange in Vietnam.

A Call to Action

I don't want to live in the dark future I predicted at the start of this chapter. I don't want my daughters and their children to return to a new and revised

1984. There is still a reason to hope and to fight for a better future for our children and the world, but we are running out of time.

We need to take control of our money, our investments, and our democracy. We need to act now as investors, as voters, as philanthropists, as executives, as consumers, as activists, and most important of all, as human beings concerned about the survival of our planet, our economy, and our struggling democracy. James Madison, Alexander Hamilton, John Jay, Thomas Jefferson, and other founders of our Constitution and Declaration of Independence could never have imagined that our form of government could become so threatened by a non-competitive, centralized economic entity called a corporation, an immortal economic entity given the same legal rights as living, breathing human beings. This economic entity is so unsurpassed in power that it roams the earth, manipulating governments, buying politicians, setting economic policies, and most recently, establishing and dominating a global government that is erasing sovereignty of nation states and marginalized people throughout the world.

While more and more people do not vote, it is not a bad tradition to revive. Perhaps voter turnout will improve following the 2004 reelection of Bush. Maybe the youth vote will materialize in the future. We must make sure that it does. We may indeed be frustrated with the process (especially using paperless electronic voting, not to mention outright fraud and intimidation at polling places), but we should not abandon democracy. Too many people have fought and died for this sacred right that many of us now take for granted. We should also open our wallets and donate to progressive candidates' campaigns at all levels. We can't begin to compete with corporate largess and lobbying, but we can start to make a difference, especially if we tie our dollars with a commitment to work for candidates in their campaigns. While presidential elections are important, the most impact we can have is at the local and state government levels, grooming candidates who will later run for higher office. We must make democracy work at the local, state, and national levels, and encourage progressives to run for public office.

Just about everybody under the sun has recommended publicly financing campaigns. Teddy Roosevelt's recommendation one hundred years ago was to eliminate corporate campaign contributions. It is still a great idea, but as long as incumbent politicians and their corporate friends within the beltway and in state houses control the levers of power, it won't happen. If corporations can't kill public financing of campaigns in congress and in state legislatures, they outspend campaign financing proponents in referendums, and their attorneys win in court to overrule legislative action or referendums supported by the people. Anytime one tries to prohibit or severely restrict campaign donations, or the supposedly God-given right corporations have to spend as much money as they want to exercise their "freedom of speech," it falls under constitutional scrutiny by the courts. Keep in mind that those that have the gold, rule, and it is no different in getting the right judicial decision, or "justice," as long as it is adequately paid for.

One clever way of approaching the problem of corporate contributions controlling the electoral system is a recommendation that *all* campaign contributions be made to a blind trust and then made to the candidates. The donors names are anonymous so that the political candidates don't know to whom they are beholden. Nicholas D. Kristof, in a November 20, 2004 op-ed for the *New York Times*, wrote "such a system of shielding names of donors exists in ten states, to some degree, for judicial candidates," and Bruce Akerman, in his book *Voting With Dollars*, makes the case that such a plan can be adopted more broadly starting at the state level. Kristof noted that Chile is holding its first election using a new law with a blind trust for campaign donations of more than $500. Perhaps this is worth a try.

The United States was one of 189 countries that signed the United Nations Millennium Declaration, a manifesto to eradicate poverty, hunger, and disease that afflicts one billion people in the world. The goal for developed countries is to give 0.7 percent of national income for development aid for poor countries by 2015. The United States is at the bottom of the list of industrialized countries, providing only 0.14 percent, Britain is at 0.34 percent, France at 0.41 percent, while Norway and Sweden are at 0.92 percent and 0.79 percent, respectively. The U.S. government spends $450 billion annually on the military—not including the war in Iraq—and $15 billion on development assistance for poor countries, a thirty to one ratio.[56] This must change, and Americans who personally give generously to nonprofit charities must work hard to force our government to change its priorities.

More important, however, is to contribute to, and volunteer for, progressive community-based nonprofit organizations. This is where you will be handsomely rewarded and your dollar will be leveraged tenfold. You will have influence in the organization and be able to insure that the mission of the organization reflects your views and commitments. Not all 501(c)(3) organizations are sterling examples of the democratic process, but your odds are much better if you actively participate. The world can only change if you give both money and *time.*

We must all become full-time philanthropists. I'm not talking about giving to charities, but making long-term commitments and annual pledges to nonprofit, community-based, social justice, environmental, and human rights organizations of all stripes. This is a necessity if we are to control our money, our lives, and our future.

As discussed in the previous chapter, as with all non-liquid, private placement investments, investors experience higher risk. Whether the investments have positive social or environmental returns or not, investors need to limit total exposure to higher risk private placements, but there is a place for such investments in a diversified SRI portfolio. Direct investments in organic, or truly sustainable agricultural practices, as well as in alternative energy clean technologies, will have the most positive impact for not only the recipient of capital, but also for the entire community. The creation of jobs and a healthier environment are not only compatible but synergistic.

Investing in local family businesses in urban and suburban communities as part of an overall personal diversified investment strategy makes sense. Businesses that incorporate family and friends and those which are modeled on community sustainability add credibility to further diversification of non-liquid investment assets. This does not mean the socially responsible investor ignores traditional business management skills, ignores reviewing a well thought out marketing and business plan, or ignores the quality and quantity of local, regional, and global competition. Seeking to make a profit, reasonably growing a business and becoming financially sustainable does not eliminate innovative and creative new business models that can be developed to be consistent with community standards and environmental quality. Not unlike affirmative action, these factors in new business opportunities must be actively pursued by socially responsible investors. Unfortunately, they don't necessarily fall into your lap. You must make the time to look for pro-active SRI investment opportunities.

As Berle and Means recognized sixty-five years ago, when investors invest in the stock market (secondary market), they give up control for liquidity. While Berle and Means focused on the loss of "control" of corporate management by owning liquid common stock, social investors are more apt to discard the need to control a small business enterprise. Control, however, can take the form of ensuring that the manager of a small business recognizes that the acceptance of social capital from investors establishes a relationship built upon the overall social and environmental mission shared by both investors and management. This shared acceptance of the mission of the enterprise needs to be not only the company's mission statement, but also an integral part of the business plan, offering document, articles of incorporation, and by-laws of the business. It is an agreement not only between investors and management, but also one that is necessary for all stakeholders—including customers.

Business opportunities similar to Upstream 21, and other non-traditional competitive business enterprises, are important to consider when diversifying one's personal portfolio. Investing in a company that shares your values is especially important and essential for ensuring trust and sustainability.

There is a need in our society today for community and the building of an alternative, local economy, where businesses support each other, as well as compete. All of our business transactions do not need to be part of the global banking and big box store oligopolistic corporate tradition. Most of the money spent by the customers at Wal-Mart and most of the money deposited at Citigroup leaves the local community. Money that consumers spend on products of local businesses is usually leveraged in the community many times over. This is the reason that the Business Alliance for Local Living Economies (BALLE), comprised of local businesses across the country, is growing by leaps and bounds. BALLE strengthens local businesses, the economy, environment, and communities through education and net-working. Unlike the Chamber of Commerce, BALLE opposes big box enter-prises like Wal-Mart, which destroy competition and local free enterprise.

Big corporations, such as Wal-Mart, also manipulate small business for their own gain. Wal-Mart donated $600,000 to defeat a proposal on the 2004 California November election ballot that would require medium and large businesses to provide their workers with health insurance. Proposition opponents aired a TV ad showing an actress portraying an owner of a small Mexican restaurant complaining that she would be required to cover the health care costs of her employees. The ad neglected to explain that because the restaurant was a small business it would be exempt from the proposition.

Social investors need to make a commitment to invest within their com-munity. This can take the form of an investment in a CDFI, by opening up a personal account at a community bank or credit union or investing in an insured CD or an unsecured promissory note in a loan fund which, in turn, lends your money to a nonprofit organization, rehabilitates a home, or lever-ages your investment in a mortgage in a low-income neighborhood project. In the San Francisco Bay Area, we are fortunate enough to have the Northern California Community Loan Fund to serve these purposes. A loan fund, such as Seattle-based Cascadia, can directly leverage your loan by lending to a small community business, such as a rural daycare in Southeast Oregon or a recycling center in Seattle. If a CDFI is not in your community, the second best depository is a locally-owned bank or credit union.

Thanks to the Calvert Foundation, investors can now purchase Community Investment notes through their broker, funding CDFIs throughout the United States and the world. CDFIs in the United States are represented by the National Community Capital Association (NCCA), which is comprised of 150 CDFIs in all fifty states, representing loan funds, community banks and credit unions, microenterprise development loan funds, and community development venture capital funds.

Green investing is growing by leaps and bounds, as is the production and consumption of organic products and food. For three years, Global Exchange has been co-sponsoring and organizing a Green Festival in San

Francisco, and in 2003, held the first Green Festival in Austin, Texas. In 2003, attendance at the Green Festival in San Francisco grew 50 percent over 2002, where almost twenty thousand people attended workshops and seminars and purchased fair trade items. In 2004 the first Green Festival was held in Washington, DC. The 2005 Green Festival was again planned for Washington, DC and San Francisco.

Kevin Danaher, author, activist, and co-founder of Global Exchange, and Jason Mark, his Global Exchange colleague, recently released an anti-corporate, pro-democracy call-to-action titled *Insurrection: Citizen Challenges to Corporate Power*. In their book, they acknowledged the growing power of an alternative consumption model: "A green/fair economy is already sprouting at the grassroots to meet this demand for better ways of living. Organic farming is growing far more rapidly than chemical farming, with sales expected to top $11 billion in 2003. Sales of fair trade-certified products broke the $100 million mark for the first time in 2000, while 'no-sweat' garment manufacturers such as Ben Cohen's Sweat-X in Los Angeles are reporting dramatic sales gains. The Co-Op America Business Network has more than two thousand green/fair trade companies as members, while socially responsible investment funds now control $639 billion in assets."

As in any social movement, the public usually leads the "leaders." Seldom do politicians lead the way towards progressive change, but they will follow an angry, vocal, and engaged electorate. The same can be said of the SRI movement. A few leaders, and many more investors, have been able to get us where we are today. The journey has been tough, but the gains have been substantial. There remains, however, much to be done. Many of us are unsure if the present members of the SRI community are ready to engage and challenge corporate wealth and power.

In 2003, I placed an ad in *Business Ethics* magazine as well as in several programs of nonprofit organizations holding annual fundraising events. It was a call to action for the SRI community to begin to think about coordinating more social responsibility activities with other participants in the social and environmental justice community. It was also a warning that we are running out of time and there is a need to develop an overall corporate campaign strategy to confront the almost omniscient power of global corporations.

Of the many responses I received, two of my colleagues in the SRI financial services industry deserve to be quoted, since they pinpointed their specific concerns about the contemporary SRI community. One person responded by saying: "SRI has a lot of power to change corporate behavior (perhaps now more than ever), but our power is largely limited to achieving incremental changes that are definitely steps in the right direction, but will likely not be enough to achieve anything approaching sustainability. I see us as one tool in the toolkit of corporate change, and a tool that can do real good, but again, not a powerful enough tool to build the world I want to live in."

Another colleague who also manages SRI assets wrote: "Shareholder resolutions take on one corporation at a time and that's wasting time, effort, and resources. Action to raise the consciousness of Americans (do it here and we can then handle the rest of the world's corporations) and political action to severely limit the power of corporations (a la Marjorie Kelly's *The Divine Right of Capital Dethroning Corporate Aristocracy*) is the only goal that is sufficiently broad to be effective. However, I fear that SRI professionals will not lead; they won't even follow. Their livelihood would be threatened, especially if the aristocracy of wealth was ultimately questioned as well, and that is a natural sequel. I have been told that some have been so bold as to give that reason for their objections to the issue even being raised at a conference of SRI professionals. I'm afraid that I don't have confidence that SRI professionals will be well represented in this effort. Some of us will be there, however."

The current thinking is not that SRI can do it alone, but that a new beginning will be the confluence of many forces including those in the SRI community who have the courage to challenge the princes of corporate management and the plutocracy of America's current Tweedle-dee and Tweedle-dum political party system. Government bureaucrats will not lead, nor will politicians. Shareholder advocates will play a role, as will activists in the streets, NGOs in the community, labor in the workplace, and peasants, farmers, and workers in the fields of developing countries. There will be very little access to the corporate boardroom. We cannot count on the SEC. Political force must move towards change in Congress and in state legislatures. As James Krohe Jr. wrote: "A growing number of activists and scholars argue that the best way to change a misbehaving corporation is to change it right out of existence, by revoking its corporate charter."[57]

State legislatures elected by the people are responsible for chartering corporations. State laws can be changed by legislatures or by the people directly through referendums. State attorney generals are elected law enforcement officers responsible for policing corporate conduct. State charters can and should be revoked when corporate management violates the public trust. Federal chartering of corporations should be demanded.

Public interest lawyers have an important, if not crucial, role to play in the courtroom, challenging corporate power through litigation pursuant to the Alien Tort Claims Act, commercial speech, class action claims regarding all forms of discrimination, and even pursuing shareholder derivative suits. Personal liability suits and violation of fiduciary duty should also be pursued against corporate management. The SRI community, similar to the human rights community, needs to educate attorneys specializing in corporate law to sue corporate management, not represent them. Instead of lawyers trained and retained by corporate management to manipulate the law, lobby, and find lucrative tax loopholes for corporations, we need public interest corporate lawyers to represent the public, owners, and other stakeholders.

Business groups, including Business Roundtable, representing corporate CEOs, had hoped that the Supreme Court would eliminate the use of U.S. courts to enforce international law pursuant to the Alien Tort Claims Act. In June 2004, the Supreme Court ruled in favor of human rights advocates, "saying that suits alleging corporate complicity in crimes such as summary execution, torture and slavery were exactly the type of international standards the court cited."[58]

No doubt the United Nations has been compromised by its agreements, voluntary codes, and joint ventures with corporate management, but we shouldn't give up on establishing international justice based on human and labor rights through U.N. agencies. Nor should citizens give up on abolishing the WTO and similar organizations created by agreements negotiated or that are currently being negotiated if such agreements and organizations cannot be democratized and transparent. If national sovereignty has been eliminated by the WTO, NAFTA, and GATT, then we must create international sovereignty whereby citizens will regain power through international courts and U.N. agencies.

If "SRI in the Rockies" can invite World Bank representatives to a conference of SRI professionals, we should begin to earnestly develop a long-term, working relationship with organized labor, immediately inviting the highest ranking labor leaders to not only speak to all of our professional associations, but to strategize and work with us to decentralize our economy, invest in our communities, create jobs, and provide improved wages and benefits for all workers everywhere. Collective bargaining, healthy working conditions, and the rights of working men and women should be honored, encouraged, and strengthened. Too many people fought, bled, and died for these rights over the last two centuries.

Organized labor has a major investment in our economy and our political system, and has played a key role in the socially responsible investment movement from its inception. SRI has to pro-actively engage labor as a major partner in challenging corporate power and investing in our future.

Shareholders are no longer the only stakeholders in a corporate enterprise, but are legally still responsible under current law. Government alone will not challenge corporate management, so we must. Investors should not only challenge corporations as a last resort, stock should be purchased specifically to challenge corporate management when these business enterprises engage in egregious conduct, violate state and federal law or regulations, or abuse human and labor rights. Corporate management should not be able to get off the hook by paying small fines simply as the cost of doing business. The *ante* must be raised to a much higher level as well as the bar of unacceptable corporate conduct. We can no longer tolerate corporate abuse of the public trust. White collar criminals should go to jail, corporate executives and directors should be held personally liable and pay financially for corporate misconduct, and charters should be revoked.

We must ignore many of the useless secondary market smoke-and-mirrors of esoteric SRI products that make money for only a few in the financial community. Many do not create competitive businesses or quality employment. On the other hand, we should encourage innovative secondary market instruments that leverage SRI assets into high social impact investments such as microfinance and low-income housing.

SRI investors should take advantage of numerous screened mutual fund opportunities that provide competitive returns that also include CDFIs in the portfolio investments targeted to the community. All SRI investors need to take responsibility and educate ourselves about specific environmental and social criteria, a fund's shareholder voting record, and how the fund supports direct investments in the community. SRI investors must demand comprehensive screening based upon personal or institutional social and environmental guidelines, and a commitment to long-term community investing.

Shareholders need to exercise control over corporate management with the help of other stakeholders and constituencies. The primary role of the SRI community, in representing the owners of capital, is to bring these forces together as one constituency. We need to change corporate by-laws, advocate for pro-active state charter control, and complimentary federal chartering of corporations. We must take public control of federal and state regulatory agencies, demand total transparency, full corporate disclosure, and join with other stakeholders to litigate and engage in coordinated and targeted corporate campaigns to protect the public interest under a new universal stakeholder fiduciary standard.

The mobilization of economic and political pressure against South African apartheid and its corporate allies was successful because a coordinated divestment campaign, including a capital strike or bank boycott and institutional and government selective purchasing laws were new, and corporate management was totally caught off guard. Corporate power has not eliminated selective purchasing power by local governments. Local and state governments can still buy fair trade products and encourage local enterprises. The city of Los Angeles and the Los Angeles Unified School District have adopted selective purchasing laws to insure that products are not purchased from companies utilizing sweatshops. The city and county of San Francisco will soon consider a sweeping selective purchasing ordinance banning sweatshop products, encouraging a living wage, and encouraging the purchase of fair trade organic and non-genetically modified products.

What is now needed is a strategy that is a "systems" approach that coordinates all the stakeholder strategies at one time to overload the corporate system. "System overload" essentially means that corporate management will not be able to deal with all stakeholders at one time: shareholders, other investors, vendors, contractors, labor, community activists, NGOs, regulators, litigators and legislators, all united to encompass a total corporate campaign. The results: system overload. Corporations will not be able to deal with campaigns coordinated at the local, state, national, and international levels. Corporate power seems omnipresent to us, only because we see it through our individual eyes, not collectively as stakeholders and communities across the globe. We can act as a sovereign country and as a sovereign people against undemocratic and unpatriotic corporations. We can also act as citizens with others across the globe. Corporations, as they are presently constituted, present a clear and present danger to democracy and a free enterprise economy.

Ethics and morality must be part of a new corporate code, but one that is consistent with public policy and civil society, based on democratic principles. A universal corporate code must be mandated and must be part and parcel of federal and state chartering, enforceable, and mandatory. The rule of law enforcing such chartering must be global and part of the international legal system.

Stakeholders that are shareholders need to use whatever means available to influence corporate management to improve corporate conduct. We must demand a deconstruction of the corporate structure and return to a market economy that is reliant on democratic decision-making, community economic needs, and stakeholder values. Economic democracy must accompany participatory democracy.

Shareholders must continue to introduce resolutions and demand, not beg, that corporate management be accountable to shareholders and other stakeholders. Raising important issues about human, labor, and environmental rights is as important for fiduciaries as board member nominations, executive compensation, and other corporate governance reform issues.

One of the most important results of shareholder action is the creation of a historical record of fiduciary involvement and concern which later may be a key factor in litigation as well as legislation.

For SRI, in the short-run, corporate governance is important, but not the heart and soul of the movement and the community. Investing and shareholder advocacy have to return from whence they came; back to the community and to serve the public interest and civil society. SRI, in addition to participating in a "systems overload" campaign against corporate domination, has to use its skills, education, and unique history to become innovative again, utilizing our activist roots to develop both profit and not-for-profit ventures to decentralize world economies and rediscover true free enterprise and global fair trade. We must create new local and global economies. This includes social, as well as private and public sector innovation and entrepreneurship.

Leadership at the community level is already there. Financial structures already exist, from community loan and microenterprise funds to community banks and credit unions, including international fair trade and cooperative housing and lending organizations. We need liquid secondary markets to leverage larger investments to fund community businesses, microenterprise firms, and nonprofit organizations, not useless products to spin money out of money and provide cover for "best in class" oil, chemical, and tobacco companies. If we can invest in ShoreBank CDs and Calvert Community Investment notes through our brokerage accounts, surely we can create the same opportunities for investors to fund individual targeted investments in community loan and microenterprise funds, as well as in private placements and social venture securities.

Most important of all, to SRI and to the future of our global society, is the individual investor.

You are the center of the universe, because you are also a shareholder, a voter, a consumer, a saver, a worker, a retiree, and a philanthropist. All of the roles you play put you in a pivotal position. You are what you invest, what you buy, what you eat and drink, who you are, and who you and your children and your grandchildren will become. Your decisions as a shareholder and a voter are crucial, but no more important than what kind of nonprofit organization receives your donation. Your donated dollar is just as important as your invested dollar. If you support politicians and mutual funds that reflect your values, you should also support nonprofit organizations that reflect your ideals, ethics, and morality.

Socially responsible investors must be just that: socially conscious and responsible. Our integrity, our children's future, and the global community's future depend upon the decisions we make in all of our multiple roles. It is time for a new beginning. It is time to use our money, our investments, and our votes to change the world.

TRIBUTE

Traditionally, authors acknowledge special people who have inspired or led them to greater accomplishments in their chosen fields. As an author, I acknowledged several friends, colleagues, clients, staff, and family in my first book, *Investing With Your Conscience: How to Achieve High Returns Using Socially Responsible Investing* (John Wiley & Sons, 1992). I wish to do so again, but more as a tribute to extraordinary individuals than simply acknowledging them.

There are people in my life who have not only inspired me, but deserve enormous recognition on their own because of their many great accomplishments, both personal and professional. Each of them deserves a comprehensive biography, not just a few words, but obviously that is someone else's task, not mine. Many others in the socially responsible investment (SRI) community should be recognized who played an important and pivotal role in growing SRI from a small community to a global movement. I hope that someone will write their stories someday.

Two men I want to pay special tribute to are both in their eighties—Bob Schwartz, who lives in New York City, and John Dunlap, who lives in Napa, California. Three other great human beings and leaders in the SRI community are no longer with us: Margaret Cheap, Chuck Matthei, and Jack Corbett; Margaret and Chuck left us in 2002, while Jack's passing was in March 2003 at the age of eighty-two.

Bob Schwartz has spent his entire life working for social justice in government and in the financial services industry. Even though he was a Marine veteran in World War II on Okinawa, he was run out of his job in the U.S. Treasury Department by McCarthyites because of his liberal political views. This, however, didn't stop him from running for Congress on an anti-war platform during the Vietnam War. In his eighty-seven years, he helped establish the American Veterans Committee, Peace Action (formerly SANE), Wall Street Executives Against the War; coined the phrase "socially responsible investing"; and co-founded Economists Allied for Arms Reduction. He recently authored a book entitled *Can You Make a Difference? A Memoir of a Life for Change,* (Lantern Books, New York 2002). He is recognized as the grandfather of SRI.

John Dunlap, my mentor, father figure, and great-grandson of one of the city founders of Napa, California, has been a great inspiration to me and a largely unrecognized figure in the history of SRI due to his work in the 'California legislature, where he served from 1966 until 1979. He was not only responsible for the California Agriculture Labor Relations Act, working with Cesar Chavez to provide farm workers collective bargaining rights, but wrote successful legislation protecting the California mountain lion, providing public access to the state's coastal resources, and introduced other environmental and socially responsible investment legislation, eventually leading to the present CALPERS and CALSTRS shareholder activism. When few in the California legislature had the courage to advocate for economic democracy, John Dunlap was calling for the divestment of state funds from companies in South Africa, the creation of a state bank, and the elimination of regressive taxes in California. A partner in an old Napa law firm, his entire life has been one of leadership and public service.

I first met Margaret Cheap when I was a consultant to Senator Dunlap's Select Committee on Investment Priorities and Objectives in the late 1970s. She was organizing the Santa Cruz Community Credit Union and had asked me to meet her organizing board to share information. She was a dynamo, committed to creating locally-based financial institutions to provide credit for everyone in the community as well as ensuring that local folks controlled their own economic destiny. She went on to work in Washington, D.C., in the 1980s, joining the newly created National Consumer Co-Op Bank and later serving as president and CEO of NCB Development Corporation. Margaret ended her career in Chicago, continuing to build on her earlier successes through her work as president and CEO of South Shore Bank when she was hired in 1998. We lost a great human being when Margaret died of brain cancer at the age of forty-nine. Her humor, commitment, and love of people will always be remembered and she and her work continually honored.

Another tireless crusader for local community economic development was Chuck Matthei, the executive director of Massachusetts-based Institute for Community Economics (ICE). Chuck never slowed down, being totally devoted to the cause of empowering people at the local level to attain economic self-determination. He almost single-handedly convinced thousands of people across the country to create their own locally-based loan funds, credit unions, and community development banks (Chuck never, ever stopped talking). He was founder and director of Equity Trust, focusing on alternative models of land tenure and economic development and providing technical and financial assistance to projects throughout the United States, Central America, and Kenya. Chuck was an amazingly engaging human being devoted to nonviolence and philanthropy and was convinced that SRI would only work if it met the needs of the poor by directly investing in community economic development. Chuck died at the age of fifty-four after a 2½ year fight with thyroid cancer. He will be missed and can never be replaced.

Reverend Dr. Elliot "Jack" Corbett was an early pioneer of SRI and, along with Reverend Dr. Luther Tyson, organized and opened Pax World Fund, the first SRI mutual fund, in 1971. A letter from a woman in Ohio asking Jack and Luther how to invest her pension money in a way that would avoid defense and war-oriented companies led them to create the Pax World Fund.

Jack also created Pax World Service, a non-profit organization promoting peace, international reconciliation, and small-scale sustainable development. Pax World Service provided Americans a way to become citizen diplomats, visiting the Middle East, Central America, and Cuba. He also founded Pax International in 2001 after Pax World Service merged with another organization.

Jack served as a United Methodist pastor in churches in New Jersey, Pennsylvania, and Illinois and authored *The Prophets on Main Street* and four other books. He was loved by all those who knew him.

Certainly no less important in my life are those family members and staff closest to me. Diana Lynn, my wife, and my daughters, Brenna Lee and Brianna Lynn, have all been very supportive. My mom, Jean Frances Turner Harrington, who was excited about my second book, passed away on August 27, 2003. She was my biggest supporter, and I miss her more than words can express. She was a Texas beauty, representing the best the state has to offer. I'm also very grateful for the work of Dawn McGee Esquire, who was on the staff of Harrington Investment's social venture fund, Global Partners, LLC and now serves as consultant. I also appreciate her "words of wisdom" in helping me pontificate about corporate person-hood in chapter 1.

Nothing would have been written without my back office chief, Chris Vallejo, and social researchers extraordinaire, Alana Smith Johnk and Peri Payne. Portfolio managers Susan Bogar and Rebecca Long also gave me the support, encouragement, and advice to finish this book in my lifetime. Congratulations also to Monica Nelson for keeping me on track, data pro-cessing this mess, and taking responsibility for bringing the book together in readable form. I also wanted to thank a great team assembled to help me with the book, including Napa editor Mick Winter, Michael Shellenberger, and Erin Malec at Lumina Strategies, Dan Strickland, and Lisa Luke and Landis Designs (who produced the wonderful cover), San Francisco attorney Marc Libarle, Beth Rosales and Jessica Boos, Sandy Close, and Nell Bernstein of Pacific News Service, and president and publisher Margo Baldwin and consulting editor Safir Ahmed at Chelsea Green.

Guard at government building, Pretoria, South Africa. Working Assets won't use your savings to support legalized racism.

If you've left your money in an ordinary bank or money market fund, chances are that some of it's working night and day to strengthen apartheid in South Africa.

Money you've set aside could also be financing missiles and warheads, nuclear power, or job discrimination in the United States. Because bankers invest your savings where *they*—not *you*—see fit.

A Practical Alternative

Now there's a sure way to earn high current interest—without supporting apartheid. At Working Assets Money Fund, your money works *for*, not *against*, your principles. For example, we carefully avoid investing your money in companies that have operations in South Africa, manufacture weapons or produce nuclear power.

Higher Interest, Too

What's more, Working Assets pays *higher interest* than most banks*. You can write an unlimited number of *free* checks...withdraw at *any time* without penalty...and know that your money is *safe*.

To learn more, simply write or call for a free prospectus. You have nothing to lose. And what you'll gain is worth far more than money.

*Based on 1984 yields of money market checking accounts at America's 50 largest banks and thrifts, as reported in *Bank Rate Monitor*. Working Assets' yields fluctuate daily and principal is not insured. $1,000 minimum investment.

WORKING ASSETS

Assets now over $60 million

WORKING ASSETS MONEY FUND
230 California Street, San Francisco CA 94111

☐ **Yes!** I want to get free check-writing and earn high current interest—without supporting apartheid. Please send me your free prospectus including more complete information about management fees and expenses. I'll read it carefully before investing.

Name

Address

City/State/Zip

Earn Interest On Your Principles
800-543-8800. Toll-free night or day.

APPENDIX B

Working Assets Money Fund: Social Criteria

Social Investment Criteria

We invest in money market instruments that we believe have a positive social and economic impact.

Jobs. We purchase instruments that we believe create jobs and develop the U.S. economy rather than rearrange existing assets through mergers and acquisitions. Also, to the greatest possible extent, we choose instruments of financial institutions that reinvest deposits in their local communities.

Housing. We purchase securities of the Federal Home Loan Mortgage Corporation (Freddie Mae), the Federal National Mortgage Association (Fannie Mae) and the Federal Home Loan Bank. We also purchase certificates of deposit in savings and loan associations and other institutions that finance moderate-income housing.

Higher Education. We invest in securities that promote higher education, such as those of the Student Loan Marketing Association (Sallie Mae).

Family farming. We purchase securities of the Federal Farm Credit System that finance U.S. agriculture and loans guaranteed by the Farmers Home Administration.

Equal opportunity. We seek out firms that promote the economic advancement of women and minorities. At the same time, we do no knowingly invest in companies that discriminate on the basis of race, religion, age, disability or sexual orientation, or which, to our knowledge, consistently violate regulations of the Equal Employment Opportunity Commission.

Labor. We seek to invest in companies that bargain fairly with their employees and have policies that promote the welfare of their workers. At the same time, we do not knowingly invest in companies that consistently violate regulations of the National Labor Relations Board, appear on the national AFL-CIO "Do Not Patronize" list or have a record, according to the AFL-CIO, of hiring "union-busting" consultants. We also avoid multinational firms that have fewer than half their employees in the United States, unless a majority of their eligible U.S. employees are represented by organized labor.

Nuclear power. We do not knowingly invest in companies that generate nuclear power or manufacture nuclear equipment or materials.

Weapons. We avoid investing in firms that manufacture or distribute weapons as a principal business activity. Similarly, until there is a more prudent policy of defense spending, we have no intention of investing any of our assets in U.S. Treasury securities. In our view, U.S. Treasury securities are used primarily to finance a federal deficit caused in part by wasteful defense spending.

Repressive regimes. We do not knowingly invest in corporations that have a substantial presence in or are part of a strategic industry in a foreign nation controlled by a repressive regime (e.g. the Republic of South Africa) or which finance such a repressive regime.

Environment. We do not knowingly invest in corporations that consistently violate regulations of the Environmental Protection Agency or the Occupational Safety and Health Administration.

Small business. We seek out investments such as Small Business Administration guaranteed loans that finance the dynamic small business sector of the economy.

Charitable contributions. We seek out firms that are creative and generous in their charitable contributions, particularly with respect to investment in their communities.

Capital flight. We do not purchase Eurodollar instruments that drain capital from productive use in the United States.

Other criteria. When buying banker's acceptances, we purchase only those that are backed by banks that meet out social and economic criteria. We do not invest in companies that knowingly and deliberately violate Section 8 of the Export Administration Act of 1979.

APPENDIX C

Fund Descriptions

EQUITY FUNDS

Ariel and Ariel Appreciation Funds

Since 1983, as the founder of Ariel Capital Management, Inc., John W. Rogers, Jr., has overseen the growth of Ariel Capital Management's assets. Ariel and Ariel Appreciation Funds were launched in 1986 and 1989, respectively. As of January 31, 2005, the two socially screened funds had assets of more than $7 billion and, annualized over ten years, outperformed all other SRI funds profiled in this book.

Fund	Expense Ratio	Assets ($ Mil.)	10 Year Perf. (%)
Ariel	1.10	4,000	15.44
Ariel Appreciation	1.20	3,170	14.75

As of December 31, 2004, Ariel had about 82 percent of the fund invested in stocks, while Ariel Appreciation had about 96 percent invested in U.S. stocks. Ariel Fund is invested in small-cap value companies, and Ariel Appreciation is a mid-cap blend fund.

The Ariel Mutual Funds do not invest in companies involved in the manufacture of weapons, the production of nuclear energy, or whose primary source of revenue comes from the production of tobacco products. For social screening purposes, the funds utilize the research of Trillium Asset Management (formerly Franklin Research and Development), to insure that companies are making a positive contribution to the environment. Ariel also considers a company's commitment to community involvement, children's programs, preservation and development of parklands, involvement in the local school system and company diversity issues.

John W. Rogers serves as chairman, CEO and chief investment officer of Ariel Capital Management and manages both Ariel and Ariel Appreciation funds. While maintaining a relatively low profile within the SRI community, he has been involved in a number of nonprofit organizations, including the Illinois Council Against Handgun Violence, the Urban League of Chicago (chairman), the Library Board, and the Field Museum. He also serves as a trustee of the Chicago Symphony Orchestra and the John S. and James L. Knight Foundation.[1] Rogers started out his financial services career as a stockbroker for William Blair & Co. He currently serves on the board of directors of several corporations including Aon Corporation, Bank One, Burrell Communications Group, Exelon Corporation, and GATX Corporation.

Domini Social Equity Fund

The closest thing you'll get to a socially screened S&P 500 Stock Index is the Domini Social Equity Fund, which has grown to more than $1.3 billion. It has four hundred stocks, about half of which are S&P 500 companies, and about 150 are added to insure that Domini's portfolio is comprised of a broad representation of S&P 500 industry sectors. This means that Domini's sector weighting is as close as possible to the S&P 500 Stock Index. Domini invests 100 percent of the assets of the fund in equities.

In every year since its inception, and certainly for the past ten years, the Domini Social Equity Fund's performance has been closely aligned to the S&P 500 Stock Index's performance. Below is the comparative ten-year performance:

	1994	1995	1996	1997	1998	1999	2000	2001	2002	2003
Domini	-0.36	35.17	21.84	36.02	32.99	22.63	-15.05	-12.76	-20.69	27.13
S&P 500	1.32	37.58	22.96	33.36	28.58	21.04	-9.10	-11.89	-22.10	28.67

Domini excludes companies involved in tobacco and alcohol, gambling, nuclear power and weapons. It includes companies that have a good record in environmental performance, employee relations, diversity and product-related issues.

Domini has been a strong pro-active shareholder, introducing and co-filing dozens of resolutions every year. Amy Domini has also been the leading spokesperson for mandatory public disclosure of investment adviser and mutual fund shareholder votes at annual shareholders meetings, a version of which was adopted by the Securities and Exchange Commission in January 2003, and became effective in August 2004. Since 1999, the Domini Social Equity Fund has disclosed its proxy voting record.

While Amy Domini and her SRI allies were successful in gaining SEC approval requiring disclosure on mutual fund websites of proxy votes, in all likelihood large mutual fund families such as Vanguard and Fidelity will continue to vote consistently with management. For example, Fidelity, which owned 5.3 percent of Tyco stock, also earned $2 million in 1999 for its part in running Tyco's 401(k) plan. In 2001, over 50 percent of Fidelity's $9.8 billion in revenues was generated by administering 401(k) plans and other employee services for about eleven hundred companies including Philip Morris, Shell, IBM, Monsanto, and Ford.[2]

The composition of the Domini Social Equity Index utilized by the Domini Social Equity Fund is determined by Kinder, Lydenburg & Domini Research & Analytics, Inc. (KLD), and the Submanager for Domini is SSqA Funds Management of Boston, Massachusetts. Domini Social Investments publishes a very comprehensive semi-annual report, which provides useful social profiles of Domini portfolio companies and information on shareholder advocacy and SEC regulatory activity. KLD has also published a very useful 2004 guide to "Sustainable Socially Responsible Investing," which discusses KLD's rating criteria, indexes, and proxy voting topics and guidelines.

Amy Domini has been successful in growing assets in the Domini Social Equity Fund by breaking into 401(k) retirement plans and, as of June 2003, about 39 percent of the more than $1.7 billion in the fund comprised of retirement plan assets. Domini Social Investments, LLC, had a profit of over $1 million last year on revenues of $11.3 million.

Amy Domini is founder, CEO, and president of Domini Social Investments, LLC; a private trustee associated with Loring, Wolcott & Coolidge in Boston, MA; and a founder of KLD, specialists in corporate accountability research. Domini has worked in the investment field for more than twenty years and is a Chartered Financial Analyst (CFA). She holds a degree in International and Comparative Studies from Boston University. She has written several books, including *Ethical Investing* (Addison-Wesley,

1984); serves or has served on several for-profit and nonprofit boards; and currently sits on the Church Pension Fund of the Episcopal Church (USA). She has been instrumental in gaining support of church pension funds and targeting some of their assets to community investment opportunities.

Dreyfus Premier Third Century Fund

A screened fund that has been around since 1972, the Dreyfus Premier Third Century Fund (originally Dreyfus Third Century) has more than $426 million in assets with about 98 percent of the portfolio invested in equities.

Dreyfus does not have a rigid exclusionary screen (other than excluding tobacco), but instead focuses on companies that enhance the quality of life in America by considering their record in: environmental protection and proper use of our natural resources; occupational health and safety; consumer protection and product purity; and equal employment opportunity.

Dreyfus' managers use publicly available information from watchdog groups and government agencies to assist them in their social research, but do not currently examine: corporate activities outside the United States; non-business activities; secondary implications of corporate activities (such as the activities of a client or customer of the company being evaluated).

Paul Hilton, the primary portfolio manager at Third Century Fund with respect to social screening, was previously a research analyst in the social awareness investment program at Smith Barney Asset Management, a division of Travelers Group.

L. Emerson Tuttle has been senior portfolio manager and chairman of the investment oversight and policy committee for Mellon Growth Advisors LLC, an affiliate of Dreyfus, since September 2001. In October 2001, he became a dual employee of Dreyfus and Mellon Growth Advisors. For more than five years prior to September 2001, he was a portfolio manager and principle of State Street Global Advisors.

New Alternatives Fund

The oldest of the environmental funds, New Alternatives was founded in 1982 by Maurice Schoenwald and his son, David. The fund was originally named the Solar Fund, which was incorporated as a limited partnership in 1978.

New Alternatives is best identified with its investments in alternative energy and related new technologies. Obviously, the fund's portfolio does not include oil, coal, or atomic energy. Products and technologies the fund does include are batteries for solar energy, natural gas, resource conservation (including biomass), recycling, photovoltaic cells, and fuel cells.

New Alternatives Fund is a small cap blend, and as of the end of June 30, 2004, it had more than $36 million in assets, increasing to over $51 million by January 31, 2005.

Both Maurice and David Schoenwald are practicing attorneys—David has been a journalist and an attorney with Law Services (a poverty law agency), while Maurice has taught law, practiced commercial law, and written extensively about investing. The Schoenwalds received financial and consulting help in founding the fund from friends and neighbors. Since opening the fund, they have actively sought and received advice from shareholders. This is the American pie family business success story.

Parnassus and Parnassus Equity Income

Jerry Dodson's Parnassus family of funds has been around for more than ten years, and up until a couple of years ago, Jerry managed all of the funds personally. Now he manages only the original Parnassus Fund, as he has very successfully done for twenty years.

Parnassus is labeled a large cap growth fund, but its $346 million fund as of June 2004 still had 25 percent invested in cash; in January 2004 that number was about 82 percent. Of the stocks in Parnassus, most are invested in financials and health care.

The Parnassus equity funds avoid companies that manufacture alcohol or tobacco products or are involved with gambling. The funds also screen out weapons contractors and nuclear power producers. Dodson looks for companies with social policies that treat employees fairly, provide sound environmental protection policies, are good equal opportunity employers, provide quality products and services, have a record of civic commitment, and conduct themselves consistent with ethical business practices.

In addition to Jerry Dodson's unique SRI contrarian investment style, his down-to-earth shareholder reports and personal opinions are worth reading, especially his discussions of the personalities and histories of his staff and the ever-changing collection of interns that pass through Parnassus.

Parnassus has a history of investing in community banks and credit unions, including Albina Community Capital Bank, South Shore Bank Cleveland, Self Help Credit Union, Community Capital Bank, Vermont Development Credit Union, and Community Bank of the Bay, among others. Jerry also invests in community loan funds, including Vermont and Boston Community Loan Funds.

On the other hand, the $712 million Parnassus Equity Income Fund, managed since 2001 by Todd Ahlsten, is a mid-to-large blend fund investing 90 percent of the portfolio in common stocks. Over the last five years the Equity Income Fund, which invests in mid-and large-cap stocks that pay dividends, outperformed 99 percent of its large-cap competitors, and in 2002 declined only 3.7 percent when the S&P 500 was down 22 percent.[3]

In addition to heading Parnassus and Working Assets, Jerry Dodson served as president and CEO of Continental Savings of America where he started the "Solar T-Bill" program to finance solar energy installations, and also developed programs to finance low- and moderate-income housing. From 1966 through 1969, he was a foreign service officer with the Department of State, serving with the American Embassy in Vietnam and as the American Consul in David, Panama.

Dodson, a graduate of the University of California at Berkeley and Harvard Business School, is board chairman of the San Francisco Haight Ashbury Free Clinics and a former director of the Social Investment Forum. He has also served on the board of Project Open Hand, a nonprofit organization that prepares and delivers meals to people with AIDS. Parnassus launched three new funds in 2005: a small cap, a mid cap, and Parnassus Workplace Fund, which invests in the Fortune 100 Best Companies to Work for in America, with advice coming from Milton Moskowitz.

Calvert Social Investment Equity Fund

Founded in 1976, Calvert Group, Ltd., operates twenty-seven funds with more than $10 billion in assets and has one of the largest socially responsible fund families in the country. It is owned by Ameritas Acacia Mutual Holding Company.

One of Calvert's many socially screened funds, the Calvert Social Investment Equity Fund, with assets of $790 million is managed by Daniel W. Boone, III Most of the portfolio is invested in stocks, with almost 20 percent invested in health care, over 18 percent in consumer services and 13 percent in financial services as of June 30, 2004.

Calvert Social Investment Funds are very proactive shareholders, engaging in dialogue with corporate management and filing and co-filing shareholder resolutions, and voting their stock consistent with their overall social guidelines.

The funds seek to avoid investing in companies that Calvert determines to be significantly engaged in: supporting repressive regimes; nuclear energy; weapons systems; alcoholic beverages or tobacco products; gambling casinos; a pattern and practice of violating the rights of Native Americans and other indigenous peoples.

In June 2004, Calvert announced the launch of the Calvert Women's Principles, a code of corporate conduct focusing on gender equality and women's empowerment. The principles cover such issues as wages and benefits; health, safety and violence; discrimination in the workplace; civic and community engagement; management and governance; hiring, promotion, and professional development; business and supply chain practices; and monitoring and reporting. Calvert will integrate the Women's Principles into its funds' screening criteria.

CSIF invests primarily in debt obligations issued or guaranteed by agencies or instrumentalities of the U.S. Government whose purposes further, or are compatible with, the fund's social criteria, such as obligations of the Student Loan Marketing Association, rather than general obligations of the U.S. Government, such as Treasury securities.

From an inclusive criteria standpoint the Calvert funds seek to invest in companies that:

- Deliver safe products and services in ways that sustain our natural environment

- Manage with participation throughout the organization and that offer employee stock ownership or profit-sharing plans
- Negotiate fairly with their workers, provide an environment supportive of their wellness, do not discriminate on the basis of race, gender, religion, age, disability, ethnic origin, or sexual orientation, do not consistently violate regulations of the EEOC, and provide opportunities for women, people of color, disadvantaged minorities, and others for whom equal opportunities have often been denied. The funds consider both unionized and non-union firms with good labor relations
- Foster awareness of a commitment to human goals, such as creativity, productivity, self-respect, and responsibility within the organization and the world (for example, the funds look for companies with an above average commitment to community affairs and charitable giving)

Calvert has also publicly committed to invest a small portion of the funds' assets to High Social Impact Investments (HSI), Special Equities (SE), and the Calvert Manager Discovery Program (MDP). Calvert's HSI investments are primarily invested in loan funds, credit unions, and community-based financial intermediaries that support business creation, housing, and the economic and social development of urban and rural communities. These investments are made through the purchase of Community Investment Notes from the Calvert Social Investment Foundation, which is a nonprofit organization that invests directly in community development financial institutions.

Calvert's SE investment program allows several of the funds to support social venture capital privately placed in small, pre-IPO companies and in private social venture funds. Calvert's MDP allows the Calvert Social Investment Balanced Fund to allocate up to 5 percent of the fund's assets to minority and women-owned money management firms.

Daniel Boone, the fund's manager for five years, has been with the sub-adviser to the fund, Atlanta Capital Management Company, LLC, for twenty-two years. He received his BA Degree from Davidson College and an MBA from the University of Pennsylvania's Wharton School of Business. He is a Chartered Financial Analyst (CFA) and a Chartered Investment Counselor.

Calvert World Values International Fund

In September 2002, Calvert's $1.8 million South Africa Fund was merged into World Values, and as of June 30, 2004, total assets of the fund were more than $212 million. In March 2002, the Calvert World Values trustees approved the appointment of Grantham, Mayo, and Van Otterloo as the Subadviser of the fund. In May of the same year the trustees dismissed Arthur Andersen, LLP, as their independent auditor and hired KPMG.

While over 90 percent of the fund's assets are in foreign stocks, it has made investments in the common stock and corporate notes of Soluz, Inc., and Soluz Dominicana, a small solar retrofit company operating in Honduras and the Dominican Republic. The fund also has high social impact investments, including Calvert's own Foundation Community Investment Note and the Mennonite Economic Development Association. The fund has also invested in Forward Foreign Currency contacts and futures to hedge the portfolio.

The social criteria for the World Values Fund is similar to Calvert's other socially screened funds, but its standards are less stringent, because of inadequate corporate disclosure, different regulatory structures, environmental standards, and differing national and cultural priorities. The fund, however, has inclusionary criteria and attempts to invest in companies that: achieve excellence in environmental management, and take positive steps towards preserving and enhancing our natural environment through their operations and products; have positive labor practices, considering the International Labor Organizations basic conventions on worker rights as a guideline; hire and promote women and ethnic minorities; respect the right to form unions; comply, at minimum, with domestic hour and wage laws and provide good health and safety standards; and whose products or services improve the quality of, or access to, health care.

Calvert World Values seeks to avoid investing in companies that contribute to human rights abuses; produce nuclear power or nuclear weapons;

have more than 10 percent of revenues derived from the production or sale of weapons systems, alcohol or tobacco products; are significantly engaged in a pattern and practice of violating the rights of indigenous peoples.

Thomas Hancock and Christopher M. Darnell co-manage the portfolio for sub-adviser Grantham, Mayo, Van Otterloo & Co., LLC.

Hancock joined the firm in 1995 and is currently engaged in global quantitative equities portfolio management. He has a BS from Rensselaer Polytechnic Institute and PhD from Harvard University. Darnell joined the firm in 1979, serving as a research analyst, and became Head of Quantitative Research in 1996. Darnell earned his BA at Yale University and MBA from Harvard University.

Smith Barney Social Awareness Funds

Smith Barney Equity Funds, a Massachusetts business trust, and Salomon Smith Barney, a subsidiary of Citigroup, manage Smith Barney Social Awareness A and B. The primary difference between the A and B is that the Class A fund is a front end-loaded 5 percent and the Class B fund is a 5 percent deferred loaded fund. Smith Barney manages sixty mutual funds altogether with $200 billion in assets. This is the company's social niche.

Social Awareness excludes companies involved in tobacco production, weapons production or ownership of nuclear facilities. It attempts to invest in companies that exhibit the positive attributes of fairness of employment policies and labor relations; involvement in community causes; embracing alternatives to unsafe polluting and wasteful activities or products; being responsible and fair in advertising and marketing practices.

Smith Barney's analysis of a company's performance is based on present activities, and the managers will not exclude securities solely because of past activities. Managers will monitor the social progress or deterioration of each company in which the fund invests.

The Social Awareness Funds invest in large cap blend, or growth and value companies, investing over 80 percent in stocks, and about 18 percent of its assets in bonds as of June 30, 2004; the Social Awareness Class A has more than $271 million in assets, while the Class B fund has more than $105 million.

The Smith Barney investment team of Charles P. Graves, III, and Ellen S. Cammer has managed the Social Awareness Funds for eight years. Graves has more than eighteen years of securities business experience and holds a BA from Hamilton College and an MBA from Columbia University. Cammer has more than twenty years of securities business experience and has earned a BFA from Windham College and an MBA from Fordham University.

Amana Income Fund

The Amana Income Fund opened in 1986 and has about $35 million invested in large value companies that are operated consistent with Islamic principles, including companies that share in profit and loss and receive no usury or interest. "Amana" means "trust" or "protection" in Arabic. Businesses that are excluded from investment include alcohol, gambling, pornography, insurance, pork processing, and Internet-based banks or finance associations. Also excluded are bonds, debentures, or other interest-paying obligations of indebtedness.

Amana does invest in dividend-paying domestic and foreign stocks. Over 98 percent of the portfolio is invested in stocks.

Monem Salam is the fund director of Islamic Investment, traveling from his Bellingham, Washington office to market to mosques and other venues across the country.[4]

Nicholas Kaiser is director and president of Saturna Capital Corporation, the portfolio manager of Amana Income Fund. He and his family control Saturna Capital through its voting stock. He has been managing the portfolio for more than fourteen years. A graduate of Yale College with an Economics degree, Kaiser has an MBA from the University of Chicago with dual majors in International Economics and Finance. He is a chartered financial analyst. Kaiser's industry activities include service with the Investment Company Institute (past governor), Association for Investment Management and Research (past chapter president), International Association of Financial Planners (past chapter president), and No-Load Mutual Fund Association (past national president). His voluntary activities include Mt. Baker Council of the Boy Scouts of America (executive vice president), St. Paul's Episcopal School (president), British Columbia's Island Trust Fund (advisor), Fourth Corner Economic Club (founder), and the Bellingham, Washington, Rotary.

SOCIALLY SCREENED BALANCED FUNDS

Most SRI mutual funds invest in stocks, while many funds allocate assets into one or more asset classes, such as stocks, bonds and short-term debt securities, including money market mutual funds. Of the twenty-two funds represented here, three are considered "balanced;" that is, a significant portion of the fund's assets are allocated to fixed-income securities: Pax World Balanced, Green Century Balanced, and Calvert Social Investment Balanced.

Pax World Balanced Fund

Founded in 1971, this is the elder statesman of socially responsible mutual funds in the country and has the best ten-year performance record of the three balanced funds.

Because of the deep religious roots of two of the fund's founders, Jack Corbett and Dr. Luther Tyson, and the fact that the fund was created at the height of the Vietnam War, the social criteria is wedded to an anti-weapons, anti-defense department exclusionary approach. The fund not only excludes U.S. Treasury securities because the proceeds are used to manufacture defense or weapons-related products, but specifically excludes securities of companies: engaged in military activities; if 5 percent or more of their gross sales are derived from Department of Defense (DOD) contracts; that derive revenue from the manufacture of liquors, tobacco, or gambling products.

Pax World invests in fixed income securities that are consistent with the fund's overall social objectives such as the Federal Home Loan Bank, the Federal National Mortgage Association, and Federal Home Loan Mortgage Corporation certificates.

As of June 30, 2004, Pax World invested more than 69 percent of its portfolio in stocks and about 25 percent in bonds, and also invested in certificates of deposit in South Shore Bank and Self Help Credit Union. As of that date, Pax World's total assets were more than $1.3 billion; by January 31, 2005, assets reached $1.47 billion.

Pax World's stock diversification by sector was weighted to favor health and consumer goods and services. Balanced fund annualized performance numbers for Pax World, compared to Green Century and Calvert, appear below:

Fund	3 Year	5 Year	10 Year
Pax World Balanced	2.18	2.92	11.43
Green Century Balanced	-3.05	10.87	10.82
Calvert Social Investment Balanced	0.31	0.03	7.17

Christopher H. Brown was named the co-manager of the Pax World Balanced Fund in April 1998 and has served as manager since October 2001. He is a senior vice president of H.G. Wellington & Co., Inc., the fund's distributor. Prior to joining Pax World Management Corp., the fund's adviser in 1998, he was an investment consultant at Fahnestock & Co., a New York Stock Exchange brokerage firm from 1987 to 1998, and a first vice president from 1994 to 1998. Brown is a graduate of the Boston University School of Management with a concentration in finance.

His father, Anthony Brown, was one of the founders of Pax World and remained as portfolio manager until his retirement in 1998.

Pax World has the distinction of being one of the least expensive of the SRI balanced funds, and is not only ranked the best ten-year performer of the three SRI funds reviewed here, but also received top rankings by Lipper Analytical Services and Nelson's Directory of Investment Managers in 1990.[5] Historically, Pax World Balanced Fund has been a low-cost, inexpensive, well performing mutual fund for more risk-averse social investors. Annual portfolio turnover is also reported to be low (38 percent), especially compared to Green Century and Calvert.

Following the U.S. invasion of Iraq, Pax World came up with a unique idea to allow its shareholders to provide humanitarian aid to Iraqi citizens affected by the war. Through voluntary contributions of percentages of capital gains or dividends, investors in the fund can contribute to the Iraqi aid and assistance work of Pax World Service, which is an affiliate of Mercy Corps, a relief and development organization operating in the Middle East and throughout the world. Mercy Corps uses contributions from Pax World Balanced Fund investors to provide refugees with food, shelter, and sanitation facilities, as well as to establish medical clinics for displaced families. The groups also assist with re-establishing utility power grids, hospitals, and water supplies.

On a worldwide basis, investors in the fund have already contributed $775,000 over four years to Pax World Service/Mercy Corps humanitarian efforts in more than thirty countries, including, most recently, assistance for civilians in the rebuilding of post-war Afghanistan.

Green Century Balanced Fund
Originally opening balanced and money market funds, environmental organizations in 1991 saw an opportunity to have an environmental impact and to use the profits from portfolio management to support environmental advocacy. Green Century Capital Management is owned and was founded by Paradigm Partners, a California general partnership, whose partners are all nonprofit environmental advocacy organizations, including California Public Interest Research Group (CalPIRG), Citizen Lobby of New Jersey, Colorado Citizen Lobby, ConnPIRG Citizen Lobby, Fund for Pubic Interest Research, Massachusetts Public Interest Research Group (MassPIRG), MOPIRG Citizen Organization, PIRGIM Public Interest Lobby, and Washington Sate Public Interest Research group (WashPIRG).

This $66 million fund invests in smaller growth companies that protect the environment and promote a sustainable future. Until recently, many of the portfolio companies were involved in renewable energy, recycling waste, providing appropriate technology for sustainable agriculture, and "leading edge" smaller environmental companies. A review of the Green Century Balanced Fund's portfolio in 2002, showed several alternative and renewable energy companies' stocks, as well as health care and medical products companies, and food companies such as Whole Foods Market and United Natural Foods. On the fixed-income side of Green Century, names such as Calpine, Kindercare Learning Center, and Nebraska Book Company appeared.

According to *Morningstar*, more than 68 percent of Green Century Balanced was invested in stocks, and over 27 percent was in fixed-income as of June 3, 2004.[6] Jackson Robinson, the portfolio manager, said that most of the fixed income securities were in non-investment grade bonds. "We don't own Treasuries because the biggest polluter in the world is the U. S. government," Robinson told *The New York Times* in a report published on June 6, 2003. "There are some wonderful green companies whose debt has junk status, but we are looking at companies where the credit situation will improve. Being a balanced fund has nothing to do with the nature of your equity or debt portfolios."

Robinson is the president of Winslow Management Company and has been the sub-adviser to the Green Century Balanced Fund for nine years. Winslow, a division of Adams, Harkness & Hill, Inc. (AHH) since April 1, 1999, was formerly a division of Eaton Vance Management. Robinson has served as the day-to-day portfolio manager since July 1, 1995, and previously served as president of Reiser, Robinson, and Harrington and the National Gardening Association. He was a partner at Trinity Investment Management. Currently, he serves as a director of Spartech Corporation, Jupiter International Green Investment Trust, and the Jupiter European Investment Trust, as well as serving as a Trustee of Suffield Academy.

Robinson is also the manager of the new "hot" Winslow Green Growth Fund, a $37 million small cap growth fund that is fully invested in predominantly small health care companies. The portfolio of Winslow and Green Century are similar, but where Winslow is fully invested, Green Century has a balance of bonds and cash. Since last year, Green Century's portfolio composition has changed radically, as has its performance. Both Winslow and Green Century lost over 37 percent of portfolio value in 2002. For Green Century, 2003 was a great year, gaining 65 percent, while the Winslow Green Growth increased over 91 percent. For the first seven months of 2004 Green Century was at −11.80 percent, Winslow −14.10 percent.

The "green" label may be stretched a bit by Green Century, and it certainly is for Winslow, whose link to environmental investing, and small cap healthcare companies may be based on the premise that cancer and other serious illnesses are caused, in part, by a deterioration of the environment. The portfolio of both Green Century and Winslow includes stocks in companies such as PolyMedica, a direct-to-consumer medical products and services company, which, among other things, delivers diabetic testing strips and insulin, and Staar Surgical, which makes foldable intra-ocular lenses used to replace natural lenses removed in cataract surgery. Another company that popped up in both portfolios in 2003 was Conceptus, which develops and markets proprietary non-incisional, permanent birth control devices for women. I'm not quite sure what these companies have to do with environmental or "green" investing. Both Winslow and Green Century have about 35 percent of their portfolios in the Health Care sector. Instead of "green" investments, these should probably be considered "health care."

Green Century Balanced Fund conducts itself as a responsible fiduciary by shareholder advocacy—introducing resolutions and dialoguing with corporate management—and implementing an inclusionary environmental screen. At the 2001 and 2002 annual shareholders meetings, 11 percent and 13 percent, respectively, of British Petroleum (BP) shares were voted in favor of a Green Century shareholder resolution urging the company to reconsider its plans to drill in the Arctic National Wildlife Refuge. BP agreed to cancel its membership in Arctic Power, the lobbying group whose sole goal is to open the Refuge to oil drilling. Green Century agreed not to re-file the resolution in 2003. It introduced a similar resolution at Conoco Phillips Petroleum, asking the company to report on its plans to drill in the Refuge, and received 5.3 percent of the shareholder vote. Green Century also filed a resolution with Campbell Soup Company calling on the company to prepare a report on genetically engineered foods.

In 1991, Mindy Lubber, the former president of Green Century declared that she hoped to be profitable in five years since the fund would have to attract $100 million to break even.[7] Mindy left Green Century and was hired by the Coalition for Environmentally Responsible Economies (CERES) to replace Robert Massey as executive director. After eleven years, Green Century has attracted about $66 million in the balanced fund and still trails the three-year performance records of the other two SRI balanced funds reviewed here as of June 30, 2004. On the other hand, it is the best of the three in five-year performance, and beat out Calvert for the number two performance spot for ten years.

Unfortunately, there may be some additional trouble ahead for Green Century. In December 2002, the Sierra Club announced the launching of two environmental mutual funds—Sierra Club Balanced Fund and Sierra Club Stock Fund—that will be marketed to its seven hundred thousand-plus members and the general public. Publicly, the Sierra Club's executive director announced that the funds would not invest in any oil or tobacco companies or companies that violate worker health and safety standards, but would invest in alcohol.[8] In material distributed at the 2004 SRI in the Rockies conference, Sierra Club Mutual Funds also stated that oil and natural resource extraction companies were excluded. In reviewing the prospectus, however, there are no exclusionary criteria. It states that investment activities are to be conducted ". . . in a manner consistent with the principles and standards espoused by the Sierra Club," and that the Sierra Club has developed a list of guidelines for investment but such guidelines do not appear in the prospectus. According to *Green Money Journal*, the Sierra Club has nineteen different screening criteria including production of renewable energy, nuclear and chemical waste management, contribution to global warming, and manufacture or distribution of military weaponry.[9]

The prospectus does list the core objectives of the Sierra Club, which, from an environmental investment standpoint, are extremely vague and ambiguous: protecting the wild lands; stopping urban sprawl; ending commercial logging on federal lands; controlling population growth; developing appropriate trade policies; protecting human rights; ending concentrated animal feeding operations; and stopping global warming.

The problem is that the core objectives would all be open to extremely subjective interpretation. What company operations do or do not protect wild lands, stop or limit urban sprawl, limit or encourage population growth, or protect or violate human rights? How do the funds end concentrated animal feeding operations or stop global warming? Unlike most screened funds, there are no clear exclusionary or inclusionary criteria. Publicly, Carl Pope has said they won't invest in tobacco or oil companies, but the prospectus is silent on these specific exclusions. What if Carl Pope or the Sierra Club changes its policy? Perhaps a new executive director would consider a weapons manufacturer or a tobacco company contributing to population control and include such companies' stocks in the portfolio.

While it appears that the "team approach" to investment management is sound, as are the portfolio managers, social and environmental investors may want to see very specific criteria in the prospectus. Otherwise, all of the Sierra Club's investment decisions may be open to question relative to social and environmental research and analysis.

Calvert Social Investment Balanced Fund

The Calvert Group's family of socially screened funds was launched in 1982 and one of the founders, Wayne Silby, remains board chairman of Calvert Social Investment Fund.

The Balanced Fund's $502 million is managed by a team including Brown Capital Management, SSqA Funds Management, Profit Investment Management, and Calvert Asset Management Company, Inc. As of June 30, 2004, the fund's assets were allocated 60 percent stocks and almost 28 percent in bonds. More heavily weighted stock sectors included financial services (22 percent), and health care (14 percent).

Calvert's commitment to high social impact investing leads to its $4.9 million investment in Calvert Foundation Community Investment Notes as well as its $482,876 investment in CDs of community banks and credit unions.

The Calvert Social Investment Fund family is the oldest and largest of the SRI family of mutual funds in the U.S. Calvert Foundation Community Investment Notes currently invests more than $42.5 million in Community Development Financial Institutions (CDFIs) which include international and domestic loan funds, community banks, credit unions, and microenterprises.

Calvert's Balanced Fund criteria are the same as that outlined earlier regarding the Calvert Social Equity Fund. The balanced fund is also permitted to invest in private placement investments, which would be considered venture investments in small, pre-IPO companies that provide promising and innovative approaches to meeting Calvert's social goals. The balanced fund can invest up to 10 percent of its portfolio in these higher risk, social companies, and up to 5 percent of the portfolio in strong performing, minority and women-owned money management firms.

The leading equity manager for Calvert Social Investment Balanced portfolio is Douglas Homes, a CFA and a Principle of State Street Global Advisors, the sub-adviser to the fund. He specializes in portfolio construction and risk control, and has been working in the investment management industry since 1980. He has a BS in Mathematics from Northeastern University. Holmes is part of the investment management team of Holmes, Broun, Habeeb and Alexander, responsible for portfolio management.

BOND FUNDS

There are four bond funds with ten-year performance track records that will be profiled here: three taxable and one California tax-exempt.

Taxable Bond Funds

The $184 million Calvert Social Investment Bond Fund was opened in 1987 and is the largest of the fixed-income funds profiled for individual investors. Citizens Income and the Parnassus Fixed-Income taxable funds were both launched in 1992. Below is a performance comparison of the three funds and total assets as of June 30, 2004.

	3 Year	5 Year	10 Year
Calvert Bond	5.91	7.11	7.03
Citizens Income	3.11	4.09	5.67
Parnassus Bond	6.96	6.39	7.09

The Calvert Social Investment Bond Fund invests in U.S. government agency debt obligations that are generally compatible with Calvert's overall social criteria, e.g. Student Loan Marketing Association rather than U.S. Treasuries. Almost 56 percent of the fund is invested in AAA corporates and 95 percent investment grade. As of June 30, 2004, the bond fund was the most liquid of the socially screened taxable bond funds, holding almost 15 percent in cash. Calvert's had the highest turnover of any of the SRI bond funds with at least a ten-year track record. The manager, Greg Habeeb, turns over the entire portfolio 955 percent a year, compared to 227 percent for the average intermediate bond fund.[10]

The bond fund also held a CD in South Shore Bank and more than $1 million in Calvert Foundation Community Investment Notes.

The fund avoids investing in companies that: are major polluters; are primarily engaged in nuclear power; have a record of employment discrimination, aggressive anti-union activities, or provide unsafe workplaces; and are significantly engaged in the manufacture of weapons, tobacco, alcohol, or in gambling operations.

The Calvert Bond Fund seeks to include companies that: strive to manage their operations in an environmentally sustaining manner; have a good record of labor relations, including strong equal employment opportunity programs; are responsible corporate citizens in the communities where they operate.

For five years the portfolio manager of the Calvert Social Investment Bond Fund was Reno Martini who has been chief investment officer of Calvert Group since 1985 and has over twenty-two years of experience in the securities industry. Bond management has been turned over to Habeeb and Nottingham, part of the same team that manages Calvert's Social Balanced Fund.

In reviewing Citizens Income Portfolio as of September 30, 2004, bonds comprise almost 95 percent of the portfolio. Up to 35 percent of the portfolio may be invested in lower grade bonds.

Citizens Income has been managed for almost four years by Susan Kelly, a graduate of Purdue University. She is a CFA and earned her MBA at New York University, with a double major in finance and strategic management. Before joining Citizens in 2000, Kelly was a vice president and assistant equity portfolio at Hancock Advisors, Inc. She worked as a vice president and assistant fixed income manager, managing five closed-end balanced funds with over $1 billion in assets. Previously, she was vice president and taxable fixed income portfolio manager at Smith Barney, Inc., in New York where she developed long- and short-term investment strategies for two corporate bond portfolios.

On June 30, 2004, the Parnassus Fixed-Income Fund had only a little over 32 percent in corporate bonds and 5 percent in cash. By January 31, 2005, the fund was 69 percent in cash and under 22 percent in bonds. The Parnassus Fixed-Income Fund credit quality is AAA and the average bond duration is a short 4.24 years. This portfolio is also managed by Todd Ahlsten.

Citizens and Parnassus both have exclusionary and inclusionary social criteria. Citizens avoids companies that are involved in manufacturing alcohol, tobacco products, nuclear power, and weaponry. Citizens also avoids companies that lack diversity on their corporate boards or in senior management, as well as companies that test on animals beyond what is required by law.

Citizens, however, does focus on companies that protect human rights, have a history of environmental stewardship, and have strong employee and community relations.

Parnassus excludes companies that manufacture alcohol, tobacco products, or are involved in gambling, as well as companies that produce nuclear power and weapons. On the inclusionary side, Parnassus uses its best judgment to find companies that (1) treat employees fairly; (2) adopt sound environmental protection policies; (3) have a good equal employment opportunity program; (4) produce quality products and services; (5) have a record of civic commitment; and (6) ethical business practices.

Parnassus California Tax-Exempt Muni Bond Fund

The Parnassus California Tax-Exempt Fund has had positive investment return for eight of ten years and for at least five out of the last ten years has outperformed either the Lehman Brothers Muni Bond Index or the Lehman Brothers California Muni Bond Index. It also has the distinction of being the only socially-screened California tax-exempt bond fund in the United States.

The $25 million fund invests in California intermediate-term municipals bonds, about 8 percent in housing, almost 14 percent in public transportation, 11 percent in education, almost 15 percent in environmental bonds (primarily waste water and water projects), 3 percent in health care, and about 13 percent in California General Obligation bonds. In addition, it specifically targets investments that have positive social and environmental impact, such as bonds that finance schools, hospitals, mass transit, and housing.

Social investors should be able to sleep soundly, and, also, probably safely at night with this portfolio, since it has no prison bonds.

Jerry Dodson runs a family business. His son, Stephen J. Dodson, and colleague, Ben Liao, until recently, managed the portfolio. Liao now manages the tax-exempt fund while Stephen is Parnassus' chief operating officer.

APPENDIX D

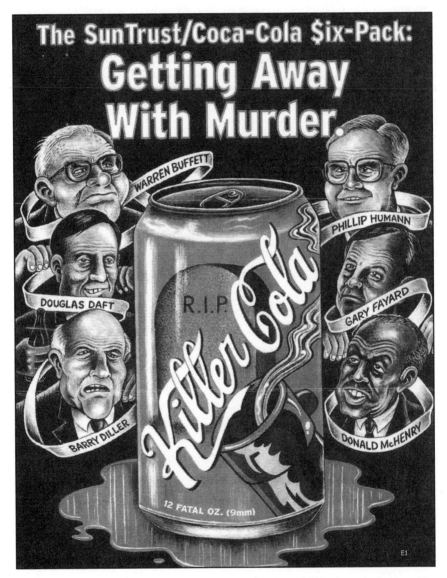

This ad was part of the Campaign to Stop Killer Coke (www.killercoke.org), developed by Ray Rogers.

NOTES

Introduction

1. Thom Hartmann, *Unequal Protection*, p. 149.
2. bid.
3. "With Interest Rates Stable, Credit Card Fees Rise," *New York Times*, April 20, 2003, p. B9.
4. "Consumer Debt Rises to $2.12 Trillion," *Wall Street Journal*, March 8, 2005, p. A2.
5. "Personal Bankruptcies Hit Record High," *San Francisco Chronicle*, November 15, 2003, p. B1
6. "In Bankruptcy, Getting Laid Off Hurts Even Worse," *Wall Street Journal*, September 30, 2002, p. A1.
7. "The Largest Bankruptcies 1980—Present", www.bankruptcydata.com.

Chapter 1

1. "Voting and Registration in the Election of November 2000," U.S. Department of Commerce, Economic and Statistics Administration, U.S. Census Bureau, p. 11.
2. Ibid.
3. "Dithering Democrats," *In These Times*, August 19, 2002, p. 10.
4. "Analysis of Green Party Vote," Mike Wyman, November 7, 2002 email.
5. "Voting and Registration in the Election of November 2000", U.S. Census Bureau
6. *Austin American Statesman*, October 26, 2003, pp. A-21, 23, 24-26.
7. "Study of Ethnicity, Civic Involvement," *San Francisco Chronicle*, Cicero A. Estrella and Venessa Heia, April 27, 2004, p. B-3.
8. Thomas E. Patterson, *The Vanishing Voter: Public Involvement in an Age of Uncertainty*, New York, 2002, p. 85.
9. Ibid., p. 82.
10. "Campaign Finance as a Civil Rights Issue," Lake, Snell, Perry & Associates, May 2002, 62 pages.
11. Gregory Palast, *Buzzflash.com*, Nov. 4, 2002.
12. Ibid.
13. "Gerrymandering Gets Focus," *Wall Street Journal*, December 4, 2003, p. A4.
14. "No More Sham Elections", *New York Times* op-ed, November 20, 2004, p. A 31.
15. Ibid.

16. Thomas E. Patterson, *The Vanishing Voter: Public Involvement in an Age of Uncertainty*, New York, 2002, p. 115.

17. Mark Green, *Selling Out: How Big Corporate Money Buys Elections, Rams Through Legislation and Betrays Our Democracy*, Regan Books, 2002, p. 16.

18. "Corporate PAC's Backed Republicans 10 to 1", *New York Times*, November 26, 2004, p. A26.

19. "*San Francisco Chronicle,* September 24, 2002, p. B1, and "Dithering Democrats", *In These Times*, August 19, 2002, p.11.

20. Ibid.

21. "Frontlines Against Biotech in Philadelphia", *Earth First! Journal, Eostar*, March-April 2005.

22. "US Flip on Patents Show Drug Makers' Growing Clout", *Wall Street Journal*, February 6, 2003, p. A4.

23. "Heartfelt Advice, Hefty Fees," *New York Times*, August 11, 2002, Section 3, pp. BU1, BU14.

24. "FDA Comes Under Fire From Prestigious Medical Journal", *Knight Ridder Newspapers*, November 22, 2004, www.tallahassee.com/mld/tallahassee/news/politics/10248723.htm?template=conte

25. "FDA Painkiller Panel Advisors Linked To Pharmaceutical Firms", *San Francisco Chronicle*, February 25, 2005, p. A15.

26. Lee Drutman and Charlie Cray, *The People's Business: Controlling Corporations and Restoring Democracy*, p. 222.

27. "Ex-senator Say He Won't Lobby His Government-Official Brother", *New York Times*, May 13, 2003, p. A19.

28. "Lee Enterprises to Buy Pulitzer In a $1.46 Billion Agreement", *Wall Street Journal*, January 31, 2005, p. A2.

29. Molly Ivins, "Rotten, Old-Fashioned Corruption at the FCC", *AlterNet.org*, May 29, 2003 (Independent Media Institute).

30. *The Ecologist*, "Getting the Government on Your Side," Vol. 28, No. 5, Sept/Oct 1998, p. 283.

31. Ibid.

32. Vijay Prashad, *Fat Cats and Running Dogs, the Enron Stage of Capitalism*, 2003, p. 122.

33. "Dithering Democrats", *In These Times*, August 19, 2002, p. 11.

34. *Alecwatch.org*

35. Ibid.

36. "Consumer Privacy Bill Dies", *San Francisco Chronicle,* September 1, 2002, p.1 and "Banks Defeat Privacy Bill Yet Again", June 18, 2003, pp. A1, A14.

37. "Davis Backs Banning Trades of Personal Financial Data," *San Francisco Chronicle*, June 3, 2003, p. A14.

38. "Banks Lose Bid to Overturn Financial Privacy Law", *Napa Valley Register*, July 2, 2004, p. B1.

39. "Private Entities Already are Playing Big Brother," *San Francisco Chronicle,* December 23, 2002, pp. E1, E3.

40. "New High Tech Passports Raise Concerns of Snooping", *New York Times,* November 26, 2004, p. A20.
41. "Do Not Call' Roster Debuts Today", *Wall Street Journal,* June 27, 2003.
42. "Outsourced UCSF Notes Highlight Privacy Risk", *San Francisco Chronicle,* March 28, 2004, pp. A1, A22-23.
43. "Overseas Listener On Your Call", February 25, 2004, http://www.sfgate.com/cgi- bin/particle.cgi?file=/c/a/2004/02/25/3ugdd57f7a1.dtl
44. "European Firms Capture Big Win In Outsourcing," *Wall Street Journal,* January 13, 2005, p. B5.
45. "Post – 9/11 Security Fears Usher in Subdermal Chips: VeriChip Recipients Can be ID'd, Monitored Anywhere in the World," *World Net Daily*, February 4, 2002.
46. "Looking for Ways to Curb Snoops," *San Francisco Chronicle*, July 14, 2003, pp. E1,E3.
47. "Pentagon Retreats From Terror Futures in Face of Criticism," *Wall Street Journal*, July 29, 2003, pp. C1, C9.
48. Ibid. and "Proposal to Trade in World Events Junked," *San Francisco Chronicle*, July 30, 2003, pp. A1, A5.
49. Ibid.
50. Kevin Phillips, *Wealth and Democracy: A Political History of the American Rich,* Broadway Books, 2002.
51. For an excellent read on corporate complicity between IBM and the German Third Reich, read *IBM and the Holocaust: The Strategic Alliance Between Nazi Germany and America's Most Powerful Corporation*, Edwin Block, Crown Publishers, New York, 2001.
52. Molly Ivins, "Politicians for Sale – at Low Prices," *Baltimore Sun*, January 30, 2003, Common Dreams News Center.
53. "Firms Pay No Tax But Get Refund", *San Francisco Chronicle*, December 28, 2004, p. C1.
54. Vijay Prashad, *Fat Cats and Running Dogs, the Enron Stage of Capitalism*, Common Courage, 2002, p. 14.
55. "Leasing deals cost U.S. billions in tax revenue," *San Francisco Chronicle*, October 22, 2003, p. B4.
56. "U.S. Overseas Tax Is Blasted", *Wall Street Journal*, May 5, 2004, p. A4.
57. "Thanks for Nothing," *San Francisco Chronicle*, May 28, 2003, pp. B1, B4.
58. Matthew A. Crenson & Benjamin Ginzberg, *Downsizing Democracy: How America Sidelined Its Citizens and Privatized Its Public*, John Hopkins University Press, 2002, P. 37.
59. "Wealthiest Americans Hold Rising Share of Income, IRS Finds," *Wall Street Journal*, June 26, 2003, p. A3.
60. "Very Richest's Share of Income Grew Even Bigger, Data Shows," *New York Times*, www.nytimes.com.
61. "Tech Giants Profit From Tax Break", *San Francisco Chronicle*, September 12, 2002, pp. B1,B4.
62. Vijay Prashad, *Fat Cats and Running Dogs, the Enron Stage of Capitalism*, Common Courage, 2002, p. 29.
63. Ibid., p. 31.

64. "A Guardian of Jobs or a 'Reverse" Robin Hood?", *New York Times*, September 1, 2002, pp.1, 12.
65. Ibid. p. 12.
66. "Halliburton's Sweet Deal," In *These Times*, September 16, 2002, p. 5.
67. "Halliburton Makes a Killing on Iraq War: Cheney's Former Company Profits from Supporting Troops",www.corpwatch.org, March 20, 2003.
68. "Army's Iraq Contracts Under Fire: No Bidding by Subsidiary of Halliburton," *San Francisco Chronicle*, May 30, 2003, p. B2.
69. "New Iraq Contract for Halliburton," *San Francisco Chronicle*, January 17, 2004, p. A8.
70. "Of U.S. Foreign Policy and Corporate Interests, *San Francisco Chronicle*, September 4, 2002, p. A21.
71. "Nation Builders for Hire," *New York Times Magazine*, June 22, 2003, p. 35.
72. "SRI New Assets", www.socialfunds.com, August 3, 2004.
73. "Our M.B.A. President and His CEO Sidekick," *Utne*, May-June, 2003, p. 52.
74. *Wall Street Journal*, December 19, 2002.
75. *Utne*, May-June 2003, p. 52.
76. "Baker Hughes Gets Subpoena From SEC on Foreign Dealings,", *Wall Street Journal*, August 11, 2003, p. B5.
77 "Halliburton's Contracts in Iraq Face Investigation by Pentagon," *Wall Street Journal*, December 12, 2003, pp. A1, A6.
78. "Halliburton Uncovers Bribe Plan", *www.cnnmoney.com*,, September 2, 2004.
79. "Halliburton Say Nigerian Payments Were Possible", *Wall Street Journal*, November 8, 2004, p. A5.
80. "Army Awards Halliburton Subsidiary Million In Bonuses", *San Francisco Chronicle*, February 25, 2005, p. A7.
81. "Military Is Facing Wide Budget Gap With Halliburton", *Wall Street Journal*, February 1, 2005, p. A1.
82. "Anti-war Group Plans Bechtel Protest," *Napa Valley Register*, June 2, 2003, p. A4.
83. "Bechtel: Profiting from Destruction," report from Public Citizen, Global Exchange and CorpWatch, June 2003.
84. "At War: Sean Penn finds getting out of Iraq even tougher than getting in," *San Francisco Chronicle*, January 15, 2004, p. E4.
85. "Dirty Warriors: How South African Hit Men, Serbian Paramilitaries, and Other Human Rights Violators Became Guns For Hire For Military Contractors in Iraq", *Mother Jones Magazine*, November & December 2004, pp. 30-32.
86. "Global Security Firms Fill in as Private Armies", *San Francisco Chronicle*, March 28, 2004 p. A-1, A-2.
87. "Wives of Civilians Working in Iraq Forge Out Support System", *Wall Street Journal*, August 3, 2004, p.A1.
88. "10 U.S. Contractors in Iraq Paid $300 Million in Fines Since 2000", *San Francisco Chronicle*, Associated Press, April 27, 2004, pp. C-1, C-4.
89. "Unusual Pentagon—Boeing Deal is Attacked," *New York Times*, June 10, 2003, p. C3.
90. "G.A.O. Faults Cost Estimates on Boeing-Air Force Jet Lease," *The New York Times*,

July 24, 2003, p. C7.

91. "Documents Show Extent of Lobbying by Boeing," New York Times, September 3, 2003, pp. C1, C7.

92. "Air Force Ex-Official Had Ties to Boeing During Contract Talks," *Wall Street Journal*, October 7, 2003, pp. A1, A16.

93. "Boeing Dismisses Two Executives for Violating Ethical Standards," *Wall Street Journal*, November 25, 2003, p.1.

94. "Boeing Penalty Costs the U.S.," *Wall Street Journal*, July 28, 2003, p. B4.

95. "Lockheed Settles Case on Air Force Contracts," *New York Times*, August 28, 2003, p. C2.

96. "Air Force Spends $2.6 Billion on Planes That Don't Meet Requirement, Investigators Say", *Napa Valley Register,* Associated Press, July 25, 2004, p. B4.

97. "Pentagon Brass and Military Contractor's Gold", *New York Times,* June 29, 2004, pp. C1, C5.

98. Ibid.

99. "NASA Finally Gets Down to Business Side of Space", *New York Times*, July 21, 2004, p. C-2.

100. "Missile Defense System Fails", *San Francisco Chronicle*, December 16, 2004, pp. A1, A14.

101. "Making Crime Pay," *San Francisco Chronicle Magazine*, August 17, 2003, p. 16.

102. Ibid., p. 17.

103. "How Many Strikes Do Big Corporations Get?", National Lawyers Guild International Law Project for Human, Economic and Environmental Defense, Los Angeles, CA.

104. "The Case Against Unocal in One Page," Professor Robert Benson, HEED, September 10, 1998, *www.heed@igc.org.*

105. "Unocal CEO Denies Human-Rights Abuses During Pipeline Construction in Myanmar," *Wall Street Journal*, May 29, 2000, *online.wsj.com*

106. Ibid.

107. International Labor Rights Fund, "Burmese Workers Suing Unocal in Los Angeles Will Have Their Day in Court," 733 15th St. NW #920, Washington, DC 20005 (202-347-4100).

108. Ibid.

109. "Colombian Killings Land U.S. Company in American Court," *Wall Street Journal*, October 6, 2003, pp. A1, A6.

110. "International Labor Rights Fund Statement Re: U.S. Supreme Court Sosa V. Alvarez-Machain (case no. 03-339 and 03-485), Allen Tort Claims Act, June 29, 2004.

111. "If Nike Lied, Is it Fraud or Free Speech?" *TheStreet.com*, May 6, 2003.

112. "The Implications of the Nike and Kasky Settlement on CSR Reporting," *www.social-funds.com*, September 18, 2003.

CHAPTER 2

1. "Grubman Still Gets Pay From Unit of Citigroup," *Wall Street Journal*, August 18, 2003, pp. C1, C9.

2. "Pressuring Analysts: Hard Habit to Break," *New York Times*, August 11, 2002, p.B1.

3. "WorldCom's Ebbers Wants Co. to Pay Bills", *Associated Press*, October 13, 2004, http://news.findlaw.com.
4. "Another Slap at Democracy from Wall Street," *New York Times*, September 1, 2002.
5. "B of A Paid for Research Linked to Bad Deal," *San Francisco Chronicle*, May 30, 2003, p. B3.
6. Ibid.
7. "SEC's Oversight of Mutual Funds Is Said to Be Lax," *New York Times*, November 16, 2003, p.1.
8. "Hostilities, Disclosures in Mutual Fund Cases: Potent Industry Lobby Failed to Finesse Overhaul Bill; It Never Got Close to Oxley," *Wall Street Journal*, November 26, 2003, p. C1, C10.
9. Ibid.
10. "CEO Pay Still Outrageous," *North Bay Progressive*, May 26-June 27, 2003, p. 9.
11. "What Bay Area Executives Made Last Year", *San Francisco Chronicle*, December 28, 2004, pp. C1, C4.
12. "Big Severance Pay For B of A Chairman", *San Francisco Chronicle*, December 28, 2004, p. C4.
13. "Back Off! Businesses Go Toe to Toe With SEC", *Wall Street Journal*, October 27, 2004, pp. C1, C3.
14. "Outsourcing Corner Offices", *New York Times*, September 5, 2004, p.2.
15. "Charles Schwab Corp.", *Wall Street Journal*, November 9, 2004, p. C6
16. "It Still Pays to be a Conseco CEO", *Wall Street Journal*, August 17, 2004, p. C1.
17. Ibid, p. C6.
18. "SEC Chairman Wants Details of Compensation Paid to Grasso," *New York Times*, September 3, 2003, pp. C1, C8.
19. "Overgrown NYSE Board Needs a Trimming," *San Francisco Chronicle*, September 18, 2003, pp. B1, B5.
20. "Pensions Fall—Not CEO's Bonus," *Wall Street Journal*, June 18, 2003, pp. C1, C2.
21. "No Wonder CEO's Love Those Mergers", *New York Times*, July 18, 2004, Section 3 p 1.
22. Ibid.
23. "Gillette CEO Payday May Be Richer", *Wall Street Journal*, February 3, 2005, p. B2.
24. "Stocks, Pay and Videotapes: The sequel," *New York Times*, November 28, 2004, p. B1.
25. "Case Could Redefine Board Members' Liability," New York Times, June 14, 2003, pp. B1, B4.
26. Ibid.
27. "Judge Rules Special Oracle Panel Had Conflicts of Interest," *Wall Street Journal*, June 17, 2003, pp. C1, C14.
28. "A Glutted Market Leaves Food Chains Hungry for Sites," *Wall Street Journal*, October 1, 2003, p. 1.
29. "White House opposes WHO anti-obesity campaign," *San Francisco Chronicle*, January 17, 2004, p. A4.
30. "Shedding 'Baby Fat' Through Surgery", *New York Times*, November 26, 2004, p. C6.
31. "Coke, Pepsi, Fight Product Contamination Charges in India," *Wall Street Journal*, pp. B1, B4.

32. "Study Links Sugar-sweetened Soft Drinks and Diabetes", *Wall Street Journal*, August 25, 2004, p. B1, B2.
33. "KFC Seeks a Crisp Take on Its Ads," *Wall Street Journal*, August 1, 2003, p. B6.
34. "Coke Moves With Caution to Remain in Schools," *New York Times*, September 3, 2003, p. C1.
35. "If You Pitch It, They Will Eat," *The New York Times*, August 3, 2003, Section 3, pp. 1, 11.
36. "The (Agri)Cultural Contradictions of Obesity," *New York Times Magazine*, October 12, 2003, p. 48.
37. "It's a Fat World, After All," *The New York Times*, July 20, 2003, pp. BU1, BU11.
38. "Trans-Atlantic Legal Cultures Clash," *International Herald Tribune*, December 4, 2002, pp. 1, 4.
39. "U.S. FDA to Require Trans Fat Information on Food Packaging Labels," www.net-impact.org, BSR Monitor, July 21, 2003.
40. "It's a Fat World, After All," *The New York Times*, July 20, 2003, pp. BU1, BU11.
41. "Famous Brands Can Bring Benefit, or a Backlash," *New York Times*, October 19, 2002, p. B7.
42. "If You Pitch It, They Will Eat," *The New York Times*, August 3, 2003, Section 3, pp. 1, 11.
43. "Expect a Food Fight as U.S. Revises Dietary Guidelines," *Wall Street Journal*, August 8, 2003, pp. B1, B5.
44. Ibid., p. B5.
45. "Socially Aware Investors Mull Junk Food Debate," *Reuters*, July 11, 2003.
46. Ibid.
47. Hawley & Williams, *The Rise of Fiduciary Capitalism*, p. 25.
48. Ibid.
49. "SEC Eyes 3-Percent Threshold for Board Nominations", *Shareholder Action Network, www.issproxy.com*, August 18, 2003.
50. Community Health Councils, Inc. website *www.ehc-inc.org.*
51. "Economics Can't Solve Everything, Can It?" *The New York Times*, August 3, 2003, p. BU4.
52. "SEC Opts for Quick Settlement in Corporate Fraud," *San Francisco Chronicle*, May 27, 2003, p. B3.
53. "PriceWaterhouseCoopers to Pay $50 Million to Settle Lawsuit", *Wall Street Journal*, May 26, 2004, p. A2.
54. "Tyco Auditor Settles Charges by SEC," *San Francisco Chronicle*, August 14, 2003, p. B8.
55. Ibid.
56. "Price-Waterhouse Partner Named to Key SEC Post", *New York Times*, August 15, 2003, p. C5.
57. "Keeping the Accountants from Flying High", *Wall Street Journal*, May 6, 2003, p. C1.
58. "We Need More Than The 'Big Four'," *Wall Street Journal*, January 25, 2005, p. B2.
59. "Oversight Board's Bad Start," *San Francisco Chronicle*, January 28, 2003, p. B1.
60. Ibid.

61. "Did Ties That Bind Also Blind KPMG?" Wall Street Journal, June 18, 2003, pp. C1, C5.

CHAPTER 3

1. "First, the War; Now, Investor Consequences", *New York Times,* April 30, 2003, p. C1
2. "Small Firms Shortchanged on Federal Contracts", *Wall Street Journal*, December 28, 2004, p. B2.
3. "Blue Gold: Earth's Liquid Asset," *The Guardian*, August 22, 2002
4. "Summary of Project Information (SPI)", *International Finance Corporation*, February 24, 2004, http://ifcln001.worldbank.org/IFCExt/spiwebsite1.nsf/0/f8lb-c93eb0010f4785256e44007e...
5. "Grupo Omnilife Reaches Tentative Deal to Acquire Body Shop for $500 Million," *Wall Street Journal*, June 7, 2001.
6. "Mexican Mogul Offers Omnilife as the Answer to Poor Diet, Poverty," *Wall Street Journal Europe*, March 3, 1999, p. 4.
7. "Ben & Jerry's Didn't Sell Out; They Got Bought-In-Lock, Stock, and Social Mission," *Green Money Journal*, Fall 2003, *www.greenmoneyjournal.com.*
8. "Stay Funky, Chunky Monkey," *grist magazine, www.gristmagazine.com*, April 17, 2000.
9. "A Statement From the Ben & Jerry's Foundation Trustees," www.benjerry.com, October 16, 2001.
10. "Stay Funky, Chunky Monkey," *grist magazine, www.gristmagazine.com*, April 17, 2000.
11. Ibid.
12. "Ben & Jerry's Didn't Sell Out; They Got Bought-In-Lock, Stock, and Social Mission", *Green Money Journal*, Fall 2003, *www.greenmoneyjournal.com.*
13. "The Legacy Problem; Why Social Mission Gets Squeezed Out of Firms When They're Sold, and What to Do About It," *Business Ethics*, Vol. 17, no. 2, Summer 2003, pp. 11-16.
14. "Greens Launch Unilever 'Disloyalty Card' to Protest at Genetic Beans Food Experiment," Friends of the Earth press release, March 27, 1998.
15. "The Legacy Problem; Why Social Mission Gets Squeezed Out of Firms When They're Sold, and What to Do About It," *Business Ethics*, Vol. 17, no. 2, Summer 2003, pp. 11-16.
16. *Articles of Incorporation of Upstream 21 Corporation*, Article 3.1, "Best Interests" Defined.

CHAPTER 4

1. "Maverick Broker Specialized In Stocks For 'Socially Responsible' Investments", *The Wall Street Journal*, May 1, 1979, p. 6.
2. "Panel Attacks Firms Offering Union-Labor-Only Investments", *Pensions and Investment Age*, October 17, 1983, p. 16.
3. "U.S. Mutual Fund Developments in 2001," *www.ici.org/paf/02fg_ch3.pdf*, p. 24.
4. "Stock Rally Seems Like Déjà Vu," *Wall Street Journal*, July 14, 2003, p. C1.
5. "Looking at the Obscure World of Fund Middlemen," *The New York Times*, October 12, 2003, p. BU10.

6. 2003 Report on Socially Responsible Investing Trends in the United States, *Social Investment Forum*, Updated December 2003.
7. "Good Vibes: Socially Responsible Investing Is Gaining Fans . . And Clout", www.online.wsj.com/*barronsarticle,* July 7, 2003.
8. "Retirement Funds", *Wall Street Journal*, June 23, 2004, p. D9.
9. Guide: Screening and Rating Sustainability: The Hague: Ministry of the Environment, 2002, IV. "From Prudent Man to Prudent Person: An Essay on Sustainability and Institutional Investment," revision of a lecture given at the Harvard Seminar on Environmental Values, Cambridge, MA, p. 4.
10. "Industry Unveils New Data Demonstrating CDFIs Stepped Up During Recession of 2000-2002", *www.communitycapital.org/community_development/finance/statistics.html.*
11. "Good for Your Conscience, If Not For Your Wallet," *www.newyorktimes.com* , July 20, 2003.
12. Ibid.
13. "Good for the Soul, Good for the Wallet," *Washington Post*, May 25, 2003, p. F1.
14. "Is it Finally Time to Invest Green?" *Fortune Small Business*, June 4, 2003, p.1.
15. "The Perils of Chasing Performance," *Christian Science Monitor*, September 8, 2003, *www.csmonitor.com.*
16. Letter to author dated June, 23, 2003 from George Sapp, Senior Vice President, U.S. Bancorp Fund Services, LLC.
17. "As Scandals Mount, Boards of Mutual Funds Feel the Heat", *Wall Street Journal*, March 17, 2004 p. A1, A6
18. Ibid.
19. "SEC Is Sued Over Fund –Board Rule", *Wall Street Journal,* September 3, 2004, p. C17.
20. HSUS, Rob Blizzard, August 9, 2002, *http://www.animalawareness,org/pages/invest_funds.html.*
21. The Humane Equity Fund Prospectus, January 28, 2002, pp. 2-3.
22. Yahoo! Finance, http://yahoo.com/p/f/FIESX.html.
23. "New CERES Study: Mutual Funds Give Climate Change Proxy Resolutions a Cold Shoulder, Even As Pension Funds Warm Up To Them", www.ceres.org, December 7, 2004.
24. *Morningstar*, quarterly report, released June 30, 2003, PIMCO Total Ret. III Inst.
25. "Huffington: Mutual Funds—Corporate Crime's Narcoleptic Giant," Alternet.org, August 27, 2002.
26. Ibid.
27. "Is Your Money Where Your Heart Is? The Truth About SRI Mutual Funds", *Common Ground*, October 2004, Paul Hawken, p. 14.
28. Ibid, p. 17.
29. "Proxy Fights, Rarely Successful, Still Tempt Holders," *Wall Street Journal*, November 7, 2002, Dow Jones & Company, Inc.
30. "Fool on the Hill: How Does Your Fund Vote?" TMF Otter, September 24, 2002, Motley Fool per TracyRembert@socialinvest.org.

31. "CERES Coalition Achieves Major Victory in Mutual Fund Proxy Voting Disclosure," CERES newsletter, January 2003, p. 4.

32. "Mutual Fund Votes Show Limits to Change", *Boston Globe,* September 5, 2004, www. bostonglobe.com.

CHAPTER 5

1. "U.S. Studies Cite Abuse by Thousands of Priests", *International Herald Tribune,* Laurie Goodstein, February 28-29, 2004, p. 2.

2. "Ex-Boston Cardinal Gets Plum Post in Rome", *San Francisco Chronicle*, Al Baker, May 28, 2004, p. A4.

3. Ibid.

4. "California Diocese Settles Abuse Cases; Record Sum Is Seen", *New York Times,* December 4, 2004, pp. A1, A14.

5. "William Aramony is Back on the Streets," *The Non Profit Times,* March 1, 2002.

6. "United Way Head Resigns Over Spending Habits," *The Washington Post*, February 28, 1992, p. 3.

7. "United Way May Feel Heat Over its Records," *San Francisco Chronicle*, June 6, 2003, pp. A1, A20.

8. ChristianityToday.com, October 27, 1997, Vol. 41, No. 12, P. 86.

9. "Charities In Feeding Frenzy," *The Plain Dealer,* December 21, 1997.

10. "Ex-Goodwill Bigwig Charged," *San Francisco Chronicle,* p. A1.

11. "Beard Foundation Accuses Ex-Chief of Looting Coffers", *San Francisco Chronicle,* December 6, 2004, p.A11.

12. "California Attorney General's Summary of Charitable Solicitations by Commercial Fund-Raisers," Year Ending 2001, p. 1.

13. Ibid., Table I, pp. 1-6.

14. Summary, SB1262 "The Nonprofit Integrity Act", Chapter 919, Statues of 2004, California Association of Nonprofits (CAN), http://givevoice.org/cannonprofits/ notice-description.tcl?newsletter_id=2933849

15. SB1262, Sher, Legislative Council's Digest, http://www.leginfo.ca.gov/pub/bill/sen/ sb_1251-1300/sb1262_bill_20040930_chaptered

16. "How Donated Dollars Turn Into Pennies", *New York Times,* August 15, 2004, p. BU5.

17. "On Corporate Boards, Officials From Nonprofits Spark Concern", *Wall Street Journal,* June 20, 2003, A1, A10.

18. "Charity Begins at Home, and You Live in the World," *New York Times,* December 3, 2003, p. B8.

19. "Gifts to Charity in 2002 Stayed Unexpectedly High," *New York Times, NYTimes.com,* p. 1

20. Ibid

21. "Social Change Philanthropy," *Greenmoneyjournal.com.,* Fall 2004 Vol. XIII, Issue 1.

22. Ibid

23. "In Charity, Where Does a CEO End and the Company Start?" *The New York Times,* September 22, 2002, Section 3, pp. BU1, BU12.

24. Ibid.
25. "Citigroup Probe Now Leads to an Elite Nursery School," *Wall Street Journal*, November 14, 2002, p.1.
26. Ibid.
27. "Social Change Philanthropy", *Greenmoneyjournal.com*. Fall 2004 Vol. XIII, Issue 1.
28. Mark Dowie, "Passive, Dissonant or Making a Difference: Which Way for Foundation Investing?" Financial Markets and Society, Financial Markets Center, Philomont, Va., p. 4.
29. Mark Thomsen and Doug Wheat, "The New Fiduciary Duty", *Business Ethics*, Vol. 17, no. 1, Spring 2003, also *www.ishareowner.com*.
30. Uniform Management of Institutional Funds Act, Section 4106, State of Maine.
31. *Social Responsibility and Investments*, pp. 56-57.
32. Ibid., p. 57.
33. Ibid., p. 59.
34. "Intel Impact on Air Studied," *San Francisco Chronicle*, September 2, 2003, pp. B1, B2.
35. Ibid.
36. "We're Owners, Not Traders," *Foundation News & Commentary*, Lance Lindblom, May/June 2002.
37. "Foundation, Bank, and Environmental Group Introduce Shareholder Resolution Using Smithfield to Examine Environmental Impacts of Hog Factories," Joint Press Release, May 1, 2003, Sierra Club, Amalgamated Bank, and the Nathan Cummings Foundation.
38. "Sarbanes-Oxley and Enron's Legacy: New Environmental Accountability", Gordon Arbuckle, May 2003, p.3-4, http://www.emsnet.com/emsnet-docs/Sarbanes-Oxley.pdf.
39. Ibid.
40. "SEC to Expand Environmental Disclosure", *Publishing Corporation*, Steven Taub, CFO, July 19, 2004, http://www.cfo.com/printarticle/0,5317,14688/T,00. html?f=options.
41. "As the Earth Warms, Will Companies Pay" *New York Times*, August 18, 2002, p.BU6, 7.
42. "U.S. Conservative Takes Aim at NGOs," *OneWorld.net*, June 20, 2003.
43. Ibid.
44. Ibid.
45. "Reining in Activist Funds," Harvard Business Review, March 2003, www.harvardbusi-nessonline.org, copyright American Enterprise Institute for Public Policy Research, the American Enterprise, September 1, 2003.
46. Ibid.
47. "We the Peoples or We the Corporations? Critical Reflections of UN-Business part-nerships," Judith Richter, IBFAN-GIFA, Geneva, January, 2003.
48. Ibid.
49. *Wall Street Journal*, June 21, 2001, *www.canamuck.org*.
50. "The New Fiduciary Duty," *Business Ethics*, Vol. 17, no. 1, Spring 2003, Mark Thomsen & Doug Wheat, also *www.ishareowner.com*.
51. "Passive, Dissonant or Making a Difference: Which Way for Foundation Investing?"

Financial Markets and Society, Financial Markets Center, Philomont, Va., p. 7, Mark Dowie.

52. "The Heartland University Labor-Capital Summer Fellowship Program," *www.heartlandnetwork.org.*

53. "The New Fiduciary Duty," *Business Ethics,* Vol. 17, no. 1.

54. Unions Use Big Stock Investors as Weapon," *Wall Street Journal,* September 23, 2003, pp. C1, C5.

55. Ibid.

56. Ibid.

57. "Business Interests Push Back Against Public Pension Funds", *Associated Press,* December 31, 2004.

58. "Building on Past Success: Labor Friendly Investment Vehicles and the Power of Private Equity," Michael Calabrese, research paper presented to the Board of Governors of the Federal Reserve System, Flow of Funds Accounts, March 1999 2nd National Heartland Labor-Capital Conference, April 29, 1999, p. 3.

59. "Screening and Rating Sustainability," The Hague, Ministry of the Environment", Steven Viederman, from a lecture given at the Harvard Seminar on Environmental Values, Cambridge, Massachusetts and paper, 2002.

CHAPTER 6

1. "DJSI and FTSE4 Good Index Licensing Continues to Expand," November 8, 2002, *ishareowner.com*, SRI World Group.

2. "Johannesburg Securities Exchange to Introduce Socially Responsible Investing Index", William Baue, http://www.socialfunds.com/news/print.cgi?sfArticleId=1271.

3. "News Briefs", www.socialfunds.com, August 17, 2004.

4. "Analysis: A new phase of corporate responsibility in Asia", www.ethicalcorp.com, August 9, 2004.

5. Ibid.

6. www.iso.org/iso/en/AboutISO/introduction/index.html#two.

7. "Beyond BP's Catchphrase," *Wall Street Journal,* November 25, 2003, p. B1, B11.

8. Ibid., p. B11.

9. "The 21st Century NGO: Poised for Change?" *Green at Work,* July/August 2003, p. 41.

10. "EnvironDesign 7: Sustainability in Action," *Green at Work,* July/August 2003, pp. 26-32.

11. Ibid.

12. "New UK Index Rates Corporate Social Responsibility Performance," by William Bave, press release, www.iosreporting.org.

13. "Business of Betrayal: Greens Who Defect To The Corporate World Jeopardize The Very Survival of Environmentalism," George Monbiot, *The Guardian,* January 15, 2002,

14. Ibid.

15. "UN Meeting Marks Launch of Global Compact,"www.socialfunds.com/news/article.cgi/article326.html.

16. Ibid.

17. "Verité in China," Statement of Mil Niepold, Director of Policy, Verité, Inc. before the

Congressional Executive Commission on China, April 28, 2003.

18. Ibid.

19. "Migrant Worker's Rights At Risk. The Challenges of Doing Ethical Business in the People's Republic of China", Soledad Mills, ICCR, *The Corporate Examiner*, Vol. 32, No. 5, August 16, 2004, p.18.

20. Ibid.

21. "News and Issues," Christian Brothers Investment Services (CBIS), June 17, 2003.

22. Ibid.

23. "Citigroup Yields to Pressure by Environmentalists," <u>OneWorld.net</u>, Jim Lobe, April 18, 2003.

24. "Shell Discloses Payments to Nigerian Government; Transparency Initiative Gains Support," Net Impact CSR Weekly, BSR News Monitor, June 30, 2003.

25. "UN Proposal Requires Companies to Comply with Human Rights Standards," Net Impact CSR Weekly, www.net-impact.org, August 25, 2003, no. 32.

26. Ibid.

27. Ernest & Young News Release, August 27, 2002, "Corporate Social Responsibility: Unlocking the Value."

28. "Levi's to Close Last U.S. Plants," *San Francisco Chronicle*, September 26, 2003, pp. B1, B6.

29. Ibid.

30. "Huffington: Would Things be Any Different if Women Ran Corporate America?" AlterNet, May 14, 2003, *www.alternet.org*.

31. Ibid.

32. "New Financial Study Shows Stocks Can Reflect Investor Values Without Sacrificing Performance: Study Measures Effect of Positive Corporate Behavior", *PR Newswire*, July 7, 2004, p.2

33. Financial Analysts Journal, July-August 1986, p. 27.

34. "Quarterly Return," Newsletter of Shared Interest Limited, Issue 47, Spring 2003, p. 1.

35. Blue Orchard Finance s.a.,Dexia Micro-Credit Fund, April 2004 Newsletter.

36. Blue Orchard Finance s.a., Microfinance Investment Advisors, July 2003 Newsletter, p. 3.

37. Ibid. p. 2.

38. Ibid.

39. "A Path to Helping the Poor, and His Investors," *New York Times*, August 10, 2003, p. BU4.

40. "Developing World Markets", conversation with Brad Swanson, www.dwmarkets.com, October 25, 2004.

41. "Building Mission Into Structure at Equal Exchange," *Business Ethics,* Summer 2003, p. 13.

CHAPTER 7

1. "A Shareholder's Guide to Grilling Companies," *Wall Street Journal*, September 2, 2003, pp. D1 & D2.

2. James R. Hawley & Andrew T. Williams, *The Rise of Fiduciary Capitalism: How*

Institutional Investors Can Make Corporate America More Democratic, University of Pennsylvania Press, 2000, p. 5.

3. TMF Otter, "How Does Your Fund Vote?", Motley Fool, September 24, 2002 per traceyrembert@socialinvest.org.
4. "Proxy Fights, Rarely Successful, Still Tempt Holders," *Dow Jones Business News*, November 7, 2002, Wall Street Journal Online.
5. "Election Run-up Could Slow SEC's Chief", *Wall Street Journal Online*, August 13, 2004.
6. "Opening the Board," *Wall Street Journal*, October 27, 2003, *www.online.wsj.com*.
7. "Looking Over Managers' Shoulders, by Law," *The New York Times*, July 6, 2003, pp. BU11, BU 18.
8. Ibid., p. BU 18.
9. "Fidelity Uses Voting Threats to Fight Excessive CEO Pay," *Wall Street Journal*, http://online.wsj.com , June 12, 2002.
10. "Pick Up the Proxy, Fill It Out and Exert Some Control," *New York Times*, August 25, 2002.
11. "Shareholder Proposals Reach Record Pace," *Bloomberg News*, August 18, 2003, *www.startribune.com*.
12. "Constructive Dialogue Marks Proxy Season", *Investment News,* David Hoffman, June 28, 2004.
13. "U.S. CEO Pay Averages $12 Million Annually," *Bloomberg News*, August 18, 2003, *www.bloomberg.com*.
14. "Victory for Gay Rights," *San Francisco Chronicle*, July 3, 2003, pp. B1, B5.
15. Lance Lindblom, "Foundations Should Behave as Responsible Corporate Shareholders and Utilize an Ignored Asset – the Proxy Vote," *www.foundationpartnership.org*.
16. James P. Hawley & Andrew T. Williams, *The Rise of Fiduciary Capitalism*, p. 30.
17. "The Battle for Corporate Power", *Across the Board*, James Krohe, Jr., Vol. 41, No.2,March 2004/April 2004.
18. "Pitt Sides with Shareholders; Wants to Change SEC Oversight Rule," *Newsday*, New York, NY, September 24, 2002.
19. Ibid.
20. "China's Chip Policies Trigger Challenge by Industry Groups," *Wall Street Journal Online, http://online.wsj.com*, June 6, 2003.
21. Ibid.
22. Ibid., p. 193.
23. "Behind China's Export Boom, Heated Battle Among Factories.", *Wall Street Journal*, November 13, 2003, p. A1.
24. "Verite's Online Newsletter", Fall 2004, www.verite.org.
25. "As End of Quota System Nears, Bangladesh Fears for Its Jobs," *Wall Street Journal*, November 20, 2003, p. A1.
26. Ibid.
27. "China to See Windows Code," *CNET Asia,* www.asia.cnet.com, February 28, 2003.
28. "U.S. Companies Moving More Jobs Overseas," Reuters, December 23, 2003,David Zielenziger.

29. Ibid.
30. "China's Golden Shield: Corporate Complicity in the Development of Surveillance Technology," *China Rights Forum*, No. 1, 2002, p. 40.
31. "China's Golden Shield: Corporations and the Development of Surveillance Technology in the People's Republic of China," International Center for Human Rights and Democratic Development, 2001, p. 12.
32. "RW Members Bring Reality to Disney Annual Meeting," email from Responsible Wealth, re: Disney Meeting of February 19, 2002, dated February 22, 2002.
33. "China Readies Super ID Card, a Worry to Some," *New York Times*, August 19, 2003, p. A3.
34. "You've Got Dissidents? AOL Weighs China Market . . . and Rights Issues," *Washington Post*, August 29, 2001, p. A1.
35. "Mandatory Labeling Seen as Killing Off AG Biotech Industry," *Food Chemical News*, no. 20, vol. 44, July 1, 2002, p. 1.
36. "Gene-altered Foods Failing to Whet Sales, Firms Find," *Chicago Tribune*, June 28, 2002.
37. "Monsanto Fined $700 Million," Organic & Food Tidbits with an Edge, Issue #19, Organic Consumers Association, August 25, 2003, *www.organicconsumers.org*.
38. "Solutia Files for Bankruptcy," *stltoday.com*, December 17, 2003.
39. "Solutia Seeks Chapter 11 Status, Blames Former Parent Monsanto," *Wall Street Journal*, December 18, 2003, p. B2.
40. "Monsanto: A Checkered History," *The Ecologist*, Vol. 28, No. 5, Sept./Oct. 1998, p. 256.
41. "Leukemia, Agent Orange Link Found," Yahoo News, January 24, 2003, *http://story.news.yahoo.com*.
42. "Genetically Modifying Consumer Rights," Organic & Food News Tidbits With an Edge, Issue #17, July 16, 2003, www.organicconsumers.org.
43. "Flaws in Monsanto's Safety Assessment of Roundup Ready Soybeans," Third World Information Service, www.twnside.org, July 28, 2003.
44. "The Wheat, the Whole Wheat, and Nothing but the Wheat," Organic Consumers Association, Issue #20, September 17, 2003, *www.organicconsumers.org*.
45. "GE Cotton Bites," Organic Consumers Association, Issue #20, September 17, 2003, *www.organicconsumers.org*.
46. Ibid.
47. "Justice Department Ends Probe of Possible Industry Antitrust", *Wall Street Journal*, August 19, 2004, p. B8.
48. "Getting the Government of Your Side," *The Ecologist*, Vol. 28, No. 5, Sept./Oct. 1998, p. 285.
49. "Plans to Introduce Genetically Modified Wheat to the Canadian Prairies are Meeting Fierce Resistance From Some Farming Groups," BBC news, http://news.bbc.co.uk, July 31, 2003.
50. "Farmer Who Lied in Dispute with Monsanto Will Go to Prison," *STL Today, St. Louis Post Dispatch*, May 8, 2003.
51. Ibid.
52. Ibid.

53. "Mississippi Council Rules Against Monsanto," *Natural Foods Merchandiser*, September 1998, p.18.
54. "Modified-Crop Makers Faulted on Safety Data Sent to FDA," *Wall Street Journal*, http://online.wsj.com, January 7, 2003.
55. Ibid.
56. "Genetically Modified Democracy: Corralling the Critics," Biodemocracy News #43, Organic Consumers Association, www.organicconsmers.org, August 2003.
57. "FDA Seeks Altered-Gene Piglets Sold as Food," *USA Today*, February 6, 2003, Yahoo News; http://story.news.yahoo.com.
58. "Zoellick Slams EU for 'Immoral' View on Biotech Crops," *Wall Street Journal*, January 10, 2003, p. 1 and "U.S. Delays Suing Europe Over Ban," *The New York Times*, www.nytimes.com, February 5, 2003.
59. "China Soybean Ban Reverses WTO-Compliance Fears," *Wall Street Journal*, August 11, 2003, p. A7.
60. "Thirty-Two Food Producers Commit to Non-GM Material in China," *BSR News Monitor, www.net-impact.org*, August 8, 2003.
61. Ibid.
62. "Trade Pact on Gene-Altered Goods to Take Effect in 90 Days," *New York Times*, June 14, 2003, p. B3.
63. "Talks Collapse on U.S. Effort to Open Europe to Biotech Food," *New York Times, www.nytimes.com*, June 20, 2003.
64. "UN Adopts Fist International GM Food Safety Guidelines," Net Impact CSR Weekly, BSR News Monitor, July 21, 2003, no. 27.
65. "Codex Adopts Guidelines", SocialFunds.com, July 22, 2003.
66. "EU Court Upholds Ban on GMO Corn in Italy," *Wall Street Journal*, September 9, 2003, *http://online.wsj.com*.
67. "EU Approves Biotech Corn for Use in Food Products", *Wall Street Journal*, October 27, 2004, p.A14.
68. "Genetically Modifying Consumer Rights," *www.organicconsumers.org*, July 16, 2003.
69. "Monsanto, Bayer, Syngenta Exploiting Child Labor, Says Report," *www.CBGnetwork.org*, July 8, 2003.
70. "EU Approves Rules on Labeling Biotech Foods," *Wall Street Journal*, July 3, 2003, p. A7.
71. "Organic-Food Labeling Rules Help Guide the Health-Minded," *Wall Street Journal*, August 20, 2002, *www.mindfully.org/food/organic-labeling-health-minded20Aug02.htm*, "What Consumers Should Know About the New USDA Organic Labeling Standard," *The Pulse of Oriental Medicine, www.pulsemed.org/usdaorganic.htm* and "Labeling - Regulatory Text" Section 205.300-205.311, www.usda.gov.
72. Ibid.
73. "Genetically Modified Democracy: Corralling the Critics," *www.organicconsumers.org*, July 28, 2003.
74. "FDA Allows Company to Drop Food Label Warning on Olestra," *Wall Street Journal*, August 4, 2003, p. B6.

75. Ibid.

76. "Objective Science Does Not Exist Here," *www.organicconsumers.org*, August 6, 2003.

77. "Monsanto's Roundup Herbicide Contaminates Danish Drinking Water," *North Bay Progressive*, Volume 2, Issue 5, July 25-August 21, 2003, p. 1.

78. "Monsanto Acquisition Remains Breed Apart", *St. Louis Post-Dispatch*, stltoday.com, January 6, 2005.

79. "Monsanto Agrees To Fines Over Bribes In Indonesia", *St. Louis Post-Dispatch*, stltoday.com, January 6, 2005

80. "Disney Rides Shuts After Accidents", *newsbbc.com.uk*, Updated July 10, 2004.

81. "Flee buyer to add jobs – in India," October 30, 2003, *http://business.bostonherald.com/businessnews/business.*

82. "B of A to send tech work, data to India," October 29, 2003, *www.sfgate.com.*

83. "Bank of America Consumer Data Tapes Lost", *Associated Press*, February 25, 2005.

84. "Shifting Sands In Data Leak", *San Francisco Chronicle*, February 25, 2005, p.C1.

85. "Data Providers Lobby To Block More Oversight," *Wall Street Journal*, March 4, 2005, pp. B1, B2

86. "Faith-based Funds Make Gains But Stay Small; Assets Jump To $4.7B Through October", *Investment News*, Volume 8, Number 48, Crain Communications, December 20, 2004.

CHAPTER 8

1. "At (Your Name Here) Arena, Money Talks", *New York Times*, May 30, 2004, pp. BU1, BU4.

2. *Downsizing Democracy*, p. 202.

3. 2003 Report on Socially Responsible Investing Trends in the United States, *Social Investment Forum*, Updated December 2003, p. ii.

4. "Dialogue: Divide and Rule," Andy Rowell, *Battling Big Business:* Countering Greenwash, Infiltration, and Other Forms of Corporate Bullying, Edited by Evelin Lubbers, p. 39.

5. Ibid., p. 42.

6. "ISIS Product Offers Shareowner Action Without Portfolio Management," SRI World Group, October 1, 2003.

7. "Vanguard Gives Corporate Chiefs a Report Card," *Wall Street Journal*, November 10, 2003, p. C1, C3.

8. "SEC Corporate Reforms Use Old-Fashioned Shame," *San Francisco Chronicle*, November 21, 2003, p. 33.

9. "U.K. Money Manager Lifts Veil on Shareholder Votes," *Wall Street Journal Europe*, May 15, 2003, p. 1, and "Annual Voting and Governance Report," 2002, ISIS

10. "Foundations Should Behave as Responsible Corporate Shareholders and Utilize an Ignored Asset – the Proxy Vote," Lance Lindblom, The Nathan Cummings Foundation, *www.foundationpartnership.org.*

11. "Fool on the Hill: How Does Your Fund Vote?" TMF Otter, September 24, 2002, per Tracey Rembert, SAN.

12. "Labor Puts Pressure on Funds," *Wall Street Journal*, March 3, 2003, p. R1, R5.

13. "Pension Relief Passes," *San Francisco Chronicle*, October 9, 2003, p. B1, B6.

14. *Unequal Protection*, p. 143.

15. Ibid., p. 145.

16. Ibid, p. 147-148.

17. "WTO Talks Collapse, Future Uncertain," *Reuters News Bulletin*, September, 15, 2003.

18. Ibid.

19. Ibid.

20. "US Reaches a Trade Agreement with 4 Central American Nations," *Wall Street Journal*, December 18, 2003, pp. A1, A8.

21. "Think Globally, Eat Locally", *New York Times* Op-ed, December 18, 2004, P. A35.

22. "As U.S. Food Aid Enriches Farmers, Poor Nations Cry Foul," *Wall Street Journal*, September 11, 2003, ppA1, A8.

23. "The Rigged Trade Game," *New York Times*, September 22, 2003, *www.nytimes.com*.

24. "In Shift, U.S. Investors Intensify Criticism of China Trade Policies," *Wall Street Journal*, 10-6-03, pp. A1, A5.

25. "RAN: The Mosquito in the Tent", *Fortune*, May 17, 2004.

26. "U.S. Conservatives Take Aim at NGOs", Jim Lobe, www.oneworld.net, June 12, 2003.

27. Ibid.

28. "Federal Suit Targets Greenpeace for Members' Actions. Experts Say Conviction May Dampen Dissent," *San Francisco Chronicle*, October 11, 2003, *www.sfgate.com*.

29. "U.S. Conservatives Take Aim at NGOs", Jim Lobe, www.oneworld.net, , June 12, 2003.

30. "Is This America's Top Corporate Crime Fighter?" *www.thenation.com*

31. Ibid.

32. Ibid.

33. "SEC Near Compromise on Shareholder Board Plan", *Wall Street Journal*, www.reuters.com, August 11, 2004.

34. "Now, Execs Pay For Firms Sins", *Christian Science Monitor*, www.csmonitor.com, January 31, 2005.

35. "A Campaigners' Guide to Financial Markets Effective Lobbying of Companies and Financial Institutions," Nicholas Hildyard and Mark Mansley, p. 27.

36. "Eco-activists begin to take action against employees of companies they oppose," *Napa Valley Register*, May 28, 2003, p. A4.

37. "A U.K. Lab Company Is Besieged by Protests Against Animal Testing," *Wall Street Journal*, April 27, 2001, p. A1.

38. Ibid.

39. "Green Group Works to Push Ranchers Off Federal Lands," *Wall Street Journal*, November 11, 2002, http://online.wsj.com.

40. Ibid.

41. "Colombian Union Leader, Targeted by Death Squads, to Confront Coca-Cola at Houston Annual Meeting," Corporate Campaign, Inc., Press Release, April 15, 2003.

42. "Assassination Is An Issue In Trade Talks", *New York Times*, November 18, 2004, p. W1.

43. "Doug Grow: Labor Activist Bubbly Over Coca-Cola Fight", Doug Grow, Startribune. com, April 25, 2004.

44. "Stakeholder Theory of the Modern Corporation," R. Edward Freeman, *Business Ethics: Readings and Cases in Corporate Morality*, 1992, p. 161.

45. "Concerned Shareholders: Ford Acknowledges Global Warming Issue, General Motors Yet To Do So," *www.hastingsgroup.com*, May 7, 2003.

46. "Environmental Groups Gain A Company's Vote on Issues," *New York Times*, May 29, 2003, p. C1, C12.

47. "State Aides Mull Pension Funds and Environment," www.wsj.com, November 21, 2003.

48. "The Ripple Effect – The Campaign Helps Change Behavior on Climate Change," CERES Newsletter, June 2003, p.3.

49. "Members of Congress Consider Social and Environmental Disclosure in SEC Filings," *www.socialfunds.com*, July 11, 2003.

50. "The Spotlight Project, The Rose Foundation discussion paper, 2003.

51. Ibid.

52. "Evidence Grows That Global Warming Is a Priority", *Wall Street Journal*, September 8, 2004, p. A2.

53. "Insurers refuse to cover GM farmers," *The Guardian*, October 8, 2003.

54. "FDA Clears Facility to Make Artificial Hormone for Cows," *Wall Street Journal*, October 13, 2003, p. A9.

55. Ibid.

56. "America, The Indifferent", *New York Times* Editorial, December 23, 2004, p. A26.

57. "The Battle for Corporate Power", *Conference Board, Inc.*, James Krohe Jr., Vol. 41 No. 2.

58. "Court OKs Foreign-Abuse Suits", *Los Angeles*

APPENDIX C

1. "The Virtues of Patience," *Investment Advisor*, Megan L. Fowler, November 2002, p.1.

2. "Huffington: Mutual Funds – Corporate Crime's Narcoleptic Giant," *Alternet.org*, August 27, 2002.

3. "Is it Finally Time to Invest Green?" *Forbes Small Business*, June 4, 2003, p. 1.

4. "A Few Mutual Funds Follow Narrow Path Set By Islamic Law," *Sacramento Bee*, March 13, 2005, pp. D1, D8.

5. *Investing With Your Conscience*, p. 199.

6. *Morningstar* report on Green Century Balanced Fund, Release 06-30-2003 portfolio data, as of July 31, 2002.

7. *Responsible Investing News*, August 19, 1991.

8. "Sierra Club to Sponsor Two Green Mutual Funds", *San Francisco Chronicle*, December 22, 2002, p. G1, G7.

9. "SRI Mutual Fund Profile," *Green Money Journal,* Fall 2003, p. 11.

10. Ibid.

BIBLIOGRAPHY

Ackerman, Bruce, and Ian Ayres. *Voting with Dollars.* New Haven and London: Yale University Press, 2002.

Alperovitz, Gar. *America Beyond Capitalism: Reclaiming Our Wealth, Our Liberty, and Our Democracy.* Hoboken, NJ: John Wiley & Sons, 2005.

Bakan, Joel. *The Corporation: The Pathological Pursuit of Profit and Power.* New York: Free Press, 2004.

Barber, Randy, and Jeremy Rifkin. *The North Will Rise Again: Pensions, Politics and Power in the 1980s.* Boston: Beacon Press, 1978.

Barlow, Maude, and Tony Clarke. *Blue Gold: The Fight to Stop the Corporate Theft of the World's Water.* New York: The New Press, 2002.

Benson, Robert. *Challenging Corporate Rule: The Petition to Revoke Unocal's Charter as a Guide to Citizen Action.* New York: The Apex Press, 1999.

Berle, Adolph A. Jr., and Gardiner C. Means. *The Modern Corporation and Private Property.* New York: The McMillan Company, 1932.

Black, Edwin. *IBM and the Holocaust.* New York: Crown Publishers, 2001.

Black, Edwin. *War Against the Weak: Eugenics and America's Campaign to Create a Master Race.* New York: Four Walls Eight Windows, 2003.

Bowie, Norma E., and Tom L. Beauchamp, eds. *Ethical Theory and Business.* Englewood Cliffs, New Jersey: Prentice Hall, 1979.

Bruno, Kenny, and Jed Greer. *Greenwash: The Reality Behind Corporate Environmentalism.* Penang, Malaysia: Third World Network, and New York: The Apex Press, 1996.

Bruno, Kenny, and Joshua Karliner. *Earthsummit.biz: The Corporate Takeover of Sustainable Development.* Oakland, CA: Food First Books, 2002.

Bruyn, Severyn T. *The Field of Social Investment.* Cambridge: Cambridge University Press, 1987.

Camejo, Peter. *The SRI Advantage: Why Socially Responsible Investing Has Outperformed Financially.* New Society Pub, 2002.

Chan, Anita. *China's Workers Under Assault: The Exploitation of Labor in a Globalizing Economy.* Armonk, New York: M.E. Sharpe, 2001.

Collins, Chuck, and Felice Yeskel. *Economic Apartheid in America: A Primer on Economic Equality & Insecurity.* United for a Fair Economy New York: The New Press, 2000.

Collins, Chuck, Betsy Leondar-Wright, and Holly Sklar. *Shifting Fortunes: The Perils of the Growing American Wealth Gap.* Boston: United for a Fair Economy, 1999.

Council on Economic Priorities. *Rating America's Corporate Conscience.* New York: Author, 1987.

Cray, Charlie, and Lee Drutman. *The People's Business: Controlling Corporations and Restoring Democracy.* San Francisco: Berrett-Koehler Publishers, Inc., 2004.

Crenson, Matthew A., and Benjamin Ginsberg. *Downsizing Democracy: How America Sidelined Its Citizens and Privatized Its Public.* Baltimore: The Johns Hopkins University Press, 2002.

Danaher, Kevin, and Jason Mark. *Insurrection: Citizen Challenges to Corporate Power.* New York & London: Routledge, 2003.

Danaher, Kevin. *Corporations Are Gonna Get Your Mama: Globalization and the Downsizing of the American Dream.* Monroe, ME: Common Courage Press, 1996.

Deal, Carl. *The Greenpeace Guide to Anti-Environmental Organizations.* Berkeley, CA: Odonian Press, 1993.

Domini, Amy L., Peter D. Kinger, and Steven D. Lyndenberg, eds. *The Social Investment Almanac: A Comprehensive Guide to Socially Responsible Investing.* New York: Henry Holt and Company, 1992.

Domini, Amy, and Peter Kinder. *Ethical Investing.* Reading, MA: Addison-Wesley, 1986.

Donaldson, Thomas, and Patricia H. Werhane, eds. *Ethical Issues in Business: A Philosophical Approach.* Upper Saddle River, New Jersey: Prentice Hall, 1999.

Dowie, Mark. *American Foundations: An Investigative History.* Cambridge: The MIT Press, 2001.

Eveline Lubbers, Ed. *Battling Big Business: Countering Greenwash, Infiltration and Other Forms of Corporate Bullying.* Monroe, ME: Common Courage Press, 2002.

Fredrick, Robert E., W. Michael Hoffman, and Mark S. Schwartz, eds. *Business Ethics: Reading and Cases in Corporate Morality.* Boston: McGraw Hill, 2001.

Friedman, Milton. *Capitalism and Freedom.* Chicago: The University of Chicago Press, 1962.

Green, Mark. *Selling Out: How Big Corporate Money Buys Elections, Rams through Legislation, and Betrays Our Democracy.* New York: Regan Books, 2002.

Gunnemann, Jon, Charles Powers, and John Simon. *The Ethical Investor.* New Haven, CT: Yale University Press, 1972.

Gutmann, Ethan. *Losing the New China: A Story of American Commerce, Desire and Betrayal.* San Francisco: Encounter Books, 2004.

Harrington, John C. *Investing with Your Conscience: How to Achieve High Returns Using Socially Responsible Investing.* New York: John Wiley & Sons, 1992.

Hart, Kathleen. *Eating in the Dark: America's Experiment with Genetically Engineered Food.* New York: Pantheon Books, 2002.

Hartmann, Thom. *Unequal Protection: The Rise of Corporate Dominance and the Theft of Human Rights.* Rodale, 2002.

Hawken, Paul, Amory Lovins, and L. Hunter Lovins. *Natural Capitalism: Creating the Next Industrial Revolution.* Boston, New York, and London: Little, Brown & Company, 1999.

Hawken, Paul. *The Ecology of Commerce: A Declaration of Sustainability.* New York: Harper Business, 1993.

Hawley, James P., and Andrew T. Williams. *The Rise of Fiduciary Capitalism: How Institutional Investors Can Make Corporate America More Democratic.* Philadelphia: University of Pennsylvania Press, 2000.

Hill, Steven. *Fixing Elections: The Failure of America's Winner Take All Politics.* Routledge, 2002.

Huffington, Arianna. *Pigs at the Trough.* New York: Crown Publishers, 2003.

Human Rights Watch. *The Enron Corporation: Corporate Complicity in Human Rights Violation.* New York, 1999.

Judd, Elizabeth. *Investing with a Social Conscience.* New York: Pharos Books, 1990.

Karliner, Joshua. *The Corporate Planet: Ecology and Politics in the Age of Globalization.* San Francisco: The Sierra Club Books, 1997.

Katz, Michael, Robert Levering, and Milton Moskowitz. *Everybody's Business.* New York: Doubleday, 1990.

Katz, Michael, Robert Levering, and Milton Moskowitz. *The 100 Best Companies to Work for in America.* New York: Doubleday, 1994.

Kelly, Marjorie. *The Divine Right of Capital: Dethroning the Corporate Aristocracy.* San Francisco: Berrett-Koehler Publishers, 2001.

Kieschnick, Michael Hall, and Julia Ann Parzen. *Credit Where It's Due: Development Banking for Communities.* Philadelphia: Temple University Press, 1992.

Korten, David C. *The Post-Corporate World: Life after Capitalism.* Connecticut: Kumarian Press, Inc., and California: Berrett-Koehler Publishers, Inc., 1999.

Korten, David C. *When Corporations Rule the World.* Connecticut: Kumarian Press, Inc., and California: Berrett-Koehler Publishers, Inc., 1995.

Lappé, Marc, Ph.D., and Britt Bailey. *Against the Grain: Biotechnology and the Corporate Takeover of Your Food.* Monroe, ME: Common Courage Press, 1998.

Lowry, Ritchie P. *Good Money.* New York: W W Norton & Co., 1991.

Manheim, Jarol B. *The Death of a Thousand Cuts: Corporate Campaigns and the Attack on the Corporation.* Mahwah, New Jersey: Lawrence Erlbaum Associates, 2001.

Miller, Alan J. *Socially Responsible Investing.* New York Institute of Finance, 1991.

Mokhiber, Russell, and Robert Weissman. *Corporate Predators.* Monroe, ME: Common Courage Press, 1999.

Moore, Gary. *The Thoughtful Christian's Guide to Investing.* Grand Rapids, MI: Zondervan Publishing, 1990.

Moskowitz, Milton. *The Global Marketplace.* New York: Macmillan, 1987.

Nace, Ted. *Gangs of America: The Rise of Corporate Power and the Disability of Democracy.* San Francisco: Berrett-Koehler, 2003.

Nestle, Marion. *Food Politics: How the Food Industry Influences Nutrition and Health.* Berkeley, CA: University of California Press, 2002.

Palast, Greg. *The Best Democracy Money Can Buy.* London: Pluto Press, 2002.

Patterson, Thomas E. *The Vanishing Voter: Public Involvement in an Age of Uncertainty.* New York: Alfred A. Knopf, 2002.

Phillips, Kevin. *Wealth & Democracy: A Political History of the American Rich.* New York: Broadway Books, 2002.

Powers, Charles W. *People/Profits: The Ethics of Investment.* New York: Council on Religion and International Affairs, 1972.

Powers, Charles W. *Social Responsibility and Investments.* Nashville, TN: Abingdon Press, 1971.

Prashad, Vijay. *Fat Cats and Running Dogs: The Enron Stage of Capitalism.* Monroe, ME: Common Courage Press, 2003.

Roddick, Anita. *Take it Personally.* Berkeley, CA: Conari Press, 2001.

Schwartz, Robert J., Ph.D. *Can You Make A Difference?* New York: Lantern Books, 2002.

Sparkes, Russell. *Social Responsibility and Investment: A Global Revolution.* West Sussex: John Wiley & sons, Ltd., 2002.

INDEX